DONE
DEALS

DONE DEALS

VENTURE CAPITALISTS TELL THEIR STORIES

EDITED BY

UDAYAN GUPTA

Harvard Business School Press
Boston, Massachusetts

Library of Congress Cataloging-in-Publication Data

Done deals : venture capitalists tell their stories/edited by Udayan Gupta.

p. cm.

Includes index.

ISBN 0-87584-938-5 (alk. paper)

1. Venture capital—Case studies.   2. Businessmen—Case studies.

I. Gupta, Udayan, 1950–

HG4963.D667 2000

332'.0415'0922--dc21

00-033454

The paper used in this publication meets the requirements of the
*American National Standard for Permanence of Paper for
Publications and Documents in Libraries and Archives* Z39.48–1992.

CONTENTS

PREFACE

SINCE THE MIDDLE of the '90s, the financial markets have been on a roll. A bull market in technology and a roaring market in Internet stocks have been two of the most distinct signs of the times. In both instances, the engine behind the phenomenon is venture capital.

Venture capitalists have backed some of the most visible investments in recent years—from Netscape, the company that wrote the book on Internet browser technology, to Amazon, the company that defined e-retailing, to search engines such as Yahoo! and Lycos to eBay and Priceline. And who can ignore the ultimate irony—the acquisition of media giant Time Warner by Internet upstart America Online?

In a business that now attracts more than $30 billion annually, separating fact from fiction becomes difficult. And media coverage hasn't helped. By predictably focusing on venture capitalists as gods or demons, the nature of their exact impact on the U.S. economy over the last fifty years has mostly gone unexplored. News stories often offer knee-jerk coverage or fixate on the new "new thing."

There have been a few histories of venture capital. In 1985, after the first high-tech boom, *Business Week* writer John W. Wilson published *The New Venturers,* an excellent record of the industry as it had evolved until then. But the book focused mostly on Silicon Valley and underplayed the accomplishments of the rest of the venture capital universe. Since that time, the industry has exploded—both in total assets and in the number of players. Within the last year or so, a number of new books have appeared, focused on the roles of specific venture capitalists and entrepreneurs, but the light they shed on the industry as a whole is faint.

Given the role venture capitalists have played—and continue to play—in shaping the U.S. economy, it is important to capture not only the dynamism of contemporary venture capital without ignoring its roots, but the voices of the early practitioners and the champions of the present. Thus began *Done Deals* as an attempt to meld past and present by letting the players themselves tell their stories.

The seeds of this effort began in 1998 after a discussion with Bill Sahlman, a professor of entrepreneurship at Harvard Business School. We both wanted to find a way to describe the explosive growth of the venture capital industry, a business that has rapidly become the engine of technological change in the United States. The idea of first-person narratives—venture capitalists telling their own stories—struck the right chord.

The subjects selected were chosen to span the history of venture capital. From September 1998 through September 1999, each subject was interviewed in person or on the telephone; the interviews were then transcribed and edited. Each subject had the opportunity to review his own narrative and to offer comments and make factual corrections. Some of the subjects let the interviews stand pretty much as they were transcribed. Others provided extensive suggestions. The final version of *Done Deals* is a collaborative effort between the venture capitalists and myself as editor.

This book would not have been possible without the cooperation of an army of people who gave freely of their time and energy. I would like to thank all of the subjects included in the book as well as those whose contributions don't appear here: Derek Jones, Joe Bartlett, Steve Gall, David Morgenthaler, Walter Channing, and Barry Weinberg. Special thanks go to Ed Mathias and Robert Knox, who read more than their share of the work and provided helpful comments on its organization. Steve Galante, publisher of *Private Equity Analyst*, and William Marbach of Technologic Partners provided the statistical context that enriches these stories. And the entire Harvard Business School Press staff, especially my editor Hollis Heimbouch and her assistant Genoveva Llosa, provided the patience and skills to make *Done Deals* a reality.

INTRODUCTION

UNTIL A FEW years ago, most people would have been at a loss if asked to explain the field of venture capital. With the focus on Wall Street maneuverings, leveraged buyouts, and investment banking, venture capitalists were hardly on anyone's radar screen. Even in the mid-1980s, venture capitalists operated mainly behind the scenes in a relatively narrow segment of the economy; mostly unknown outside their industry, they were nevertheless powerful deal makers and arbiters of change.

How the world has changed. Today the words "venture capital" are on the lips of virtually every entrepreneur, investor, and journalist—every dreamer. Fueled by the Internet boom, there is perhaps no better time to be a venture capitalist or an entrepreneur, as witnessed by the 80 to 90 percent return rates enjoyed by many a fund in the late '90s and the instant wealth conferred on start-up champions such as Jeff Bezos of Amazon.com or Meg Whitman of eBay when their companies went public.

The catalyst for this newfound infatuation is undoubtedly the Internet. Add a dot-com to a business, and its potential takes on unparalleled dimensions, at least in the eyes of stock market investors. But without the investors' willingness to buy shares in venture-backed companies at phenomenal prices and valuations, the record returns being posted by venture capital partnership after venture capital partnership simply wouldn't occur.

Indeed, success fuels the drive for even greater success. As venture capitalists show returns far in excess of other asset classes, institutional investors pour even more money into the industry. Once grudgingly allocating 2 percent of their total assets to venture capital, investors now consider allocations as high as 5 percent. And venture capital partnerships, once accustomed to raising a new pool of capital every five to seven years, today raise new funds every two years—funds that are often double or triple the size of the previous ones.

The size of the venture capital industry has nearly doubled in the last ten years. Steve Galante, who publishes the *Private Equity Analyst*, estimates that in 2000 there are as many as 7,500 private equity practitioners, including some 5,000 pure venture capitalists and many buyout veterans, such as Thomas Lee and Henry Kravis, who now have venture funds of their own. And, of course, the amount of money in play is much greater. In 1999, venture capital funds raised $30 billion and invested nearly the same amount. At the beginning of the decade, only $3 billion was raised, of which about $1.5 billion went into deals.

The First Fifty Years

The first venture capitalists, coming into being in post–World War II America, worked at a time when high-tech was a nascent industry and the stock market was just beginning to embrace "new issues," the initial stock offerings of technology companies.

These early practitioners were pioneers working in a rarefied climate. Their investors, mostly wealthy individuals—the Rockefellers, the Whitneys, the Phippses—and asset managers of foundations and universities, were excited by the chance to bring new technology to bear on commerce and to reshape the economic environment. As a new asset class, venture capital promised to deliver financial returns greater than the stock market to those select investors willing to take the risk.

The setting and the rules are different now. Contemporary venture capitalists, with few exceptions, talk about their ability to generate mammoth financial returns—home runs, ten baggers, and grand slams—and to build huge capital pools. Talk of collegiality and building businesses, once common in the industry, has been supplanted in some cases by cutthroat competitiveness and the drive to land deals first. But the differences between the East Coast and the West Coast are even sharper than those between the old and the new.

The East Coast, the financial center of the world, has traditionally been fixated on financial engineering. There, with a priority placed on the structuring of deals, it has often mattered less what a company did or what would be involved in ensuring its long-term success than whether the deal would provide tax benefits and financial returns. On the West Coast, by contrast, the driving spirit has been innovation in science and technology. Technologists and investors, many of whom are refugees from the East, have long gathered around the campuses of Stanford University and Caltech to create a new economy and a new entrepreneurial culture. They were soon followed by investment bankers such as Sanford Robertson, George Quist, William Hambrecht, and Thomas Weisel, and lawyers such as Larry Sonsini, who provided the financial and legal support to help turn great ideas into many now-legendary businesses.

There was a time when venture strategies were straightforward and self-evident. Venture capitalists would provide equity or a combination of debt and equity to a company and get paid back when the company went public or was acquired. If such "exits" didn't happen, the investments were written off as unrecoverable. In this approach, one hoped that the returns from the good deals exceeded the write-offs from the dead and nearly dead deals.

Venture capitalists once were a close-knit community, a collegial group that shared information, deals, and even entrepreneurial talent. Today the venture capital community is more diverse, not only because it has expanded well beyond its early boundaries along Route 128 in Boston and Sand Hill Road in Silicon Valley, but also because its practitioners don't necessarily fit the same mold as their predecessors; nor do the deals they make follow any particular uniform structure. More significantly, the provision of venture capital is no longer left to traditional venture capital funds. Instead, angel investors, corporate venture funds, pension funds, foundations, and university endowments are investing directly in entrepreneurial ventures. Everyone wants a piece of the action, and big institutional investors in particular are beginning to play a key role in the explosion of the capital pool. They shower successful funds with even greater pools of capital and if shut out of a particular fund are often instrumental in the initiation of breakaway funds such as Redpoint Ventures, the Geoffrey Yang–led fund that cut loose from Institutional Venture Partners at the end of 1999.

The preponderance of new sources of funding and of practitioners has forced a differentiation in investment strategies. Venture capitalists are no longer the only investors in early-stage technology companies, nor are they the sole providers of capital to a wide range of entrepreneurial start-ups. Early-stage venture capital funds won't go away, but much of the industry now resorts to a mix of investments—

early stage as well as late stage, buyouts as well as turnarounds—that provide high returns with a measure of safety. Many have turned to the public markets to find value in venture-backed companies that have foundered, which was the strategy behind the launch of Silver Lake Partners, a $2.3 billion pool financed by investors such as Kleiner Perkins for private equity buyouts and recapitalizations. With billions under management, venture capitalists seem poised to become hybrid creatures: investors doing deals in both the public and the private markets, signaling a departure from the industry's original charter to invest only in privately owned companies.

Crowded arenas, however, don't necessarily signify a greater pool of talent in the venture capital ranks. Where once venture capitalists were veteran investors with technology or management experience under their belts, many of today's new venture capitalists are inexperienced journeymen rushing into an industry short of able bodies and full of promises of quick riches. And for all the prestigious venture firms that stand tall because of their achievements and track records, hundreds go unnoticed; for them, visibility will be absolutely necessary to attract deals and do business. Just twenty years ago, the total industry invested $1 billion in portfolio companies, and independent partnerships raised slightly less than $700 million. In 2000, industry observers such as the *Private Equity Analyst* expect venture capitalists to surpass last year's investment of over $30 billion in portfolio companies and more than $30 billion raised in new funds.

Capital is a commodity today. Consequently, marketing, once an unspoken word in venture capital firms, has taken on greater importance. To be sure, funds such as Kleiner Perkins and Benchmark need no publicity, but for middle-tier firms, selling their story to prospective entrepreneurs is an important aspect of managing their business.

With the growth of new funds, the prices of private transactions sky high, and large pools of capital almost forcing deals upon investors, some observers expect another shakeout in the industry. The first one occurred in the early 1960s, fueled by a flood of capital and inexperienced investment strategies. In the aftermath of the bumper stock market of 1982 and 1983, many funds began to inflate prices for private transactions, only to discover that they couldn't recoup their investments, especially in a stock market that quickly cooled off. Many funds disappeared, unable to raise new pools of capital. In other funds, partners left to resume careers in traditional industries or simply to take to the hills. Whatever the outcome in this latest phase, the venture capital industry has clearly risen to a new plane. Venture capital partnerships aren't simply a group of investors raising a pool of money and doing deals; they are full-fledged organizations—often frustrating bureaucracies—requiring infrastructure and effective business processes and dependent on their ability to find a distinct competitive advantage.

AS MANY OF the early pioneers report, venture capital funding after World War II was a liberating experience, a noble business offering a chance to change the economic landscape. It didn't suffer from the stigma that investment banking faced as a practice often dependent on structuring young companies cheaply to sell to the highest bidder, where too often the bankers and their clients made all the money, and the buyers of the stock were lucky if they got their initial investment back.

Early venture capitalists such as Lionel Pincus rebelled against such practices. For them, venture investing was a way of providing capital to entrepreneurs, working with them to shape a business, and cashing out in a public offering or by selling out to a corporate buyer. Working with new ideas, bringing them to fruition, and reaping the financial benefits of the successes seemed far more exciting and uplifting than the alternatives.

Most of the early venture capitalists were businesspeople looking to entrepreneurs for ideas. They understood finance, but not necessarily as much about managing businesses or managing technology, the industry segment that soon became the staple of venture capital investing. For pioneers such as Eugene Kleiner and Arthur Rock, the early days of venture capital were a heady time of discovery and profit. Kleiner found himself moving into biotechnology—an area he now confesses he knew little about—with the founding of companies such as Genentech and Hybritech. For Rock, an early investor in Intel and Apple, his excitement was derived from the chance to create new opportunities for a new generation of Americans and his willingness to take a bet on people as much as technology. Others such as Lionel Pincus, Peter Crisp, and Peter Brooke were financial specialists without much training in running companies. But they were all united in a belief that if they could bring the right people together and structure a business effectively, the rest would fall in place. More often than not, they were right.

Many of the early venture capitalists, including Arthur Rock, Peter Crisp, Charles Waite, and Steve Lazarus, got their venture capital education at Harvard Business School, at the feet of General Georges Doriot. Doriot, a French-born business professor, established some of the first principles of entrepreneurship in the 1940s and 1950s, and brought together many of his students to form American Research and Development (ARD), a publicly traded venture capital partnership. But Doriot was not solely a businessman. He saw ARD as an attempt to change the economic landscape of the United States—and perhaps the world—through entrepreneurial efforts, and he expected his students and employees to share in the same vision. A look at some of Doriot's class notes from this era only goes to prove the eclectic quality of his early teaching.

> *One of our hopes is to manage effectively, profitably, and constructively an organization . . . sometimes even to create one.*

> *We know that when we speak of managing, we are talking about a man or men's actions—their behavior. Organization as a skeleton can be conceived in theory without men but to give it life and effectiveness, men must be picked, and placed in a relation not only to the work to be done but also to one another.*

> *Work is part of living. It must be hoped that work can be considered not as an activity necessary for existence but as a worthwhile part of existence.*

> *We have to judge a man and an idea. The two cannot be divorced. We say that we judge a man plus an idea as of today, the day we see them. That in itself is difficult but, more than that, since our task is to give life to the combination of man + idea, we have to try to attempt to determine the type of evolution, the type of goals, the problems of that particular combination. It is not a static study. It is the study of a life to take place in the future—under strict and hard competitive situations.*

> *Judging, measuring, evaluating a man as he is today is not too difficult. There is a record of what he has done under the circumstances.*

*Where the problem is very much harder is when one wants to foresee
how the person to be considered to create and build an enterprise will
behave and perform in an entirely new and changing environment very
often, if a new technique or method or idea is involved a new environment has to be created.*[1]

In Doriot's and the early practitioners' estimations, venture capital
depended on bets placed on individuals. If all the factors worked—if
the individual, the ideas, and the marketplace came together—the
future would be not only different, but better.

The East Coast Pioneers

Venture capital began with wealthy families, but it wasn't until the
Small Business Investment Company (SBIC) Act came into being in
1958 that a different kind of money and a different set of goals started
to shape venture investing. The SBIC Act was Washington's attempt
to boost the economy with tax-advantaged capital. Prompted by a
desire to catch up with the breakneck pace of the Russian economy,
the Eisenhower administration pushed hard to get the Act passed,
and banks, financial institutions, university endowments, and foundations soon became the primary sources of capital for the technology industry, which badly needed risk capital. The carrot was that the
Small Business Administration (SBA) would leverage the capital put
in with loans of its own. So for every dollar that a fund put together,
it would have three dollars to invest.

For a brief period, the fantasy of government leverage attracted all
comers. Then the cracks began to show. Many of the early SBICs fell
by the wayside, hurt by poor management and even poorer investment decisions. The SBA, like most government agencies, seemed
more interested in keeping the accounts straight than in fostering
entrepreneurship. A myriad of rules and regulations prevented SBICs
from investing in some of the more interesting technologies—to do so
would have violated SBA guidelines that pertained more to busi-

[1] *Georges F. Doriot, Manufacturing Class Notes, Harvard Business School, 1927–1966.
Compiled from the Board of Trustees, the French Library of Boston.*

nesses in mature industries than to unproven high-technology businesses. And violating the SBA's guidelines was the path to liquidation and extinction.

Perhaps because the early excesses hurt the industry and because many of these SBICs still had ties to the SBA, the appetite for risk on the East Coast was low, especially when compared to the chances taken by their West Coast counterparts. Even more significant, many of the firms began to shun the partnership model that many venture capital funds had championed and instead adopted a hierarchical corporate structure.

Still, the East Coast venture capitalists were among the first to recognize the appetite for venture capital and its higher-than-market returns not only among U.S. investors but among international investors as well. Similarly, they were among the first to move away from early-stage investments to the idea of private equity—investing in everything from early- and late-stage companies to private purchases, public stock, roll-ups, and consolidations. Indeed, the pure venture capital fund that only invests in early-stage companies is becoming a rarity on the East Coast. Today many funds invest in so-called special situations in the public market—undervalued companies that once were venture-backed, undervalued assets, or corporate cast-offs.

These days it would be easy to sell the East Coast venture capitalist short. But without the large sums of capital provided by the East Coast funds, many deals on the West Coast would have been still-born. Still, when all is said and done, venture capital is only an asset class on the East Coast—it is the culture of the West Coast.

The West Coast Mavericks

Venture capitalists on the West Coast offer a different portrait from their East Coast counterparts. In their philosophy and style, they are akin to members of artists' colonies or ateliers, albeit with a high-tech slant. Firms such as Sutter Hill, Mayfield, Institutional Venture Partners, and Kleiner Perkins have shaped the course of U.S. technology by taking chances on often unproven and untested technologies and betting the store that they will succeed.

Until a few years ago, however, West Coast investors often were perceived by their East Coast counterparts as financially irresponsible investors who would overpay to get a deal done, or so the rap went. But they were also admired as high-tech dreamers who structured companies and marshaled ideas and people—for deals that East Coast investors would have most likely discarded without a second thought. They are different from their East Coast counterparts in style, in risk profile, and in the levels of success they have achieved, and perhaps more than their East Coast counterparts, they are accustomed to using intuition, hype, jargon—whatever best suits their goals.

Historically, Silicon Valley investing was a model in which a few Stanford nerds were mentored by Stanford professors and then handed off to the professionals on Sand Hill Road. That model has changed since the days of David Packard and Bill Hewlett, but the template remains the same: take a chance on a fledgling technology and nurture the scientists. When you have a proof of principle, hurry up and build a company and its products.

Technology investing has flourished in the Valley because the environment has been receptive to new ideas. Stanford University and the University of California system have provided the financial and human resources necessary to forge a new frontier. Fred Terman, a professor of engineering at Stanford and the Valley's General Doriot, helped his students, engineers Hewlett and Packard, to create an enduring company by offering guidance, establishing a set of values, and providing the necessary financial connections. The efforts of Lee de Forest, who in 1909 co-founded Federal Telegraph Company, California's first technology company, and later of Intel co-founder Robert Noyce, also made this particular strip of land particularly friendly place to those escaping the corporate trappings that characterized much of America in the '50s and '60s, especially on the East Coast.

Companies like Intel, Hewlett-Packard, and National Semiconductor, in turn, became the engines of change for the next generation of companies. Venture capitalists such as Tom Perkins and John Doerr of Kleiner Perkins Caufield & Byers got their technology grounding at these institutions, as did dozens of entrepreneurs who went on to launch new start-ups. With the success these companies continue to enjoy today and the abundance of technology spawned by other high-tech giants, including Cisco, Boeing, and Microsoft, the West Coast continues to lead the way in funding technology start-ups.

The Next Fifty Years

As industries grow and expand, it is inevitable that they themselves will fragment and subdivide. The same is true of the venture capital industry, which once profited mainly from taking risks on emerging technologies. As a consequence of the first flood of money in the 1980s, the industry gravitated toward late-stage investing and into undervalued public market stocks. But still fund sizes didn't change drastically. Early-stage funds stayed relatively small, and late-stage funds ballooned. And why not? Who could resist the opportunity to charge a 2 to 3 percent management fee and earn a quarter of profits made—for doing many of the same things that stock fund managers do for a fraction of the charge?

But these days, when even so-called early-stage funds manage hundreds of millions of dollars, one can't help wondering whether it is viable for any one fund to make thirty to forty labor-intensive seed investments per year. Such a scenario evokes concerns about the role of venture capitalists: Will they ultimately be in the game of selling inflated shares in technology companies or will they return to their early focus on company creation and superior financial returns?

To be sure, technology will continue to anchor the venture capital business, given that the scalable nature of technology—its ability to defy conventional financial analysis—makes it the perfect vehicle for venture capitalists. But even though the ability to spot early-stage technologies—especially the not-so-obvious ones—remains the venture capitalist's ultimate weapon, the need to develop a competitive advantage will drive venture capitalists to greater and greater specialization. The industry has already seen specialized funds such as the Java Fund, started by Kleiner Perkins, and an explosion of Internet-only funds. Of course, specialization may not solve all the challenges: one has only to look at the rise and fall of biotechnology-only funds in the '80s to realize the perils and pitfalls of specialization. One-time high flyers such as Delphi Bioventures and CW Ventures have become virtually irrelevant, and even Healthcare Investment Corporation, which created the buzz around genomics, is an insignificant force in the world of venture capital.

Feed the fad while it exists, but what do you do when it is gone? Amid the euphoric talk, disparate and competing scenarios of the future co-exist. One group sees venture capitalists as an unruly band, with more capital than ever before, patching together entrepreneurs and technology simply to exact returns—often oblivious to whether the deals make business sense or whether the entrepreneurs are equipped with the managerial skills to operationalize the venture. Still others assert that venture capital is no longer a financially attractive means of technology development but yet another asset class on par with leveraged buyouts and savings and loans. And for those who continue to believe that innovation is time intensive, not capital intensive, there are concerns that hurrying ideas to market may produce phenomenal short-term windfalls—as they have in the case of the Internet—but they may not create the sustainable companies and businesses necessary to produce the next generation of venture start-ups.

As we look to the next few decades, there are more questions than answers: Will the romance of radically changing the economic landscape, financially empowering a new breed of economic players, and generating returns superior to the market be replaced by the stability of being simply another financial asset class, albeit the most profitable in history?

Telling Their Stories

By bringing together the voices from the first fifty years of the industry's existence, *Done Deals* highlights two themes: the sharp contrast between the practitioners of early venture capital and those practicing today, and the coastal divide—the difference in venture capital culture and practice between the West Coast and the East Coast. The thirty-five venture capitalists from thirty-one different firms gathered together in *Done Deals* represent all facets of the industry's evolution, and their diversity highlights the industry's changing reality.

As such, the book is organized into five thematic parts: In the first section, Fast Forward, we meet deal makers Robert Kagle, Mike Volpi, Bob Knox, Cleveland Christophe, Ann Winblad, Geoff Yang, and Mitch Kapor. Together these voices represent the newest incarnation of venture capital, a world dominated by technology deals but populated by diverse venture philosophies. In the next section, Beginnings, early pioneers of venture capital—the late Benno Schmidt, Eugene Kleiner,

Peter Crisp, Lionel Pincus, Herbert Wilkins, Sanford Robertson, and Arthur Rock—explain how they got their starts, and they offer their impressions of the industry's more recent success and notoriety. In the next section, focused on the West Coast, the contrasts between the first forty-five years and that past five are made clear through the voices of long-time practitioners Paul Wythes, Don Valentine, Reid Dennis, Richard Kramlich, Grant Heidrich, Kevin Fong, and Larry Sonsini as they recall the early days in Silicon Valley and explain the unique set of circumstances that enhanced its entrepreneurial process. In the section on East Coast venture capitalists, we meet early practitioners Charles Waite, Richard Burnes, Peter Brooke, Kevin Landry, William Egan, Mort Collins, and Ed Mathias as well as relative newcomers Steve Arnold, Jon Flint, and Terry McGuire from Polaris Venture Capital. Finally, in a section entitled Visions, the focus is on the future and on where the industry is headed in the next fifty years, with perspectives from Jim Breyer, Jon Callaghan, Steve Lazarus, and John Doerr—all leaders in the industry today.

FAST FORWARD

ROBERT KAGLE
Benchmark Capital

 Since 1995, when it was first launched, Benchmark Capital has established itself as one of the industry's leading players, with spectacular results from investments in Internet companies such as eBay, E-LOAN, and Ariba. On the basis of financial returns, Benchmark's investment in eBay is one of the most successful venture capital investments to date. Their initial $5 million investment in the company was valued at well over $4 billion in mid-1999.

The success is no accident. In an industry where few firms stand out, Benchmark has embarked on a deliberate strategy to differentiate itself. Several major university endowments and foundations are limited partners in the firm, and some of the top names in retailing, such as Louis Vuitton Moet Hennessey, are its corporate partners. The hiring of David Beirne, one of Silicon Valley's top executive recruiters, as a partner has given the firm even more attention as a major-league player. To top it all, the firm recently announced that it had raised a new $1 billion fund, ostensibly to fuel the Internet frenzy.

Benchmark has resisted being a generalist, focusing more on technology, especially the transactional side of the Internet with e-commerce companies such as Ariba, eBay, eBags, PlanetRx, and Scient. Until recently, it stayed away from writing the high-valuation "$10 million check" to focus, instead, on smaller early-stage investments. As one of the more marketing-conscious funds, Benchmark is always sensitive to the need for public relations and the importance of branding for itself and its portfolio.

Kagle, one of the founding partners, talks about the steps Benchmark took to quickly establish itself as one of the Valley's most prominent investment partnerships and how its focus on the Internet has paid off with spectacular returns.

I ENDED UP in venture capital quite by circumstance. I was at The Boston Consulting Group and was beginning to get frustrated with the nature of the work there. It was, in many ways, three months and a cloud of dust. I found this unsatisfying for two reasons. One, you couldn't see your ideas through to their implementation. Second, your relationships with clients were rather temporary. You'd be involved in all these interesting and stimulating intellectual issues and challenges, but then you would quickly be moved on to the next project. So I went to Dave Marquardt, who had been a friend of mine in business school at Stanford, for career guidance. I asked him if there were any young technology companies that he thought I would be a good fit with as a marketing executive. I've always been a marketing guy at heart—I'm really a consumer marketing junky.

Dave introduced me to a few companies, and I would visit these companies and then come back to Dave and say, "Here's some interesting issues with these companies." After two or three of these visits, he asked me, "Have you thought about the venture capital business?" I said, "Dave, I am looking for a *real* job."

The only thing I could imagine to be less satisfying than consulting was financial services. Fortunately, Dave persuaded me that the venture business was really something quite different, that it was an opportunity to combine the intellectual stimulation and the variety that I enjoyed about consulting with the ability to form enduring relationships and the real responsibility associated with making venture investments. I liked the fact that you sat on the boards of these companies and were involved with them for five, six, seven years or more. Ultimately, you could know whether or not you were doing the job by calculating the difference between the money you put in and the money you took out. So in 1983, I joined Dave at Technology Venture Investors, along with Burt McMurtry and Jim Bochnowski, and have never looked back.

Starting in Difficult Times

My introduction to the venture capital business occurred during a difficult period. Many industries had been overfinanced and there were a lot of me-too companies. It was the time when tens of disk drive companies were financed all at once. It was similar to the environment we find ourselves in today—a very capital-rich environment where fewer of the disciplines of venture capital, such as due diligence, research and the like, are being applied.

It was a very sobering time. A number of companies were going out of business, while others were having a difficult time getting financing. It was a time when you could see what life was like on the other side. The interesting thing about the venture capital business today is that many of the venture capitalists have not seen that kind of a difficult environment. Lately, it's been really hard not to be a successful investor in the venture business. I think there are many people in the business today who don't understand what a challenging environment is, much the same way many mutual fund managers have not seen a genuine bear market.

One of the disadvantages of having so much capital in an industry—other than financing too many competitors—is that venture companies are more prone to try a broad range of things, rather than focus in on what it is that they do best. Having ample resources, ironically, will many times prevent a company from finding its power alley, or reason for being. I've seen a lot of companies fail for lack of focus. I've rarely seen a company fail for being too focused.

We seem to have re-entered the early 1980s in this Internet age. Some companies literally shy away from profitability, because many of the analysts on Wall Street say, "If you're showing profitability, it must mean you're not being aggressive enough about pursuing the leadership position in your segment. We want to see you aggressively invest in the marketing and branding of your service or product so that you can guarantee that leadership position. Lose money now— you can make it later."

I was at TVI for twelve years. In early 1995 we decided, as a group, not to raise another fund together. It was a collective decision in which we, in some sense, declared victory, because the partnership had been tremendously successful. We were investors in Microsoft, Sun, and Compaq Computer. I think at one point in time we had twenty-five companies each with more than a $250 million market cap. We had a string of very successful investments. But as a group we didn't have a shared commitment to being the best in the business going forward. We also represented a broad range of generations at

TVI, with Burt (McMurtry) being the most senior, and Dave (Marquardt) being next, and then me being the youngest.

Establishing Benchmark

I really felt there was an opportunity to build the best venture firm in the business, so I established Benchmark with four others who shared the same vision. Two partners, Andy Rachleff and Bruce Dunlevie, were originally at Merrill Pickard, a Silicon Valley venture firm that focused on technology. The other founding partner of Benchmark was Kevin Harvey, who was a twice-successful entrepreneur. Kevin started his first company while in college and sold it to Apple Computer. The second company he started, Approach, he sold to Lotus. Bruce was on the Board of Directors with him at Approach. The fifth partner, Val Vaden, has since left Benchmark.

We formed Benchmark around a couple of very basic principles. First of all, I had read Jim Collins's book *Built to Last* right at the time that TVI was deciding to declare victory. I was saddened that TVI had been a very successful firm but wasn't going to be an enduring enterprise. Reflecting on Jim's book, and Jim's principles, I felt we ought to apply his thinking to Benchmark as we put it together, so that we could create a firm rather than a partnership, and ensure that it had lasting values. So we spent a lot of time together discussing the values and principles we were basing the firm on.

We observed that the most successful investments in the venture capital business were in companies that were built to last. In many cases, it was the culture of these companies that really gave them this quality of endurance. What, we asked ourselves, are some things we can do differently at Benchmark to really distinguish ourselves from other funds, and to make us really unique in the venture business?

The Benchmark Principles

We had a couple of market segment insights and a couple of guiding principles. The market segment insights were that, if you invest early—if you're there at the company-creation moment—you are assured a proper seat at the table. So, we decided to focus on early-stage companies.

Also, this was at a time when all the venture firms were raising ever-increasing amounts of money. They were raising hundreds of millions of dollars on top of hundreds of millions of dollars. We asked ourselves, can these firms afford to write a million-dollar check when it's just one guy and a napkin? We observed that in many cases they had so much money that they couldn't do the small deals. So we decided that we were not going to raise more than $100 million so we wouldn't feel pressure to put money out. In terms of capital per partner, we were going to be among the lowest in the industry. That would give us the opportunity to write the half-million-dollar check without feeling guilty about it. We went out and raised money on that basis.

Consistent with our view that we were targeting ourselves to be the best, and the fact that we were building a labor-intensive business, we asked for a premium carry structure.[1] We decided that, not only was it a bold statement, but if we were going to invest all this time and energy into the early-stage process, we wanted to be fairly compensated. We were able to get a 30 percent carried interest, even though we were a first-time fund—which, I think, was unprecedented.

The second insight we had was that we felt that consumer markets and technology businesses were coming together, and that the consumerization, or democratization, of technology was going to be a very fundamental thing.

A Partnership of Equals

We founded the firm on the notion of equal partnership. We decided that we didn't want anybody at this firm to ever feel like they haven't been treated fairly. We want everybody to feel maximum empowerment. We observed that many entrepreneurs, in fact, do go out and start companies because they don't want to report to anybody. They don't want somebody else calling the shots. Every investment professional at Benchmark should have that same entrepreneurial feeling, because we are a start-up company. We need everybody to feel a sense of ownership and a sense of commitment to the cause.

---

[1] A carry structure, or carried interest, is a venture capital fund's share of the profits in a partnership. Traditionally at 20 percent, some funds are now commanding 30 percent.

This has created real teamwork at Benchmark, so that we're constantly helping one another achieve success. We're not trying to outperform one another to get a bigger slice of that next pie. We had observed, both at TVI and at Merrill Pickard, that inequality was not a constructive situation.

Equal partnership means totally equal in every way: same economic interest in the firm, same salaries, and an equal vote on all administrative issues. Some people, when we were raising our first fund, declared our structure a sociology experiment. But it really works, because there's a lot of joint leadership that's displayed at Benchmark, coupled with a tremendous amount of individual freedom and responsibility. I think it brings the best out in everybody.

The only way to get financial leverage in an equal partnership is if the next guy you bring in is actually better than the guys already there. It's the only way the pie gets any bigger. That led to our attracting David Beirne, one of the top recruiters in high-tech, and our subsequent hiring of Bill Gurley, both of whom have taken Benchmark up a notch. That's a very different outcome than trying to find someone you can "leverage," and hire as an associate, or a junior partner, and make money off of while they're out doing the work. I think that is the model much of the venture business has operated on over a long period of time.

We now have a totally flat partnership of six general partners and no associates. The way we position that with the entrepreneur is, when a Benchmark partner is on your board, you're getting a decision maker, one of the most influential people in the partnership.

When we started Benchmark we were a start-up, so we went into full-gear hustle, and we were out there pounding the pavement like crazy, just trying to put ourselves in a position to see as many interesting investment opportunities as possible. For example, eBay came to us through the referral of its founder, who had worked with Bruce at a company called E-Shop, which TVI was also an investor in. It was a classic case of a relationship that already existed.

Venture Capital as a Service Industry

When we founded Benchmark we conceptualized our business as a service business rather than as an investment business. We observed that many venture capitalists had begun to see themselves as the center of the universe. They were the power brokers, the kingmakers, and all power and goodness emanated from them. We think the opposite—that the entrepreneurs are the people who deserve to be at the center of the universe. When we're doing our job really well, we're the stagehands and the entrepreneurs are the stars. If you have that philosophy—and you believe it's a privilege to invest in these companies—then you try to earn your keep every day by showing that you can help. That brings the very best entrepreneurs to you, because they don't want to answer to anybody, and you've got this partnership, service-oriented philosophy. If you're helping them build their companies, they're more than happy to share that information with their friends. Our best marketing tool is our list of portfolio companies.

Zeroing in on Information Technology

We focused. We decided when we started Benchmark that we would do no health care investing. Many venture firms had half their house doing biotech, and half doing information technology. We said no. We had a slide in our presentation that was a picture of those snakes with wings—the medical symbol—with a big red circle slashed through it. We said, "We don't understand what goes on in test tubes, so we're not going to pretend we do. We are going to focus all of our energy on information technology. By doing that, we're going to have more coverage in information technology, specifically the Internet, and then subsequently e-commerce, than anybody else." We've very much executed that plan.

About a year into Benchmark, at one of our off-site meetings, we drew the conclusion that e-commerce was going to be really significant. So we, in some ways, caught that wave early, and got out in front of it. I think we have something like fifteen investments in e-commerce right now.

An interesting thing that has been happening in recent months is that a lot of very significant brick-and-mortar companies are coming to us and saying, "We really want a partner to help us 'dotcom' our business, and to build an e-commerce capability. We are not sure how to do it, and we'd like to partner with you." Some of these situations have led to relationships with our portfolio companies and enhanced opportunities for everyone.

More recently, we've had some discussions about starting whole new businesses in partnership with large corporations that are looking to build effective e-commerce offerings, and to provide the proper incentive to recruit the best and the brightest to go do it. They have decided that to do so internally would be difficult to accomplish for cultural reasons.

Dollars and Cents

We first raised $100 million and invested that in about twenty-two companies. We invested the fund quicker than we expected to, because it was such an opportunity-rich environment. Then we raised a subsequent fund from the same investors. We've increased the amount we manage from individuals—which has been a strategic pool of capital for us—from $10 million in the first fund to about $50 million in our most recent fund; however, we've kept the institutional contributions at about the same size. Our third fund, which was just raised last fall, was exactly the same size from an institutional point of view as our second fund, at $125 million. We could have raised much more, but we decided not to raise too much capital. We don't want to have to feel pressured to write the $10 million check. We want to stay in a position to do the earliest stage investing.

In that very first fund, we put in three times as much capital as most typical venture capitalists do in their funds. A venture capitalist usually invests 1 percent. We invested 3.5 percent of that fund because we wanted to show our investors we believe in ourselves as well. As a result of our investment, Benchmark was cash-flow negative for the first three years.

But the results of our first fund have been worth it. It's a $100 million fund, and today on paper it's worth almost 100 times that. I think that the eBay investment could turn out to be the most rewarding venture investment ever—a $5 million investment that's worth over $4 billion today. You have to realize that eBay is a very fortunate experience. We aided the company's development by helping to recruit the management team and helping them sort through some important strategic issues. But returns like that don't happen very often. And, the great thing about eBay is that it's not only Bob Kagle's success—each of my partners has contributed to the company in meaningful ways, so it's Benchmark's success. Just think about how often you hear about Benchmark versus hearing about any of the individuals in the firm. That is a measure of our effectiveness in building our brand and our firm.

Early Stage, Early Tech

I would say there were a couple of principles that made us want to invest at an early stage, one of which is that it is more rewarding to be part of the company building process from the ground up. Just in terms of your emotional connection to the entrepreneur and your involvement with the process. Ariba is going to be a fantastic company, and it was started right here in our offices. Keith Krach was our first EIR[2] at Benchmark. Before he left, he had twelve employees working here full-time, elbow to elbow with us over a four-month period. You can't buy the kind of connection and the kind of relationship that that develops.

The most important characteristic to have as an entrepreneur? There are really two characteristics—well, maybe three. You have to have a tremendous amount of resilience, because these are very challenging endeavors. You also have to be very flexible, and you have to listen very carefully. I like to say the characteristic I look for most in entrepreneurs is big ears, because nobody's so smart as to have the right answer from the beginning. Most of our companies go through fundamental transformations between the time they're started and the time in which they achieve some degree of success. What we try to do is just encourage that process as much as we can, and to be a resource, not only as a sounding board, but also as a conduit for these entrepreneurs to connect to other constituencies that can be helpful to them in developing their plans and their businesses.

eBay—The Deal That Changed Internet Investing

Amazon was just starting to show up on the radar screen. They were a company we learned about a little too late. But, here's the insight

---

[2] *An Entrepreneur in Residence. Many venture funds are discovering that it pays to have an entrepreneur on the premises incubating the next idea.*

that drove our thinking there. We looked at the Web and said, wait a minute, the Web is mostly about the ability to make a one-to-one connection efficiently. Why is it that most of the people who are using the Web are using it in a broadcast fashion—using a broadcast media–oriented model, an ad-driven model, to charge for eyeballs that are undifferentiated? Not that it doesn't make sense, but it doesn't realize the full potential of the Web.

The fabric of the Web is really about being able to make these one-to-one connections. You have to achieve a degree of relevance to the user of the system by putting things in front of them that are of extremely high value. The best measure of that value is whether or not they are willing to transact.

So we started to think about the Web as a transactional fabric. If we looked to where the transactions were happening, we were much more likely to find lasting and enduring online business models. It was that kind of thinking that helped us realize the value and potential of eBay when we first saw it, because here was a project that had an enormous number of page views, but no banner advertising.

I can tell you what the revenues were then. A couple of hundred thousand dollars a month. The revenues the second quarter of 1999 were some $30 million. There's been a tremendous amount of growth in just a little over two years. What we observed was that the dogs were eating the dog food. This thing was working, it was growing organically. We weren't spending a tremendous amount of money on customer acquisition. A lot of the growth was word of mouth. You just couldn't deny the fact that it was showing a tremendous amount of vitality of its own accord. Wherever you can find natural organic growth, and you find momentum in these businesses without a tremendous amount of marketing effort, then that generally indicates that you're on to something.

We felt that online banner advertising was probably not the promised land. But thinking about what *could* be the promised land led us to consider transactions as an indicator of that. Then we just started looking for the transactions online.

There are a lot of things we look for in e-commerce business opportunities. One of the things that we like is when something is being accomplished online that just cannot be accomplished in the real world. eBay was a good example of that.

The Internet: A Transactionally Enabling Medium

The fact that the Web is an enabling medium is a fundamental element of the proposition. Another thing we look for is where the online experience can add enough, in terms of the user experience, to be compelling. We think about that along a number of dimensions. First of all, convenience. If something is just totally convenient online, relative to what you have to do in the real world, then that's very appealing to people. And, I like to use the illustration, "If the real world experience feels like a root canal, then what you want to do is find a way to use the Web's efficiency to reduce the pain."

Online mortgages are a great example. We're investors in the leader, E-LOAN. You talk to people, and they hate the process of getting a mortgage. It's a bunch of paperwork. And there are all kinds of stages in the process where you don't know what's going on, and you're not sure exactly what you're supposed to do next. It can be a really frustrating experience for the consumer. Well, our ambition for E-LOAN is to have a product called Mortgage Now which would allow customers to apply online, get approval a day later, and get the funds a week later. That will be a totally compelling offering, not only for consumers, but also for the real estate agents whose livelihood depends on closing these deals. There's an example of a process online that looks incredibly different from the one in the real world, because it's much more convenient and much more efficient.

The considered purchase, where the gathering of a significant amount of information in order to make an intelligent decision is necessary, is facilitated greatly online. Because in the real world you have the very separate exercises of doing the research, finding the information, and making the purchase. On the Web that can be managed in a pretty unified way.

There are a number of businesses in the terrestrial world that have very inefficient distribution channels, have inventory spread at various layers around the country or around the world, and are turning that inventory at a very modest or slow rate. My favorite example here is luggage. We've just invested in a company in Colorado called eBags. Luggage in a department store turns on the average of twice a year. That says you have $50 of inventory sitting on the floor to create $100 of sales. Well, if you centralize and manage that inventory in a single location, you can achieve inventory turn something on the order of twenty to twenty-five times a year. You can live on one-tenth the margins the traditional brick-and-mortar retailers do, and still achieve the same level of profitability on a return-on-assets basis.

You have to select categories where customers can be satisfied by a remote shopping experience and next-day delivery. There are clearly some things that are never going to be sold online. I don't think you're going to see many cups of Starbucks coffee sold online anytime soon. But there's a whole host of merchandise for which it will make sense to fundamentally change the distribution structure and the economics of the business to support a much more efficient and effective method of distribution. And soon next-day delivery will turn into same-day delivery.

Louis Borders of Borders Books is launching a company by the name of Web Van. If you think of groceries and drugs and general merchandise that are brought to your door in two hours, you'll have the idea. You'll have these large distributed warehouses that will run large trucks to local depots. The trucks will cross-dock into vans, which will travel through your neighborhood dropping off your groceries and everything else you've ordered within the last several hours. It's a business where Web ordering is an absolutely pivotal enabling technology. Because if you think about it, any other user interface that you would use to collect those orders would be highly inefficient.

I think what we're doing is stealing back bits of time that otherwise are wasted driving back and forth to the dry cleaner's. And we're giving people that time to invest back in family and community, in terms of interaction and relationships. Most of these online businesses are designed to add back time for what you and I might consider the more important things in life.

Funding Web Blockbusters

I would say that we're trying very much to stay focused on the company-building process, and on the real process of knitting together a team of executives that have the ability and the passion to build a really significant company. Having said that, the competitive intensity of these segments at the early stages is such that you can't afford not to shine the light on them in order to get early visibility and create a following for these companies. In many ways, branding is more important in the venture business now than it ever has been. And so, "mind share" is what you're trying to capture. Returns in these segments have always gravitated toward the leader. And so, there's a tremendous premium that comes from being the first well-executed play in many of these segments. What it means to be the first well-executed play is not just to execute the business, but to communicate the early success of the business, in an effective and broad way, so as to feed that success. Success does breed success in the venture capital business.

It used to be true that the pioneers often had the arrows in their back, back in the late '70s and early '80s. I think that's less true today, although you could certainly argue that the first online services were CompuServe and Prodigy, and where are they today? But, I think that you could also take the counterpoint that Amazon.com was the first truly effective e-commerce solution for books, and they've been able to parlay that into a tremendously successful and leading business. So, being early is important, but being the best and being perceived as the leader when the category begins to become legitimized are the most important things.

Moving Forward

I think the main thing we have going for us is that we have a tremendous team spirit. We really want to be the best, and we want to be widely recognized as being the best. We want all our companies to be very happy that they did business with us, and to feel that they made the right decision when they picked Benchmark. It's really not about the money. That's one of the taglines around here. I mean, we've made more money from our first fund than I think any of us would ever have imagined having. But it hasn't changed a thing that we do. I think part of it is that we're still a start-up. In our own minds, we've still got a tremendous amount to prove to the world, to one another, and to ourselves. And, I think that we wake up every day thinking about that. It's the same kind of energy you get when you're starting a company.

I kept telling Bruce that the only thing I would rather do than be a venture capitalist is start my own company. Well, that's what we did. We started our own company, which turned out to be a venture capital firm. But, we have much the same magic as a start-up, with people who are working incredibly long hours but yet not resenting it. They jump out of bed in the morning, instead of dragging themselves out, and they spend their time in the shower thinking about the next strategy challenge, rather than their next trip to Europe or that new jet.

We said, "Look, it's not about the money anymore. There's money everywhere. We have to provide value to these companies. What we do for these companies has to be worth a lot more than the check we write." By thinking of ourselves as a service business, all of a sudden you're working harder to return a phone call, and you're offering to meet the entrepreneurs in their office rather than dragging them into yours. It's a subtle thing, but I do think that entrepreneurs are by and large a pretty savvy customer base. And if you genuinely believe in the spirit of partnership, you'll behave that way. That means that when really important decisions come up, you state your case persuasively, but you defer to their judgment and their decision, because it's their company. If you do that, then I think that word gets around that you are someone people want to work with.

We're not planning to get much bigger. I'm not sure our model scales above the six partners that we have in the firm right now. So what we have to do is work smarter. We have to be more selective in the projects that we get involved with, and we have to continue to aim high and develop the full potential of the companies that we invest in. I don't think it's likely that you're going to see us raise billions of dollars, and do something radically different.

MICHELANGELO
VOLPI
Cisco Systems

 In high-technology industries, where the Microsofts, Intels, and Ciscos of the world dominate their respective spaces, corporations play an essential and pivotal role; they are test sites, partners, customers, references, and sources of capital for a vast number of start-ups.

In the past, the question for corporations when it came to new products and technology was whether to buy or build. For the innovative high-tech company today, it's buy and build—not in the old-fashioned acquisition mode but as corporate venture capitalists: invest so that the technology and the products of a start-up become available to you and to your customers.

Since the beginning of its venture capital program in 1995, Cisco Systems has made over fifty investments in start-ups worth about $250 million. The value of those investments in August 1999 was well over $1 billion. To be sure, the strategic importance of corporate venture capital is well recognized at Cisco; instead of diverting scarce resources into playing catch-up—at the risk of not catching up at all—the network giant invests strategically in companies that provide some of its customers' solutions.

Some contend that corporate venture capitalists such as Cisco or Intel are now competing with mainstream venture capitalist investors. But at Cisco, the feeling is that corporate investors are best suited to work alongside venture capitalists. According to Mike Volpi, who runs Cisco's venture investing group, corporate venture capitalists are not a substitute for traditional venture capitalists, but a complement; they offer a different set of assets for the entrepreneur to use. Of course, the question of whether and how corporate giants such as Cisco and their entrepreneurial investments

29

actually co-exist is still up in the air. Some argue that companies such as Computer Associates and even Cisco buy companies for their products and often have no use for the people who helped develop those products. On the other hand, companies such as Microsoft want to integrate the companies they acquire into their own operations—and often the task can be a painful one. Whatever the outcome, the idea of a partnership with a corporate power such as Cisco can be an extremely important event for a small company, providing capital and customers with one fell swoop.

I GOT INVOLVED with venture capital at Cisco because it's always had a fairly active business development process of looking outside the company to augment the solutions we can offer to customers.

In 1994, when I came to Cisco, it had made one investment and one acquisition up to that point in time. Both the investment and the acquisition worked out well. The acquisition worked very well from a revenue perspective. As for the investment, we built a pretty good partnership with Cascade, the company we invested in. From a financial perspective, they were heading toward an IPO, and sure enough they did one. Things worked so well with the first two that Cisco felt it should institutionalize what it had done. In other words, make it a repeatable process. So, the company jumped into that, and I was the first hire that it made to help that process.

Since that time in 1994, Cisco has acquired fifty companies and invested in about one hundred, with total investment amount of about $500 million. My guess is that the market value of that investment dollar is upwards of $3 billion by now. So, our work has yielded a very good financial return for us. But that wasn't the fundamental driver of why Cisco decided to do corporate venture capital.

Why Cisco Ventures?

The fundamental driver was two or three key things we wanted to accomplish. One was to build strong partnerships with relatively small companies and give them credibility. We wanted to be able to take them to a customer and say, yes, we know they're a fledgling company, but they're our partner, and they offer an important part of the solution. The assumption was that we don't believe we can do everything ourselves—by working with other people, we can build a better solution for the customer. That's why we invested in Cascade, and why we've invested in a number of other companies. Of course the thought also was, while we make these "strategic investments," we don't want to make stupid financial decisions. At the end of the day, if we make a strategic investment and the company fails financially, then there is no strategy around it anymore. There has to be some financial success that's associated with a strategic investment as a secondary benefit.

Our venture investing differs from others such as Intel and Microsoft. Intel, for example, primarily invests as a demand-creation vehicle for their products. Their corporate development group is not as tightly knit with the rest of the corporation. They act as venture capitalists. We, on the other hand, make fewer investments, and are more oriented toward a close coupling between the external company and the operating unit within Cisco. Ours is more a strategic investment and less the demand-stimulation investment that is Intel's mission. For Intel, anything that uses more MIPS is good, so they invest in anything that uses more MIPS. If you look at the history of our investments, you'll see that they're all tied to what we do. We don't invest in a Yahoo!, for example, because they are not tied to what we do. We actively pass on opportunities that may be very good financial investments—and are very good at 50,000 feet for demand creation—but are not necessarily directly coupled with our business.

We were early investors in Broadcom, as was Intel. We actually sat down with them about two and a half years ago and said, "We think that cable modems are going to be a really interesting technology. People are going to want to have high-speed Internet access in their homes. You have cable modem chips and we should jointly develop a product." So, we invested in the company at the time, and together started building a product that actually consisted of two parts. One was a cable modem head end—a big box that sits in the cable company's central office and spits out high-speed data. The other was a subscriber piece that sits on the customer side. The investment worked out. Broadcom went public, and we made a lot of money.

Clash of Values?

We are extremely conscious that corporations and entrepreneurial ventures can be in conflict. At Cisco, we won't invest in companies that we compete with, so a lot of the companies we approach feel much more comfortable working with us. But if they don't know us or have never interacted with Cisco, there is an initial concern that needs to be overcome.

We've overcome such concerns by building a track record. We have enough references within the venture capital community that we can say, "Hey, why don't you talk to John Doerr or go to Don Valentine and ask them what they think about having Cisco as an investor." Pretty unanimously we get over that hurdle. When we do end up competing with a company we've invested in, we become a passive investor and stop exchanging information. That's happened a couple of times. If possible, we'll divest the stock. We don't want to put ourselves or our partner into a compromising position.

Fitting In

How does Cisco, as a venture capitalist and corporate partner, see the world of computers and computer technology?

We break down the communications segment into two big businesses. There's a classic software-type environment, where a distribution partner is very useful. And there's a hardware environment where distribution doesn't always necessarily make sense because of the cost associated with pass through. So, if we pursue an OEM arrangement, I will take the start-up's product and re-sell it through my distribution channel.

For software, partnering works well because there's enough margin in software for a small company to make money, and for a big company to make money distributing the software. That has worked well historically. Taking a small company into our distribution channel—not necessarily re-selling the product, but saying, "Hey, work with these guys"—that works very well too. AT&T would never consider putting a product made by a thirty-person company into their network. But if it was recommended by Cisco, and Cisco was standing behind it, they would certainly look at it as a much more realistic option. The credibility that a large corporate partner brings definitely helps.

New Markets

We first look at new market areas where we want to expand our presence. Then we look at the type of solution that a customer looks for in that area. We evaluate what we can do internally and what we can potentially acquire. We see if it's part of a competence that we should have, and we look at where we need to partner. Then we actively look for people in that new market segment we can partner with. That then becomes the source of future venture investments.

We don't usually invest in venture capital funds. We have invested in only two of them. One was the Java fund with Kleiner Perkins, and the other was an IVP fund called the Broadband fund. The intent behind investing in those funds was so we would see more of the opportunities that were out there. The reality turned out to be that you don't learn much unless you're involved firsthand. So about two years ago we decided to not invest in funds, but to do the investing ourselves. We invest alongside venture capitalists frequently. In 80 percent of the circumstances, Cisco and the venture capitalists are together, investing in the same round. But we don't want to invest directly in their funds, because a limited partner in a fund basically is only looking for a financial return. Since that's not our primary objective in investing, we don't benefit by investing in funds.

A lot of venture capitalists invest in things that are competitive for Cisco. We don't want to fuel price competition by investing independently. We figure we have more control over the process if we invest hand in hand with venture capitalists. Corporate investors like Cisco, Microsoft, Intel, and others have enough deal flow that they see everything. We don't need to be a limited partner in a fund to create access.

Entrepreneurially Friendly

Entrepreneurs are entrepreneurs because many of them want to avoid the bureaucratic processes of the large corporation. There clearly are corporations that are impossible for entrepreneurs to work with. On average, the cards are stacked against an entrepreneur getting a corporate investor. There are specific steps that we've taken at Cisco to avoid that.

First, we created a process by which investments can be approved with a very small decision-making body. This consists of three people, basically. Big companies move slowly because decision-making is so distributed that any time you have more than three or four opinions, you can't get to a consensus quickly. Our solution is to keep the decision-making body small and give that body the authority to invest sig-

nificant chunks of money. The tricky part is how to staff that decision-making body. You need to staff an internal venture capital program with generalists who understand the things we do, are well connected and networked horizontally within our own organization, and
are judicious about learning and understanding all that's going on in
the company and in the industry. Because they are a small group that
behaves as a proxy for the rest of the company, they have to have the
trust and the knowledge of the company, and the ability to make decisions about fairly sizeable—millions of dollars—investments.

Entrepreneurship Begets Entrepreneurship

Cisco is where it is today because we organically grew it into this position. When we started we were a small company. Everybody knew me.
Everybody knew my boss. We put this program together, and we've
been working with the company forever. So, everybody says, "Well, if
those guys tell me I should be working with them, I will." Other companies come together and twenty-five years into their development
decide that they're going to create a venture fund. They say, "We're
going to hire a couple of guys from the outside to come in and invest
money." That almost never works, because those people aren't tied into
the rest of the company. They have no organizational credibility; the
company is not culturally open to accepting outside input and outside
technology. Everything is stacked against them. So, the fact is that we
evolved into the place where we are today, versus somebody who just
decided one day to start a fund. That's where I think we have a significant competitive advantage over most other people who try to do this.

The most challenging portion of doing corporate venture capital is
keeping up with the growth of the company. Our company has been
reaching new areas so rapidly that knowing everything we are doing is
challenging. It's hard for me and my team to be continuously relevant to
everybody in the company, because there's so much going on. But, in
terms of organizational resistance, we've never had a challenge with that.

Deep Pockets

Big, important players see corporate venture capital either as a company that wants to create demand—like Intel—or as a company that

uses venture capital as a sourcing mechanism. I think that we—and probably Microsoft—are the exception. We do things differently.

Previously when a venture capitalist started a company, you needed $5 million. Now you need $30 million. But investing $30 million in something can get pretty ugly. So venture capitalists need an investor that gives them distribution and gives them a lot of money to invest. I think most venture capitalists think of corporate investors as great, because their money comes in at a higher valuation, and more important, they get access to a distribution channel that can be very useful. So, it helps them at the latter stage of developing a company. In large part, I think that most corporate venture capitalists will play that role.

Does the infusion of corporate venture capital also speed up the development process? I don't think so. Start-ups go about as fast as they can go right now, with or without corporate partners. Most corporate investors are fairly detached from the operational reality of their investment. And because they hire people from the outside to spend their money, those people are inherently not knowledgeable about what's going on in the corporation. On average, big corporations make mediocre venture capitalists because of that disconnect.

I think Microsoft, Intel, and Cisco are exceptions to the rule. We are doing things in a way that only we are capable of because of the specific way we've evolved into this business. We are capable because of our knowledge set and because we invest very early. We see things before venture capitalists at times. But when it makes sense we come in after venture capitalists. We have also achieved intellectual equality with venture capitalists in many circumstances, where they do not view us as dumb money that comes in later, but as smart money that can invest with them.

Where will Cisco be two to three years from now? How much of the model that we and Microsoft and Intel have fine-tuned can actually be used by other people? Will the underlying conditions we've operated under be there two to three years from now?

We have a model that we feel pretty comfortable with at this point. So, if anything, we're going to be doing more of the same. We will never have an exclusive fund. We will continue to invest our own money and focus on technology areas we want to get into. We will probably increase the number of transactions we do at a modest pace, maybe 20 percent more a year.

Is our model repeatable elsewhere? I think it's very challenging. It will be difficult for other people to replicate what we've done, again because we have grown into where we are. It's not something you can start from scratch when you're a big company.

There always will be a place for corporate investing. Keep in mind that for corporations there is an arbitrage opportunity. Money sits in the treasury and earns 4 percent a year. And for many corporations there's a lot of money sitting in the treasury. So if these companies spend $100 million or $200 million in the venture market, it doesn't impact them at all. They are valuation insensitive, and they play a key role in the evolution of companies.

The Yin and Yang of the Corporation and the Entrepreneur

A lot of entrepreneurs run from the bureaucracy of a big company. What they try to do in receiving investments from big companies is to achieve some of the benefits of a big company—brand, status, distribution, and so forth—while not having to bear the burden of the bureaucracy of a big company. What inevitably happens is that life is not that black and white. You can't only extract the parts that you want out of a big company and leave behind the things you don't want. If you really want to leverage the big company and have access to that distribution channel, you have to engage their sales force, understand the politics, and all that stuff. You do have to engage the bureaucracy to some level. In other words, there is no Nirvana. Take the good things of a big company, get a little bit of investment from them, and leverage those good things.

Cisco has been a successful company. We still are very entrepreneurial internally, so folks who work with us don't get mired in the same type of bureaucracy that they do in a lot of traditional big companies. Because of that we have success. Ironically, we ourselves have a tough time dealing with the bigger companies, and I don't think that sort of conflict ever goes away.

Ten years ago, which is not that long a time in corporate evolution, we were 200 people and pre-public. Today we're a big company. We're 15,000 people. One out of every five of our employees is an employee that came in via acquisition. And most companies we've acquired have been start-ups. In fact, 90 percent of the companies we acquire are start-ups. So, most people who work here remember being small. Some of the people that are here now were small three weeks ago. So there is a certain amount of intellectual bonding that goes on, because everybody remembers being there. And everybody remembers the pressures and the urgencies of entrepreneurship.

BOB KNOX
Cornerstone Equity Investors

 The first venture capitalists were mostly private equity investors who evaluated privately owned companies and invested in those that could be financially transformed into public companies by infusions of capital. Risk and speculation—measured by today's standards—were low. Most of the companies financed were already going concerns—with customers, sales, and even profits. But the advent of computers and computer technology put venture capital investing into the realm of start-ups and early-stage companies, where the speculative nature of these enterprises required a different level of risk. Now as the technology business has matured, venture capital has undergone still another redefinition, returning at least in part to its early roots in funding mature businesses, in technology and in other segments as well. Consequently, the lines between private equity and venture capital investing have blurred, especially when it comes to bigger deals and higher valuations.

Few private equity/venture capital investors have had the success of Cornerstone. It began as a subsidiary of Prudential Insurance in 1982, but soon established its own identity with a new fund in 1984. Cornerstone demonstrated that technology investing, late-stage financing, and private equity are not mutually exclusive strategies. Over a sixteen-year period, the principals at Cornerstone have made investments in more than 100 companies, with an aggregate equity value of over $3 billion. In some cases, Cornerstone has taken a minority position in high-tech growth companies such as Dell Computer, Conner Peripherals, Linear Technologies, and PictureTel; in other cases, the firm has taken controlling positions by providing equity for leveraged buyout transactions such as StorMedia, Centurion Health Management Associates, and True Temper Sports.

Investments are made in both private and public companies, but all investments in public companies are privately negotiated and structured. Typically, Cornerstone's partners hold two board seats in each company. While treating management as partners, Cornerstone institutes board structures and governance processes that are as sophisticated as any found in well-run public companies.

One of Cornerstone's unique strategies has been to identify privately held market leaders, such as FAO Schwartz and Novatel Wireless, and structure deals that help them grow and forge new markets. Indeed, for many family owned, privately controlled companies, the private equity strategy articulated by funds such as Cornerstone may well become a key liquidity and exit strategy. Here Bob Knox, one of the founding partners of Cornerstone, describes his transformation from an institutional investment manager to a full-fledged venture capitalist and discusses Cornerstone's evolution into one of the industry's largest private equity players.

WHEN I WAS in high school, even though I was very actively involved in sports, I used to follow the stock market in the *Wall Street Journal*. I commuted to school by train and was surrounded by business executives—guys in suits with their heads buried in newspapers on their way to their offices in New York. My mother often reminds me that at the time I vowed I would never become one of the suits—someone I viewed as married to a corporation.

I liked the idea of ownership, of owning assets. I was strongly influenced by my father, who was a real estate broker and investor. He would buy and renovate residential and small commercial properties. He was always making deals, and the fact that he had complete control of his time made quite an impression on me. He was also an amazing risk taker, and not just in business. He was a seat-of-the-pants type Navy pilot and started me flying airplanes when I was about fifteen years old. Some of the flying stunts I pulled when I was a kid frighten me more today than they did then, when I was too young to know better. In any event, from a very early age I had decided that I wanted to own a business and take risks for myself.

How I ended up at Boston University is a story by itself, as my college career started after several months serving as a deckhand on a freighter ship. I was an economics major but during my junior and senior years, I increasingly elected to take courses in investments and portfolio theory at the business school. I decided that I needed to get an M.B.A. to get into the investment business, but I was extremely anxious to get out of school and start working. At BU, I was able to waive a good number of core M.B.A. course requirements in economics and math by taking special exams. So I graduated with an M.B.A. and B.A. in five years. I was twenty-three years old and I went to find a job on Wall Street.

I don't recall being consciously aware of venture capital at that point in 1975. I ended up going to work at Prudential, which at the time was just beginning to add M.B.A.s to its investment staff. I was one of a handful of M.B.A.s hired that year for what was then called the Corporate Finance Department. At the time, Prudential was by far the largest investor in private placements, annually purchasing over $3 billion of private debt and equity securities. The mid-to-late '70s were also the very beginning of the investment form called leveraged buyouts and Prudential quickly became the leading mezzanine-level equity player in the early LBOs.

Baby Venture Capital Steps

About the same time, one of my college friends started a software company in Boston that needed venture capital. At Pru, I had started to take a real keen interest in leveraged buyouts, and had worked as a number cruncher on a number of KKR[1] deals. I remember being at an investment conference speaking on leveraged buyouts—how we constructed them, participated in them, and so on—and meeting some venture capitalists. While my friend was forming this company, he really had no idea how to raise venture capital, so I became the natural person to design the financial strategy and capital structure, and to lead the fund-raising effort. It was one of the first software companies that produced business graphics. We raised a $2 million first round from a group of venture capitalists that included Russ Carson of Welsh, Carson, Anderson & Stowe, which was at that time

---

[1] *Kohlberg Kravis Roberts, one of the leading leveraged buyout firms of the '80s and '90s.*

investing their first fund, Venrock, and Greylock. Through the process of raising that money, I got a firsthand understanding of what the venture capital business was all about. That was around 1980 or 1981. And 1981 was the first year that institutional investors committed over $1 billion to venture capital funds.

That billion-dollar commitment level became an important milestone in the evolution of the private equity markets. Until then, an institution like Prudential, which had hundreds of billions of dollars of capital, couldn't be convinced that venture capital was an industry that had sufficient depth and growth potential to be a permanent and powerful capital market with institutional-scale investment opportunity as opposed to being just a cottage industry.

In 1981 I proposed the formation of a venture capital investment unit to Bill Field, who was then running all of Pru's private investment activities. We received the enthusiastic support of Garnett Keith, Pru's chief investment officer. We formed a venture capital investment unit as part of the private placement area and got Pru's board of directors to approve an investment program where, beginning in 1982, we committed to invest over $500 million in venture capital funds. Bill Field is retired, but two of the individuals who I brought into the group in 1982, Mark Rossi and Dana O'Brien, are my co-equal senior partners at Cornerstone today.

Our investment strategy was to proactively seek out the general partners of venture capital firms and become large—in most cases the largest—limited partners of a select number of venture capitalists practicing on both the East and the West Coasts. This approach reflected two views we had about the venture capital business.

First, we viewed the industry even then as being a steeply sloping pyramid with a few outstanding firms at the top and many mediocre firms at the base. So we created a core portfolio of what we thought were the leading venture capital firms in the country. Typically, we invested $10–$30 million and provided from 10 to 20 percent of the total partnership capital. In the early '80s, commitments of this size were unprecedented. We wanted to earn superior rates of return by investing in the top-tier funds. Second, we wanted to look into the portfolios of these established venture capital firms and identify mature companies that were still growing rapidly but needed amounts of capital that the general partners were neither willing nor able to provide, as these were larger rounds at higher valuations. We started our own direct investment program by making relatively large investments in portfolio companies from those venture funds. Eventually we sourced deals from elsewhere as well, but initially our limited partner status was a strategic linkage for our direct investment deal flow. Today that's called co-investing, and a lot of institutions do it. Back then, we called it late-stage venture capital investing.

We possessed the kind of skills needed to find, select, and evaluate late-stage investments—we were good financial analysts, we could do comparable analysis, and we understood managements and business strategies. Late-stage investing required skills that are traditionally associated with public stock market investing rather than traditional start-up venture capital investing. We aggressively built the venture capital program with Pru's capital for a couple of years, and it turned out to be a very effective way for a large institution to invest in the venture capital industry.

One of the issues that we soon confronted was that of compensation. At that point the venture capital unit that we had begun within Pru had probably ten or so employees. It became clear to us and to Pru that if we were going to build this business for the long term, we had to do it with a compensation structure that had, if not the same, then very similar features to the one that was standard in the venture capital partnership world. What we came up with—which at the time I think was pretty unusual, if not unique—was a structure where we formed a subsidiary of the insurance company, and that subsidiary became the corporate general partner of what turned out to be a series of limited partnerships, where Pru had a special carried interest[2] but allowed the individuals to also have a significant part of the carried interest. Through this arrangement, we had an opportunity to create wealth for ourselves if we were successful. In each partnership we formed, Pru put up about 20 percent of the total capital, and we raised the other 80 percent from other institutional investors, which included Fortune 100 corporate pension plans, large state retirement systems, and foreign institutional investors.

---

[2] A special carried interest is a company's share of the profits the partnership generated.

Why was the Pru strategy successful when other institutions have stumbled in venture capital? There was agreement as to what the objective was, which was to maximize the rate of return on invested capital. There were no other objectives. We were not trying to execute any kind of business strategy on behalf of Pru. We, the individual officers of the subsidiary, were acting as the general partner and were purely motivated by achieving the best rate of return that we could for our limited partners, one of which happened to be Prudential.

What are the lessons for a corporate venture capital investor? Most corporate venture capital investment programs are widely viewed to have been failures, in part because their rate of return objective was subordinate to their corporate objectives—the industries they wanted to be in, the intelligence they wanted, the strategic corporate relationships they wanted. So, from an investment perspective, I think corporate venture capital—at least as practiced in the 1980s—has generally not been too successful. From a financial institution standpoint, I think it's very difficult, too, because at some point the interests of the individuals diverge from the interests of the financial institution.

In our case, we had managed a series of partnerships successfully, but we were still sharing the carried interest with Prudential. Eventually we felt we didn't need to do that anymore, and to their credit, they recognized that as well. Ultimately, we separated from Pru and formed Cornerstone. We did that in a complicated, but amicable, set of agreements with Prudential, under which we continued to manage the partnerships and assets we had created as officers of the corporate subsidiary.

Our Investment Rationale

Our approach to the direct investment private equity business has always been driven by underlying assumptions about the nature of capital markets in the United States. The initial assumption that we made, which turned out to be correct, was that there really wasn't a deep supply of capital for rapidly growing, capital-intensive, private companies in the mid-'80s. As an example, two of our well-known investments, Dell and Conner Peripherals, were companies that were growing extremely rapidly, but could not access the public market because they didn't have the characteristics that were necessary to achieve public offerings. But they still needed huge amounts of growth capital. The rounds that were done in the mid-'80s in these kinds of technology companies could be anywhere from $20 to $50 million. Equity rounds of that scale weren't going to be supplied by even large venture capital funds, which in that era would have been funds that typically had only $50 to $100 million in total capital. So, we came in and played the lead role in providing relatively large amounts of capital to these companies. And, of course, we usually exited when those companies became public companies and provided us with liquidity. Obviously, similar conditions don't exist today. In the case of Dell, we led a round of financing that totaled $27 million in 1987. Michael Dell was twenty-two at the time and the company had just crossed the $100 million revenue mark. We ended up making about six times our money by the time Dell went public in 1989. While this was a good investment for our fund at the time we distributed the stock, it turned out to be spectacular for those who held the stock after the distribution.

The easier the access to the public market, the fewer opportunities there are going to be on the private side. There's also a very close correlation to the levels of prices in the public market and the valuations one can negotiate for private companies. That's always been true. Clearly, the formation of new companies in technology, particularly in the telecom and Internet sectors, has exploded. So the opportunities and the need for capital continue to be very large.

Partnering with Entrepreneurs

As we evolved, we increasingly made a lot of investments in companies that didn't have traditional venture capital backers—companies that had been grown by sweat equity and sometimes financed by smoke and mirrors—but had become reasonably large. Most of these companies were run by entrepreneurs who were fiercely independent. Our philosophy was, and still is, that we wanted to be partners with these executives. We spent a lot of time figuring out if we could work with them, if their vision was the same, and if their scenario for liquidity—whether it be an IPO or an acquisition—was really going to be acceptable. Although you can try to memorialize intentions in securities documents, that doesn't mean the frame of mind of the entrepreneur or the controlling shareholders won't change over time—it often does. So a lot depended on our ability to assess whether the entrepreneur would share our objectives and would react with us to opportunities for liquidity.

One of the things that we've done—and I think many people in our business have done the same over the last five to ten years—is to become very specialized, in terms of knowledge, in the industries that we're interested in. That's the only way you can stay competitive when there's an abundance of capital. In dealing with entrepreneurs, we've learned to make fairly accurate judgments about people and developed the ability to understand whether there is a match and whether we can work with people. I think one of the things we've learned, and maybe we've learned it the hard way, is that life is too short to do a deal with a management team you don't trust. Even if we find a deal that's attractive, if we can't work with the entrepreneur or if we don't agree with his or her values, we step away from that situation.

We try to spend as much time as possible with management on their home turf, to see who they are, how they fit, in their company and in their community. We try to get as much of a handle on who they are as individuals while we study the business. Even after having done all that, we sometimes completely misjudge someone.

Late-Stage versus Early-Stage Investing

Early-stage venture capitalists very clearly have a vision for the companies they invest in. They are very good at organizing new companies and setting the company out on its initial course of development. There are a lot of very mundane aspects to that, like leasing office space, hiring the first employees, and so forth. Founding entrepreneurs often do not have the skills, interest, or inclination to be the CEOs that will go through the next growth stage. Those skills are the skills we would associate with growth managers, or a professional manager, which is the kind of management that we more frequently encounter or recruit.

One of the other things that's changed dramatically over the last ten years, and it's still changing, is the level of sophistication and experience of management teams. We are now finding that the management teams we back in many cases have already raised private equity once or twice before. So they're tremendously more sophisticated than the kind of management teams you would run into ten years ago. There are pros and cons to this new level of experience and sophistication. The pro is that you have a management team that's lived through the experience of having a private equity partner, may have lived through the experience of operating under leverage, may have lived through the experience of doing a high-yield deal, and may have gone through an IPO process. Those are all very positive experiences because your management team isn't learning as you go along. The negative side is that managements are incredibly sophisticated about valuation, and very familiar with the kind of activities we do. This management sophistication is one of the powerful reasons that the private equity market is much more efficient than it was in the past.

Where Private Equity Is Headed

If you asked me five years ago where the private equity business would be today, I would have completely mis-predicted the current situation. Certainly, no one who is a student of the private equity market would have predicted that in 1998 approximately $100 billion would be raised by private equity funds. It's just an astonishing number. I think again back to 1981, when $1 billion was raised, and remember that as a huge milestone. We have experienced a hundredfold increase in capital raised in a period of sixteen or seventeen years. And the demand by institutional investors for private equity remains very strong. Some of the largest pension plans and institutions actively investing today have an issue as to whether they can deploy enough capital into the private equity markets to meet their own increased asset allocation targets despite the fact that the industry has become much bigger.

I think as long as the rates of return in the private equity business continue to be good for top-tier managers—I think the average rates of return may change quite dramatically in a negative way—then there will be capital available to be managed in early-stage venture capital, expansion capital, mezzanine, buy-out, distressed, and probably several new categories. That reflects the trend of increasing specialization.

I also think that more talented, intelligent people will enter the private equity business. One more trend that we're seeing some evidence of is that large institutions—global scale investment banking firms—will attempt to be more active in the business as principals. Goldman Sachs is a prime example of this trend.

One of the things that's happened is that the number of private equity firms has not expanded as rapidly as the amount of dollars in aggregate under management. Therefore, the amount of dollars under management by the average firm has expanded greatly. That has caused—and will continue to cause—a shift in focus toward larger deals. The more capital you have under management, the more you have to look at bigger companies and bigger transactions. That doesn't mean that companies that are seeking less than $10 million of equity won't have an abundant source of supply, but strategies will change for firms as their capital under management gets larger. But I don't see any part of the spectrum being abandoned, because success has been had in all stages of investment.

CLEVELAND CHRISTOPHE
TSG Capital Group

The Minority Enterprise Small Business Investment Companies (MESBIC) Act was enacted in 1968 in the aftermath of the Watts riots and the Kerner Commission report on race relations in America. When President Lyndon Johnson and Commerce Secretary Maurice Stans helped enact the recommendations of the report into law, no one would have predicted that it would help establish a minority venture capital industry and a culture of minority entrepreneurs. Indeed, it took nearly three decades and many changes before minority-focused funds could carve out their own niche; it took academics such as Michael Porter to extol the competitive advantages of inner cities, and it took pension funds such as the California Public Employees Retirement System and New York State Common Retirement Fund to insist that investment advisers include minority-focused funds in their total asset allocation mix.

Of the funds that have benefited from this money, Stamford's TSG Capital is the largest. TSG traces its roots to being the MESBIC of Equitable Life Assurance Society, eventually being acquired by its managers, Duane Hill, Cleveland Christophe, and others in 1992. In the subsequent years, it has acquired its own identity as a major provider of capital to minority-focused businesses—ranging from early-stage communications companies to apparel retailing.

TSG has demonstrated that investing in minority-focused businesses can have wider impact than currently thought. There are a host of investment opportunities, but they need to be properly scouted and structured,

and even then exit strategies for investors are the same as those in every
other segment—IPOs, sales, or mergers.

TSG's institutional investors include the state pension funds of New
York and California, Chase Capital Partners, and the Mellon Foundation.
Christophe himself has emerged as one of the leading voices of his indus-
try niche—an investor with an enviable track record and a champion for
increasing capital to the minority investment segment.

I GREW UP in Arkansas in the segregated South. I graduated from segregated schools, then went to Howard University for undergraduate work. My initial thought had been to be a lawyer. When I was in my sophomore year in college, Mr. Sadler, a fellow who owned a supermarket chain in Savannah, Georgia—which is where I was living at that time—wanted to know how I was doing in school and what I was going to major in. When I told him I was thinking about majoring in business administration, this look came over his face, and he said, "Cleveland, I like you and I think you're a smart boy. Don't do that. You should be a doctor. You should be a lawyer. You should be a dentist. Or you should be a preacher. You will do extraordinarily well, but your type will never make it in business." That was in 1963. I got into business administration because at Howard they had business law courses. I figured that if I was going to be a lawyer, I might as well try to get a head start. That's how it all started.

Toward the end of my junior year, I learned that there was something called an M.B.A. I was urged by one of my professors to speak with a dean who was visiting Howard from the Harvard Business School. Two things came out of that. The first was that I became even more interested in business, and I thought that maybe an M.B.A. was the way to go. Second, I knew I wasn't going to Harvard Business School. I went to the University of Michigan Business School instead. I had a singular focus as to what I wanted to pursue—finance, and more specifically, investments. I wanted to invest in public equity securities. I even went a step further. I wanted to be on the buy side, as opposed to the sell side.

I felt that I wanted to be someplace where—as I would have put it then—the market would be the judge, as contrasted with skin color or that type of consideration. I felt that the public securities market would be unbiased in its assessment of my skills. I particularly wanted to be on the buy side, where there was no emphasis on peddling stuff. I wanted to be in research. So as I prepared to come out of the University of Michigan, I interviewed with about twenty organizations. I ended up joining the investment research department of the Trust and Investment Division of First National City Bank (today's Citibank). I was the first African-American there.

I worked there from 1967 to 1969, and then was recruited by a retail conglomerate by the name of Kenton Corporation, which had been put together by the two heads of ITT's acquisition effort during Harold Geneen's most active acquisition period. I was with them for the better part of a year. We had a lean corporate staff of six or seven people. We assembled a $100 million public retail conglomerate with companies like Cartier Jewelers, Valentino, and Family Bargain Centers. It gave me my first inside look at what management and strategy—or the absence thereof—were really all about. I left Kenton, telling them they were going to drive the company over the cliff; and within two years, that's exactly what they did.

Entrepreneur/Short-Order Cook

In leaving Kenton I became an entrepreneur. Three young M.B.A.s— two from Harvard and one from Columbia—had started a restaurant business called Soul Stop that they hoped to build into a fast-food franchise chain serving inner-city markets. They raised a bit of venture capital from friends to launch the business. They approached me to consult with them on raising additional capital. I took one look at what they were doing, and said, "You guys have so screwed this whole thing up that you don't need a consultant, you need somebody to run the operation. The only basis on which I would consider working with you would be to run Soul Stop; and even if you decide that you want me to do that, I'm not convinced that I want to be in the restaurant business."

I ended up doing it. They sold me on becoming their partner and the CEO of the outfit. At the time we had one unit operating in Harlem. What a learning experience! I learned about operations, vendor relations, labor relations, fund-raising, accounting, and partnership. Shortly after I joined Soul Stop, my three partners all but deserted me. While they maintained their economic interest, I was left with the thrill of trying to make the business work. I've never worked harder.

Soul Stop's original thesis was a good one. Provide a clean, customer-responsive environment, quick service, and quality, along with employment opportunities and franchising across the landscape, to underserved markets. Nice in theory, but damnably difficult to implement in practice.

By day I wore a suit and sought venture capital to support our business expansion plans. By night I wore a smock and cooked fried chicken. Our restaurant was at 126th Street and Seventh Avenue in Harlem, in 1970. I learned a lot about a lot of things, and I learned fast. I learned about accounting during that period, because I had to keep my own books. I learned about people management, because it only took six people to run that operation, but at the end of the year I had to prepare 106 W-2s. Some I fired; others simply didn't return to work after receiving their first paycheck.

Toward the end of the year, I had convinced Phil Smith, who then was the president of FNCB Capital Corporation, today known as Citicorp Ventures, to invest a little bit of venture capital into Soul Stop. I'll never forget the day Phil said, "Cleve, I buy it and I'm prepared to put some money behind you." I hesitated and said, "Phil, thanks. Let me come back to you." Two days later, I told Phil, "Thanks, but no thanks. I've made a mistake. I think that I can build this business, create value and make money—but my heart is not in it."

While I had not been responsible for bringing anybody's money into Soul Stop, I wanted to salvage as much in the way of value or value potential for the investors as I could. In the next few months, my attorney and I put together the sexiest stock swap for a penny-ante little restaurant in Harlem that you'd ever want to see. It was a very sophisticated transaction that preserved value for all of Soul Stop's constituents—lenders, the trade, employees, and investors. My lawyer was Reginald Lewis; the same Reg Lewis with whom I would work seventeen years later to raise $1 billion to buy Beatrice International Foods from KKR. Dating from the Soul Stop days in 1970, Reg and I became best friends. As I was exiting Soul Stop, Phil Smith asked me to consider returning to First National City Bank. At first I thought he was crazy. Why would I do that? I had certainly enjoyed my time there, but that was part of my past. His response was, "I want you to join us in the venture capital business at FNCB Capital Corporation."

So, in 1971, I rejoined FNCB Capital Corporation, now known as Citicorp Venture Capital Corporation. As you know, this was an SBIC. Over the years FNCB Capital became one of the major private equity and venture players. Among my teammates in 1971 were Russ Carson and Pat Welsh, who would later found the highly successful Welsh, Carson, Anderson & Stowe. Others were David Arscott, Larry Lawrence, and Bill Reilly, each of whom would start venture capital firms. Finally, there was one other person whose career certainly had its ebbs and flows. His name was Bob Swanson, who was a founder of Genentech.

In any event, by 1973 there was a real question about whether FNCB Capital would survive. The head of investment policy for the trust division also had oversight responsibility for FNCB Capital. One day he said to me, "You've got some friends that would like you back in Investment Research." He said, "I know you're having fun at FNCB Capital, and I'm not going to tell you that you shouldn't continue, if that's what you choose to do. But," he said, "I will suggest to you that the jury is very much out on this bet because it has not turned a dime, and the bank may not be prepared to fund it much longer." So I ended up going back to dealing with publicly traded securities in the Investment Research Department.

I worked at Citibank in investment research, then in France where I became involved in commercial banking, and in San Francisco where I became directly engaged in corporate lending and relationship management. During the height of the Third World debt crisis, I became country head of Citibank's floundering business in Jamaica, and then in Colombia. By 1987, I could truthfully say that I had achieved everything in the bank that I wanted to achieve.

Entrepreneurial Again

My initial thought after leaving Citibank was to seek to acquire a small platform business. Things didn't turn out quite that way. Within fifteen days of being back in the United States, my best friend of seventeen years, Reginald Lewis, convinced me to join him as his partner. At that point, he owned the McCall Sewing Pattern Company, having acquired it in a 1984 buyout. He was doing quite well with it, and was thinking of exiting. Reg's appeal to me was, "Cleve, given your experience and strengths, and the strength of our relationship, we will make a great team. You understand the financial aspects, and I have the deal and legal experience—and I already have a platform through TLC Group [Reg's company] and McCall. Join me, and let's build something great together."

And so on June 15, 1987, I joined TLC Group. Within days we started looking at KKR's planned sale of Beatrice International Foods. On June 19, I told Reg that I thought this could be a great deal and that we should bid $950 million for it. On June 23, we bid just that—$950 million. And we won. It sounds simple, but obviously it was not that easy. There were many challenges and obstacles to overcome, starting with an absence of credibility, mapping through a field of well-known and well-heeled competitors, and ending with having to keep the financing glued together through the market crash of 1987. But we prevailed, raised over $1 billion, and acquired a corporation with over sixty operating companies doing business in more than twenty countries.

I won't go into all of the complexities of putting the Beatrice International transaction together or the challenges that arose in my relationship with Reg, but it was clear to me even before we closed the deal that I would not stay with Reg. We were on divergent paths in terms of the way we saw the world. I decided to return to my original strategy of building something myself.

Finally, Venture Capitalism

I left Reg in early 1988. I worked from my home office over the next two years pursuing acquisition opportunities. I came dangerously close to buying a failing bank in Connecticut in 1989 with backing from some specialized SBICs. My principal supporter was Equico Capital Corporation and its president, Duane Hill. Equico was a wholly owned investment subsidiary of Equitable Life Assurance Society. In the fall of 1989, after I had made the decision not to buy the failing bank, Duane asked me what I was going to do. I told him I was committed to the entrepreneurial path. I asked Duane what he intended to do longer term. He responded by saying that he had considered leaving Equico but really believed now that there could be a rewarding future in backing minority entrepreneurs. To which I said, if you feel that way, why don't you buy Equico. Duane looked at me but didn't say much. Two weeks later we had that same conversation. And I said the same thing. Why don't you buy the company? This time he asked if I really thought that seeking to acquire Equico made sense.

Two months later I went back to Duane with a book I had prepared and said, "Here is why I believe it makes sense, and here is a road map for doing the deal. Equico could become the platform from which to build a real presence in financing minority entrepreneurs in building strong, wealth creating businesses. And if you are serious about pursuing Equico, and you want a partner, I know where you can find one. But," I said to him, "it's going to take you more than the measured moment in order to pull this off, because my bet is you're going to find yourself ping-ponged between a large, bureaucratic insurance company that right now doesn't know it wants to be a seller and the U.S. Small Business Administration, which as regulator will have to approve the change of control. I'm not going to be hanging around on the outside, waiting for that to happen." So in February 1990 I joined Equico with one objective in mind—to buy the company.

From Corporate to Independent Venture Fund

Our long-term strategy had four components. Step one was to acquire control of Equico and transform it into a minimerchant bank imbued with entrepreneurial spirit, that we had total control of and a significant economic stake in. Step two, once we had Equico, was to gain the flexibility to operate outside of the regulatory morass of the federal government, or the SBA, because it was too difficult to work within those strictures. Step three was to amass a sizeable pool of capital with which we could do transactions of scale with companies that had solid strategic positioning in their industries—companies that would have the capacity to attract managerial talent and financial resources. The fourth part of the strategy was to gain the capacity to sponsor transactions, taking controlled positions—something we we couldn't do operating under SSBIC regulations.

In June of 1990, within days of Dick Jenrette having become CEO of Equitable, we put an offer on the table to acquire control of Equico. There were four of us: Duane, who was president and CEO of the outfit, Larry Morse, Divakar Kamath, and myself.

Upon receiving the offer, Equitable said they were going to take it very seriously. What then ensued were the longest two years of my life. That's how long it took, working our way through the bureaucracy, to effect the change of control. It was the most arduous negotiation in which I have ever been involved. It should have been such a simple deal. A lot of learning, a lot of experience came out of those two years. May 14, 1992, was emancipation day—we acquired control of Equico Capital Corporation and renamed the company TSG Ventures Inc.

We hocked practically everything we had to get a bank to back us with a loan representing our equity infusion into the deal. It was not easy to find a bank that would lend us the $600,000 we needed. Interestingly enough, it was a minority controlled bank, Boston Bank of Commerce, run by Ronald Homer, that provided the support. Where other large banks had turned us down, Ron said, "If I can't lend you $600,000 on the strength of second mortgages against your homes, and even more importantly, your background, your experiences, and, frankly, my belief that you could get another job someplace and pay me back, then I ought not to be in business." It was with that small but critical financial backing that we were able to do a recapitalization transaction and acquire a controlling position in Equico.

Operating as TSG Ventures

We moved TSG Ventures from New York City to Stamford, Connecticut, the following year. In July of that year, we succeeded in raising our first limited partnership. We raised $5.7 million, and used the proceeds to totally redeem Equitable's residual interest, and to ensure that we had control of the organization with somewhat greater flexibility than under the agreements with Equitable.

The pace of events quickened as we moved against the three remaining elements of our four-part strategy for building our business. In early 1994, we launched fund-raising for TSG Capital Fund II, L.P., a traditional private equity buyout fund with no ties to the federal government. With the support of our placement agent, Beacon Hill Financial Corporation—one of the best in the business—we raised $225 million in less than a year. With Fund II, we were no longer restricted to financing minority entrepreneurs or minority controlled companies. Our strategy broadened and, very importantly, focused on companies that operated in underserved ethnic markets without regard to the ethnicity of the management team. We saw a huge private equity opportunity without having to compete against every other buyout shop. We understood these markets and believed in the force of the demographic trends.

Demographers tell us that African-Americans, Hispanics, and Asian-Americans will represent pretty close to 50 percent of the United States' population by the middle of the next century. Even in 1994, the purchasing power of these three segments of our population represented something like the seventh largest economy in the world, larger than any of the so-called emerging markets—larger than Brazil, larger than Mexico, larger than Canada. Our investment strategy is to capitalize on these underserved markets. We also capitalize on our access to ethnic entrepreneurs and managers, who represent a largely untapped base of talent.

By August 1998, we were fully invested with Fund II and had our first closing for TSG Capital Fund III, L.P. With a final close in February 1999, Fund III has $515 million in committed private equity capital. We have five excellent portfolio companies in Fund II. Presently, we are readying each for liquidity events. Moreover, we are almost 50 percent invested with Fund III. Between the two large funds, our four-partner team—three of whom are African-Americans—controls almost $750 million of private equity funds. We can invest up to $100 million of equity in single deals, with all decisions made inside TSG.

Envirotest

Let me turn back to the challenges of attempting to do transactions of even modest size a few short years ago. Envirotest, led by an African-American entrepreneur, Chester Davenport, is a prime example of entrepreneurial talent applied to a mainstream opportunity, and then pushed, pushed, pushed to make a private equity success story.

Envirotest began as a $56 million acquisition of Hamilton Test Systems from United Technologies Corporation in 1990. Hamilton Test was one of the leading companies in providing centralized motor vehicle emission testing services to states and municipalities. It took $6 million of equity capital to do that initial deal. We had to put that together the hard way. At Equico, I took the lead in raising the majority of that equity capital. It took a syndicate of five funds, with Equico being the largest equity investor at $2 million. This was the largest single equity deal that Equico had ever done. The other investors were UNC Ventures, led by Ed Dugger; MESBIC Ventures with Don Lawhorne and Tom Gerron; and Wally Lennox and John Doerer of

Amoco Ventures (now Polestar Capital). Even then, we almost got muscled aside by my former employer, Citicorp Ventures, who at the last minute asked Chester why he needed a bunch of small investors in his deal. I said to Chester, "Yes, Citicorp Ventures can put all of the money in, but we've worked long and hard at your side in order to pull this acquisition together and if you're going to build the value of this business over the longer term, there are going to be many times when you're going to really need to know who your partner is, and to know that you've got somebody who you can count on. If we are your partners, we will be there. We may not always agree with you, but we'll be there. You'll know where we are coming from. You've got to make your own judgments as to whether or not you would know that with other players." Chester decided to stick with us. And I think that he would say that we were true to our commitment and that he never regretted the decision. I assure you there was plenty of drama and trauma over the eight years we were in Envirotest.

The Envirotest acquisition closed in December 1990 at an investment cost of $0.77 per share. In 1991, through Envirotest, we went to work on acquiring its largest competitor, itself a subsidiary of a U.K.-based, publicly held company. That was quite exciting. We succeeded in closing that transaction in 1992. In 1993, we had a very successful IPO at $16 a share. We got our initial investment back shortly after that, and the stock was shooting the moon, trading at over $28 per share. Then the Federal EPA started to change the emission testing industry's operating rules and life got very challenging.

In 1997 Envirotest shares traded as low as $1.625. This was after the Commonwealth of Pennsylvania had unilaterally decided to walk away from a signed contract pursuant to which Envirotest had invested over $180 million in setting up testing facilities in the state. It was a bit of a challenge, and it took a lot of time, but we convinced Pennsylvania to give the money back. Many investors thought Envirotest was on its deathbed. But Chester is a fighter, and we fought at his side. We turned the company around and successfully exited in late 1998 at $17.25 per share, or a total of about $600 million. Chester rightfully made a lot of money—and we didn't do too badly either.

Investing in Urban Companies

So, what are the deals that we have in TSG Capital Fund II? One is Urban Brands, Inc., a women's apparel chain whose principal division is Ashley Stewart. Ashley Stewart's focus is providing apparel to the full-figured woman, with a particular emphasis on African-American and Hispanic women. When we made Fund II's initial $30 million investment in April 1996, Joe Sitt, Ashley Stewart's young founder and CEO, had twenty-one stores operating here in the east. Today, through Urban Brands, we have about 170 stores. These are quality stores delivering merchandise and service quality to ethnic women in their communities. Ashley Stewart has built a powerful brand. We expect the company's financial success will lead to an outstanding investment success. We also are invested in Z-Spanish Media Corp., a Spanish-language radio broadcast company that now owns thirty-four stations and has another thirty-five affiliates. Incidentally, Hicks Muse felt so strongly about what we were doing with Z-Spanish that, through their Chancellor Media operations, they became a minority investor with us in Z-Spanish.

A third portfolio company is Vista Media, which owns outdoor advertising, billboards—but not just any billboards. Vista's focus is on the smaller eight-sheet boards that are six feet by twelve feet in size. Vista owns more of these than anyone else in the country. Where are these boards found? In the urban centers. So, through Vista, we own over 6,000 boards in Los Angeles, and over 2,000 boards in New York City. Who lives in the urban centers? African-Americans and Hispanics. The whole strategy behind Vista's appeal and approach to its markets is being able to deliver to the national advertiser, or the large regional advertiser, saturation coverage of those ethnic markets in major cities.

The three decades since business school have been a hell of a journey. There are too many stories to recount. I am deeply grateful to partners I have had along the way who contributed so much to my success, especially Duane Hill and Reg Lewis. But the saga isn't over. Along with my partners, Darryl Thompson, Mark Inglis, and Lauren Tyler, I will continue to establish TSG as a premier private equity investment institution. Simply put, we aim to be the best at what we do.

ANN WINBLAD
Hummer Winblad
Venture Partners

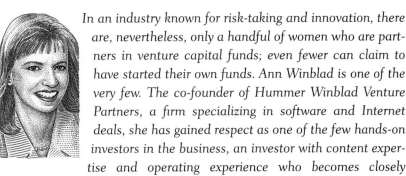 In an industry known for risk-taking and innovation, there are, nevertheless, only a handful of women who are partners in venture capital funds; even fewer can claim to have started their own funds. Ann Winblad is one of the very few. The co-founder of Hummer Winblad Venture Partners, a firm specializing in software and Internet deals, she has gained respect as one of the few hands-on investors in the business, an investor with content expertise and operating experience who becomes closely involved with many of the firm's portfolio companies.

To be sure, Winblad isn't the only female partner at a venture capital firm. Others include Jacqueline Morby at TA Associates, Ginger Moore at Oak Investment Partners, and Patricia Cloherty at Patricof & Associates. But Winblad is the only one who has moved from success at building a high-tech business into a full-fledged role as high-tech investor. She started as a programmer and in 1976 founded Open Systems, an accounting software company. Winblad operated the company for six years, sold it for over $15 milllion, and moved to Silicon Valley. She then worked as a consultant for a number of companies, including IBM and Microsoft, before joining John Hummer to start Hummer Winblad, a software-only venture capital firm.

Hummer Winblad continues to specialize in the software arena, creating successful companies such as Wind River Systems, Homegrocer, and IMX. A relatively small partnership that currently manages a fund of approximately $500 million, Hummer Winblad's future, like all firms, depends on its ability to attract new partners and new deals. Its focus on the Internet has revitalized the firm, but having recently lost one of its senior partners,

Bill Gurley, to Benchmark, Hummer Winblad still has to prove that it can
be one of the bigger and more influential players in Silicon Valley.

I DIDN'T INTEND to become a venture capitalist. I viewed venture capitalists from a software-industry perspective—which was that venture capitalists did not understand or appreciate the software industry and that they didn't deliver value. In the software industry that certainly was true. There were hardly any venture-backed software companies. At the time we were raising our first fund, one of the biggest hits of venture-backed software was Digital Research, and it was far from a big success.

When I moved to California from Minneapolis, my intent was to actually take a year or two off—not to sail around the world but to have a job that demanded less intensity—and then to be an entrepreneur again. Almost at the same time that I moved to California I met John Hummer, who was at a small venture firm called Glenwood.

John was a first-round NBA draft pick out of Princeton and played basketball from 1970 to 1976, took some time off, and then graduated from Stanford in 1980 with his M.B.A.—the same class as Scott McNealy of Sun Microsystems. Vinod Khosla of Kleiner Perkins was in that class as well. The venture industry was growing then, and many of John's classmates became venture capitalists. 1980 was the first big boom in venture capital.

John wanted to leave Glenwood, which was a small diversified venture firm, to start a software-only venture firm. He had decided to raise a new fund. The difference between 1980 and 1987—it was mid-'87 when John made this decision—was that there were no new funds being created. Returns had gone down. Many segments had become overinvested. In fact, today venture capitalists still speak of the meltdown in the disk drive industry. In fact, when we were raising our fund in 1988 and 1989, people complained that some of these firms were returning passbook-savings-type yields. We're talking four to five percent returns.

When I moved to California, venture capitalists were calling me like crazy to go do checkups on software companies. "I don't know you, but I've heard you know a lot about software, so will you go see if this company is dead?" I didn't move to California to nursemaid ailing venture-backed software companies. But, one really great guy called me up. He said, "Look, Ann, I just want to explain this to you. I know you're turning everybody down to go look at these venture-backed companies, but it's a little different here in northern California than it is in Minneapolis, in that venture capitalists really are part of the fabric of this industry. If you want your future company to be financed, you need to do something for the VCs."

So, this guy convinced me to go look at a software company where his venture firm and John Hummer's venture firm, Glenwood, were invested. It was a horrible mess. It was in the hospitality industry and they'd installed their software at twenty customers. It was like grenades going off—each customer's site was blowing up, and they didn't know what was going on, and couldn't seem to fix it. I had ten years experience in the software industry by then; the approach to finding the problem was fairly obvious to me. I said I'd like to speak to the VP of engineering first. So I asked him to show me the source code. He said, "Well, there was a problem there." And I said, "Well, what's the problem?" As it turned out they never finished a Release 1 of the product, so every time they got a new customer, they would create a different finished product. They had twenty or more piles of source code. Since none of it was commercial-grade software, they could never figure out what had gone wrong. There was no one way to fix the software, because there were twenty-some paths for this software. I reported this back. I said the only choice is to regroup, get a release truly done, and then install it simultaneously in all of these companies. In the meantime, assign a programmer to each customer. But somehow that didn't seem feasible to me. So, John immediately went in and shut the whole company down. The twenty companies they had acquired as customers they lost to a larger competitor. John sold the rights to the customers and recovered the venture capitalists' money, which I think was the right choice.

Despite this experience, John wanted to start a software venture firm. This was in 1986, shortly after I had moved to California. For the next year and a half, John hounded me to start a venture capital firm based on software. It was an interesting time to be hounded, because we really had nothing new in software. We had Windows, but we didn't really have distributed computing. Distributed computing didn't really happen until 1989 and 1990. So we started formulating our plans to start Hummer Winblad.

Going against the Grain:
Launching a Software-Only Fund

When we raised our fund, the growth of software sales was huge, but the worldwide market for software was maybe a tenth of what it is today. Software technology was not considered the centerpiece of the U.S. economy yet. No one wanted to touch software companies. Software did not require much capital and in the industry capital itself was not a competitive advantage. Most venture capitalists feared building companies based on intellectual capital and thought the assets would walk out the door at night. They preferred hardware companies where huge amounts of capital were a competitive advantage. The software category was also a younger industry with less experience. John felt we had a wide-open segment and that I could easily make the transition from entrepreneur to coach.

In our first fund, we invested in sixteen companies with a $35 million fund, which after management fees gives you $29 million to invest. The management fee was used to run the fund over its ten-year life. By 1995, the value of the fund had grown to $260 million. We had four big winners there. The first company that we took public was Wind River Systems. Wind River was, for a long time, a sort of Rodney Dangerfield. They were doing embedded systems from the beginning. But people didn't believe in embedded systems. We did. We helped the company get its business plan and its management team tuned up. We helped take the oxygen out of competitors, and we developed a strategy that worked. So we took them public. We made ten times our money, so we had a $10 million gain, which in today's market seems meek.

Wind River went public with a market capitalization of $80 million, which was then considered quite large for a systems software company in a vertical area. They now have achieved a market cap of $1.6 billion.

The next company we took public was Powersoft. We made some $60 million on that deal, or twenty times our investment. Then we took Arbor public. Arbor was a spectacular public offering. We made sixty times our money. Both companies reached billion-dollar market caps—even before the Internet! By this time we had also had a couple of small IPOs that did well for us. We were passive investors in a company called Farallon (now Netopia). We made a small amount there. Then we took Scopus public, and we made another $30 million. All of these deals, remember, were raw start-ups.

We also had one write-off—a deal we called Slate. We wrote off $1.5 million. That was a pen-based computing company. It taught us a good lesson: If the risk is a market risk, as opposed to a technology or a people risk, don't do the investment, because you can't push markets to happen faster than they're going to happen.

An Early Strategy for Software Investing

The performance of the first fund was stellar, primarily because of our focus on software companies. There wasn't much competition for deals. We were early in enterprise computing. We did some CD-ROM companies and actually made money there, because we got in and out at the right time, although the window was tight. If you do a great job in building a company as opposed to saying, "Hey, I think I can make money here," then even if market conditions change and you can't take the company public, you still have an asset, and that asset will be valuable to someone else who already has to perform on the market. If you're not doing company-building, and there's not an opportunity for an IPO-liquidity path, you may not have an asset.

There are some people who say, "Let's fund a whole bunch of companies and see what happens." But you have to carefully, yet rapidly, build asset value in these companies; good products, good teams, good strategies. We've benefited from that. In the early '90s, we took companies public only if they had four or five quarters of profit, with 20 percent growth per quarter in revenue and earnings. Several of our companies were some of the first new companies in the 1990s with billion-dollar market caps. Everything changed after that.

It took us four years to invest our first fund of $35 million. Four years. During that period of time, we were selective investors. We had two partners, and an associate, Mark Gorenberg, who later became a partner. Mark and I had already spent ten years each in the industry building software. Mark started at Boeing, right out of MIT, and when the New York blackout happened, helped to fix the software. The results for us were cumulative. We didn't have a fund maker—which means that we made it all on one deal—we had multiple fund makers and only one minor loss, Slate. That was our goal. It was not to get one to win so we could make a lot of money on the fund. We really liked the job of building these companies and building the software industry.

What happened next? As we approached 1994, we started to see this Internet platform become a reality. In fact, most venture firms that did Internet investing made their first investments in '94. We were doing very well and our fund was bearing fruit from the pre-Internet era of distributed computing. Three of those four companies went public with nice gains, in the thirty times your money, forty times your money range like we had with Powersoft, Arbor, and Scopus.

The next generation of automating the enterprise was clearly happening. We started to get a sense of a rocket booster coming from the Internet. It all of a sudden looked like an enormously fertile and visible field, and then the land rush started. We raised our second fund, of $65 million, in 1994, and our third fund, of $100 million, in 1997. Our third fund was invested in two years' time. We raised our fourth fund, of $320 million, in 1999.

Selective venture capitalists have not changed their strategy. We asked ourselves, "We have a huge area of opportunity here—should we do something different? Should we inflate all the valuations to get as many deals as we can? Are we willing to walk away from deals where the price is too high—even if we know they're great deals? Are we willing to do more deals, because there's some uncertainty of which deals are going to make it?" Our answer to all those questions was no. But we did decide that we needed to hurry up, that speed was important. We needed to audition more companies, grow the companies faster, and invest more money at each round.

Investing in the Age of the Internet

Cash became extremely abundant for software and Internet companies as more and more funds turned their attention to this segment. Cash is not *the* competitive weapon, but without cash, you don't have a company. The era of the sweat-equity start-up had disappeared. So, we've seen companies mow through $10 million, and say, well gee, that strategy didn't work, let me go get another $10 million. And, because there was so much more money coming into the low end of the private sector—seed, first stage, or second stage—the ability for even questionable companies to get step-up valuations was unbelievable. Even if you didn't help the company, and it started veering off track, or if it crashed, you could just go buy another new train for Tommy the CEO.

Venture capitalists have overcommitted to the Internet. I can tell you what's happening now behind closed doors at those venture firms that have forty private companies at the seed level. They're saying, "Who are our winners? Who is going to get money and who needs to find a home? Who are we going to give the money to? Which ones should we go out and get extra money for now, because we really want to build these companies, and for which ones should we wait and see what happens?" Companies are being pruned, whether they know it or not.

There's an assumption that a lot of companies can go public at a billion-dollar-plus valuation. This assumption continues to be validated in the booming tech economy. The window closed abruptly in the autumn of 1998, causing a surge of panic in the halls of venture firms plump with Internet start-ups, but the closure was only for six months and it was off to the races again in 1999.

Investing in People—Software Style

In every deal, investors talk about how important people are. But in software they're everything—it is an intellectual capital business. The VP of development is a make-it-or-break-it hire. That is the person that runs your factory. In this case, it's not a shoe factory; it's a software factory. So, that person has to really understand how you build the best software factory and how you get products out on time with quality, at the same time adapting to the needs of the market. Development has become even more important in Internet companies where software is not shipped, it is available 24 hours a day, 7 days a week, 365 days a year, it changes in real time, and is subject to performance needs simultaneously. And you have to coddle each customer. The process is very quick and adaptive, and you have to understand when you have a product and when you don't—when you have moved far enough along the development cycle so that there is enough value to the customers that they will absorb some of the risk in future development. If you ship too early, all hell breaks loose; if you ship too late, your market is gone. The timing—the decision of what is a product—is experience oriented. Besides, product companies need partners. None of these software companies can work alone. The company that gets the partners wins. You also have to declare victory early now, which means that a company has to have a very clear position of what it owns to differentiate itself from the thicket of entrants.

In comes important person number two—the marketing person. This person has to go out and declare the battles you've won, before you've won them, and deliver the results quickly. They have to tell the world, "We are going to do this, we will therefore own the universe." And, all of this—claiming a market, shipping the product, building the partners—has to happen simultaneously within a very short period of time. By the time these companies are two years old, you either have a company or you have nothing. Sometimes you're delivering a product in twelve months or less from the time the two-person start-up team is standing in front of you. That velocity is unfamiliar to most people.

Four years after we first invested in Arbor, it went public. We went from two guys standing in my office to a management team running a company with several thousand people. But even Arbor had to ship their product quickly, and had to get their partners. They had an important partnership with Comshare, which was reselling the product. Arbor also had to claim the market. They said, "If we call ourselves decision support, then we'll be in this polluted pond of companies with low valuations. This is a new generation decision support. What is it? How do we define it? They came up with the term OLAP—for Online Analytical Processing—and built the OLAP council. They did all of the necessary things—declared what they owned in the thicket of start-ups, built the product, got the partners, saw it off, and shipped it. Interestingly enough, the first customer who we shipped the product to—whom I will not name—didn't know what a server was, and asked Arbor to buy one and bring it in. So Arbor bought a server, loaded their software, and dropped the server off to the customer. They did what it took to get the first customer site installed.

Facing the Music

Has the music stopped? Clearly venture capital is an important part of the economic food chain. People think that there are millions of us out there, but there aren't. In fact, only a very small number of people are instrumental to company creation, whether they're good or bad investors. At the end of 1998, $50 billion of unspent capital was in the hands of venture capitalists, so there is a lot of entrepreneur rocket fuel out there. By mid-1999, $300 million was being invested in Internet companies each week.

My belief is that it will take a while before we go back to funds being invested over four to five years. The opportunities that the Internet platform has brought to the software segment are just too numerous to slow down the investing process right now. Some of the mezzanine-stage investors will likely go back to where they were and see better bargains in the public markets, watching the hundreds of newly public Internet companies. I think the acquisition market—where for every company that went public, eight were acquired—will become even more active. Everybody has currency to acquire.

Vertical Portals and Other Internet Strategies

The thing that's really interesting for us as venture capitalists—for Hummer Winblad specifically—is that we've always done what I'll call foundation software—the toolshed, which includes system software, development tools, and applications. We've been pretty good at sorting out those opportunities. We've missed some, but the ones we've picked have been good ones. That will continue, because we still are a young software industry. In the early '90s, we varied our focus a little and did some of these entertainment companies. They aren't part of the toolshed—they're software as fun. And we made money there.

Now, what makes the Internet challenging for me as a venture capitalist, but opens the opportunity field, is that as we become more connected, we can look at whole industries to see where we can better leverage the power of bits.

We can build these companies with the same kind of funds that we built software companies. We have a company called IMX, Industry Mortgage Exchange, which is a neutral third-party trader between commercial lenders and brokers. It's doing extremely well. We funded a company in Chicago called the National Transportation Exchange, which is an exchange for all of the trucking companies, tying back into the logistic companies of Fortune 500 companies. We have investments in Pets.com and TheKnot.com, each of which represent $50 billion-plus industries.

And then there's Homegrocer, which represents the huge grocery industry. We invested in it with Kleiner Perkins. It is a different twist on the grocery business, which consumers love. Our firm, like other VCs, does not have any indigenous knowledge of any of these industries. Before we did IMX, we had one of our associates spend three months making sure we really understood the economics and the suppliers.

So, with the Internet we can find a lot of these what I'll call vortals—or vertical portals. Let's take IMX for example. If they had come to us in 1990 and said, "The way that commercial lenders deal with brokers is really flawed; we built an application and we're going to sell it to banks," we would have said, "Gee, that seems like a small market, just selling it to banks so that they can then make it easier for the brokers." And we would have turned that deal down. That same company coming to us in 1998 or 1996, said, "Look, we've found this flaw in the banking food chain, and we think we can serve as a neutral third party between banks and brokers. Everyone will use our software and pay a usage fee, and we can take a cut of the transaction, because we facilitate all this." That's a lot different from what we could even consider in 1991.

Traditionally, venture capitalists have shied away from vortals because these businesses fall in the vertical market with few customers, versus if you effectively serve all the constituencies of customers and actually change the way things work. Vortals are risky deals, because if there are some government regulations that you didn't know about, or if you don't know the food chain well enough, then you may miss some behemoth in that chain who can muscle you out.

So, the challenge for us is to figure out which opportunities to attack. This means understanding the existing economics, the existing players, and the opportunity to reach the ultimate customer using the Internet.

Venture Capitalists as Salespeople

As a venture capitalist you're always in a selling mode. Even Kleiner Perkins has been turned down on deals where they did a bad selling job.

Or people thought they were going to get John Doerr, and they ended up with somebody else. So we're all in the selling mode. That's been a given since 1989. Our selling mode was different in '89 than it is now—given the ascendancy of software and the Internet to center stage in the new economy. Our selling mode was harder in '89. I was new in the venture industry. Nobody knew who John Hummer was, except the inside venture capital community, and we'd never done a deal before. That was really hard. What we have to sell now is our commitment to working as hard today as we did before, and our commitment to keeping our companies funded. We've never failed to raise money for companies or to secure capital for a company. No company in our portfolio has ever gone under for not securing capital, even when our funds were smaller. We can also bring to the table an incredible diversity of strategic partners. I think our companies are still amazed today at the flow of intellectual capital that we have—we are always recruiting people, and we're always bringing people to the table, and frequently we're not paying head hunters for them either. And last but not least, we are not confused about what our job is; we are coaches, not visionaries. Our primary job is to bring extraordinarily good business practices to these companies so that they don't fail. We are hard-nosed about this. There may be some times an entrepreneur works with us when he or she would say, "Gee, this board meeting wasn't that fun." But that entrepreneur would also say, "I'm going to have the best company that there is." You can call all of our entrepreneurs, and they will tell you how we work.

We have to use our entrepreneurs to sell to other entrepreneurs as well. They are our references. Many people coming into this industry need the selling, not because of the competition from capital, but because they are at the same point that I was in 1989—they think venture capitalists are generally not valuable and should be avoided if possible. And if they can't avoid them, they'll try to get the least-involved firm. These are new people, people who have not been in the technology industry before, coming into these vertical markets, coming into the Internet.

Success

We've had some interesting Internet deals that have been less glamorous than others but grand successes. And we have had our share of glamorous companies as well. We created Global Center, which was acquired by Frontier for hundreds of millions of dollars, at month thirteen. But it wasn't HotMail, so it didn't show in the media. We created Net Dynamics, another company acquired for hundreds of millions of dollars in year two. Then we have had Net Perceptions, a two-year-old company that went public with a $700 million-plus market cap, and Liquid Audio, a three-year old that also debuted in the public markets with a $700 million market cap. Both of these companies were raw start-ups when we funded them and we are proud to be associated with them.

Have venture capitalists created their own chaos out there with these Internet deals? I think we've been more selective than most. We have picked up the necessary speed to audition 7,000 (1999) versus 500 companies (1990) per year. I think there have been some enormous successes built with good coaching from VCs—I'm quite fond, for example, of Amazon.com. We fought hard to be the venture capitalist in that deal, but John Doerr won the deal. In fact, it was at the peak of John Doerr's fame and fortune, and John Doerr is an extraordinary venture capitalist. If our firm over time can be as good as Kleiner Perkins has been historically, we'll be happy.

GEOFFREY YANG
Redpoint Ventures

In August 1999, Geoffrey Yang made a sudden and surprising announcement. He and two other partners from Institutional Venture Partners (IVP) were joining three partners from Brentwood Venture Capital to form a venture capital fund focused on next-generation and broadband Internet called Redpoint Ventures, capitalized at $500 million. "We're taking the spindle that turns yarn into gold and breaking it up," Yang told the Wall Street Journal. "But we think we can make a new spindle that will spin a bigger amount of yarn."

Under Reid Dennis's tutelage, Institutional Venture Partners became one of Silicon Valley's most established venture partnerships. But Dennis, who's been in the business since the 1950s, is from the old guard, most of whose members believe that a diversified portfolio is a better long-term strategy than a narrow focus. With Geoff Yang, IVP re-invented itself, forcing the firm to redefine its strategy and goals along the way. This interview was conducted in 1998 while Yang was still at IVP, but his comments shed light on his decision to form Redpoint a few months later.

The future, Yang likes to say, is in specialization. With the pace of technology change frenetic and the demands of building a technology business more complex than ever, the generalist fund can only provide capital and not much added value. The returns from a fund focused specifically on next-generation and broadband Internet are likely to be far greater—at least for the moment—than a diversified fund, Yang and many others believe. Representing both the industry's present and its future, Yang is a technology specialist and also a one-time entrepreneur; he embodies the focused approach to venture capital, the complete concentration on technology and, for the present, on communications and the Internet.

I WAS RAISED on the East Coast and went to college at Princeton. Both my parents were engineers. My mom, who was a math major, worked at IBM and got me interested in computers and technology in general. She also was an early entrepreneur. In the '60s she and a bunch of IBMers tried to start a time-sharing company. I had fun visiting her while she was working on weekends, punching computer cards and loading tapes. I was hooked on computers.

We had a family friend who was in the venture business at Time Life and then at Menlo Ventures, who started a firm, Abacus, and then ended up retiring from the business. I always thought what he did was really pretty neat, because I'd get to see all the stuff that Time Inc. had invested in. So, I went to Princeton as a double major in engineering and in economics. I was interested in technology but I didn't think I wanted to be a design engineer, and I was also interested in business. I thought it was an interesting combination. In college, I ran a small business selling and restringing tennis rackets. I also did some quantitative research for a savings and loan, doing mathematical modeling for branch site selection and then designing financial instruments.

Big Blue

After college I worked at IBM, mainly because my mother had worked there, and she had a lot of friends there. I spent the summer between my junior and senior years as an intern, then joined full-time in New York after graduation. I worked selling computers between '81 and '83, which was a really fun time to be at IBM, as they were on a roll. I learned about the information technology business. They gave me the PC to introduce and to sell because as far as they were concerned, it was a toy; it wasn't a real machine.

When I was in college, I thought I would be interested in getting into the venture business and decided business school would be a good thing after some work experience. So I decided to go to business school at Stanford. Part of the reason I wanted to do that was to see what the West Coast was like. I had a bunch of friends at Stanford Business School who were working with early-stage companies. So I came out to Stanford, spent some time writing business plans for a couple of companies, got some stock in the companies—one of which went public—and in the middle of all that spent the summer interning at Goldman Sachs.

Venture Capital—Investment Banking Style

Before going to business school, I had made a personal commitment to family and friends to go back to New York. So after Stanford, I went back to New York, joined the venture affiliate of Smith Barney, called First Century Partners, and spent a couple of years there. But in New York the mind-set was more financial engineering and we kept looking at buyouts. Even the way people looked at deals was different—it was more running spreadsheets and running models. Maybe it also was the fact that I was at a venture capital affiliate of an investment bank, which I didn't like.

At the time there were few technology companies in New York, so I'd be in Boston a couple of days a week. After doing the same routine for a couple of years I decided I had to get closer to the companies. If you're really going to do venture capital, you should do it as a partnership and do it where the companies are. So I made the decision to move either to Boston or Silicon Valley. Serendipitously, a headhunter doing some work for Institutional Venture Partners called up, referred by a business school classmate and friend, and offered me a job as an associate.

Institutional Venture Partners

It was a great opportunity and a chance to come to Silicon Valley. I came out with the notion that I might move to a company after a couple of years. This was in '87, when it was in vogue to hire people for a couple of years and then spin them out into portfolio companies. I figured if I didn't like it I always had that option. But after three or four years at a venture capital firm, you're no longer suited to do anything other than venture capital, because you're a jack of all trades and master of none. After a year and a half at IVP, I was starting to think about where I was going to go when one of the CEOs of an IVP portfolio company tried to convince me to go and work in marketing there. I was mulling the offer over when IVP offered me a partnership position. I thought thought long and hard and decided I really liked what I was doing.

What I liked about the venture business was that it is very entre-preneurial. Your only task is to do a good job, make money for investors. How you do it, what your style is, or what you look at is up to you. I liked the notion that you could drive down the street, see something, and decide that the world needs X, and then you could go and try to start a company to build X, or offer X service. I really liked that. I liked the notion that everywhere you go, you're always trying to see where the holes in the market are. I think it's a very intellectually stimulating business where you get to meet a bunch of people who think they can change the world.

Our job is basically pattern recognition. We get a bunch of very smart people giving us points of data but they don't get to see the whole picture—the whole elephant. They get to see a leg or they get to see a tail. Part of our job is to be able to step back and take a lot of data from some of the world's smartest people, and put together this image of an elephant. There are a lot of opportunities out there, and how the pieces fit together is really interesting.

Becoming a Venture Specialist

I only recently realized that there is a piece of the venture business that goes beyond making good investments to being able to shift industries. When I started in the venture business in '85, there was a different mentality. An investment would come to you and you'd ask if it was a good investment. But as time passed, the focus changed from a specific investment to whole industry segments. The need to specialize was becoming more critical. So when I came into the business, I specialized.

I decided I couldn't compete with the guys who'd been around for five, ten, or fifteen years. As a generalist, people aren't going to want to come see me. Why should they come and see Geoff Yang, who just started in the venture business. I decided I should develop a industry specialty in an emerging industry to use as my currency—either a knowledge of an industry, or deals that I could use to parlay into working with the kind of people who really know what they are doing.

My strategy was to focus on the communications business in general, and networking specifically.

Industry Benchmarks

When I first came into the industry, the standard metric was making ten times your money in five years, or a 58.3 percent internal rate of return. You ran all your numbers on a $100 million market capitalization. If you got to a $100 million market cap, that was outstanding.

Look at the business today. We just distributed Excite, where we made 300 times our money in three and a half years. We distributed MMC Networks, where we made 100 times our money in four years. What I look for now in deals is twenty or thirty times your money in two or three years; ten times your money in five years is really not that interesting.

One other thing that's different in the industry is that, you used to look at merits of individual investments. That's the reason people were generalists. However, the industry has grown so much and become so much more complex that it's hard to keep up with all segments of technology. Entrepreneurs are much more demanding in what they're looking for in venture capitalists, so you now have to have domain knowledge in order to sell yourself. There are a few people who can still sell themselves as generalists—they're the industry legends.

When I got into it, the venture business was much more reactive. Deals would come to you and you'd look at them as part of a portfolio. Now we've realized that the venture business moves in waves. That's the way significant market values are created. So now we're trying to pick what the waves are, and we're going to invest in every company, every segment of company that rides that wave.

The velocity of the business has increased dramatically. It used to be you'd raise a fund, invest the fund in three or four years, start getting returns in year four through year seven or eight, and then you'd wind down—or try to wind down—the portfolio by year ten. Often you'd need extensions because it actually took twelve years to earn back the fund. Today, fund investment cycle is one year for the most part and you start getting returns in year two. By year two through year four, you really know the story of the fund, and you're in distribution mode in years three through six. It's going to be much easier to wind funds down in ten-year periods.

Going for the Fences

We're at a very interesting point in time. The business has become much more of a home-run business. Every thing is risk return, and the risk return is what the market pays you to play. Where we are right now, home runs have an incrementally small risk but an incrementally huge return.

At this point in history, technology is really becoming mainstream. Early-stage companies are changing the world, not just the back office. It used to be that for the most part IT companies changed the back office by reducing costs, but now they are pervasive in people's everyday lives. You look at the way people receive media and receive their goods and services. Look at the way communications providers are architecting their networks. Look at the way people get information.

We have an opportunity at this point in time, if we can visualize what an industry's going to look like, to change the way people live their lives. One of the things we didn't do in the past but we do today is say, "Okay, if we believe that vision, let's fund all the companies that will shape that vision. It's not because of us that this new industry will be created, but it might be accelerated because of the things we do. If nothing else, it's a great investment." It's very interesting to think that you can have a big impact in helping create new industries and new industry segments by the things you do. So, if you believe in the Internet, for example, you'd say, "Okay, to make the Internet work you can't do without fast routers. If you're going to use fast routers, you really have to have fast servers. And if you have fast servers and fast routers, you need fast access. So if we believe in the vision of the Internet, let's invest in all the pieces that make that a reality."

Changing Styles—From Passive to Active Investing

The first deal I ever did was in '86; it was a company called Concord Communications, and they were doing a local area network for manufacturing. This company had a product that implemented what was known as Manufacturing Automation Protocol, which automated factories. I looked at that deal and did a lot of due diligence, talked to a lot of customers. I saw the deal at AEA[1] and that got me interested. But the deal was very typical of what I was just saying: it was very reactive.

After they presented their vision to me, I thought it was interesting, invested in the company, and hoped that it would work. Interestingly, Concord's initial market turned out to be a disaster. But Concord transformed itself and just went public. I guess at the end of the day, the deal worked. But it took a really long time, and the original concept I invested in didn't work.

Contrast Concord to the second deal I did called Applied Digital Access, which was a seed deal, where a guy came to us to do testing and monitoring for telephone companies. It ended up that the deal worked great, went public, and we made a lot of money, but again, it was just following.

Fast forward to Excite and MMC. In '93, I'd been doing a lot of networking deals. At the end of the year, it became pretty clear that the networking business was in between waves, so I decided to go look around at other spaces, and this whole Internet thing seemed pretty interesting.

I began to think. All these people are connected over e-mail— there had to be something cool you can do with a mail-enabled application. That caused my interest in a company called Collabra Software, which we ended up investing in. We started looking at this stuff and started meeting all these people. This was before the World Wide Web—that came in late '94 or '95 with Mosaic.

I decided I was going to spend all my time looking at all the things that were going on in the Internet because I felt there was something there. At the time, I was signed on through PSI Net, using something called Chameleon to FTP to servers, and I had an account with MCI Mail. It was one of these things where we decided that this Internet thing could really be interesting, given all the people who are con-

---

[1] *American Electronics Association, a high-tech membership organization that holds an annual meeting in Monterey.*

nected to it. The way I got into the Internet was because all the high-speed networking guys had worked on ARPANET, the precursor of the Internet. So I started meeting all these guys who were in their fifties or late forties and who had worked on ARPANET. It was very interesting to hear them talking about it from a transport point of view, and what would be possible. Then, I started meeting these kids, these twenty-year olds. And they started talking to me about all the things that you could do on top of this new medium, and then the Web came along.

Internet! Internet!

It was really interesting to see the potential of the Internet. We were at a point in time when we always used to say we would only invest in people who had done it before. But this was a whole new platform with a whole new paradigm. Having a knowledge base or a set of traditional experiences held you back, because conventional wisdom was wrong. So I invested in Excite. We bought a good chunk of the company for a small amount of money. I figured if it works out, great; if not, we wouldn't have invested that much.

We had a big internal debate because Internet deals really stretched the way we thought about deals. So we developed a model that says there are two types of companies in the world. One is called Faster, Better, Cheaper, and the other one is called Brave New World.

Faster, Better, Cheaper represents the typical venture business. Something that's ten times the performance at two or three times the price. It's something that does it faster, better, cheaper, and smaller. The whole bit. You know what the business model is. You know where to get the management—they've done it before and can do it again. You start with a great product and then it's execution, execution, execution.

Contrast that with Internet, which is really Brave New World, where people came in and when we asked them, "What's the business model?" they would reply, "I don't know." "Well, what's the paradigm?" "I don't know." "Where do you recruit people?" "No clue." People used terms like paradigm shift and enabling platforms.

There were no proven business models for the Internet. There were no easy places to get people. If you looked at the two types of deals as if they were the same, it wouldn't work. Because if I do a

Faster, Better, Cheaper deal, and the entrepreneur doesn't know what the business model is or where to get people—that's a recipe for disaster. If I do that in a Brave New World deal, where if you ask the entrepreneur about the business model the answer is, "I don't know but I'm going to figure it out as I go along," that's okay. You just finance them differently. On the Faster, Better, Cheaper deals, it's okay to put in a lot of money and bet on execution.

These Internet companies were clearly Brave New World investments and my strategy was to put a little money in a bunch of companies, try to own a big percentage of the companies, and then have the guts to say, "Feed the ones that work, and bury the others."

Excite: Our First Internet Home Run

The interesting thing for me was how quickly the whole Internet thing took off. To get Excite off the ground, we gave them Mark Vershel, who was VP of Engineering at Borland, to be an entrepreneur-in-residence and to see if the idea was scalable. Darlene Mann became interim VP of Marketing. We introduced the deal to Kleiner Perkins because we were working on another deal together.

The Web took off so we funded Excite at the end of '94. All of a sudden it became clear what their technology was really good for: navigation of this mess called the World Wide Web. I think it signaled a change in mentality for us in two regards. One, we really decided we were going to go after the Internet to figure out what our strategy was and be more proactive. Two, it signaled a new way of thinking—Brave New World versus Faster, Better, Cheaper—and that it was okay not to have a model but just figure it out as you go along.

Toward a Comprehensive Internet Strategy

I think my mistake on the Internet was that I made only two or three investments, and thought that was enough. Right around the time the Internet started to explode, the networking business came back. I was pulled back into the networking business where I was the only guy working on networking, and I felt like I had enough Internet investments. I should have realized this thing was really huge and gone for the whole space. What we are doing today is identifying key areas, marking them as firmwide initiatives and having everybody in the firm working on these areas. I shouldn't be the only one doing this. I should have gotten everybody else working on it because it was a really fruitful area.

If I could do it again, I would say, "The Internet is a huge initiative. We're going to do content deals, we're going to do commerce deals, we're going to do membership deals, and we're going to do networking deals. We need to get the whole firm moving as a group, because if you believe in this notion of investing in big markets, and investing in initiatives—and the fact that one person can no longer carry a firm as they used to with small funds—the whole firm has to act together."

Today, venture capital is much more of a team business than it was ten years ago. Ten years ago, it was a business of individuals excelling, and I think today it's much more about teams having to excel because that's the only way you can multiply these huge funds we have. $350 million. I've got to return $1.4 or $1.5 billion. A single person can no longer carry funds, whereas before, if you had a $100 million fund and one person has a good investment, you could carry the whole fund. So I think that part of the business is really changed.

At the end of the day, entrepreneurial teams are the ones that will make this all happen. As venture capitalists we're in a support role. But having said that, if we can help shape the thinking of entrepreneurs—like shaping an arrow or moving the aim of an arrow—we can have a lot of impact early on. I don't want to forget the fact that the entrepreneurs are the people who really make this happen. They're the ones that have to execute, and they're the ones that have to own the vision.

MITCH KAPOR
Accel Partners

Mitch Kapor founded Lotus in 1981, which went on to become the first software company to succeed in the PC marketplace and the first to prove that software companies were deserving of venture capital. On leaving Lotus in 1987, Kapor started ON Technology, a developer of GroupWare systems. Kapor left ON, saying he didn't have the heart and the energy to run another start-up. He turned angel to invest in start-ups on his own and to launch the Electronic Frontier Foundation, an nonprofit advocacy group that has been described as the ACLU of the software industry. Since those early forays into angel investing, Kapor has become one of the more sought after angel investors, and he has worked closely with such funds as Accel Partners and Polaris Venture Partners as an investor and at Kleiner Perkins and Sevin Rosen as a special partner. But in 1999, Kapor, believing that the needs of entrepreneurs were wide-ranging and could not be adequately addressed by angels alone, became a partner with Accel.

Kapor has been on both sides of the street. His perspective is one of an entrepreneur, an angel, a venture capitalist, and an activist. Kapor talks candidly about his experience with the venture capital process and about some of the venture capitalists with whom he has worked.

A S A KID, I was very good at math. It also became the primary focus in my life—a sort of "safe place"—something I was good at and could get rewarded for. I was also fortunate enough to have early hands-on exposure to computers in the mid-'60s, at school and in some enrichment programs. I loved it but had no thoughts of making a vocation out of it.

I went to college in the late '60s and graduated in '71, so for a number of years I was distracted with adolescence and the general upheavals—external and internal—that took place at that time. I wound up working briefly in the early '70s as a programmer, but I wasn't very good at it.

About the same time I read Ted Nelson's book, *Computer Lib*, which had the vision of the personal computer even before there were any. In '77–'78, I got into the Radio Shack TRS-80 Model 1 as a hobby, and that led to the consulting gig that actually began my career.

Growing up, I never thought of myself as entrepreneurial. Part of it was because "business" was just not cool then. In fact, however, my father ran a small business and my maternal grandfather was also a small businessman. I have since been reminded by friends that even though I didn't know it, I was always thinking about starting a little something—a used record business, actually, in college.

Entrepreneurship just came naturally. It was in my genes. And the interesting thing for me was discovering—this is now '78–'79, that not only did I have an aptitude for computation, but also I just seemed to understand better than most people around me what would make a good business and what wouldn't. It became obvious to me that there were huge rewards to being successfully entrepreneurial. That's when I really got serious about it.

From 1978, when I started with PCs, to 1982, I had a very extensive introduction to business, personal computing, and management. I did a lot of different things in quick succession: I was a consultant; I ran a cottage industry software shop out of my apartment where I wrote a large program in Basic—the first graphics and statistics package for the Apple II—and sold it by mail order; and I worked as a program author for Personal Software, Inc., the publisher of VisiCalc.

I had contracted with Personal Software to do work on VisiPlot and VisiTrend, which were companion products to VisiCalc. Before those two products were even complete, I went out to Silicon Valley in 1980 and lived in Sunnyvale for six months, working as the new product manager for Personal Software.

That was my first direct experience with Silicon Valley venture capital. I remember meeting Arthur Rock, who came into a Personal Software board meeting I was attending. That's where I really learned the structure and the who's who of venture capital. I then moved back to Boston to finish the products I was authoring, and Personal Software published them. I was getting royalties, so I had some money. I put some of it into working on new products.

I teamed up with a guy named Jonathan Sachs. There are several Jonathan Sachses in the computer industry, all of about the same age. This was the one who started out at MIT and Data General, who had actually written an early spreadsheet for Data General minicomputers. And he was in a start-up that failed.

So Jon and I started working together. The IBM PC was announced, which gave us a focus because it was a next generation machine after the Apple II. That's when we began. In the fall of '81 we started working on what became *Lotus 1-2-3*. I had made a bunch of money—after taxes and settling with my partner, I was left with $600,000. I had sold back the royalty stream to Personal Software for a large sum. I said, "Okay, I'm gonna put half of it aside for myself. I might buy a house and put some money in the bank. But I'll take half of it and start funding this project." When I could see that I was running out of the $300,000, I said, "I better go raise some money." But I was very ambivalent about venture capital.

Dealing with Venture Capitalists

Bill Sahlman of the Harvard Business School wrote a case about the Lotus financing. Part of the case is the seventeen-page letter I wrote to Ben Rosen, which was essentially the first draft of the business plan. I had gotten to know Ben because he had been a customer of *Tiny Troll*—my first product—a graphics and statistics package. And he was the first Wall Street person to notice VisiCalc and to say, "Hey, there's really going to be a business in personal computer software, particularly in PC applications." He was a guru. And he also had a small investment in Personal Software and was a brand-new VC. I had met him two or three times.

I was terrified of the standard-issue venture capitalist. I had met Arthur Rock and found him very scary. And I had met Pat Lyles, late of Charles River Ventures, who was teaching at Harvard. At one point while I was in Boston, I had gone to visit Charles River as a favor to a colleague who was pitching a business plan. I wasn't a part of the business, but I was there to add credibility. You knew it had to be a pretty raw start-up, if I was adding credibility. It wasn't a very good plan, and the venture capitalists just took this guy apart! Looking back, I would say it was more of a "surgical dissection" to prevent blood loss. But even so! I mean, I was a former "flower child."

I knew Ben Rosen and he seemed like a nicer person. He had just started Sevin Rosen. In this letter I wrote—and this is famous through Harvard Business School for its honesty—"Look, I want to tell you about this business I want to start. But first you need to know that there are some things which are as important to me as making a profit—if we're going to be in business together." I did this for self-protection. I was so scared of getting dismembered, that I just felt it was best to be completely honest with the whole thing! When people at Harvard read the plan now, they're mystified by this. There's often speculation as to whether this was some negotiating plan on my part to somehow get a higher valuation. People just don't understand.

I didn't shop the plan. I was highly inexperienced. It was a funny thing. I was simultaneously highly experienced and highly inexperienced. It was now 1982. I had been in personal computers for four years, which is longer than almost anyone except Bill Gates or Gary Kildall. I had authored a commercially successful product. I had been a product manager and done a good job for a hot start-up. I was somewhat well-connected. And I had a co-founder who had technical experience and who was really excellent. So if you were going to invest in PC software start-ups, we were quite experienced.

On the other hand, I had no management experience to speak of. I didn't have a deep technical background. I have a pretty good background now, but at that point I had no industry experience, hadn't worked at Digital, hadn't been at Intel. And I was a kid. But Ben didn't know much more about venture capital than I knew about being an entrepreneur. That's why he brought in Kleiner Perkins as a co-investor. Much of Kleiner's specific advice in the early days was not useful. But that's because PC businesses were a different model and they hadn't learned the model yet.

I showed the plan to Ben. He said, "Please write us a business plan. And make it short, because—y'know." So I did. And then I didn't hear anything for a while. Four to six weeks later I get a call from L. J. Sevin, his partner: "Mitch, I'm in town. I'd like to have dinner with you tonight. Is that possible?" I said, "Absolutely!" rushed home and changed, and made a reservation at a very fancy restaurant in town.

We get through the salad course and we are just making chit-chat. And I'm waiting for him to get to the point. Then we're done with the appetizers, and I was thinking that if he didn't get to the point by the main course, I was just going to ask him, because I couldn't stand the suspense. Right about then he said, "Mitch, Ben and I would like to invest in your company. How much do you think it's worth?" I dropped my fork, I was so shocked! They decided to take a chance on me.

Working with Sevin Rosen

There were only six people at Lotus at the time. Jon was already hard at work on *Lotus 1-2-3* itself. In fact, before we closed the venture deal we had a working prototype. We had actual code up and running that you could see. We were Sevin Rosen's third investment. They had done a later round at Osborne and they had done Compaq before us. I felt at the time that Sevin Rosen was atypical of venture capitlists based on my small sample. Ben was very genial. And he was going up the learning curve as well. So he had a lot of "value-added" in media, Wall Street, marketing, communications, and positioning the company, because that was what he knew. And he also had an enormous amount of enthusiasm for the product. He was really a product champion.

I thought that was great. There wasn't any friction. And he was the board member. Ben's partner L. J. recommended that Alex d'Arbeloff, the CEO of Teradyne, sit on the board. As Alex was running Teradyne then, he had significant operating experience.

Alex and I butted heads a few times. I appreciated a lot of Alex's practical wisdom, but he was also very opinionated and I didn't take criticism very well. Over the years our relationship wasn't always that great, but I always found him quite valuable. Alex made more of a contribution on operational issues.

The Kleiner folks were passive: no board seat. We had a couple of meetings. They tried doing a couple of things, like pushing us to offer

IBM exclusive distribution rights. Jim Lally of Kleiner came with me to IBM. They wouldn't even consider the offer—fortunately for us!

So, as far as Sevin Rosen's "added value" to Lotus, I would say it was the fact that Ben believed in the venture and supported it. That meant an enormous amount. By my standards now—and I'm sure by Ben's standards—it was just a beginner's performance all the way around! There was a lot that was left out. There were a lot of things that they weren't good at.

When I compare the relationships companies now have with VCs to what Lotus's relationship was to Sevin Rosen, there's a real contrast. Companies now can get much better, deeper, and broader support in all different areas—strategic stuff and improving partnerships—than what we got. What helped us was that Lotus became successful very rapidly. We were cash-flow positive on our first quarter of shipments.

The business plan that Sevin Rosen had invested in projected first-year revenues of $8 to $10 million. My first plan was $3 to $4 million, but I raised the estimates. We actually did $53 million in revenue in the first year. In 1983 dollars! And then we tripled that in '84. We couldn't have done it without the money from Sevin Rosen. And Ben's help was invaluable.

I left Lotus in '86. Then I founded ON Technology in '87. It was very ambitious and technically ahead of its time. I raised money from Kleiner Perkins and Cole Gilburne. ON had a high valuation at $10 million. I also put in a bunch of my own money—over $3 or $4 million. A year into it, I realized that I just didn't have a "fire in the belly" about it. It was a huge mistake. I tried heroically to turn the company in a different direction. We changed strategies from being a platform company to producing applications. And then I wound up leaving.

Being an Angel Investor

My being an angel investor goes back to the mid-'80s. First, I became a limited partner in a couple of venture funds. I was in something called The Masters Fund. I was in the next Sevin Rosen fund. And in KPCB IV.[1] I started co-investing with Kleiner Perkins and Sevin

---

[1] The fourth venture fund of Kleiner Perkins Caufield & Byers.

Rosen on some of their deals. I invested in PictureTel alongside Kleiner Perkins and Accel. I also invested in Avid Technology. I co-invested in Shiva's first round with Cole Gilburne—I actually had 5 percent of Shiva at one time, which was a big position. I did some other whimsical things, most of which didn't work.

As an angel I'd have a relationship with the CEO. I'd spend a certain amount of time talking to the company and visiting it. But if that was three or four times a year it was a lot. I was in Digital F/X— that one didn't work. It kept on missing, and we kept on raising money. I learned a lot. I always learn more from the losers than the winners.

As to my less-considered deals, I did some curious things, like Reliable Water. That was started by Ed Fredkin out of MIT. It was a desalination system powered by an expert system. It failed. That was $100,000. And I put money into Dynabook, a failed laptop start-up. That was a big bust. So I started getting an education. I learned a lot in that period, from the mid-'80s up until the early '90s. Some things worked well. Avid made money and PictureTel made money. Shiva ultimately made a lot of money because we sold near the top.

GO: An Entrepreneurial Failure

I invested in GO Corporation, one of the pen computing companies. GO was overly ambitious, and not well enough thought through. I put in a lot of money and sat on the board initially. There wasn't a business plan. The business was too early, technologically. John Doerr and Vinod Khosla of Kleiner Perkins were both on the board. We were all in the mode of "swing for the fences, hit a home run." And so it got ramped up very big. It also had a huge burn rate that it just couldn't sustain. The funny thing is if it had been more modestly capitalized, it probably would've been alive today, as it might have eventually found its way—or so I told myself. But at the time it was either "out of the ballpark" or "shut it down." One day it was IBM that was going to save the company, the next day it was Intel, then it was AT&T. And the measures got increasingly desperate. I'm glad Jerry wrote the book *Startup* because it really gave the flavor of what it was like. He left some of the good parts out, though.

Getting Institutionalized

In the early '90s I wasn't very active in venture investments as a limited partner. I was sort of seeking to broaden my investment base. So I wound up being approached by Accel Partners. I didn't know them. But Joe Schoendorf made the connection in 1993. They were raising a new fund. I felt a very positive chemistry within the firm from the outset. I liked the people, and I felt especially comfortable with Jim Breyer.

The first thing I did was to refer an Internet project to them—UUNET. John Doerr had declined my invitation to take a look at it. I was a seed investor and very excited about the company, so I called Jim. Accel did the deal and it wound up being enormously successful.

In 1995 I referred another project to them—RealNetworks. I was an angel investor and Accel did the first round. I was on the Real-Networks board with Jim Breyer for four years, and I became more and more impressed with him. In addition to being smart—he is off-the-charts smart—and experienced, he has always acted with 100 per-cent integrity, which is impressive. That's my standard, too, but you don't see it all the time in operation.

At Accel, which I joined as a full-time partner in 1999, I feel very comfortable with the culture. Voices are rarely raised despite every-one around the table being highly competitive, Type-A personalities. People are not treated or mentioned with disdain. There's intellectual honesty and candor, but it doesn't get personal. And there is really a partnership culture of collaboration that goes back almost twenty years to Jim Swartz and Arthur Patterson, who established that tone for the firm. And I think Jim Breyer, as the managing general partner, not only fits in but carries the culture on, and will carry it on into the next generation.

As to joining Accel, Jim Breyer had made it clear for a couple of years that Accel would be delighted for me to work more closely with them in any capacity. I got to a point where I was ready to do that. I had decided that I was tired of working alone and I wanted to work in a team context. I also think that with an aggregation of resources you can get a synergistic effect where the whole is greater than the sum of the parts. I don't think it's an accident that the fundamental form of venture capital has been a partnership—in part because you need it for judgment balance.

Angels Revisited

Angel investors have become very important. There are a lot of successful entrepreneurs and executives with money to invest who want to be active in the very early stages. I see it as a complement to, and not as competitive with, the kind of institutional venture capital Accel does. We work with angel investors regularly. They are one of our best sources of new projects.

I am doing this because I get very passionate about helping build companies, helping entrepreneurs, and taking my twenty years of experience and applying it toward new ventures. The influx of new money is increasing more rapidly than the influx of smarts. That's because smarts is not a fungible commodity—it's in part a product of experience. And I think, ultimately, the value-added—the non-financial contribution—is going to continue to be material. I think it will be *more* material—because money is money is money—and everybody will have money. It'll be even harder to win on the virtue of having dollars in the bank.

Success is going to be about strategy, execution, and building a company's infrastructure quickly. I would hope, for instance, and this is something that's been really worked on at Accel, that the next frontier could be in VC firms helping with people issues—human resources issues.

We ran a focus group at Accel for portfolio CEOs, and it became clear there is an opportunity for venture firms to take the initiative to help portfolio companies deal with people issues. They can identify appropriate resources and steer people to the companies.

BEGINNINGS

BENNO SCHMIDT
J. H. Whitney & Co.

 *The organization of the venture fund J. H. Whitney & Co. by John Hay (Jock) Whitney in February 1946 is arguably the official starting point of private venture capital in the United States. At the time, Whitney was considered one of the richest men in America, a champion polo player, a horse breeder, and a frequent backer of Broadways shows and Hollywood movies, including Gone with the Wind. The idea to raise a private pool of capital for venture investing was Whitney's, but it was the execution by Benno Schmidt in his role as managing partner that made the fund the most significant of its time.*

The firm's mission statement, crafted by Jock Whitney, read: "We are here to invest in companies that we believe can succeed, companies with both management teams and purposes that we can wholeheartedly embrace, companies that it will be fun to work with as we build and companies of which we will be justly proud when we succeed." By the late '50s, however, Whitney had departed to become ambassador to the Court of St. James, and Schmidt was left to chart the firm's independent course as a venture capital firm, without any further support from Jock.

In subsequent years, J. H. Whitney has gone through significant changes—investing in start-ups, technology restructurings, and in buyouts. Today, it is once again a diversified fund that invests in start-ups as well as in mature companies, and it continues to be one of the industry's most influential investment funds, long after Whitney's death in 1981.

Benno Schmidt completed this interview in 1997, two years before he died at the age of eighty-six. His re-telling of the almost whimsical story of how Whitney began emphasizes the pioneering spirit the industry has taken on over time.

I N LATE 1945 I had returned from a three-year stint in the army in Europe and was serving as general counsel to the economics division of the State Department when I got a call from Jock Whitney. When I answered the telephone, the voice at the other end said, "Hello, my name is John Hay Whitney, you may have heard of me as Jock. . . . If I came to Washington could we have dinner together?" When we met for dinner at the Mayflower Hotel a few evenings later, the conversation had nothing to do with State Department matters.

Jock told me that during World War II, particularly when he was a prisoner, he had given a great deal of thought to what he should do after the war. He had been fortunate enough to inherit a substantial amount of money and was anxious to use both his time and resources as constructively as possible upon his return to civilian life. He had given a lot of thought to the absence in the economy of any organized source of capital devoted to financing new ideas, ideas that might have great promise but also carried substantial risk.

Jock pointed out that neither commercial banks nor investment banks provided such a source of funding, and if corporations found new proposals worthy of funding, they would normally swallow up both the entrepreneurs and the idea. Prior to the war Jock had been presented with various proposed new ventures and in fact had even funded a few. But that effort was not particularly satisfactory because he had not had an organization to do the due diligence necessary for sound decisions. He also observed that, with respect to the new enterprises he had financed, he had lacked the ability to provide professional assistance to the new organizations he was putting together.

He said he had decided to use $10 million to capitalize a small private firm that would be devoted to financing new enterprises found by the firm to have appeal and merit. It was his belief that a free enterprise economy such as ours would lose its dynamism unless there existed somewhere in the economy a source of new money for prospective entrepreneurs seeking to start worthwhile new enterprises.

Jock strongly emphasized to me that there was no guarantee that such a firm would succeed, and referred to the fact that some of his advisors had expressed doubts about such a firm's chances of success. The advisors had suggested that some form of regular income business needed to be added to his plan, such as a bond business or investment counseling business, in order to "pay the rent."

Jock was determined to proceed with the plan as he had originally conceived it, without provision for continuing current income. He then said: "If I am wrong and my plan doesn't work, I will be $10 million worse off, but that will not change my life materially. However, you should give some thought to where you would be if this proposed organization is unsuccessful."

I replied, "In the first place, I believe that the business as you have outlined it will succeed. Secondly, if it doesn't succeed, you will be $10 million worse off, I will be right where I am now, so I believe I can handle the risk part okay. However, there is one thing you should know." "What is that?" Jock asked. "I've never had a day of business experience in my life, unless you call roughnecking or rig building in the oil field business experience," I said. Jock's reply was, "Why don't you just decide whether or not you'd like to come with us and leave it to me to pass on your credentials."

"Fair enough," I replied, "I just didn't want anyone to be surprised if they took out a balance sheet and I said, What's that?" Jock replied, "We'll learn together," with that wonderful modesty, wry smile, and quiet sense of humor that I came to know so well.

On February 1, 1946, we opened for business. Jock, Dick Croft, Web Todd, Malcolm Smith, Sam Park, and I were partners in the firm. Venture capital was born and Jock took his place in history as the founder of what was to become the most positive economic development of the post–World War II era.

The question as to whether or not J. H. Whitney & Co. would succeed was decided at a very early date. Our first investment was Spencer Chemical Company. This investment involved the purchase of a surplus war plant in Kansas by a Kansas native named Kenneth Spencer. Spencer had operated the plant as a munitions plant during the war and, under the Surplus Property Act, he was entitled to first refusal of the plant at the price fixed by the Surplus Property Administration, a government agency set up after the war to dispose of surplus war plants, materials, and supplies. Kenneth Spencer proposed to use the plant to manufacture ammonium-nitrate fertilizer and the price placed on the plant by the Surplus Property Administration was quite reasonable, as it was in most such cases in order to encourage the conversion of surplus war plants to civilian use.

Kenneth had arranged with the First National Bank of New York to borrow the money necessary to buy the plant, but they required that he put in $1.5 million of working capital. He came to J. H. Whitney & Co. for this investment. We put up the $1.5 million, $1.25 million as preferred stock and $250,000 for one third of the equity in the business. Spencer owned the other two thirds. The plant was rapidly and effectively converted. The fertilizer business was booming, and well before the end of the first year our preferred stock had been redeemed, and it was clear that the $250,000 that we had put in as equity was worth more than the $10 million of capital with which Jock had started the firm. After that, there was never a concern about capital, and no outside capital went into the firm until after Jock's death thirty-six years later. The successful Spencer Chemical Company was eventually acquired by Gulf Oil.

The term "venture capital" emerged in a very interesting way. When J. H. Whitney & Co. was formed, we described ourselves as a private investment firm. Unfortunately, the *New York Times* was not onboard, and they regularly referred to us as "J. H. Whitney & Co., New York investment banking firm." Since we were not investment bankers this reference was, of course, incorrect. Jock particularly disliked being referred to as an investment banking firm and at lunch in our dining room on a day the morning *New York Times* had referred to us as a New York investment banking firm, Jock said, with particular emphasis, "We've got to find a better description for ourselves so the *New York Times* will stop describing us as an investment banking firm."

In response, one of our partners, Alex Standish, said, "I think we should get the connotation of risk into the description of our firm." That remark prompted Bill Jackson to say: "I think the most interesting aspect of our business is the adventure." Putting those two thoughts together, I said, "How about private venture capital investment firm?" Jock's immediate response was, "That's it! From now on we will use 'private venture capital investment firm' to describe ourselves." Soon the term venture capital was being used not only to describe J. H. Whitney & Co., but also to describe the small industry group that formed after us. This group included Payson & Trask,

Henry Sears & Co., and American Research & Development—all part of what became and is now known as the venture capital industry.

In our initial discussions at the Mayflower Hotel in Washington, Jock had emphasized the role that he hoped J. H. Whitney & Co. could play in making our free enterprise economy more dynamic. However, he recognized that we alone would have a relatively small impact on the dynamism of an economy the size of the United States' economy. In our discussion that very first night, he expressed the hope that, if J. H. Whitney & Co. were a success, others would follow our example so that there would be a real impact on the national economic scene. Farsighted as this thought was, I don't believe that Jock could ever have imagined that the venture capital industry would become what it is today.

EUGENE KLEINER
Kleiner Perkins Caufield & Byers

Together with Tom Perkins in 1972, Eugene (Gene) Kleiner launched one of the industry's most successful venture capital organizations—first called Kleiner Perkins, now known as Kleiner Perkins Caufield & Byers. Today, the firm is the industry standard-setter, despite a host of challengers and the successes achieved by both newcomers and veterans of the industry.

Founders Kleiner and Perkins both came to their new endeavor with strong backgrounds in technology. The Kleiner family left Vienna in 1939, and Gene himself first worked as an apprentice at a tool and die maker after coming to the United States. He later received an engineering degree and in 1955 went to work for William Shockley's semiconductor laboratory. Soon he had financed his own company, sold it to Raytheon, and become a private investor in the myriad of technology deals that floated around Silicon Valley, including a 1968 investment in Intel.

Kleiner operated at a time when entrepreneurs needed firms such as Kleiner Perkins not only for their money, but for the company-building skills and the technical advice they could provide. As the industry grew, Kleiner and the firm that he helped launch grew with it and soon became one of its standouts.

Reflecting on those years and the current state of the industry, Kleiner is not completely bowled over by the success and the triumphs of the present. He believes that long-term venture capital successes will come not from increased specialization but from a more generalized approach to investing. The venture business has always been a series of hot sectors, one after another. But long-term strategy, Kleiner maintains, means taking the hot with the cold.

I WAS NOT a stranger to venture capital. I worked with Tommy Davis on an informal basis for some time. He was a partner at Davis & Rock and I was a limited partner there. They often asked some of their limited partners to evaluate technology and asked me at times to help evaluate special situations. I enjoyed doing this and slowly got involved in the whole process. I also made some private investments, including some companies in which Tommy had invested. This was between 1968 and 1972.

Venture capital then still wasn't a big industry but many people wanted to get involved. Pittsburgh's Henry Hillman had been friends with Tommy for some time and he approached Tommy about managing a venture capital fund for him. But Tommy had been working with Arthur Rock and was already committed to starting the Mayfield Fund. He wasn't interested in doing another fund, so he referred Henry to me.

Launching Kleiner Perkins

I went to Pittsburgh to see Henry Hillman. We hit it off, and he asked me to start a venture fund. There was one hitch. He wanted me to run the fund out of Pittsburgh and I wanted to be back on the West Coast. Still, we wanted to do something together. So Hillman agreed to my operating a venture capital fund from the West Coast. He said, "I will give you $4 million if you can raise the other $4 million." I came back here and went to see Sandy Robertson, who was in investment banking, and asked him to help me raise the other $4 million. He mentioned this other fellow named Tom Perkins, at Hewlett-Packard, who also was looking for money and said, "The two of you should get together. If you get together, I'm sure we can raise the rest."

Sandy introduced us and we spent several days together to see if we had enough in common, and then decided to go ahead. We wrote a prospectus, then with Sandy's help went on a tour to raise the money. This was before 1975, when there still was the prudent man rule that didn't allow pension funds to invest in venture capital. So we had to raise the money from individuals and foundations.

Insurance companies proved surprisingly receptive. They didn't know what venture capital was, but since the amount of the money was very small we got three or four them to each put together about $800,000 or $1 million. It was such a small percentage of their total money that the impact on their total assets was minimal. They probably were extremely happy when they saw the returns they got on the first fund.

A Family of Funds

The first fund was a small one, but we had no difficulty raising the next one, which was $15 million, or the one after that, which was much larger.

We worked on a wide range of deals, all of which were technology related. I have been reading about the increased specialization that is going on in the industry. I read the other day about some people leaving some of the more generalized venture groups and setting up more specialized venture units. Some are going to do only Internet-related deals. Others are focusing on some other narrow technology area. When things are going well, such choices seem popular, but when that sector isn't as attractive, what do you do? I think you can accommodate both areas in the same partnership.

One of the things we worked on from the very beginning was planning for succession, even though we didn't think of it in those terms then. We felt that the people we brought on, such as Brook Byers, should be able to carry on without us. And now there is John Doerr, who develops ideas and gets people together. What he is doing is really remarkable. We owe this to continuity and to our limited partners.

Tom and I both had hands-on experience with doing computer-related things, but that didn't stop us from looking elsewhere in the technology sector. That is how we came upon biotechnology and Genentech. Bob Swanson, who was a co-founder of Genentech, had been working for us at Kleiner Perkins and was interested in doing a biotechnology company. There weren't too many examples, let alone successes, in the area. So we asked Bob to look into the whole field. He liked it and with our encouragement decided to set up a new company. He worked with Dr. Boyer of UCSF and began Genentech.

Pioneers

A lot has changed in venture capital since we first began. The nature of deal-making has changed, as has pricing. People are willing to pay higher prices because they feel that the public markets and company buyers are willing to pay more. The business is a lot more competitive, and people are constantly bidding against each other.

When we began, entrepreneurship was in its early stages and entrepreneurs didn't have the same grasp of business they now have. We had more experience than most entrepreneurs the first time around. As a result, we participated with the entrepreneur in building companies. We were involved in the start-up and in the corporate governance. We sat on boards, and were involved in most major decisions. It improved our learning capacity and helped the companies to learn. We saw ourselves as builders of companies rather than just investors.

We would opt out of situations where an entrepreneur didn't see us as partners. Not that we always discovered that when we were considering an investment. But some entrepreneurs are suspicious and have a mind-set that prevents you from helping them. If we saw that after the investment we would drop out.

One reason for the cooperation was the sharing of risk. We were looking for co-investors who could bring some business or technology knowledge to the table. We liked to share the risk but we also liked to acquire skills from our co-investors.

Being Proactive

We just didn't wait around for deals to come to us. You had to create the deals to be really successful.

With companies such as Tandem, which was entering a new market and offering a product that needed to demonstrate efficacy, we helped identify the market needs and even contributed to designing and making the equipment to meet the market's needs. That is what you still need in every kind of venture.

Tom knew a lot about computers. I had less experience in computers but had experience in semiconductors. But we both spent a fair amount of time at Tandem, where we were part of management—although we did not take any salaries. This was true of every one of our investments. The big advantage we had was that we were familiar with the technology and we understood how small companies worked.

Of course, our success also helped our deal flow. After a while, the entrepreneurs wouldn't shop around a deal. They would show it to us before they showed it to anyone else. Not that there were that many deals or that many entrepreneurs around. Competition with others wasn't cutthroat. There was a lot of cooperation. I think it is a mistake for entrepreneurs to keep shopping their deal around. The two or three a cents a share you'll get more are not worth it.

The way we worked required a lot of time and effort. We were always very much involved in the companies. We ran the companies as if they were smaller departments of large companies because that's where our experience was. We worked closely with the entrepreneurs to develop their business and we didn't make too many technical mistakes. It was more the question of execution. Indeed, we had very few technical failures. Things failed because of the inability to execute.

We were patient investors. We also had the luxury of having some early successes. Having early successes gives you the courage to be more patient and more tolerant about mistakes.

Are entrepreneurs today more experienced? I'm not sure they are more experienced, but there are certainly more around. We liked to breed our own. Both Jim Treybig (who started Tandem) and Bob Swanson worked at Kleiner Perkins before they went off to start their companies with our blessing and our money.

We funded Jimmy Treybig with $1.5 million, which was a lot of money in those days. In the case of Bob Swanson, we relied a lot on the promise. We didn't have a lot of technical background or experience in the area, no one did. We turned to high-school biology for help but that didn't help us very much either. We got Steve Packard on the board and he too didn't know much about about biotech.

A Different Era

Venture capital was very different then. People focused on building companies rather than on exits. Securities regulations such as Rule 144[1] have helped investors exit a firm but it may also have hurt the chances of building companies.

We had very few companies going public early. And we always worried about that kind of early exposure. Tandem Computers went

---

[1] *Rule 144 of the 1933 Securities Act regulates the redistribution of stock by persons other than underwriters.*

public rather early, which is always dangerous. The market could be very unforgiving even then. If you had a bad quarter they punished you for it, just as they do today.

One other company that went public early was Genentech, but there the attraction was the enormous promise of biotechnology. In the case of Genentech, we didn't offer any profits or sales. We simply built the company and took it public on the promise of the technology.

Silicon Carolina?

What have I missed most as I have become less active? In the beginning I was a little relieved because much of the pressure was gone. But I missed the interaction.

What I have done is help start venture groups in other areas such as North Carolina. I was quite active there in the early days. It's never going to be another Silicon Valley, but there are three major universities to draw from.

I have been working with various groups in North Carolina to help them establish an entrepreneurial and venture capital culture that is similar to California's. The area around Durham has some of the same characteristics that we have here. There are some great research universities, such as Duke. There are major pharmaceutical companies such as Glaxo Wellcome, and there is a proliferation of research activity in the Research Triangle. The difference between California and North Carolina is the number of venture capitalists. In North Carolina, Intersouth is the only game in town.

I have also been working with some European governments. A few years ago I spent some time in Ireland and found tremendous reception to entrepreneurship. But venture capital and entrepreneurship in Ireland are relatively undeveloped compared to in the United States.

Why hasn't it grown? Europeans are still more traditional. And while some countries are willing to break the mold and try new things, entrepreneurship has been slow to catch on. There's no reason why Europe can't be just as entrepreneurial as the United States. There's plenty of capital, there's a lot of interesting technology, and, most important, people are politically and culturally freer.

PETER CRISP
Venrock Associates

Institutionalized venture capital began as capital pools funded by wealthy Eastern families, and, to be sure, as somewhat of a social experiment. In the aftermath of World War II, many wondered whether it was possible to restructure the economy, make a profit, and do good all at once. The Rockefeller family, the Whitney family, and the Phipps family were among the first to establish separate venture capital programs. Laurance Rockefeller provided the initial spark in the 1930s. His interest in aviation and his access to capital helped him finance two seminal businesses: Eastern Air Lines and McDonnell Aircraft. After World War II, Rockefeller continued to invest in entrepreneurs but mostly on a deal-by-deal basis, by which time his reach extended from aviation to electronics and emerging technologies.

In 1969, Rockefeller decided to make the process of venture investing more institutionalized and created Venrock Associates to serve as the venture capital arm of the Rockefeller family. Founded with $7.5 million of funds from the Rockefeller family and several non-profit institutions that had long-standing relationships with the family, by 1998 Venrock had financed 262 companies which together employed some 440,000 workers and had total revenues of $110 billion, resulting in a market capitalization in excess of $600 billion.

The task of running the fund for nearly three decades fell to Peter Crisp, a Harvard Business School graduate, who had been intrigued by the idea of venture capital and entrepreneurs. While Laurance continued to invest in those areas that he found interesting, Crisp began to lay the groundwork for an organization that eventually became a formal fund. Many see early Venrock as a product of Rockefeller's eclectic interests in *technology and entrepreneurship, but it was Crisp who turned the family office into a lasting organization.*

I JOINED THE Rockefeller family office in 1960, straight out of Harvard Business School. At that time the people involved in venture capital were a handful of wealthy families and a couple of institutions, such as American Research & Development and Boston Capital, that were trying to formalize the process. I had been an undergrad at Yale, then in the Air Force for three years. Once I got out, I went to Harvard Business School. I wasn't sure what I wanted to do with my business life. I enjoyed aviation, but I was thinking about philanthropic work.

Between my first and second year at Harvard Business School I was working for Swissair. They asked six of us to come and rank prospective capital investments using present-value techniques. While I was in Zurich I saw a one-page article in the international edition of *Time* magazine about Laurance Rockefeller, venture capital, and aviation. It sounded interesting to me, and I thought I might combine all my interests together. So from Zurich I wrote a letter to Laurance. He shared my letter with his colleagues and decided that I might make a good addition to the group.

A Family Investment Office

The Rockefeller's investment effort at that time was led by Laurance. He had graduated from Princeton, where he had been a philosophy major. But he was also a gadgeteer and very interested in aviation. In 1938 Laurance made two investments. He responded to Eddie Rickenbacker's request for capital to acquire Colonial Airlines from General Motors. That became the start-up capital for Eastern Air Lines. About the same time, J. S. McDonnell, a young aeronautical engineer from St. Louis, came to Laurance and told him that with the invention of the jet aircraft engine he would like to design a single-engine fighter plane. Laurance indicated to him that he was interested, and if he would go back to St. Louis and put together a business plan he would respond favorably to the idea. That was the start of McDonnell Aircraft, which eventually became McDonnell Douglas—now merged with Boeing.

Laurance invested equity capital in very early-stage companies and worked with their management teams to try and help them. When World War II came he joined the Navy. In 1945, at the end of the war, he was discharged from the Navy. He concluded that many technologies that had been developed for the war effort could be applied to commercial purposes, such as blind landing systems, navigational instrumentation, and power systems. He decided to put together some companies, some investments, that would be reflective of such a strategy.

He assembled a staff of three people. One was a banker from Chase, another was General Arnold's top procurement officer, and the third was an MIT aeronautical engineer who had been a lieutenant colonel in the Air Force. That team and Laurance went looking for deserving investment opportunities—companies to start or companies to invest in—where they could do something worthwhile and provide enhanced returns at the same time.

Laurance's effort and staff was dedicated to creating and supporting early-stage companies with equity investments. His aim was to build companies for ten to fifteen years, then sell them or have them go public. Laurance invited his brothers and sister to participate. David, John, and Abby were regulars. Nelson and Winthrop pursued their own interests, though they were certainly aware of Laurance's exploits. Venrock's successes provided the participants with securities with low-cost bases, which could be used to support various charities and philanthropic activities.

There were people who tried to argue throughout the early '50s and '60s that if Laurance had left all this money in Standard Oil Co., he would have done better collecting his dividends. But the fact of the matter is that his investment results were quite outstanding and far exceeded the returns from his oil holdings.

In the pre–World War II era, he made three investments. In the post–World War II era, until 1969, he made fifty-six investments in different kinds of early-stage companies that included Alaska Airlines, Reaction Motors, and the Marquardt Aircraft Co. Itek was introduced by Richard Leghorn, who worked at Kodak and said Kodak wasn't interested in the high-altitude cameras that he had developed. Laurance invested in Itek after receiving Kodak's blessing and encouragement.

I joined the group in 1960 and from '60 till '69 Laurance was the quasi-family "underwriter" in all investments, always inviting his brothers and sister to join in the program.

Venture capital in those days was not focused on technology. Venture capitalists were all investing in small companies in industries that ranged from aviation and oil and gas to a smattering of electronics, instrumentation, and computer technology. In the business those days were J. H. Whitney & Co., ARD, the Brady Family Office, Joan Payson, and the Burden family.

Everybody worked very closely together and shared deals. We didn't make any moves or take any action without the advice and consent of our partners. We were very collegial, not competitive. Company mortality was high, but our results were excellent because we bolstered the companies we invested in with experienced managers.

As part of every deal, we met every entrepreneur and their spouse. We visited with them at their homes and spent weekends with them. We knew them very well indeed.

Building Companies

We believed in building companies. We were seeking early-stage ventures with the potential for growth. Often we financed companies with three to four years of sales and a stable management team. Among the characteristics we were looking for were increasing revenues, increasing profits, and a stable management team. So when the company went public there was a high likelihood that it was viable and public shareholders would be investing in a real enterprise.

Often the due diligence process took weeks, followed by extensive discussions about the best financial structure. We took pains to be certain that the management felt well rewarded with ownership incentives.

We calculated that if a company required $3 million before the liquidity event we didn't want to dilute the management by putting it all up up front. So we used to stage the investments towards mutually agreed-upon milestones. We would put in $500,000 to get the company through the product development, then another $500,000 for testing, and another $2 million for introduction to the markets.

I like to think that we have kept our standards high, that entrepreneurs recognize the value of our network and our experience, and that we are quality, patient investors, not out to take advantage of the relative inexperience of entrepreneurs.

Venrock has a reputation of sticking with its companies longer than most other firms. This policy may have affected our returns as we didn't quit the bad ones, but stayed with them until their problems were solved or until we could find an appropriate merger partner.

A New World Today

In today's world if there is a hot project, there will be a lot of venture capitalists competing for it. Entrepreneurs are savvy and can control the financing. Decisions are made much more quickly and on the basis of far less information. Founding investors no longer have to participate in later-round financings as others often willingly step up at higher valuations.

Years ago there wasn't a deal that we didn't see. Today that is clearly not the case. There are 300 to 400 firms that have funds ready to commit.

In today's world investors are pushing money into the hands of venture capitalists. A typical venture firm has five to six partners and won't expand because they do not want to reduce the carry for each partner. They simply don't have the bandwidth so they are much more hard-nosed and cutthroat about cutting their losses and going on and doing something else.

Venture capital has become more of a portfolio management business than it was. Investors are willing to shut down companies that are underperforming and that's unfortunate. But if you look at the overall picture and see how many companies are getting funded and the entrepreneurial opportunities that are being created in software and on the Internet, you'll have to say it's a wonderful engine for America. It has exceeded everyone's expectations.

A New Venrock

Venrock has changed. We still believe in backing great people with worthy ideas. We are looking for large hits with relatively small amounts of money. Relatively small thirty years ago was $300,000 to $500,000. Relatively small today for the first round is probably $1 to $3 million with an ultimate investment of $4 to $5 million.

We are doing our homework faster and more efficiently, but we are also committing more quickly and making many more investments than we did before. We are making fifteen to twenty investments each year, as opposed to two or three.

Do we still have the same values and the same desire? Yes, indeed we do. We are always on the cutting edge of something that is new and important.

Do we make mistakes, or get lured into quickie investments by people who aren't up to the mark? We feel we have less of a missionary role today. We feel that to be competitive we have to be responsive, but we also have to get down and compete aggressively in order to get the deals. If an entrepreneur—however loyal he is—gets a 20 percent better deal from others, we must prove that we can add more value over the long term. Entrepreneurs today have greater self-confidence and are better equipped to accept the challenges that are inherent in building companies with significant lasting value.

LIONEL PINCUS
Warburg Pincus

 Lionel Pincus is one of the first of Wall Street's dealmakers to have recognized the advantages of venture capital. He founded Warburg Pincus in 1964, led the first wave of venture capitalists on the East Coast, and parlayed that into a prominent role as a "venture banker." He expanded the expertise of his firm beyond traditional venture capital to embrace the full range of private equity investing.

In 1998 Warburg Pincus raised its latest fund, a $5 billion pool used to invest in "venture capital transactions, developing companies, buyouts, recapitalizations, and other special situations," as the fund's prospectus notes. Clearly, Warburg Pincus has moved beyond its venture capital and early-stage deal financing roots to become a leader in global institutional finance, with over $12 billion invested in more than 100 companies on four continents. But Warburg Pincus still plays a vital role in providing venture capital financing for entrepreneurial companies.

The firm has invested across many industry areas and has been a leader in information technology, media and communications, telecommunications, health care, energy, and financial services. Its operations have spread to Europe, Asia, and Latin America, as the firm has become cognizant that the rest of the world needs the same capital and entrepreneurial resources that Warburg Pincus has successfully provided in the United States for more than three decades.

Warburg Pincus may best be known for the successful recapitalizations of companies such as Mattel and Mellon Bank in the 1980s, but its strength and knowledge base continue to be entrepreneurial. The evolution and growth of Warburg Pincus suggests that even venture capital firms can become giant financial institutions.

As a young man I wanted to be a writer. But my father died when I was a freshman at Yale and I transferred to the University of Pennsylvania to be closer to my family in Philadelphia. I landed in the middle of a family feud. My father owned two businesses in Philadelphia. One was a soft goods manufacturing business, the other a retail business. When my father died, the surviving brothers got into a complicated family fight. The fight led to a court battle that fascinated me, even as I was getting my degree in literature. So I decided to get a master's degree at Columbia Business School, where Ben Graham and David Dodd, the fathers of security analysis, were both professors. That's how I got to New York.

While I was in graduate school I took a summer job in a brokerage firm. And while buying and selling securities that way was not very interesting to me, I found the people who created these securities fascinating. I had romantic visions about the creative process. I began to hear about people like J. P. Morgan and Jacob Schiff. So I finished Columbia Business School and took a job on Wall Street at the old investment banking firm of Ladenburg Thalmann & Co. General Georges Doriot, a Frenchman who I think was also a professor at Harvard, ran a closed-end, technology-oriented investment fund and briefly made his office there. His assistant in the early 1950s was Bill Elfers, who subsequently started Greylock. Arthur Rock was on the upper floor in the same building. He was then an analyst at Hayden Stone, a conventional brokerage business.

In the early 1950s, these old Wall Street houses were post-Depression firms with all the trappings of finance but very little real business. Ladenburg Thalmann had been one of the premier railroad and utility bankers in the previous era and, with $6 million in capital—a very large sum for the '50s—was a highly capitalized and well-known firm. They did deals and provided a full line of financial services such as brokerage, underwriting, and money management. It was there, as head of corporate finance, that I learned the "deal business."

Deals in those days were different from the way we understand them now. Each one was a private financial transaction, constructed by investment bankers with their wealthy family clients. They would create new enterprises or acquire old ones, restructure them, and offer them as soon as possible to the public. An investment letter then was about three weeks. All this was done part-time by people who were basically in the brokerage business.

One of the first big deals, the American drug company that became Warner Lambert, was started by Ferdinand Eberstadt and André Meyer of Lazard Freres. Harry Lake, who was my senior partner at Ladenburg, got the firm an interest in the deal. The size of a normal deal in those days was between $250,000 and $1 million.

The biggest start-up at that time was Litton Industries, founded by Roy Ash and Tex Thornton, known as "the whiz kids" during the Second World War. A million and a half bucks. Lehman Brothers shopped the deal around and couldn't raise the entire capital. They brought Burnham & Co. and Clarke, Dodge in as co-leads. Imagine Lehman not being able to raise $1.5 million today.

Electronics Race

In the late 1950s the Russians sent up Sputnik, and the United States government became very concerned that it had lost some sort of unknown battle in outer space. The government began to shape the investment climate with tax incentives like Rule 1244, whereby wealthy individuals would pay 25 percent for realized long-term capital gains and write off losses against a 60 percent ordinary income tax.

Electronics took over. Applied technological innovations came out of technology developed by the defense industry during the Second World War. The equity markets revived, and the concept of growth stocks was put forward by a guy named Sam Steadman at Loeb Rhoades. There was a strong demand for capital and the old Wall Street firms started expanding and hiring young people. My generation took charge of many of those institutions because there was now a twenty-five-year gap between the Depression and the '50s. During that period very few young people went to Wall Street unless they had a family tie or could produce in a fixed-commission environment.

Developments in finance reflected the expanding economy. Growth was becoming the operative word, or at least the illusion of earnings growth, as seen in the conglomeration phase of the '60s. Lehman Brothers did deals such as the leveraged purchase of De Laval Steam Turbine and started Great Western Financial. I went over to London to try to buy a machinery company based in the

United States called Baker Perkins. Charlie Allen emerged with a number of transactions such as Allied Supermarkets, Colorado Fuel and Iron, and Syntex. I made investments like Magnetronics; Precision Electro-Optics; Geurdon Industries, an early mobile-home builder; and Hughes and Hatcher, a clothing retailer. All this was done informally by probably a half-dozen houses on Wall Street.

I felt that the deal business needed to change. Deals were still being put together piece by piece on a part-time basis—it was very unprofessional.

A Full-Time Dealmaker

I always saw myself as a principal, not as an intermediary. I started thinking about what was going to happen to the Wall Street firms. As the business was evolving, it became apparent to me that the major firms like Goldman Sachs and Morgan Stanley would come to dominate the investment-banking business in an expanding industrial world that required financial services. But there was also a place for niche activities, including principal investing, and my personality was better suited for that. Having been a venture capital investor, I thought about starting a firm that would be dedicated to that form of investing.

It seemed to me that there was an opportunity to do deals on a full-time basis, and I started thinking about building a firm that would professionalize the deal business. It would be a firm that would have a full-time, dedicated staff, with enough permanent capital to support that staff on a reasonable economic basis and to have credibility as an investor.

I conceived of an organization that was going to be a fully professional firm in what I came to call "venture banking." It would create transactions in a variety of businesses and invest directly in new products and markets, in unusually gifted managements, or in undervalued assets as we perceived them. I had learned from my previous experience that managements and investors would both benefit when the capital providers were active partners in the ventures. My firm would be such a partner. We needed capital to invest in each tranche along with other investors, which would enable the firm to develop controlling positions and get first call on transactions. I formed Lionel I. Pincus & Company in 1964 on those premises.

I didn't have any large sum of capital in the firm. I had enough to support myself and a small staff. I brought a management consultant into the firm. That combination was always interesting to me, and I started a consulting business that provided a combination of financial and investment banking advice, management consulting, and the adversarial, advocacy, ministerial, and psychiatric functions necessary to help managers build their businesses.

I was gradually designing the firm and planned to have a few very wealthy individuals as investors. Then Donald Blinken, a friend of mine, talked to me about E. M. Warburg, where I had advised him to go some years before. Donald came to me and said, "That place is dying, why don't I come and join you, you have lots of ideas." Through him, I met Eric Warburg, and we started talking.

Eric had been a partner in M. M. Warburg, the original Warburg firm established in Hamburg in 1792. He had left Germany before the War and had become an American citizen and an officer in the OSS. In 1939 he established a small merchant bank that was populated by Europeans.

By then I knew what I wanted to do, and Eric and I spent a year talking about it. In 1966, I invested in and became president of E. M. Warburg & Company, which simultaneously merged with Lionel I. Pincus & Company. To avoid conflicts of interest as principals, we gave up all the investment banking and brokerage activities except conventional money management and concentrated on arm's-length consulting and venture capital investing.

I started bringing my friends in to join me, including John Vogelstein, a partner at Lazard Freres; John Heimann from Smith Barney, who subsequently left us and became Controller of the Currency; and Henry Bloch, who had been head of the Technical Assistance Program at the United Nations.

The Business Model

We created our business model, which was making direct equity investments, in partnership with management, at all stages of business development.

We supported ourselves by running a consulting business. We developed an annual fee income of over $1 million which enabled us to build our staff. We honed the capabilities that we needed for our direct investments by selling the capabilities professionally to companies that didn't have those skills.

We had $3 million in capital. We did not have a fund per se but were making deals the old-fashioned way, deal by deal. We would pass the hat for each deal and bring other investors in. We always made an investment, and then invited other people to buy in on the same terms. We would get more of the equity than they did for creating the venture. We did approximately eighteen transactions by the late '60s. I remember it was around 1968 when the president of White Weld called us up and offered us a participation in a deal concerning a computer-processing company in Nashville. For $2 million they were offering us the right to buy 20 percent of the company. John Vogelstein and I were flattered that White Weld had asked us over, but the deal made no sense whatsoever and price was unreal. On the way back to our office, we decided it was time to get out of the market.

Changing the Model

We then conceived the idea of further professionalizing and formalizing this business by raising $20 million in an operating corporate entity. It was called EMW Associates Inc., standing for E. M. Warburg & Associates. This was in 1969, and we got nine families that had been our backers in individual deals to join us in that operating entity. We made a substantial capital investment ourselves in a $20 million capitalization that consisted of $10 million of subordinated debentures, $5 million of common stock, and $5 million of equity.

So there we were, with a full-time dedicated staff and enough capital to support them at a reasonable cost. While we weren't charging fees on deals like the investment bankers, we did charge a management fee for the total pool we managed. Our mission was to develop and invest in new products, new markets, and existing companies in partnership with management. We would always be a principal, always an active investor. We had entered the New World of venture capital.

After we had raised more than $20 million, I felt we had to become acquainted with the new West Coast firms I had started hearing about. So I decided to call them all up. I visited Reid Dennis, who was then at American Express. I called on Tom Perkins and met his partner Gene Kleiner. I met Pitch Johnson, a classical venture capitalist of the old school and still a great friend of mine. I also got acquainted with Sandy Robertson through our mutual friend and accountant, Arthur Dixon. I made several trips to California and met with many of the West Coast group who looked at me like I was some kind of freak from the East Coast, and I looked at them as regional techies.

When Heizer Corporation came forward a year later with institutional money composed primarily of debentures and preferred stock, we understood that we needed to have access to the institutional marketplace. We decided that, since we were in a long-term equity investing business, we needed to be 100 percent in equity capital. So I visited with my old friend John Gutfreund at Salomon Brothers who helped us raise $27.5 million from institutional investors. Coupled with our existing firm's investment of approximately $12.5 million, we formed a new fund, EMW Ventures, with equity capital of $40 million. It was 100 percent in equity, with a Class A stock that had preference in liquidation and a Class B stock that was owned by the management. Warburg Pincus charged a fee of 2.5 percent of the total assets under management. This corporate structure was a direct precursor for the industry's limited partnerships that followed in later years.

NVCA

In the early '70s there were a number of attempts to get all the existing venture capital firms together. There were a strong bunch of personalities here, with all different backgrounds and focuses. While there was some suspicion among us, many common interests were emerging, such as ERISA, the Employee Retirement Income Security Act. Eventually seventeen firms that managed a total of $500 million in capital got together and formed the National Venture Capital Association in 1972. Half of that capital was in the old family firms like Bessemer and Venrock, and the rest was with new firms such as Heizer and Warburg Pincus.

We hired as our executive director a guy named Stan Rubel, who also worked with the Small Business Administration, to represent our trade group in Washington. On behalf of the NVCA, Charlie Lea and I led the negotiation with the Labor Department of the plan asset rules in 1978 and 1979. That produced the prudent man regulations and the contemporary venture operating company. These regulations made it possible for pension funds to invest directly in venture capital funds, opening a floodgate of new capital for our young industry.

From the outset Warburg Pincus has had a relatively large capital base. We were the first firm ever to raise a $100 million fund. That was in 1981, and it enabled us to continue building our professional capabilities at a reasonable economic cost and to be creditable as an investor. We raised our first billion-dollar fund in 1986, and our last fund was $5 billion, which came almost entirely from institutional investors.

The Mission

As a venture banker, I always saw us as specialized investors who provide start-up and development capital and invest in undervalued assets that need to be fixed. For example, we created BEA Systems, an information technology firm, from an idea, bringing our money together with excellent entrepreneurial management. Some other early-stage companies were LCI (now Qwest) and Covad, both communications companies. Renaissance Communications and United HealthCare both required development capital. The Mellon Bank was a major undervalued asset that had to be restructured and cleansed with a private equity infusion. So was Mattel.

Our progress has been evolutionary. We always saw ourselves as providing venture capital. You balance your risks by spreading your risks—by extensive due diligence and by establishing investing criteria and partnerships with management appropriate to the stage, industry, and geographic location of each investment.

Warburg Pincus is not a leveraged buyout firm. That's not our business. Our business is being direct equity investors. We think of creating and developing successful companies rather than financial engineering. We look for opportunities where other investors hesitate to go. We don't follow the crowd and we never want to be put in a box, which would limit our flexibility. That, to me, is an invitation to disaster. We also tend to be somewhat contrarian. Our limited partners have allowed us these prerogatives.

Building a Global Portfolio

We are now a global institution. In the early 1980s we decided we had to internationalize our firm because that was the direction in which the economies of the world were moving. We felt that international markets would present a substantial opportunity for our investment skills and our industry expertise. We spent a couple of years talking about how to do it. We contemplated and discussed various joint ventures, but none of the global institutions we approached understood what we wanted to do. So eventually we decided to build it the way we have built everything else—from the bottom up.

In 1983 we made our first European investment—$10 million in a Dutch pharmaceutical company called Centrafarm—and in 1987 we opened an office in London. Today, through our five offices located outside of the United States—London, Hong Kong, Singapore, Tokyo, and São Paulo—we have invested over $3 billion and received rates of return that compare well with our domestic investments, returns that have kept us in the top quartile of private equity firms for more than thirty years.

Warburg Pincus partners, with their diverse industry and geographic expertise, work together seamlessly to bring success to our portfolio companies. Each partner, regardless of his or her office location, shares in the successes or failures of each and every one of our investments. This allows us to bring not just capital but a depth of experience and relationships—our value added—to our portfolio companies.

We are deeply committed to the international market. Our broad industrial background and the professional techniques we've developed in this highly entrepreneurial business have enormous potential for creative and profitable investment in developed and developing economies throughout the world.

HERBERT WILKINS
Syncom Capital

Nearly two decades after the founding of J. H. Whitney & Co. and Venrock, the first minority venture funds began to take root, due to a government initiative known as the Minority Enterprise Small Business Investment Company Act. Administered by the Small Business Administration, these funds were tightly regulated and could never match the passion and the creativity of the mainstream funds they had been designed to emulate. It was left to pioneers such as Herbert P. Wilkins, Sr., to work within the system to better focus the investment direction of such funds and expand the number of minority-owned and managed venture capital firms. Wilkins also sought to expand the pool of capital available to minority-owned firms to include private equity from institutional investors in addition to SBA-supplied funds.

Richard Burnes, Jr., of Charles River Partners has suggested that until the mid-1980s, venture capital was a gentleman's club. For most African-Americans, it was a club that, by design or by neglect, ignored them. For Wilkins, a child of Boston's Roxbury neighborhood and a graduate of the Harvard Business School, the neglect rankled. But instead of taking flight to another profession, he started his own venture capital fund directed at minority-owned businesses. At a time when most similar funds were just providers of debt—with a little bit of equity sprinkled in—Wilkins focused on building a minority fund that specialized in telecommunications. At that time, most minority venture capital firms resembled the old SBICs: they were more providers of debt than equity because the financing provided by the SBA required regular payments of interest on the debt. And because these funds needed to generate income from day one to pay the SBA debt and cover operating expenses, the only investments these funds could make involved debt.

Wilkins's Syncom, based in Silver Spring, Maryland, isn't the largest venture capital fund directed at minorities—that would be Cleveland Christophe's TSG Ventures—but its pioneering effort and its investment strategy has become the blueprint for nearly all of the other funds operating in that space. Wilkins's entrepreneurial attitude toward venture capital has created a community that now manages well over $2 billion in capital.

I N 1968 Harvard Business School opened up its application process and I decided that because I got accepted into the business school I would commit my life to minority small business. That may sound corny but that's what I set out to do. I would never work for a major corporation.

When I got to the Business School there was a fashionable debate going on about entrepreneurship. Up to that point the Business School had not offered small business as an option to graduates. But there were a number of people who were starting to look at what General Doriot had done.

Raising Venture Capital

I joined a club on entrepreneurship and small business and decided with a couple of other Black M.B.A. candidates that we should spend the summer of 1969 looking at raising a venture capital fund. We got together with Charlie Cabot, who was a lawyer with Sullivan & Wooster, and Peter Brooke, who acted as an informal advisor to the effort, and began fund-raising. We were able to convince Bache & Co. to help us raise $10 million for a venture capital fund. We found the process of raising the fund rewarding and began to get a feel for the new-business development potential venture capital offered over conventional banking. We were excited, as we had looked at a whole array of career opportunities and had focused on venture capital, a brand new industry, as a single career option. The process was both challenging and fascinating. We spent the month of July writing a placement memorandum. The idea was to start marketing the fund immediately. But the market went sour and Bache told us they would not be able to place the fund.

My partners, one of whom was a C.P.A., and I were interested in accounting and consulting. After graduation, we established a C.P.A. firm. And even though I wasn't a C.P.A. I joined as a principal and handled all management services engagements. Subsequently, the firm merged with a New York City–based C.P.A. firm. I moved from Boston to New York with firmwide responsibility for management services. Although I liked what I was doing, I knew that going into a venture capital partnership would be my only career choice.

Urban National—A Minority Effort?

At the time, another group was looking at the process of venture capital for minorities—a group called Urban National. I closely followed their efforts as they were planning to do exactly what we had wanted to do. They went to J. P. Morgan and Morgan Stanley and raised $10 million. I talked to the group about the possibility of joining them, and in 1973 they offered me a job as senior vice president and investment officer. At that point I had achieved my goal to be a senior investment officer in a venture capital firm.

Early on, I found out that the firm was extremely elitist, and the people at Morgan Stanley and J. P. Morgan who backed the fund had their own particular approach to investing and only wanted to fund their type of deals. I felt they were on the wrong track. They financed steel companies, clothing manufacturers, radio stations, franchise store operators—a lot of fairly good companies, but their approach to doing business didn't make sense to me. They weren't looking at anything entrepreneurial; instead, they wanted to back Black corporate managers. These were generally good managers but they were also people who lacked the vision to grow a company. They did not have the feel of the market or business opportunity and the dynamism of leadership that entrepreneurs bring to a deal.

Decisions about investing or reacting to changes in the portfolio businesses weren't made quickly. After two years I was really having problems with the entire investment approach in terms of the deals I was bringing to the company versus the deals they wanted to do. They were turning down deals in a very sarcastic fashion. And I realized there was a fundamental difference in the way I wanted to do things. I wanted to finance the people I had grown up with—people with clear vision about the future and where they wanted to go in business. I wanted to finance forceful, strong-willed, and extremely competitive people, like many of the people I grew up with in the projects of Boston—but ones who were my peers, and had gone on to college. The differences were so intense that I was terminated in February 1975, and that was probably the best thing that could have happened to me.

Syncom

I went back to consulting and also worked on acquiring a beer franchise distributor, a deal that subsequently fell apart. But I had been talking to a group about running their new telecommunications venture fund and finally decided that I would take a crack at it. Started in February of 1977, Syncom had about $1.5 million in the bank. That was its total initial capitalization.

In coming on board with Syncom I decided to spend the first six to nine months developing a business plan that would focus on how to deploy our scarce capital and still achieve our investment objective of increasing minority ownership of telecommunications opportunities. We wanted to be in a situation where we would be considered a serious player in the financial arena and could attract some serious deal flow. Our initial intent was to focus exclusively on seed and early-stage companies that were minority-owned telecommunications enterprises.

Given our capital constraints, the business plan was probably as good a product as anyone could have done at that time. I thought I had a pretty fair understanding of what the venture capital profession was. Even with my differences at Urban National, I had really gained a lot of experience, especially from Courtney Whitin, Urban National's president, who was a former investment officer at American Research & Development Corporation (ARD). All through my trial by fire at Urban National I still considered Courtney Whitin a friend and mentor.

The first thing we did was to take the capital we had and put it into a 301(d) SBIC named SCI Media Corp., which we subsequently changed to Syncom Capital Corporation, a MESBIC. The MESBIC allowed us to leverage our capital four to one.

Telecommunications

Our business plan was to focus on those services in telecommunications where we could get in at a relatively cheap price, grow values, and achieve capital gains. I began studying signal coverage maps of media properties across the country and decided that that the best opportunities were in developing and building newly issued FCC radio station broadcast licenses. These stations generally had less power but, properly engineered, gave good coverage of communities where there were large minority populations. I began to give presentations across the country, encouraging people to apply for licenses that we could finance.

We started with a plan for FM radio and we also developed an AM strategy as well. There were a number of heritage AM stations owned by Sonderling Broadcasting Corp. that were being sold off as these companies shifted to FM broadcast. Suddenly, we were financing AM stations all along the East Coast—from Boston down to South Carolina. The AM plan was a disaster, principally because AM was a declining service. The audience was moving from AM to FM faster than we had anticipated. By and large if you invested in AM back then you lost your investment. Fortunately we had so little capital, we didn't invest in too many stations, and our losses were held at manageable levels.

Cable Markets

We also started investing in cable in urban markets. In 1978 I hired Terry Jones, who had been at the Booker T. Washington Foundation focusing on obtaining minority-owned cable franchises in major markets. We then set about this dual focus on AM-FM radio and cable in 1979 and 1980. By 1981 the number of cable franchises we financed had surpassed the number of radio deals. Still, there were questions as to whether we could ever get enough capital to make these investments work and whether we could find and develop the management talent to make these properties grow.

We realized early that plain old prejudice was sustaining a great disparity between the resources that were available to mainstream companies and to minority-owned radio and cable companies. Although in most markets there were no companies providing programming to the Black community, the existing stations still were able—through general market programming—to take most of the revenue. We had stations coming onstream in markets with large Black populations that were programming Black and were almost immediately able to go to the top of the market in ratings but could not generate any real revenue. So we had to figure out how to balance out the cost of quality programming and the lack of revenue.

I remember having a conversation with a lawyer who represented one of our radio stations in Oklahoma. I went to him and said, "Listen, we have a real problem. We're seventh in the market in terms of ratings in Oklahoma City but we're generating no revenues—our revenue is a measly $5,000 to $6,000 a month." I asked him to contact the right people and let them know of our plight. He came back after talking to some business owners and advertisers and said, "Your problem has not been completely solved but you should be able to do business." That's how we worked on closing the revenue gap in market after market.

A Level Playing Field

It dawned on me that leveling the playing field had to be an essential part of every business plan if we were to make money. We could be very successful in getting properties, we could build a cable system, but we weren't going to get favorable pricing for financing construction of cable systems or anything that was necessary to be successful in any industry without tough hard fights and strong investor alliances to achieve a change.

How did we deal with it? We decided we would hang in there and explore cost alternatives—bring the cost down to match the revenues being generated. Most of these properties were run on a shoestring, but I don't think we lost a single investment. Then in 1984 the economy started taking off, and you could see the portfolio taking shape. It was solid. The years of patience and basic business strategy had begun to pay off.

Today Syncom Capital Corp. has retired all of its SBA debt, and has achieved a compounded 18 percent return over the past twenty-one years. Syncom's performance ranks it in the upper quartile of the venture capital industry based upon recent *Venture Economics* statistical data.

SANFORD ROBERTSON
Robertson Stephens

While the more established New York bankers such as Goldman Sachs and Morgan Stanley have always been the ones to take blue-chip technology companies public, boutique bankers such as Hambrecht & Quist, Montgomery, or Robertson Stephens have helped the majority of technology start-ups reach the public market. These boutiques have provided the marketing, research, and underwriting for many companies that would never have met the more traditional—and conservative—criteria of the New York banks. In the process and by their very nature, the boutiques themselves have had to be entrepreneurial.

But in the world of high-tech investment banking, even bankers have to be entrepreneurs. As one of the founding bankers of Robertson Stephens—part of the legendary four horsemen of high-tech investment banking—Sanford (Sandy) Robertson has helped put together more venture capitalists and more deals than any other investment banker. Perhaps even more than Bill Hambrecht of Hambrecht & Quist and Thomas Weisel of Montgomery Securities, Sandy Robertson typifies the entrepreneurial spirit that bankers have had to possess to do business with venture capitalists and venture-backed companies.

Robertson thrived from the very beginning on the West Coast, where competition was thin and the demand for services high. Combine that with the almost total disregard Wall Street banks had for most high-technology companies when Robertson Stephens was launched in 1969, and you can see how Robertson and his fellow horsemen had the field to themselves. But as the industry exploded and the demand for underwriting expanded in the 1980s, the high-tech specialists suddenly found themselves competing with East Coast establishment investment bankers such

as Goldman Sachs, Morgan Stanley, and CS First Boston. They found
themselves undercapitalized by big-league standards, and they scrambled
to be more competitive. Since 1997, all of the boutiques have been
acquired by bigger firms, and their founders have gone back to their roots,
doing entrepreneurial ventures in the Valley.

W HEN I CAME to California for Smith Barney in
1965, the firm had never done any underwriting out
here. I started looking for ways to do investment
banking in this area. I found a deal called Applied
Technology, which was a defense electronics
countermeasure company. It was not exactly commercial technology, but
it was located in the Stanford Industrial Park near Hewlett-Packard and
it was a step in the right direction. A year later we ended up selling the
company and earned a fee for that as well. The deal broke the ice a little
bit with my New York partners, but it was a defense stock, not a true
technology stock. Then we did a private placement for Spectra-Physics,
which had an 80 percent share of the laser market—a huge market share.

In working with Spectra-Physics I met Tom Perkins, who had
started a company called University Labs. His company originally
made lasers for instruction in schools, but had ventured into the real
world by making lasers that helped lay sewer pipe and ceiling tile.
Finally, I persuaded Spectra-Physics to buy University Labs, which
got Spectra-Physics into the commercial world.

When we did the private placement for Spectra-Physics, I got
Smith Barney to make a $100,000 investment for its own account.
When I did go back for a partners' meeting, people were starting to
say, "Hey, Buck Rogers, how's your ray-gun company out there?" I
think it was then that I realized that I would never be able to get the
firm to look at technology. I thought to myself, "They'll never get it, or
it will take years for me to convince them that this is a valid industry."
Spectra-Physics, the "ray-gun company," eventually went public and
made it to the New York Stock Exchange. It was a great investment.
I guess I could see that there was a market out there for some of these
interesting smaller companies. This was a niche that a certain group
of institutional investors wanted to be in, that is, the newer, faster-
growing companies with a technology edge.

In the late '60s and early '70s there wasn't very much venture capital. The Whitneys and the Rockefellers had been investing moderately for years. DSV was in Princeton and Art Rock was doing deals with his partner Tommy Davis in San Francisco. Sutter Hill was in Palo Alto and Brentwood in Los Angeles, but these funds were not very big. If you had $5 million, you were a big player.

Launching Robertson, Colman & Stephens

I decided to start an investment bank in late 1969 and we did our first trading on the Exchange on the first business day of 1970. I remember the first January issue of *Business Week* had an all-black cover that said something to the effect that the stock market was dead. This obviously scared us, but it turned out to be a perfect time to start because we had no overhead to speak of and good people were available.

The '70s were, in general, a pretty tough time to invest. But we were in the right market, as technology was doing well. The companies that were getting started were doing well, and we were there ready to take them public. There were very few offerings in the '70s but the companies that did make it to the public market were quite interesting, and our overhead was low.

We had a whole group of limited partners who we thought could help us in our business. Eugene Kleiner, who was a Fairchild Semiconductor founder, was the first one to commit. When Ken Siebel and I called on him he said yes in about five minutes, as he understood what we were trying to do. When we left his office, we were as high as a kite from getting our first limited partner. Our limited partners were people who could help us out, who could bring us deals, who could provide good advice, and who could help us evaluate a technology. They were extremely valuable to us.

We raised $1.1 million. There were eight limited partners at $100,000 apiece, and three principals at $100,000 apiece. So, that totaled $1.1 million. When we started we had only ten or twelve people, but we grew quite fast. We had brokerage income from the first day. We had private placement income from the first month. Since there were not that many venture capitalists, entrepreneurs used us as an intermediary for private placements with the venture community. So we had quite a few venture placements, and would bring deals to the venture capitalists. With these two sources of income, we made money from the first month, even though we didn't have our first IPO until 1972.

The first IPO was Wangco, a tape drive manufacturer that we later sold to Perkin Elmer. And then in the fall of 1972, we did the IPO of Applied Materials, which is now the dominant factor in semiconductor equipment. At the time they had about $17 million in sales. General Electric owned 14 percent of the company and Fred Adler was chairman of the board. It was a good company serving the semiconductor industry. The stock came public just as the Dow Jones Average was hitting 1,000 for the first time. People were very worried about how high the market was and it was starting to fall precipitously. In order to get the deal done, we had to eliminate the secondary component and only do the primary. I am very proud of this offering because today Applied Materials has sales of over $3 billion annually. Twenty-five years later, almost to the day, we did a $100 million financing for them. It has been very satisfying to have them as a client—to raise money for them and then watch them thrive.

Matchmaker

I remember being in Dick Riordan's law office in Los Angeles—he's now the mayor—and running into Kip Hagopian of Brentwood. He was ecstatic. They had just finished raising a $5 million fund, which had taken them over a year. I thought to myself, there must be some venture money around at last. When I got back to San Francisco I called Tom Perkins, who had told me he wanted to spin out of Hewlett-Packard and become a venture capitalist. I said, "Maybe there's some money out there now, possibly we can get together a $10 million fund." At about the same time Eugene Kleiner, who was an original investor in our firm, and a private venture capitalist, indicated that he was talking to the Hillman family in Pittsburgh about investing some of their money. It occurred to me that Tom Perkins and Eugene would be great partners, even though they didn't know each other. Eugene had the semiconductor world covered; Tom had the computer world covered. They had heard of each other and respected each other from a distance. I suggested the three of us meet for breakfast at Ricky's Hyatt House, which used to be the place where you met to do a deal in Silicon Valley. We met there at 7:30 in the morning, and it was fascinating to see the immediate rapport. The energy of that breakfast was wonderful. The conversation was so intense we forgot about the time and finally got kicked out of the restaurant four hours later as they were setting up for lunch. Over breakfast they found that their philosophy in investing and running small companies was the same. It was a Friday morning, and they met again on Saturday and on Sunday. Monday morning they called me and said, "We're on the same wavelength. We both think the same way, and we've both been operating managers. We think we can work together, and our philosophy of venture capital is the same—let's go and raise a $10 million fund." In 1972 that was a tough job. By the first of December, after three months of fund-raising, we cut the fund off at $8.4 million, as we thought we might lose some of those dollars over Christmas and have to start over again. Interestingly, they never spent the full $8.4 million, but it was one of the greatest venture capital returns of all time. It funded Tandem Computers and Genentech. I think the best merger I ever did in my life was introducing those two guys to each other and raising their first fund.

Financial Architecture

We were just out there trying to do a good job, trying to make a living, and trying to finance these companies. It was like being an architect where you design a building and then watch it come out of the ground. We would be the financial architects. We would help finance these companies, and it was very satisfying to go down to the Valley and see a new building being built, a parking lot fill up, and new jobs being created. It has been a very satisfying business to be in, with lots of rewards. We were making these entrepreneurs very wealthy people, so they loved us for it. They were upset if we were trading their stock and it happened to be going down, but overall they were very pleased. We really felt that we were in the forefront of the American economy. There was a great deal of follow-on business, because of course the companies would need more money for further expansion.

We knew that we were doing something that was fun and important, and the people we were dealing with were fascinating. They could be tough clients, they could be demanding, but they were always interesting. They were driven, not to make money, but to make their technology the best in the world. They wanted to make whatever it was better than anybody else.

The entrepreneurs who came in and said they were motivated to start a company because they wanted to get rich were not the ones that had the best ideas. The ones who came in and said that they had an idea to make the world better or the technology better were the ones you wanted to back. The money followed the ideas.

The Archetypal Investment Banker

Nobody knew what an investment banker was, literally, until a few years ago. I don't think the general public really knew until the insider information scandals of the '80s when some investment bankers went to jail. I think the scandals of the '80s exposed the fact that a lot of people came into investment banking because it was the fastest way to make money in the '80s and '90s, not because they loved the business, loved the fascination of financing these companies, or loved the thrill of the deal. This business is so entertaining I would pay to come down to the office and do what I do. Working with entrepreneurs and their companies and watching new technologies develop is great fun and brings great satisfaction.

Investment banking is the greatest business in the world. You are looking at companies through the eyes of the chairman of the board, and you don't have to get down to the minutiae of the company. You also play God a little, saying, "I like this company," or "I don't like that company." The challenges of the marketplace are also fascinating. Everything in the world—politics, economics, sociology, and world events—is reflected in the marketplace. It's a fun place to be in the spectrum of business. I'm not sure the whole group of new investment bankers feel that way. I think they drifted into the business because it was known to be a place where incomes were high. There are still a few around who love the fascination of the business, and genetically have the right mind-set of how to put a deal together, and how to finance something. There's only a certain percentage who really have that real God-given talent. It's just fascinating working with the young people who have it. Others are perfectly capable, have all the skills from business school, but are there more to make money than for the thrill of the business. First the graduates coming out of business school wanted to be investment bankers, then they wanted to be venture capitalists, then they wanted to be in LBO funds, and today they all want to be in Internet start-ups.

Financing—'70s Style

In the 1970s, I think there was only one company that was ever started with more than $1 million, and that one exception was Amdahl. Possibly you could find others. But basically a company got $1 million to start, and if they didn't get to positive cash flow on that million, there was a washout financing at ten cents on the dollar. If additional funds went in, the poor entrepreneurs got washed out. As a result, the entrepreneurs handled their expenses very carefully. People worked out of their garages, or in very modest circumstances, and worked to try to get to positive cash flow on their first million before they were financed again.

That's all changed. With more money around, a company might start with $5 to $15 million, and when they run out of that, they still might not be at positive cash flow, but there's another round at a higher price, rather than lower, because they're "on track." Venture companies are force-fed, which gets them to the public market a lot sooner, since they've had $10 or $15 million poured into them before they even go public, rather than just $1 million. I have been worried that there's too much venture capital around chasing too few deals, but up to now the number of entrepreneurs that have sprung out of existing companies has kept up with the amount of money available. There has been a huge number of entrepreneurs and companies to invest in because of the Internet. At some point we're going to run out of quality managers.

What was the amount of money that went into venture funds last year? About $20 billion was reported by venture capital funds, and then you've got companies like Microsoft, Intel, Oracle, and Sun making venture investments. I don't know what the real number is—it may be double the reported $20 billion. But so far, so good. The entrepreneurs have appeared just as fast as the money. Somewhere between now and five years from now, there will be a shakeout in the industry—maybe because the public market is going to be tougher—and these companies won't go public quite as fast, causing the rate of return to not look so good on some funds, and those funds will have a hard time getting re-funded. So, while it's been easy for everybody to snap their fingers and say I'm doing fund V or fund VIII, at some point some of the funds raised this year or next year won't have the rate of return. They won't be able to get ten times *sales* for their Internet IPOs. It will only be fifteen times *earnings,* and therefore they'll have a borderline profit, not a 100-to-1 profit. It will then be harder for them to go back to their existing investors and say that they've given 50 percent a year in the past but this time its only 7 percent a year, or 10 percent. However, I think venture capital has become a true marketplace—one that's here to stay. It has a continuing flow of funds into it now, and it's part of the overall financing structure for the United States. It's a real advantage for the United States. The development of that venture capital stream gives the United States a significant advantage over other world economies.

Succession Planning

I think at the top-level venture capital firms the current partners are just as capable as the earlier generations. At Kleiner Perkins, Eugene, Tom, and Frank Caufield have trained and given way to Brook Byers, John Doerr, and Vinod Khosla. At Sequoia, Don Valentine and Pierre Lamond have brought along Mike Moritz and Doug Leone. This later generation seems to be grooming its successors as well.

Succession management has worked in the venture area. I think it's worked for the better funds because it's such a desirable business to get into that they've been able to have their pick of the business school graduates and technology executives they want to bring in.

The business is also spreading beyond Silicon Valley and Boston. Wherever there are technology companies, a venture capitalist has followed to catch the spin-out from these companies. Therefore there are pockets of venture capitalists in Seattle, Orange County, San Diego, and Austin, Texas. Even New York is thriving with its start-ups in Silicon Alley. These pockets of entrepreneurs often start where there's a university or a remote plant of a major company, so Silicon Valley is exporting its expertise throughout the country.

The Next High-Tech Boutiques

Now that the boutiques all have become a part of larger banks, where will the next boutiques come from?

The boutiques have been institutionalized with their purchase by larger commercial banks and the major investment banks have beefed up their technology underwriting capabilities. I believe there is a pocket of opportunity developing that was left vacant when the old Big Four were bought up. The distribution of securities is changing dramatically and some of the opportunity brought about by change may be filled by the new electronic underwriting firms who are becoming a much more important factor in securities distribution.

Our relationship with Bank of America was working out beautifully. They kept us as an encapsulated firm within the firm. Yet, we could reach out of the capsule and use their client base and capital. They were introducing us to new customers and we could double or triple our capital when we wanted to. It was a very happy relationship and seemed to be working very well. The second merger jarred that, and put everything in play again. But I think the Bank of America/ Robertson Stephens merger would have been the most successful. The Nation's Bank/Montgomery merger also seemed to be going very well, but with the merger of the two larger banks, we became gnats on two elephants' tails.

In our economy today, you look at the industry on a worldwide basis. What's happening in Japan or England or Malaysia can have the same impact as something that's happening in Silicon Valley. In a worldwide economy, or for that matter in an Internet economy, everything that happens in the world from a technology standpoint is immediately reflected in technology markets.

ARTHUR ROCK
Arthur Rock & Co.

 *If anyone stands out as one of the seminal figures in venture capital, it is Arthur Rock. The first venture capitalist to grace the cover of* Time *(January 23, 1984), Rock garners respect among his colleagues and competitors not only because he has made some of the most rewarding investments, but because the companies he has helped finance have come to form the backbone of what is now known as Silicon Valley. Think of Scientific Data Systems, Teledyne, Intel, and Apple Computer, and Arthur Rock invariably comes to mind.*

A private person, Rock has never been the media-savvy promoter that many venture capitalists have become. Rock made his first investments at a time when technology wasn't the Wall Street investment choice, a time when it took products and revenues and proven managers to go public. And although Rock himself confesses that he was never a very astute judge of technology, the people he brought together and the culture he helped influence have created a lasting economic presence in Silicon Valley. Even though Rock's partnership with Tommy Davis (who went on to launch Mayfield Fund) came at the very beginning of Silicon Valley, many of their covenants and practices became part of the partnership structure that Valley venture capitalists adopted.

I FINISHED Harvard Business School in 1951 and ended up at Hayden Stone, a New York investment banking firm that specialized in financing for companies. I was especially fascinated with smaller companies. We did quite a few deals, both public and private. Of course, the venture capital firms around then weren't called venture capital firms—they were just private family organizations, like the Rockefellers, or the Whitneys and

the Phippses. There was a group of individuals who had been following the deals I had been making, and with them I invested in a few
companies, the most notable of which was Teledyne.

You probably have read the story of the forming of Fairchild Semiconductor. Well, Fairchild Semiconductor was formed by eight scientists out of the Shockley Laboratory Division of Beckman Instruments. Shockley, of course, was one of the three people who invented
the transistor. Shockley was a difficult man, but a genius. After he
invented the transistor, he decided he wanted to change his life—he
got divorced then remarried, and then moved to California. At the
time you couldn't raise the money you can today, but he did know
Arnold Beckman. With Beckman's help, the Shockley Laboratory
Division of Beckman Instruments was created. Of course, with
Shockley's name he could recruit anybody he wanted. So he recruited
a whole group of very young super scientists. That went on for around
two years, but finally Shockley's difficult personality got to all of these
guys, and some of them decided they wanted to leave. Seven of these
scientists got together. One scientist's father had a brokerage account
with Hayden Stone. So, he wrote to his father's broker and informed
him that there were seven scientists who were going to leave Shockley, but before they did, they were wondering if anyone knew of a
place where they could get a job together.

Lucky for me, this broker showed me the letter. I talked to this scientist, and it was decided that one of the partners at the firm and I
would come out to San Francisco to meet with them. They needed $1.5
million. We thought about it for awhile, and I got the idea that we
ought to see if we could form a company and then get one of the bigger companies to finance it. So we made a second trip out to California, at which time an eighth individual—Bob Noyce—joined us and
we agreed to agree to form a company in which each of the eight scientists would own 10 percent of the stock, and Hayden Stone would
own 20 percent. And between the scientists and ourselves, we selected
about thirty-five companies to go talk to. We did zero with all of them.

This was 1957, twelve years after World War II, and all these companies were interested in expanding their technology, and they didn't
know how to do it. They all liked the technology, but they couldn't see
how it could be done without upsetting their organizations. They
didn't understand how they could set up a separate subsidiary, and

finance it, and how that would affect their organizations. All thirty-five of them passed. Then we came across Sherman Fairchild.

Sherman Fairchild was the single largest stock holder in IBM, because his father had financed Tom Watson Senior in forming the predecessor company to IBM. In any event, Tom Watson Senior had quite a few offspring. Sherman Fairchild's father had only one. So Sherman ended up as the single largest stockholder in IBM. He had a lot of money. In addition, he was an inventor. He invented the aerial camera—and then he had to invent an airplane to hold the camera. That's how Fairchild Camera and Instrument and Fairchild Aviation came to be two separate companies. Sherman liked young people and he liked new ideas, and he had a lot of patents, so when we approached him, he liked our idea. So Fairchild Camera and Instrument lent $1.5 million to this company, in return for which they got an option to buy all of the stock for $3 million. That was how Fairchild Semiconductor came to be.

The reason I got so excited about Fairchild Semiconductor was because I'd already been in the semiconductor business through General Transistor. General Transistor was the first publicly held, independent company to make transistors. To show you what kind of money was involved, the company was started with $50,000. We did a small public offering for them, and eventually that company was sold to General Instrument, and became the semiconductor division of General Instrument.

In two years, Fairchild Camera bought whole thing back. They exercised their option and paid us the $3 million, and created Fairchild Semiconductor. By the time everybody left, the subsidiary was making more of a profit than Fairchild Camera. Sherman Fairchild had died in the meantime, and the company was being run out of Syosset, Long Island, where Fairchild Camera and Instrument had its headquarters. Relations got pretty testy after Sherman died. The CEO didn't like the idea of stock options, and wanted to call the shots out of Syosset, and have everybody report to him. Finally people started to leave, and eventually Noyce and Moore left and started Intel.

It is entirely possible that there would be no silicon in Silicon Valley if Fairchild Semiconductor had not been established. The Fairchild Eight would probably have dispersed and the only other company working with silicon was Texas Instruments.

I moved to California in '61. We were doing a lot of deals in California, and it occurred to me that all of the energetic scientists were forming around Stanford. The reason for that, in my opinion—although some people will differ—is because of Fred Terman. He was head of the engineering school at Stanford, and he encouraged his students, especially the doctoral and postdoctoral students, to form companies and continue to teach at Stanford. That was an unknown concept at any other school in those days—it certainly wasn't happening at MIT, Harvard, or Princeton, or any of the good engineering schools. People got fired from MIT in those days if they started companies. All these people were entrepreneurial, and yet there wasn't any money in California. The money was in the East, and Eastern companies weren't exciting. So I decided to try to get some Eastern money and move to California to set up a company to invest in these entrepreneurs.

I don't know that there was a term called venture capital when I started out. As far as I know, I was the first to use the term, but I can't claim that I coined it or anything. I suppose venture capital actually goes back to the days of the Medici. But in any event, institutions were not interested in putting money into these companies, because they were all Eastern institutions that invested by the prudent man rule—it was just taking too big a risk. So we got individuals to invest.

Davis and Rock

I had met Tommy Davis through some mutual friends while I was in San Francisco. He was a vice president of the Kern County Land Company, which had decided they wanted to do some expansion, because they had all this cash flow coming in from their royalties. So, they hired Tommy to invest their money in corporate developments. He was responsible for the Kern County Land Company making an investment in Watkins Johnson. He had a couple more deals he wanted to do, but the Kern County Land Company said, let's wait five or six years and let's see what happens with the one deal we've done. Tommy didn't want to do that. So, we got together and raised $5 million—mostly from Eastern friends of mine who had been in deals with me before—and we formed the firm of Davis and Rock in 1961 with the princely sum of $5 million. In fact, we never invested the whole $5 million. We got pretty lucky, and made some very good investments, the most notable of which, of course, were Teledyne and Scientific Data Systems.

I suppose if I were starting out today I would do it the same way. I think venture capital today is made up of portfolio managers— except for a few of them. You know—I'll go into your deal, you go into my deal. We've raised all this money, we've got to get it invested. And if you divide up the number of companies they're invested in by the number of partners, you find that the partners haven't got ten minutes for any one company. We spent a lot of time with our companies.

As for the entrepreneurs, many of them were corporate creatures who weren't familiar at all with the outside world. We were success-ful in getting people who had been through it before. Henry Single-ton was the vice president of Litton Industries and ran one of the big divisions. And Max Palevsky at Scientific Data Systems had success-fully run the computer subsidiary of Packard Bell. But there were enough people around, and enough time for people to grow. You don't have that today. Everything is so fast and furious, and you've got to do things right away. But these people we invested in needed help. They had no idea of stockholder value.

Davis and Rock dissolved by its own terms in 1968 after a seven-year life. We had a big position in Scientific Data Systems, and the SEC laws were a little different in those days than they are now. So if we formed a new partnership, all the partners who were partners in the old partnership would be deemed insiders of SDS. I didn't want to resign from the SDS board, but we wanted to have our limited partners free to sell their stock if they wanted to. So Tommy went his way, and I went mine. We were very good friends, no problem there; it was just the way things worked out.

When institutions began seeing what kind of returns Davis and Rock had, they became more interested in investing in those entities. So, beginning in '69 and '70—maybe even '68—other venture capital firms were formed. SDS was sold in '69 to Xerox at close to $990 mil-lion. That was a humongous deal in those days.

I worked by myself for a year or so, and then I formed another partnership called Arthur Rock and Associates. That was successful, but nowhere near as successful as Davis and Rock. When that expired, I went out on my own.

Intel

It was the invention of the semiconductor and the microprocessor that really changed the world. And Intel was at the forefront.

It was Bob Noyce, Gordon Moore, and myself who incorporated Intel. Andy Grove was actually employee number two. As I said earlier, the Fairchild group became less and less happy at Fairchild Semiconductor after Sherman Fairchild died and John Carter became CEO at Fairchild Camera. John was not an easy man to get along with. He wasn't crazy like Shockley, but he was an Eastern CEO, and he ran everything by the book. He didn't want to give out any stock options, or to do the things that Bob and Gordon felt they had to do to build a business.

Fairchild was making transistors. When Bob and Gordon decided to leave they had the idea that they would make semiconductor memory. Now, you have to realize that all memory was made up of magnetic cores, and magnetic cores had to be strung by hand. So, if semiconductor memory didn't exist, but there were the same number of computers that are out today, my guess is that everybody in the world would have to be stringing magnetic cores. That's the business they went into, and they eventually replaced magnetic cores.

I was already involved in the memory core business, so I knew how difficult it would be to expand the business—to get people to string those cores. And I had known Bob and Gordon since 1957—this was '68—and Intel is probably the only company I invested in that I was absolutely, 100 percent sure would be a success, because of Moore and Noyce.

We got lucky again with Busicom, a Japanese company that came to us wanting to make a calculator. One of our engineering gurus figured out a way to put together some semiconductors to make a calculator. From that we went into the microprocessor business. The memory business turned south because of Japanese competition, with their dumping in our markets and selling below cost. So, we couldn't make any money in the memory business. To Moore and Grove's credit, at that time we decided to bite the bullet and take our losses. We let go a third of our employees, and exited the memory business. That was probably, in my opinion, the single best management decision ever made in any company. It took a lot of guts.

The lesson from Intel? The necessity of having great management. Intel has been blessed with absolutely fantastic management, with the right managers at the right time. Noyce was the first CEO, and he was a visionary and a great scientist, but he was also a good salesman and a good marketing person. His interests were all over the place. He finally got bored. Then we had Moore for ten years, and he was the ultimate scientist and really drove the technology when the technology needed driving. Then when we started to have competition and needed someone to drive the business, Grove came on the scene. The Grove years were great ones for Intel, because Grove steered the business with laser-type vision. He just recently retired as CEO, although he's still active as chairman. Now we have our fourth CEO, and hopefully he'll be as good as the others. I don't know of many businesses that have had three generations of CEOs who were really fantastic.

Apple

Really, Mike Markkula should get most of the credit for my association with Apple. In those days, I was going to staff meetings regularly at all the companies I was associated with. I used to go down to Intel every week for staff meetings. One of the people I got to know in staff meetings was Mike Markkula. He was vice president of marketing and he retired early after he made quite a bit of money in his Intel stock options. Somehow or other, he had met Steve Jobs and Steve Wozniak. As I recall, he had guaranteed a bank loan of $300,000 to Apple, and became a third partner. Then Mike asked me to take a look at it.

Steve Jobs and Steve Wozniak weren't very appealing people in those days. I kind of wondered about this, but I trusted Mike. He asked me to come down to the Home Brew Computer Show. There were going to be a bunch of computer companies there, as well as a technical show. I had been going to shows all along, so, I said, "Sure I'll go." I went down to San Jose, and there was a big auditorium full of people with circuit boards and makeshift computers. No one was actually making a computer. Many booths were empty. I walked over to the Apple booth, and I couldn't get close to it. People were piled up behind the booth. I began to figure maybe there was something to this. I stood around there for quite awhile, and listened to people talking about it, and I thought, there's really something here, and if Mike is going to be really serious about this company, I guess I'll make an investment. The Rockefellers at that time also were making an investment. I invested the princely sum of $60,000. I went on the board, and lo and behold, it just took off. We got professional management in there. Jobs is an incredible person. He is very manipulative, very political, and has fantastic ideas, and can drive a process. But, he wasn't a manager, at least in those days. He had a falling out with Wozniak, and then he had a falling out with John Sculley, and much to his credit, he came back; maybe something will come of Apple now.

I had to get off the Apple board when IBM, Apple, and Motorola jointly developed what they called a Power PC chip. I really didn't pay much attention to it. Apple had always been a Motorola customer, not an Intel customer, and that was fine, that didn't bother me. I didn't see where I had any conflicts, because they had made that decision technically and had decided that the Motorola chip was better for their purposes. But, when this consortium developed the Power PC, they took an ad in all the newspapers—a double-page ad—in the *Wall Street Journal,* the *New York Times,* the *San Jose Mercury News,* and so on, announcing the chip, and saying that they were going to kill Intel. It wasn't two days later that I resigned from the Apple board.

The main help that I tried to give Apple was getting them some seasoned managerial people. Their first president didn't work out. Then of course we went out and hired John. Sculley did great for eight of the ten years he was there. Then things started to fall apart again, and that's exactly when I left, right at the end of Sculley's term.

The Venture Philosophy

There's a huge difference in a lot of venture capital firms. I think maybe Kleiner Perkins and a couple of the other older ones still try to give some management help. There's so much money around that they're fighting to get into deals, and decisions are being made over the telephone. People are calling up saying, I've got to be in this deal, without ever knowing anything about it.

I've been quoted fairly often as saying that I invest in people, not in technology, first of all because I'm not a technologist. I think you have to be a technologist today, because there are so many different technologies converging that you have to understand where everything is coming from. When I started doing these deals, there was no competition. You could make some mistakes, and still not get very far behind. Today, if you make any mistakes, you're dead. So, you have to understand the technology. A person with a general business background would not make it in the venture capital business today. But, in any event, I was always interested in investing in people. So, I spent a lot of time with would-be entrepreneurs to see whether they were motivated and whether they were intellectually honest. I don't see that as being possible in today's markets.

It just came out of people wanting to create something. I know I wanted to create something. I knew I couldn't do it by myself because, again, I wasn't technical. But I could sure help other people create things. And I really liked the engineers, scientists, entrepreneurs. Those are the people I enjoyed being with. I got my kicks out of helping to build big companies, creating jobs, and creating new technologies that would be helpful to people.

The Internet

I have this idea that there's been a major development of technology about every fifty years, 1850–1900 was the mechanical age with the development of the engine, 1900–1950 was the age of electricity, and then the big invention in 1950 of course was the transistor, which really is responsible for all of the technology we see today. Everything new in technology is a result of the invention of the transistor. I can't think of a single technology company that would have been able to exist without the semiconductor—from medical instruments and software, to bio-tech, and so on. There is nothing that doesn't trace itself to the invention of the transistor. During the last ten years, I really began worrying about the future without a new seminal invention.

The new invention, right about the turn of the century, is the Internet. It's not an invention in terms of somebody getting a patent or developing a process, but it really is an invention where no one knows what's going to happen within five or ten years. You have no clue. Anyone who says he does is crazy. So that's the new invention, and I am just not up to it. I'm up to investing as an angel investor, and being of small help where ever I can, but not in taking the lead in doing what I did at SDS and Teledyne and Intel and Apple. I just don't see myself in that position.

As I said, the Internet is a new invention and a new platform. It's going to be a huge business, and big companies will come out of it as leaders. But in the meantime there is going to be more money lost than made before it sorts itself out.

I'm involved in a couple of companies that I think are quite exciting. One is a company called Education Partners, which is trying to change the way reading is taught in grammar schools. So far we've been successful and are profitable. I would guess we're probably the only profitable education company going. It's run by some very fine people—in fact, the CEO is a Harvard Business School graduate, Adam Berman. There's technology involved, but it's not a cutting-edge technology. It's just a new method of teaching reading.

I'm involved in a very small medical start-up, which has developed a product that we're testing which will help people with Alzheimer's. It's quite exciting because it's such a simple thing to do. The theory is that part of the reason people get Alzheimer's is that their cerebral spinal fluid doesn't circulate fast enough in the brain, and builds up pressure. If you can relieve that pressure, the brain will become more normal. People call me about these little things and I get interested in them.

Things move so fast. Big profits and successes are made not only because the venture capital firms are choosing well, but because of the IPO market. I keep on telling people, wait until the IPO market dries up. I am a great believer in the regression to the mean. I don't know what's going to happen to all of these valuations. There are all these pension funds that are going into fund one, and fund two, and fund three, based on the profits of small amounts of stock that are sold in an IPO, which causes a shortage of them, so they trade hands at higher and higher prices. Some day that's going to stop. I don't know if it will be in my lifetime, but it just can't continue. What's going to happen to all these venture capital firms—to all these investors who are investing blindly—I just don't know.

WEST COAST

PAUL WYTHES
Sutter Hill Ventures

The oldest existing venture capital firm on the West Coast is Sutter Hill Ventures, where Paul Wythes was a founder in 1964.

Sutter Hill outgrew the SBIC investment limits in the late 1960s, and its need for larger sums of capital to invest made Wythes seek out Canada's Genstar as a new source of capital. With Genstar as its sole institutional investor, Sutter Hill quickly became one of the leading investment firms in the Valley, responsible for some of the most successful companies of that time, including Diablo Systems, Xidex, Qume, and Measurex.

His firm continues to enjoy the respect of the Valley community as a venture capital firm that continues to invest the old-fashioned way, with old-fashioned principles.

I WENT TO Princeton. I graduated with the class of 1955, and was an engineering student at Princeton. I did not major in finance. I was not in English, or any of the other liberal arts areas, although at Princeton for every five students walking around the campus, only one is an engineer, and the other four are liberal arts majors. After Princeton I went right into the Navy as an officer, and spent two years in the United States Navy which I got in through the NROTC program. I got out in two years, and went on to Stanford Business School, graduating with an M.B.A. in 1959.

That was the move that took me, for the first time in my career, west of the Mississippi River.

I grew up in southern New Jersey, in a little town called Haddonfield. My father was in education. We grew up in an environment that was non-business oriented. So I ended up in California in 1957, having never been there before, knowing no one, and started at the Stanford Business School. The reason that was important, not only for getting me to the West Coast, where I've lived ever since, was because I knew when I was at Princeton I wanted to get into business. I knew I wanted to go to business school. So, I talked to the dean of the engineering school at Princeton, and he said, "You know there's Harvard, there's Wharton, there's UVA (Darden) which is getting started in a bigger way, there's Kellogg in Chicago at Northwestern, and so forth. But, there also is this emerging first-class business school on the West Coast called Stanford." And, I said, "Well, that's interesting, I've never been west of the Mississippi, so maybe I should think about it." I applied and got in. When I graduated I took a job with Honeywell in scientific sales, in their scientific instrument division. I was a salesman at Honeywell, basically, selling scientific instrumentation that related to my engineering background. I was with them for four years, then I went to Beckman Instruments in Fullerton, California. At that time, Beckman was running neck and neck with Hewlett-Packard as to which company was going to be bigger in sales and profits the next year.

I went to work with Beckman in their market research area. We were doing mergers and acquisitions, trying to find new products or areas for the company to either develop internally through their R&D program or bring in through acquisitions. I reported to the vice president of marketing.

The other turning point was when one of my classmates from Stanford Business School called me and said he'd like me to think about coming up to Palo Alto and helping to get this new firm that he and his brother-in-law had formed, called Sutter Hill, started with venture capital. This was in 1964.

To put that in perspective, in 1964 there were really only two other venture firms on the West Coast doing venture capital. George Quist was running the Bank of America's SBIC in San Francisco, and Tommy Davis and Art Rock were at Davis and Rock. There were no Kleiner Perkinses, Mayfields, or IVPs. So, Sutter Hill had roughly a ten-year head start on most of the firms that we all know today. Sutter Hill Ventures today is the oldest venture firm on the West Coast.

The Early Days of Venture Capital

There were people like Laurance Rockefeller, the Whitneys, the Bessemers, and so forth, who got an early start with a lot of family money. But with the SBIC Act of 1958 there were a few SBICs formed, such as the Bank of America SBIC, and others. They played a more significant role in getting the venture activity out of the box, so to speak, with one on every corner like Merrill Lynch, than any thing else. The SBICs filled a void from roughly 1958 until the early '70s, when the partnership format became the norm in our business. I give them a lot of credit. The business was fraught with a lot of red tape. You had to fill out forms, and all that sort of thing, but the debt was cheap. It was very long term. Some deals that were done in the SBIC framework, depending on who was running the SBIC, were very similar to deals that are done today, while others were very different. I think a lot of people that were running SBICs in the '60s would do a deal where they had to have some sort of interest payment to cover what they were paying in interest to the SBA. Others said, "The hell with that. We're going to do real equity deals." It depended on who was involved in running a particular SBIC at the time.

Today you go to a cocktail party, and somebody says, "What do you do?" you say, "I'm a venture capitalist," and they say, "Wow!" They either think you're wonderful, or they think you're a vulture. In the '60s, I can remember people asking at cocktail parties, "What do you do?" When I would reply, "Well, I'm a venture capitalist," they'd say, "What's that?" And you'd almost have to say, "I don't know." But that has changed a great deal over the years.

I think the entrepreneurs today, the really good ones, are much more knowledgeable about venture capital, what it is, who does it, and who the marginal players and the excellent players are in the field. And the really good entrepreneurs do their homework before they come in to see you much more than they used to do in the 1960s.

Pioneers

Sutter Hill pioneered some things that I don't think a lot of people realize. We pioneered the warehousing of people. Dave Bossen, who was the founder, entrepreneur, and CEO of Measurex, came and lived in

Sutter Hill's offices for six months. He had left a company in Ohio and wanted to move to the West Coast. He basically wrote his business plan in our office. I took Dave out on the road to raise the million and a quarter dollars we needed to get the company started. At Sutter Hill at the time our maximum investment was about a quarter of a million. We felt that was about all we should put into any one deal. So, we committed to that, and then I took Dave with me and we went around the country trying to raise the other million dollars. I remember going in to see George Quist, and he turned us down. We went to see Tommy Davis and Art Rock, and they turned us down. It was very interesting, because I brought Dave back to New York, and there was a gentleman at Blyth Eastman Dillon in those days, a man named Jack Kelsey, who had International Paper for a client. Measurex made control systems for the manufacture of paper and other sheet processes. Jack talked to his people at International Paper, and he thought it sounded kind of interesting, because it was a whole new way of digitizing the sensors, and building a major control system for the paper industry. So, he came back and said he'd like to go in on the deal. That unlocked a couple of other venture firms, and we had the deal done. The last person to commit to that deal was Pete Bancroft at Bessemer. It was a race between Pete at Bessemer and AllState's Ned Heizer in Chicago. They were both raising the last chunk, which I think was $500,000. It was the biggest chunk. Pete beat Ned to the punch and came in. The company was a start-up. We started nothing but high-tech start-ups. And, it became a very successful company—went on the New York Stock Exchange and recently was sold to Honeywell.

Investing on Trust: Never a Term Sheet

In the start-up business then, you had more time to do homework, due diligence, and research. The speed of decision making was a lot slower then than it is today, which gets to the competitive nature of the business today. We tended to always do straight preferred stock, rather than something with warrants or a convertible debenture. We felt we were in the equity business and wanted simply to structure deals. Sutter Hill is known to structure deals, even today, as very simple deals. We never had a term sheet. Today, there are term sheets flying around all over.

In those days—and I think it still exists today, but not to the extent it did then—it was a handshake. You'd say to Dave Bossen, "Here's what we think is fair." And, he would say, "I think that's fair," or, "Let's negotiate." And, then we shook hands, and that was the deal. And many times we would loan a company $50,000 or $100,000 before we closed the paperwork, just to get them started. It was all by hand-shake. And we did a hell of a lot of references in advance. It was very much of a face-to-face, personal kind of thing. I think it's gotten a lot more formalized these days.

As I mentioned, I come from an operating background. Every one of my partners also comes from an operating background. The people we hire who eventually become partners are not investment bankers or consultants by background. We've all worked for real companies that make things. We've all had real jobs. That tends to play into our wanting to help our companies beyond just giving them money, because our business, in my view, is not financial. You might spend a week talking to the entrepreneur about the structure of the financial deal, and you would shake hands on it, and then you spend six or seven years working on operating problems with the company trying to help it become successful.

I think one of the points I would like to make, and this is a big difference from back in the '60s and also maybe a big difference between our firm today and other firms: Venture capitalists don't create successful companies, entrepreneurs do. Some venture capitalists and some venture capital firms today think it's exactly the reverse, but they are the ones that have it reversed. I think if you can be supportive of a company as a venture capitalist, and be in the background, not up front making it look to the world like the venture capital firm made this company successful, it's much better. Let your entrepreneur reap the glory of being successful.

Investing in a Diversity of Backgrounds

If you look back through Sutter Hill's portfolio, there have been a lot of entrepreneurs/CEOs who came from very diverse backgrounds. David Lee, who is Chinese and started Kume Corporation, fled China, went to Taiwan, and then came over here. George Kasper fled East Germany through the subway into West Berlin. He started a company called Kasper Instruments that made semiconductor equipment, which we sold for a very big price. We backed a bright guy out of the Hungarian revolution, Dr. Andy Gabor, who was a co-founder of Diablo. There have been a lot of people over the years who have come from diverse backgrounds. And, we have backed women, as well as men, Donna Dubinsky, CEO of Palm Computer, which is now the Palm Pilot at 3Com. She co-founded that company, and we sold it to US Robotics, which then sold it to 3Com.

The venture capital club is bigger and broader today. When Sutter Hill got started in 1964, we were the only game in Silicon Valley. When entrepreneurs wanted to start companies, they went to midtown New York. That's where the money was. The Rockefellers, the Bessemers, Jack Kelsey, and the Whitneys were all there. Today the money is in Palo Alto and Menlo Park. I think the money, in a venture sense, moves to where the action is. If for some reason a new Silicon Valley were to start somewhere else in this country, I'm sure you would find very quickly a number of venture capital funds opening offices in that area as well.

Sutter Hill Ventures is different in that we are thirty-six years old in 2000 and we still have just one fund. We do not have fund five, or fund six, or fund seven. We've been able to grow the fund in excess of $400 million, and to provide substantial long-term returns to our limited partners, which makes us very different from other venture capital funds. We're much more like a Venrock in that sense. We have grown it to a mega-fund size, and so we have been able to generate high enough returns for our limited partners to keep them happy. That's number one on our list of objectives. Let's have great returns for the limited partners, and still have enough money left to grow the fund to the point where we can compete with anybody in the business today, in terms of size of deals. But the real reason why that's important in my view is that we are not in the business of raising numerous $500–$750 million funds every few years where the general partners sit around and say we've got $500 million, we're taking a 2.5 percent management fee, let's go out and invest that really fast, because then we can start another fund in about two years with another $500 million, and get another 2.5 percent, and we'll have a lot of cash flow coming in, pay ourselves big salaries, drive nice cars, have fancy offices, and that's going to be wonderful. In my view, it takes the eye off the ball of trying to build companies. Venture capitalists go out and invest the $500 million fast and they throw it against the wall, hope about eight out of thirty investments will stick, or whatever it takes to get the money invested, and then move on to the next fund. We have no incentive to do that. We have had only one fund. The negative is we only have one management fee. We're still doing it, like Smith Barney says, the old-fashioned way. We're still doing it for capital gains. From the entrepreneur's point of view that's very healthy. I've sat in on many board meetings over the years where the company that you're invested in with other venture firms tells you they need a second or third round of financing. Right in the middle of that meeting, these other venture firms let it be known that as they are forming their second or fourth fund, they won't be able to put any more money in this company because one company can't be in more than one fund. The entrepreneur's left holding the bag. He's got to go somewhere else. But then everybody wonders why the current venture capitalists aren't backing the company. And it really creates problems for management.

We also don't put pressure on the entrepreneur to take the company public or merge because a venture capital firm is trying to close out one of their funds. We only have one fund and it typically takes, from start-up, probably six or seven years (less these days) before we end up realizing liquidity in a company, and it's not a forced function at all. We're in the business of building businesses. We're not trying to do financial transactions.

Our Biggest Investors

We started with Genstar, a Montreal-based Canadian company, and they were our only limited partner up until 1986. In '86 they got acquired by a larger Canadian company called Imasco Limited. Imasco wanted Genstar for reasons other than buying Sutter Hill Ventures. But the CEO of Imasco talked to me, and said, "Hello, we're your new limited partner, but we don't want to stay in the venture capital business long term, because we don't understand it. Imasco is the largest cigarette manufacturing company in Canada, and is totally uninterested in high-technology venture capital." So, I didn't worry about that much, because I knew we could easily find other limited partners. During the next five years, we put together a group of seven institutions to buy out Imasco. We sat down in 1991 and said, "Okay, here's the portfolio. We, Sutter Hill, as general partners, value it at a certain price." There were 45 to 50 companies in the portfolio. Then we took it to these seven potential buyers and said, "Here's what we have to offer, or what Imasco has to offer. If you're happy with the values, you can put up the money, and put it in Imasco's pocket." No new money came into Sutter Hill. They just bought into the partnership and gave the money that they used to buy in to Imasco. It was a great deal for those coming in, because they received an instant portfolio—because they didn't start with $200 or $300 million cash, they started with a portfolio valued at $200 or $300 million. So, they received momentum in the business, and that's worth a lot. The first of the seven entities that we brought in was Power Corporation, which is a very large Canadian financial services company. It owns the largest mutual fund complex in Canada, among other things. The second was Sun Life Assurance Company, which is the largest life insurance company in Canada. We wanted the Canadians because of our wonderful past Canadian connection with Genstar. The CEO of Genstar, who was the person I basically reported to, introduced us to those two companies. That was a natural fit. Then we brought in the Irvine Foundation in San Francisco, which is the old Irvine Ranch Assets from Southern California. We also brought in four universities: Stanford, MIT, Princeton, and Yale. So we have seven institutional limited partners, all of whom have become strong and supportive partners.

Intermediaries and Gatekeepers

We don't deal with gatekeepers.[1] I think Reid Dennis at Institutional Venture Partners would say the same thing. The better venture capital firms in this country don't need, and don't want, a gatekeeper as

---

[1] Gatekeepers are investment advisors who work with institutional investors on their venture capital allocations. At one time, they were the sole arbiters of capital allocation. Today, with more fund investment data available, they have lost their market advantage.

an investor in their firm. The only reason gatekeepers exist is that they are an intermediary between some major money sources and the venture funds. They justify their existence by measuring, rating, and evaluating venture funds for the large sources of money that they're taking a fee from. That puts pressure on the venture industry and on the venture funds they put money into to come up with near-term statistics as to how they are doing, maybe even quarterly statistics. In our partnership agreement with our seven limited partners, we have a section saying they are not allowed to give our performance data to anybody else without our approval. We don't want that data to go out to these venture gatekeepers. I think the gatekeeper business has peaked in our industry. There was a time when they played a bigger role, but I think there are so many really good venture funds today around that know what they're doing, that the gatekeeper service isn't necessary anymore.

Financial Performance

We've been in a marketplace for venture capital where the last eight or nine years have been super years. And, there are a lot of people in this industry today who are under forty-five years old and in their lifetime in business they've never seen a bear market. It's going to happen. I would say if we're in the business of hitting home runs, at Sutter Hill we want to hit home runs, but we also want to hit a lot of doubles and triples—even an occasional single.

I think the internal rate of return (IRR) measurement that you show to a limited partner comparing two funds, particularly if you do them every two or three years, is really bogus, because there's value in there that hasn't been realized. It's only on paper. Realization of numbers is important in this business. It's not like real estate where you trade in for something else at a higher price and you've now made a lot of money on paper but you haven't realized profits. But, having said that, I think the IRR measurement over a finite period of time, let's say, four years, or even eight or nine for a number of venture capital firms, has been very good. I think the true test in our industry, however, is to make an exceptional IRR return, say, over 35 percent over a thirty-year period. And that's what we've been able to do at Sutter Hill.

New Investment Paradigms

Venture capitalists are now playing a game that's ultimately going to come back to haunt some of them. At Sutter Hill we still think that you can start companies and at the end of the day, you might have $5 to $10 million of equity in the company, and it's self-sustaining as a company at that point. It's in a marketplace where maybe the entrepreneur has built it to a point where it's doing $100 million in revenue, and it's making money. You could merge it, or go public at $400 million or $500 million, and you've got yourself one hell of a nice return. In a normal market, which we are not in now, if you've invested $100 or $150 million of venture capital in a company, I view that as a failure, because there's not enough left for the management. You've got to have enough ownership left in there for that entrepreneurial team to make it worth their while. If the equity value gets so large, like $5 billion, it might work out, and has worked out on occasions when companies like Amazon get so large that the valuations are okay. It would be interesting to run a computer sweep today of companies started by venture capitalists, take all that have gone public, and see how many of them today are valued over $5 billion. I will bet there are very few—the percentage is small.

Where is the pressure to do all this coming from? I think it's partly coming from the younger people in our business because—and this is really kind of a gross generalization, I'll probably eat my words—I think there's a lot less deferred gratification today. They want it all now. As a result, they invest that way. I think good things take a longer time period to develop, if they're sustainable and if they're enduring. I want to see some of these firms that got started in the 1990s after they have been in business for nine or ten years. I'd like to see what kind of an IRR they will have put together over a thirty-year period. If they can show that over thirty years they've got an IRR that's in excess of 35 percent, I'm going to be impressed with their performance. I'm going to be happy for them. I'll be delighted. And I know their limited partners will be very happy too. But if they put together over the first ten years of their life, a 50 to 150 percent IRR, and over the remaining twenty years it drops to 6 percent, I'm not so sure the limited partners will be very impressed.

The big money poured in by pension funds is a bad influence, I think, on our industry. The better institutional money in our business is not the CalPERS,[2] nor the pension funds, and that's why we have universities in our partnership. We think universities and endowments are the best source of venture capital money, because they have a long view of commitment to our asset class. I mean, Princeton University has a venture capital asset allocation, and Randy Hack, who runs Nassau Capital, has $1 billion or more under management devoted to alternative assets, including venture capital. The money will probably be there a long time because the trustees want to keep things stabilized and not move quickly in or out of these assets. They don't have a quarter-to-quarter, mark-to-market mentality. So, I think the source of institutional money in our industry can and should dictate how venture capital firms run their shop. I think the other side of it, though, is that there's so much money that some of it will be dumb money coming into our business at the wrong time. It happened in the mid-1980s coming off the peak of the early '80s. Those are the institutional sources that don't know what they're doing. That trend peaked around '85. A lot of funds got started that don't exist today because they didn't have successes in the ensuing three to four years of their ten-year life. That's when the limited partners pulled out.

Where Are We Heading?

Sutter Hill wants to provide outstanding returns per partner. One of our objectives is to create large returns per partner, and that includes not only general partners, but the limited partners. The second objective is to be known in the industry, by those who really know what's going on, as one of the top firms in the country. Our third objective is to run the firm on the basis that it's going to be around for another 100 years, and not go out of business. That's why we do not have our names on the front door. The fourth is to do the first three by working hard and doing them well, but also to have reasonable personal lifestyles. One of the things that we don't want to do is be on the front page of *Time* magazine. We do not want to be in the press, because at some point there is going to be backlash in our industry.

---

[2] *California Public Employee Retirement System.*

The best, I think, was Laurance Rockefeller. The Rockefellers were a classic example of the best—you do things quietly, you do them well, you make a lot of money, and nobody knows about it. When you do things well, make a lot of money, and everybody knows about it—that is not Sutter Hill's style.

Passing the Torch

We've done a lot of thinking and accomplished a lot. But people like me, who've been in venture capital for over thirty-five years, have started to move aside and make room for the younger partners who come up in the firm. There's a transitional period in this business. For those firms that don't realize that, it could become a transitional problem. I can point to a few that blew up because they didn't pass the torch.

I think we're doing a very good job of passing the torch at Sutter Hill. I've hired people into the firm with an age differential. I'm the old guy at sixty-six. I've got two partners that are in their mid fifties. I have another partner in his late forties, one in his early forties, and one in his early thirties. And, strategically, we're going to keep doing that.

We're never going to have eight, ten, twelve partners. We don't want that. We learned long ago if you generate outstanding returns, there will be more per partner if you have fewer partners. On the other hand, we are going to stick to our knitting and stay with high technology, and stay with the early-stage start-ups and invest throughout the United States. And, we will probably never raise a second fund.

What'll Be Different in the Future?

I really can't say what it will be like, other than the one thing I do know will be different. It will be more international. I think today we invest basically in the United States of America, like most venture funds. But it is becoming a global market. The General Atlantics already have done a lot of investing in Europe. I think our industry in the next ten years is going to be investing more internationally than we do today. That one I'm pretty sure of. I'm not sure I know that much about where we're heading as an industry, other than I do know in the ten-year period going forward, we will see a down cycle in our industry.

Angels

Angels are a competitor of traditional venture capital in some ways. It will be interesting to watch people like Jim Clarke, who have attained amazing returns of money. But he's an exception to the typical angel who puts in maybe $100,000 to $200,000 per deal. When the market downturn happens and the angel mind-set goes negative for awhile—for a few years maybe—or when angels get involved in some other type of deal like real estate that goes sour, I think these angels will go negative on venture capital very fast. The smart entrepreneur knows that and so many entrepreneurs still come to institutional venture capital money for start-up money, as opposed to getting a real sweetheart deal at the front-end from an angel. The smart entrepreneur knows he doesn't make money at the start, but he makes real money at the back end, when he comes out of the project by going public or getting acquired. And so I think here again you're going to get a lot of less-smart entrepreneurs getting money from the angels during the current cycle. If I were an entrepreneur, I'd rather have Sutter Hill in my deal when the industry slows than have Joe Blow from ABC Ventures, who all of a sudden doesn't have any more money for you. We will have more money for you and be there to help in the troubled as well as good times. It is our full-time job, whereas the angel plays in the venture capital world part-time.

DON VALENTINE
Sequoia Capital

Don Valentine was a Silicon Valley hero even before he got to Sand Hill Road. At Fairchild Semiconductor in the 1960s, he shaped the chipmaker's sales and marketing strategies and helped transform it from a struggling company into an industry leader.

That reputation stood him in great stead in his investing strategy at Sequoia, which he joined as a partner in 1971. Valentine is known and respected as a venture capitalist with a keen sense of marketing acumen— an investor who understands the market and how to respond to it. His most quoted philosophy is, "It's better to invest in a company in a market with great demand than to invest in a company that has to create it."

Not surprisingly, Sequoia, at Valentine's recommendation, was an early investor in both Apple and Atari, and was one of the early investors in the Internet, founding such financial successes as Yahoo! and Excite.

Valentine isn't simply an astute investor and a marketing guru, but he also is one of Silicon Valley's elder statesmen and one of its most outspoken observers. His strong opinions on venture capital and venture capital strategies, the influx of foreign capital and the dire implications of that money, and the pitfalls of too much money and "me-too" investing, make him one of the most controversial investors in the industry.

I WAS A very early employee at Fairchild Semiconductor, but not one of the first eight. The company was started in late '57; I joined in '59 on the sales and marketing side of things. We had infinitely more customer interest than we had resources. So we evolved a somewhat ad hoc approach to evaluating the customers, their business, and their applications. After doing that for years and getting the process somewhat refined, I began to invest in some of these small private companies personally. That's how I progressed from the operating side of the semiconductor business to part-time venture capitalism.

Those were the days when SBICs were around, when those kinds of private financings were called private placements. I don't think it was even called venture capital then.

In about 1967, I left Fairchild Semiconductor and went to National Semiconductor, and continued to do the same thing. National was an existing public company that was badly financed and virtually bankrupt. I continued evolving this selection process, and making investments on my own. And since National was public, I received enough personal exposure that a large mutual fund company in Los Angeles, the American Fund Group, approached me to determine if I would be interested in investing in start-up companies full-time. They had clients that wanted to diversify their pension fund activities by investing in some small companies. So, in the early '70s, I switched, and began to do that full-time.

Switching to Venture Capital

I wasn't looking for new horizons. I was just doing this for my own account, and unconsciously evolving a process and selection criteria. Operating from a $5 million dedicated fund, it was highly useful to have had that sort of evaluation experience in order to determine whether the prospects had a probability of success, and whether we should dedicate financial resources to them. And, basically, with minor evolutionary adjustments, I've never changed that selection criteria.

Almost none of the people in the business then, Arthur Rock included, understood anything about technology. They were all from other disciplines. Pitch Johnson was from the steel industry. Bill Edwards was from the petroleum industry. None of them was especially grounded in any kind of technology. So when I began it was very collegial. If you wanted to invest in any company, everybody stood back and invited you in, and you could invest as much or as little as you wanted. If you knew something, it was incredible. So, unlike today, where the mountains of money prevent cooperation, the environment then was total cooperation.

One of the key people that I met was Roger Kennedy, who was running the investment side of the Ford Foundation. Roger was, among other things, very visionary. He pioneered the interpretation of the prudent man rule which allowed pension funds to participate and the change in the balance in asset allocations from 80 percent fixed income to 30 or 40 percent equity. And it was he who was the original Ford Foundation limited partner. He was very helpful to me, because I've never been a finance guy. Roger helped me with a view of what was going to happen in the world of finance.

The type of instruction I got from Roger Kennedy had to do with returns—the pension world was a 9 to 10 percent total return business. So, we always were committed to a return that was approximately twice what the tax-exempt pensions and foundations achieved annually. Now remember, they were moving away from having fixed income investments as a dominant portion—as much as 75 percent—of their portfolio. That was the environment in which we began. And the returns on our first fund were over 60 percent compounded annually.

Exploiting the Microprocessor Boom

Sequoia was our name from inception. Interestingly, when I entered what was not yet the venture capital business, George Quist explained to me that I had an incredibly unfair advantage over everybody else on the West Coast, as I had just come from an environment where I had worked for Bob Noyce for years. I had been working in an environment that was the beginning of the microprocessor business. So I always knew what the future was going to be. Investing with that advantage was tremendous leverage. The early investments we made were applications of microprocessors. If you invested in a wide variety of companies, you were hard-pressed not to succeed.

Arthur Rock and I have always had sort of a very friendly debate. Arthur disclaims any ability in technology, and any understanding of it. He makes his investments based on people—and he has proven to be a spectacular chooser. I was never very comfortable with that approach. I always felt that I could understand the market and the application. I would invest almost exclusively based on market size and momentum, and the nature of the problem being solved by the company. I always

felt that trying to choose people was very difficult, as other venture people tended to change, for a wide variety of reasons. So, for a long time
on the West Coast, I had a tremendously unfair advantage, because
none of the other people understood much about technology. They
often would call me and ask me to participate, which I did.

Apple Computer

In 1977, we financed Apple. One of the people at Apple, Mike
Markkula, was someone who used to work for me. I sent him to Steve
Jobs to be president, but Mike became the marketing guy and the
chairman. The first president of the company was a guy named Mike
Scott, who also used to work for me. It was an era where knowing
about microprocessors made the evolution of the PC obvious. Steve
Jobs was an employee at Atari in its early days. So I had the advan-
tage of all that knowledge before anybody else.

I'll give you an illustration of how I looked at this computer industry, because here's an example of where I had previously no experience. From my knowledge of the microprocessor, I financed Apple.
The real issue was that Apple didn't do anything, because the memory system was an audiocassette. I don't know if people remember
that. It became very apparent that Apple needed a different memory
system. So Sequoia financed a guy by the name of Jugi Tandon to go
into a small five-inch disk drive business. That decision was clearly
driven by an application need in the PC which required a solution
that was faster, far more reliable, and had greater density than an
audiocassette. So, we financed Tandon. And it was a spectacular
investment. At the same time, recognizing a little bit about the memory business, we financed a company that made disks for the drives.
We used the need and the application structure of the PC to make
other investments in the category, in both hardware and software.

Coping with Growth

As we progressed, our funds grew larger and we faced the fairly traditional problem of needing to expand our staff. Selecting others, getting them to see the world as we did, avoiding people who were interested in financial engineering, and attracting partners who would
understand the applications side of the issue and invest from a solu-

tions point of view—these were big problems for ten years. Initially, some of the people from the Capital Guardian Trust Company, because they were directly concerned about the impact on their clients, decided to participate with me. So, over time, I added partners who saw the world the way I did.

This was at an interesting point in time because a friend of mine was at Salomon Brothers. He was determined that I was on to something, and he wanted me to talk to the Salomon people. So, he persuaded me to go to New York City, which is something I rarely do, and talk to the Salomon people. Their first question was, What business school did you go to? I said, I went to Fairchild Semiconductor Business School. Well, they were oriented toward backing brilliantly educated, financially oriented Harvard Business School graduates. I told them that the venture business was about building companies and industries. So we never did business. That was the orientation in the finance world then.

A lot of potential partners—pension funds and endowments—thought of the business initially as an asset allocation, a diversification area of financial investing. Early on, I was only interested in limited partners that understood that we were in the business of creating businesses, and sometimes creating industries; we were not in the financial transactions business. We were going to build companies. We were going to build an industry once in a while, but we were not going to do anything that required a lot of financial cleverness, because we didn't have any, and we didn't need any. That was not where we thought the opportunity was. In time, it became progressively easier to attract people to Sequoia as partners, and easier to attract limited partners who understood that we were not in the financial transaction business—we were company builders. I suspect some of them only pretended to understand it because they understood the returns, and were willing to sign up for the experience.

Setting Industry Milestones

I started in the early '70s with $5 million. By the time we hit 1990, our fund was about $150 million. In the early '80s we created the idea of having side-by-side funds in which we had major technology industry people to help us in analysis as well as by mentoring the ever younger, ever less-experienced entrepreneurs. When we hit the '90s, we now had a fairly hard-core group of partners who had been together without very much change or turnover at the partner level for quite a while. We all had operating backgrounds, having been in small companies, and so were very empathetic with the entrepreneur in the start-up world. We had a fairly strong philosophical bond, a good set of experiences, and Sequoia's funds were only limited by the amount of money we wished to accept.

The dates I always use, just for fun, are 1977, 1987, and 1997. In 1977 we helped participate in starting the PC industry. In 1987 we started the internetworking industry with Cisco. We had previously invested in 3Com and other similar companies, so we understood the connection of the Internet, and all it encompassed, probably better than most people. So we were looking for Cisco when they were looking for us. That is how we prefer to invest, in an anticipatory way. So, we financed Cisco in 1987. Well, the symmetry ends a little bit in the Yahoo! case, but I always use 1997, although it's slightly chronologically incorrect, just to establish that roughly in every decade there's something consequential that changes. And the playing field, which sometimes goes flat in terms of serious technological change, every once in a while has a dramatic moment. If you followed Cisco at all, you'll remember that the company was launched on one protocol. It is now a major standard, but when the company was launched TCP/IP was not generally visible. In the late '80s and early '90s we began looking at the IP, the Internet protocol. Through our relationship with the customers of Cisco, and Cisco's engineering, we began to get very interested in investing in this category. That is what we try to do—anticipate. So I'm comfortable with the idea that as successful as the PC industry was for twenty years, from '77 to '97, the probability is that the Internet will be even more successful, not in market cap only, but in terms of revenue, people employed, taxes paid, balance of payment, and international trade—you name it, this will provide a similar impact worldwide. You can start that period whenever you want in the 1990s. We are in what I see as the first of two decades of exploitation of the Internet.

The environment has now radically changed. If, in fact, there was too much money in 1973, the amount of money in 1993 may be two orders of magnitude too much. Almost everybody has a fund of $100 million. Part of what's happened is that a lot of the institutions have massively liberalized investing in the '90s, so that their asset bases have gone up at least five times. They have far more absolute dollars to deploy, although the percentage is still small. And, for a whole bunch of reasons, they cannot get into the funds that they want. When we take on a new limited partner, for instance, our existing limited partners are somewhat offended by the dilution they face if our fund increases without their being a part of that increment on a percentage basis. So, lots of people get funded. Investment bankers get funded. God knows what category of people who have never been in this business get funded. So, to me it's reminiscent of the money being sprayed around in the '70s by the SBA to a whole bunch of people whose only skill set was the ability to fill out the SBA form.

We have been in that era for a long time. The environment is not very collegial. One of the partners at a prominent firm in northern California recently talked to one of our guys and said, "We ought to get together, this shoot-out at the O.K. Corral is not making any sense." It is brutal out there in terms of the amount of money, numbers of practitioners, and people's interest and willingness to position companies in direct competition to each other. That never used to be the environment. It used to be we would worry about IBM, or General Electric, or some giant company. Now we spend all our time worrying about each other. We know for sure that without almost any exceptions, we can easily compete through stealth and speed against the big companies and their balance sheets, but we can't compete that way against one another. We constantly see major venture groups positioning companies against one another, dividing the market, dividing the personnel pool, paying much too much in terms of valuations, in an effort to be in certain businesses. All this will come back to haunt us at some point in time, when the IPO markets cool, valuations cool, and returns are less significant.

Too Much Money, Not Enough Good Companies

What are the consequences? We're not creating as many great companies. I'll use an old example for you which I think is symptomatic of what has happened and what will continue to happen. Some years ago now, Sequoia financed a particular kind of computer company called Convex. The category was called a super computer. Well, the nature of the application was such that it had a reasonably sized market, but not a gigantic market. Ten companies were financed to the tune of $30 million each in that same business, because of the visible success of Convex. All of those companies are gone, Convex included. None survived. Almost all of the ten lost $30 million each. Now, you can say now $300 million is no big deal. And, in part you're right, but what happened additionally was the pool of people capable in that technology, instead of being focused and concentrated on one company, was divided by ten. As the companies collapsed and began to go away, international acquirers bought the technology for nothing. The venture community lost $300 million. The country lost the pool of qualified people that should have been in one or two companies to maintain worldwide dominance. There are a lot of human side effects in addition to the financial wreckage. This is going on again now.

For approximately ten years I campaigned fairly aggressively with lots of our limited partners that they were putting out too much money. I did not make very much progress. Over the years, after getting to know several limited partners fairly well, I said, "We must talk about this, because I don't understand what you guys are doing. We have had limited partners with greater than $30 billion in assets. And, when they gave us $10 million and we compounded it at 100 percent a year, we had no impact on their fund. Why do this?" The answer was, "It is much more fun to do this than to invest in bonds. It's more fun than investing in real estate, where nothing happens for a long time." So, the reason why a significant portion of money is being deployed—for which I am eternally grateful—is that a whole bunch of people think it's fun.

After talking with more people, I recognized that I was dealing with their entertainment. I had no hope of persuading them to stop doing the equivalent of going to the movies. So, I gave up campaigning. It's hard to imagine what it is like to be someone that works in a large pension plan who chooses managers in different categories, and watches them do everything—a professional that dispenses funding, and then sits on the sidelines and waits for something to happen. So, when you think about it, they're looking for some part of their professional life that's more interesting, more meaningful, more fun.

That's what I discovered when I started interrogating our limited partners over a period of time. There was no way they were persuadable. Returns were defensible. Many of the funds had nice able teams. Anything you wanted to measure suggested that it was a useful asset allocation category. The question is how much money to deploy. In the '90s, the stock market in general—and the S&P in particular—has gone up so much that some of our limited partners have assets that have increased four to five times. So, the partners who used to invest $3 million fifteen years ago now want to invest $10 million. There is no way to stop the fund flow, from my point of view. And, as a result there are a huge number of funds, and huge amounts of money. And although this is certainly a question that has to be resolved over time, I doubt that there will be any way to stop it.

Sequoia's Greatest Hits: Cisco and Yahoo!

There's a great similarity between the two companies. When we encountered the Cisco start-up team, there were actually five employees. The thing that struck me was the cleverness of the people at Cisco—they had an appreciation of what they were really good at, and a profound recognition of what they knew nothing about. Our relationship was struck on the basis that Sequoia would provide management, a management process, and $2.5 million and Cisco would provide the technical side of things.

Interestingly, we began Yahoo! on the same basis. We encountered two individuals whose greatest strength was the recognition of their weaknesses and their lack of experience. And we struck the same kind of arrangement. We would go out and develop the management team and the management process, and we would put in the start-up money. They would work at what they were interested in and very good at. Cisco and Yahoo! are not the only two companies we have done that way, but certainly they are the ones with huge size and market value, and great returns for us. And, in part this is what we try to do—this is our game plan. We try to find combinations of people who understand the special solution to a major application. And we tend to find them and intercept them at a point in time when we can add our incremental capability. Both companies evolved from that conceptual beginning.

In the case of the two major founders at Cisco, both of them are unusual. You never know why people choose to pair up the way they do. He was and is very cerebral, very hands-off, very theoretical, extremely bright, and very introverted. She, by comparison, is extremely aggressive, much more articulate, rigidly opinionated, very hands-on, and a micromanager. And, in a sense, that's the perfect kind of team, because they're completely different. I don't know how that works at home. From eight in the morning until seven at night, it's terrific. I think from seven at night until eight in the morning it may not be so terrific. But, oftentimes we find the entrepreneurial founder team very different in composition.

The two guys at Yahoo! are very different from each other. One is far more personable, extroverted, interested in business, and the other is not. They work fine together, because they recognize what the other contributes.

The situation at Cisco was relatively easy from a demand point of view. We had invested in Apple in the PC business. We had invested in 3Com and Ethernet technology, and we understood the problem. The problem was broadcast storms—a network environment that was struggling. So, there was a desperate need for something that solved the problem—there was a market demand that was incredible. The customers would tear the hinges off the door to get the product.

In the case of Yahoo!, quite like Apple, it was a matter of market creation. In the beginning Apple's computers didn't do anything. In the beginning, at Yahoo!, Sequoia spent a tremendous amount of time and energy trying to figure out what business to be in. There was no obvious application. They were in the search engine business. That is a business where you give away the product; so, it is necessary to develop a slightly more complicated and better business model.

In a sense it's much easier to do a Cisco, because the customers are so intent on their problem that they're willing to do anything. They'll pre-pay. They'll tell you what the specs are. They'll tell you what protocols are needed or not needed. It was a great environment. I don't mean to diminish the management execution at Cisco, but they have been in a company that has seen better market timing than ever before. Management came up with an application solution and ten years of products that have solved bigger and better problems.

Yahoo!: Listening to the Customer

At Yahoo!, while we had a product that did something useful, we had to figure out how to get paid for it. The whole evolution in the first three or four years of the Internet has been amorphous in the sense that you had a hard time with the initial users who were accustomed to everything being free. You had to develop other customers who were more accustomed to paying for things. The Internet was a very flawed environment. It was a world in which everything was free. And, I have to tell you it was a very difficult problem figuring out how to get paid. Lots of companies are resolving this problem. That was the Internet environment in the early '90s. It was exclusively then used by very computer literate people, who unfortunately are very articulate and noisy when you tried to charge them for something. We are progressively, collectively bridging that gap.

What turned the corner at Yahoo! was a matter of management figuring out a few things that large corporations needed, or wanted. They wanted a Web site, they wanted one that was recognized, that was good. So, the drift toward the creation of the Web site phase, along with the advertising phase, is what propelled the economics at Yahoo! in the beginning. That wasn't so easy to figure out in a world in which 90 percent of the historic practitioners were geeks who didn't pay for things. You didn't want to offend them. You needed them. You certainly didn't want traffic on the Net that was bad-mouthing your company. You didn't want the chat rooms loaded with a whole bunch of people talking about what bad guys you were. At the same time, you had to figure out a model where customers pay for something the old-fashioned way. I think by and large people have divined categories and approaches that appeal to the non-geeks of the world. If you look at the focus of a company like AOL, which went down a particular track towards the consumer for a long time, invested in trying to build a relationship with them, and progressively sold them products over time, making them long-term subscribers. A lot of the business models during the first five years of Internet companies have been highly evolutionary. A lot of them are working okay now. The amount of profit being made in the Internet environment is still negative when aggregated. That was never true in the world of Apple, going back in time, or in the world of Cisco currently. Those companies were able to develop a profitable business model in a different kind of world, a precise product solution with a huge demand.

Using Money Liberally

I think a simplistic view of what it's all about is that venture capital nowadays is almost free. It's gone from what was a fungible commodity to a free commodity. In some respects, just as bytes of memory are free, so now is the money. It allows companies to pursue the Japanese model of market share and profit deferral. At some point in time, when the money is no longer free, I think those unprofitable companies will have to be altered in order to sustain themselves and grow.

To me, the interesting part about a subscription model, like the magazine business, or maybe the publishing business in general, is that many magazines are given away on the assumption that their revenue comes from elsewhere as long as they can maintain your interest as a subscriber. In the AOL model, what they are doing is collecting subscribers, and they've got to feed them and provide them products and services that keep them subscribed. A tough model, because you're constantly being re-evaluated for appropriateness and interest, and you know your subscribers can switch easily to some other magazine. But it's free money for the magazine world, and it always seems to me that it must be free, because magazines seem to start as often as gas stations. The Internet world has thrived on free money. Look at the IPOs and the secondaries, and convertibles that have been put in place in the Internet world versus the actual aggregate amount of earnings. It is amazingly disproportionate.

Yahoo! is one of a few companies that has earned money seven quarters in a row. It's not a staggering amount of money, but it's meaningful. The amounts lost—AOL and Amazon as examples—have been huge. They seem to be exploiting this pseudo-Japanese model, where money is free and you keep building your infrastructure and your client base gradually.

We have always maintained a broad range of investment interests. A year doesn't go by where we don't start one or more new semiconductor companies. Going back to the knowledge base that we developed in our relationship with Cisco, it's fairly clear to us what silicon is needed in the communications industry to go forward. So, we integrate backward, and start silicon companies that will continue to emerge as suppliers for all those companies that are in the execution stage. Our investments in the Internet have been like an iceberg. We have invested in more things below the surface of the water. To my way of thinking, broadly defined, Cisco is the biggest Internet company in the world, certainly the most profitable. We have been financing a raft of companies that invest and perform in the infrastructure.

I don't think they will be headline grabbers the way E*trade is, but they will be massively profitable as growth companies. And we will continue to do that. Our investments in the Internet are only a portion of what we do. It is true that they are currently a major part of the businesses we finance, but we continue to finance many other types of companies.

REID DENNIS
Institutional Venture Partners

On the West Coast, where venture capitalists with high-tech backgrounds now are legion, Reid Dennis was one of the first. Even while Dennis was employed as an analyst by the Firemen's Fund in 1952, he established an angel network among friends and colleagues, screening entrepreneurs at lunch and funding them if they fit the bill. In 1974, Reid, backed by a $5 million commitment from American Express, formed Institutional Venture Associates and raised $19 million from six institutions—nearly half of all the capital raised in the United States that year by private venture capital partnerships! Over the life of IVA, the original $19 million grew to over $180 million.

This now old-fashioned strategy made Dennis a wealthy man even before he established IVP in 1980. Among the investments in that first IVP fund were such companies as Seagate, Collagen, LSI Logic, and Stratus Computer. In time, Institutional Venture Partners became known as one of the Valley's stellar performers, and Dennis himself became one of its most respected investors. As with many other VCs of this era, Dennis talks about building companies, not simply because they produce financial returns but because that is part of the venture capitalists' complete mission. But he also is cognizant of change and its implications: a greater emphasis on financial returns and less emphasis on business building.

Ironically, this interview was completed in early 1999, only months before Dennis directly felt the impact of this new environment. In August, his heir apparent, Geoff Yang, and two other partners at IVP decided to spin out and join with three other venture capitalists from Los Angeles–based Brentwood Venture Capital to form Redpoint Ventures, a $700 million Internet-only fund.

I WENT TO Stanford and got my degree in Electronic Engineering in 1950. I went right on to the business school and got my M.B.A. in '52. I recognized early on during a course on wave theory that I was not going to be a creative engineer. I couldn't even tell which direction the waves were going. I knew I was not going to be the kind of engineer that came up with new concepts and was a great theoretical engineer. There weren't very many people around in the financial world who understood engineers or technical products, so I decided that maybe there was a role for me to play if I could bridge that gap.

After getting out of Stanford, I went to work with the Fireman's Fund Insurance Company as a security analyst trainee. I went in with the purpose of learning something about how to deal with finance and investment in order to get a job in the finance department of one of these emerging high-tech companies.

I can remember when I was being interviewed for the job, my boss told me that if they hired me they would be willing to pay me a starting engineer's wage—which was at that time about $400 a month—because he saw a lot of technical developments coming along. He thought it would be easier to teach an engineer about investing than it would be to take an investment person and teach them about technology. So he said, "We're willing to give you the job, but if we do, will you tell me you'll still be here three years from now?" I'll tell you, for a kid right out of college, three years sounded like an eternity. I sort of bit my tongue and said, "Yeah, I think I'll still be here three years from now."

So, I went to work for Fireman's Fund and the fellow I worked for was one of those people who left huge amounts of responsibility laying around on the floor. Anyone who wanted to grab a piece and run with it was welcome to. I had a ball! I had more responsibility than most people my age, and I really enjoyed what I was doing. I ended up staying with the Fireman's Fund, which became part of American Express, for twenty one years. I loved it.

I eventually got Fireman's Fund into the venture capital business in the early 1960s, and I did the same for American Express after the merger.

Starting with Ampex

In 1952 there were no publicly traded electronics companies on the Peninsula. There was a company called Eitel-McCullough, which was in the high-powered vacuum-tube business up in San Bruno and is now a part of Varian Associates. Every now and then some employee of Eitel-McCullough would sell a few shares privately to somebody. Varian Associates was a very socialistic company, and wanted its employees to own the business. For a long, long time they did not let any outsiders buy their stock. Hewlett-Packard was still private. Litton Industries was one of the first to go public, and that was a deal put together with some financing from Lehman Brothers, as a leveraged buyout deal from Charlie Litton. The major part of his business was making glass-blowing lathes for the vacuum-tube industry. There were travelling wave tubes and backward wave oscillators. People today don't have the slightest idea what the hell these products are. That was a very, very successful financial deal, and out of it came Litton Industries, and soon financing expanded into different fields. But there really were no publicly traded electronics companies on the Peninsula.

I had seen an Ampex tape recorder in an engineering seminar at Stanford, and I can still remember thinking that it ought to be a very handy technology. To be able to record things on magnetic tape seemed to have all sorts of applications.

About three or four months after I got out of college, and the month before I went to work for Fireman's Fund, I had a chance to put what was left over from my college educational fund into a private financing of Ampex. I had roughly $15,000 and I put it all into Ampex. I figured that if I lost it all, I could work the rest of my life just like everybody else. I told my wife that she was self-insured—if she was good enough to get me, she ought to be able to get somebody else to support her if anything happened. About three years later, when Ampex went public, I bought a little more stock in the public offering. I had made a little money doing some other things, so I put more into Ampex. A $20,000 investment in Ampex over five or six years became worth over $1 million, and that's what got me started.

It really had an impact on my life because I realized it was a pretty good way to make a living, so I began looking around at other high-tech companies down here.

High-Tech Tinkering

In 1952 to 1953, I was the only person working in the financial district in San Francisco who was trained as an electrical engineer. It just wasn't done at that time. People didn't go from engineering into finance, investment analysis, security analysis, or areas like that. I was the first.

For Fireman's Fund, I went up and visited Sprague Electric in North Adams, Massachusetts, which made capacitors, and companies like P. R. Mallory, which made resistors. Everything was, in effect, made of discrete components. If you wanted to start an electronics company, what you needed was some workbenches, some soldering irons, some components, a little metal work, and people. Men and women would sit at these benches and solder things together. That's the way everything was done, and it was very much a black box kind of an industry. You didn't really have to know what was inside the black box; all you had to know was what the black box did. Similarly today, the way to start a company is to get some programmers and some computers and create it out of software. In those days it was done from components.

Companies were beginning to spring up along the Peninsula, and some of their people would wander into San Francisco to see about getting financing. One of the first people mentioned on this historical map is Ed Heller. He was a senior partner of Schwabacher & Company, a local brokerage firm. Ed was the salt of the earth. He was a very wealthy individual, and if an entrepreneur came in to see him, and took a half hour or forty-five minutes to explain what it was he wanted to do, Ed would invariably write him a check for $10,000. He started a lot of people out just that way. It was a very informal business.

Lunchtime Financiers

At any rate, in the early '50s, if somebody wandered into one of these brokerage houses, and it was a technical product, they would usually call me and say, "Reid, I've got somebody here that has a black box. I don't know what it does or how it works but anyway, it's a black box, and he's looking for some money. If you talk to him and you think it's a good idea, I'd like to put some money into it." So, that's how an informal circle of friends got together. The Group—that was its name—included Bill Bowes and John Bryan from Blyth & Company; Bill Edwards and Dan McGanney from Lionel D. Edie, which was an investment counseling firm; and a friend of ours, Brooks Walker, Jr., who was running a company called U.S. Leasing.

Somebody would hear about one of these high-tech companies, or what we now call high-tech companies, and he'd call The Group together. We were all young and didn't have a lot of obligations at lunchtime. So, we'd get a table at Jack's or Sam's or one of the downtown restaurants, and the entrepreneurs would come in and have lunch with us. We'd sit around the table and make them go through their song and dance over lunch. We would then have the entrepreneurs stand outside on the street corner for five minutes while we discussed their idea. We'd say, "Well, what do you think?" "It's pretty good." "Yeah, we ought to do this one." Members of The Group, some of whom had inherited some wealth, would each put a good $25,000 or $30,000 into a deal. At that stage of the game, I was a $10,000 or $15,000 kind of investor. We could maybe get $80,000 to $100,000 just out of The Group, and then we'd go back to the entrepreneur, who invariably needed $250,000 to $300,000. We started all sorts of companies for $250,000. We'd go back to our various offices and we'd all call our circle of friends and say, "Hey, The Group has decided they're going to do this XYZ company, do you want to come along? I don't know exactly what it does, but it sounds like a good idea." Anyway we could usually raise the $250,000 to $300,000 within a week, just by making phone calls. We probably financed twenty-five companies over a period of ten years, and of those twenty-five companies, eighteen of them were wonderfully successful. A few we lost money on, and with maybe two of them we just got our money back. It was a wonderful experience. We all enjoyed doing it.

We would assign a member of The Group to be on the board of directors of this or that company. I can remember one day when Bill Edwards came to me. I said, "Bill, it's your turn to be on the board." He said, "I don't know anything about being on a board of directors." I said, "Well, neither did any of the rest of us when we started doing this; it's your turn to go learn." We essentially grew up in the business, and then they changed the name of it to venture capital, and we found out we were in the venture capital business.

Success in Venture Capital

We ran The Group on an informal basis throughout the '50s. In 1961, a friend of mine in New York had run across a deal and he didn't know what to do with it. I was in New York, and he said, "I don't want to take your time during the business day to talk about this, but can we have a drink, and I'll give you the business plan." It was a report on a company called Recognition Equipment Inc., located in Dallas, which had developed an optical reading machine. Fireman's Fund at this time had a very imaginative director of information processing, or MIS director. I brought the report back from New York just before Thanksgiving. It was a pretty thick report. I gave it to the MIS director, who was a good friend. I knew the MIS department was thinking about better ways to process insurance claims. He took it home and read it thoroughly over the Thanksgiving weekend. He came in Monday morning and said, "Reid, if these people have half of what they claim to have, this is the greatest thing since sliced bread." This company needed around $600,000, which was way out of my class anyway, so I went to see my boss at Fireman's Fund. He said, "Not only is this an interesting technology, but we could help the company a great deal by giving them their first order for one of these machines. We'll use it as an R&D project and see if we can make it work on our insurance forms." We finally got the whole thing approved and my boss was just wonderfully supportive. He told the finance committee, "We're going to place an order for this equipment anyway. Just that act of placing the first order for this equipment is going to have such a beneficial impact on the company that we ought to take advantage of it and be an investor at the same time." So, he carried the day, and we made our investment of Recognition Equipment. We eventually got to the point where we had a little over $1 million invested in the company, and that investment eventually was worth over $40 million. It was the largest single tangible asset the insurance company had. It was kind of an embarrassment because it was bigger than our holdings in General Electric or DuPont, or any of those wonderful companies that are supposed to be your core holdings in an institutional account. Here was this crazy thing that nobody understood and it was worth $40 million! I can remember, once we doubled our money, the finance committee said, "We ought to sell half and get our money back." I talked them out of that. Then it tripled in price, and they said, "Sell one-third and get our money back." This went on for a long, long time, and I kept resisting. I was supposed to get prior approval before we sold anything, but one day I came in and the market was such that Recognition Equipment was selling for ten times what we paid for it. I figured, okay, I've run this string out long enough. I went ahead, sold 10 percent and got our money back, and reported it at the next meeting of the committee. Fireman's Fund and American Express eventually took about $15 or $16 million out of that one investment so it was a very, very worthwhile deal. That opened the door to venture capital at Fireman's Fund which was very successful over a period of time.

One of the things that changed the business was a fellow named Dave Bossen. He came along with a company called Measurex that was going to make a digital paper-thickness machine to control the web on papermaking machines. He had worked for another company back in the Midwest which had an analog version of this. He came to California all by himself. He had the audacity to say that he needed $1.2 million to start this company. Well, none of us had ever heard of a number that big before. We were still doing $300,000 and $400,000 deals. He went back to New York and visited with Bessemer Securities, and Bessemer agreed to put up $600,000 of the $1.2 million. Then we said, hey, if they're going to do that, maybe we can come up with the rest of it.

It was the first time we'd seen one of the big institutions come in with a major investment in a deal that we could also participate in, and even Bessemer didn't want the whole thing. They wanted partners. They particularly wanted West Coast partners who would interact with Bossen and be helpful to his company. So that was sort of a watershed kind of investment for our group, and after that we saw more and more deals that became "institutionalized."[1]

My arrangement with my boss at Fireman's Fund was that anything that required a $25,000 or $30,000 investment I could make personally. Anything that was $200,000 or more, I had to show to the insurance company, and it was a no-man's-land in between. There was a buffer so we wouldn't have any conflicts of interest, and that system worked pretty well for a long time.

Building Companies: Investing Long-Term

We were doing long-term investing. I define long term as being generally five to eight years. Now there's much more of a feeling of wanting instant gratification: "If I can't make X millions of dollars in the next year or two, I'm not going to play in your sandbox with you!"

---

[1] An institutionalized deal is one that is syndicated among a large group of investors.

Let me back up and say that between 1980 and 1981 there were three companies that went public in a remarkably short time. One of them was Seagate, one of them was Compaq, and the other one was Lotus. Well, I know that Seagate went from start-up to public entity in less than three years. Any company that could do that in that amount of time was remarkable then. Now you talk about starting a company you may take public next year.

I can remember how Stratus Computer went public at ten times revenues. We all said, "Holy smoke, there's no way that's sustainable." The stock came out and then promptly went down, and it took another two years before it got back up to its IPO price. It was a long, hard struggle. In the meantime, those of us that owned a lot of it couldn't sell it because we were tied up, and then it got down so low you wouldn't want to sell it.

I really believed in Stratus. Bill Foster, its CEO, had never run a profit center before—he'd run a cost center. But my feeling about Bill Foster was that he would listen—he was sound, he was coachable, and he was decisive. He had a software person named Bob Friberghouse who was unusual. He wore a shirt and tie, and very few software people wore shirts and ties in those days, but he was articulate, he made a lot of sense, and he was a good manager. Gardner Hendrie was a good mechanical layout person and a mechanical design person. Stratus had all of the ingredients from a technical point of view. The question was if you could surround them with the business infrastructure that would enable them to make a successful enterprise out of it. I'm really very proud of the Stratus investment because after Tandem came along, there were five different start-up companies that came out to compete with Tandem, and Stratus was the only one that was really very successful. The other four didn't go very far.

Boom and Bust—1983

In 1983, this industry got into a mode where there were an awful lot of people in the industry who felt that the name of the game was to see how fast they could get the money. It was as easy to raise money as it is now, and it was also just as easy to spend it. Some people thought that was the whole trick. Just get as much money out there as you possibly can.

The public market was booming in '83, and one of the things that fueled the fire was the fact that the underwriters were able to sell to the public a whole bunch of junk stocks—stocks that would not stand the test of time. I've said in the past that I would hope that we would have the decency to bury our dead instead of trying to foist them off on the public. In '83, we as an industry foisted an awful lot of junk off on the public, and it all came home to roost. It took us three years to work our way through all of that, and get this business back on a firm footing again. I think we're running a significant danger doing the same thing now.

The New Environment

The stock fund manager today has more flexibility in terms of the ability to get out of part of his position. If something triples and he sells a quarter of his position, nobody is going to grouse too much about it. They're playing a numbers game of their own. One of the things that underwriting firms do—and they all do it—is say, "Look, out of the last twenty-five companies we brought to the public, twenty-three of them are still selling significantly above their offering price. If you, Mr. Investor, had just bought them all, you would be in great shape." As a result, you end up with a community of people who know the price of everything and the value of nothing. They're all playing a price game, and they're going on the fact that this, that, or the other underwriting firm has a lot of momentum and everything they've done recently has gone up. So let's hope the chain won't be broken on this one, because if you get in that chain, you're constantly playing with the house's money. That kind of investment philosophy is doomed to fail eventually.

Investment Bankers: Increasingly Transactional

One of the things we're suffering from right now is the fact that the investment banking business has gotten so overloaded that research analysts will not follow a company unless it is or it has the potential to be an investment banking client. As a result, there are a lot of orphan companies that just don't have anybody following them. That's a serious problem because you cannot get an analyst's time unless you're about to do the underwriting, and now the underwriting window is closed. It beats the hell out of me what all these people are going to do.

My old boss at Fireman's Fund used to say, "When they raid the house, they take all the girls. They don't distinguish between good girls and bad girls, they take them all." In this industry that means that all the stocks go down—good stocks go down with the bad stocks. I think there is too much money around today, and because of that we are seeing a lot of young people coming into this business because it looks like a great place to make a lot of money. They are not coming in because it's a great place to help build companies. A lot of us enjoy this business because we work with bright young people and help them build their companies, and all we've had to do was, in effect, have a cheering section and write checks periodically to keep them going. That part of the business has changed, there's no question about it.

IVP's Performance

Our rate return over all of our funds since 1980 has been over 35 percent. The 1982 fund was the worst performing. But we were helped a lot by our 1980 fund. 1980 was the best time in the history of this industry to become a new player in the venture capital business, and our 1980 fund, which was a $19 million fund, had about a 78 or 79 percent rate of return.

There were six or seven crown jewels in there. LSI Logic and Seagate were two of the big ones, and Stratus was in there also. With the tax law changes in '78 and '80, there were more entrepreneurs coming out of the woodwork wanting to start new companies than ever before. You had a lot of what I would call latent entrepreneurs coming out of big companies and starting their own—it was probably the best time in the whole span of history for the venture capital business.

Succession

I think some companies in the industry have managed succession very well. I think we're very fortunate to have some high-end people here in this firm.

My intuitive approach included my evaluation of the people. If I got to the point where I believed in the people, then I made the investment. Unfortunately, we've gotten to the point where because we now manage larger funds with more money, we have to look for larger opportunities, which means that there are a lot of good smaller opportunities that we just plain don't have the ability to deal with anymore. I really think that's sad because there are a lot of very good people that are pursuing some great opportunities, and we can't help them.

The same is true with the rest of the industry. I think that the large funds are developing the Mark McGwire syndrome—every time you get to bat, you're trying to hit another home run and not necessarily trying to win the ball game. Hopefully, there will be enough new people coming in the business and there will be enough angels working to pick up the slack.

We think of ourselves as doing seed deals, but they are bigger than ever. We have a incubation space downstairs and across the hallway. We do incubate companies. We do invite people to come in here, and we give them an office in which they can write their business plan, and we help them with their market research, and things like that. We act as sounding boards to bounce things back and forth. Yes, we still consider ourselves a seed and early-stage, first-round kind of investor. But the business has gotten so competitive, one of the best ways to control your investment pace is to incubate companies in your offices, so you're completely up to speed when the company does its first round of financing.

I used to like to champion smaller deals, but I really can't do that anymore because the firm doesn't have the bandwidth to do those smaller deals. We've gotten so large that we are running out of time before we run out of money, and when you run out of time, you're just nowhere in this business.

I don't have a crystal ball, I can't see any further ahead than anybody else. It's very hard to recognize at the beginning of a major industry just how big that opportunity is. When you're there, you're so used to looking at the next step, and the next step, and the next step that you can't see how far up the stairway goes. I think it's impossible for us to sit here today and properly gauge how big the whole Internet and e-commerce business will be. I think we're seeing a major sea change in the way people do things. A few years ago, right after Microsoft went public, who could have really foreseen—other than Bill Gates maybe—just what a huge opportunity it was?

It is an enormous opportunity. Take the microprocessor and what's happened at Intel. That was an enormous opportunity. But it's very hard to judge these things while you're right in the middle. Sure, these Internet stocks are selling at ridiculous prices relative to historical valuations, but compared to what their market value might be in three to five years, they may be cheap because the opportunities are enormous.

I don't know that I would have had the foresight to invest in Amazon.com. I like to go to a store and page through books before I buy them. Now they've got such a wonderful franchise that they're going to be selling music and CDs through that environment. Now, who could have foreseen that?

A New Age for Venture Capital

I think there are a lot of people taking chances because the rewards have gone up, particularly in this Internet space. We've seen huge gains made in a relatively short period of time. The timescale is compressed, and the rewards have been remarkable. But because the timescale has been compressed, you don't have to do as many rounds in private financing. You can actually get the thing out to the public sooner than usual.

Has the pace of venture capital gotten too fast? I don't think the pace is too fast but it's a young person's business. I used to run a hell of a lot faster—I always tried to respond to every deal that I heard of that had merit to it. We can't do that forever.

The pace gets distorted by competitive pressures. That's too bad, but it's a fact of life. The entrepreneurs play one of us against the other. They sometimes will give their perceived favorite venture capital firm a twenty-four- or forty-eight-hour head start, or a week head start. We're seeing a lot of entrepreneurs who have done it a couple of times before—they've gotten pretty savvy.

The competitiveness of the business is driving wedges between people who should be good friends. The problem is that we used to syndicate deals with ourselves and maybe two or three other venture capital firms. Three- or four-firm syndication has now become two- or one-firm syndication, and because we run bigger funds, we want to get more money invested in each deal. As a result, in a good deal there's only room for one friend at a time, and that's too bad because then you have to choose between friends. There are times when that becomes very, very tough.

RICHARD KRAMLICH
New Enterprise Associates

For the most part, venture capital funds are regional institutions. They invest nationally but keep their offices in one or two predictable major technology centers, such as California or Boston. New Enterprise Associates (NEA), with offices in Washington, Baltimore, and Menlo Park, tried to break the mold. At one time it established affiliate operations in other cities and with other funds. Indeed, it was one of the first funds to advertise itself as a national fund.

Richard (Dick) Kramlich, who in 1978 co-founded the firm with Chuck Newhall and Frank Bonsal, describes the process of building a large venture fund. Their effort came at a time when many insisted—as some still do— that venture capital was a regional phenomenon: A firm in Silicon Valley, so the argument goes, cannot properly oversee an investment along Route 128 in Boston, or vice versa. NEA hasn't tried to counter that feeling, but by creating a national infrastructure with offices close to entrepreneurial hot spots, it has managed to share in deals on both coasts.

From a group of three partners and $17 million or so in the early days of the firm, NEA has simply exploded in recent years. Today, the partners intend to raise a billion-dollar fund. If that happens, NEA will become one of the largest venture funds in the business. In the middle 1980s, however, NEA was one of the many firms to be hit by the volatility of the capital markets. It raised money in the early 1980s, invested it at relatively high valuations, and suffered as technology valuations slid and the IPO market closed down. But in the 1990s, NEA has come back bigger and stronger, and the firm kept intact, with most of its partners staying together, thus avoiding the implosion that a number of the Valley's venerable firms have suffered.

Kramlich argues that venture capital firms don't lose their vision when confronted by large pools of money. Indeed, that pool gives them the ver-

satility to cover diverse markets, instead of fixating on the fad du jour. Those firms that can manage large sums of money and be diverse in their selections at the same time, he argues, will be around long after the Internet has become a commonplace commodity.

I JOINED ARTHUR ROCK in 1969, when it was just Arthur, myself, and Marie, our secretary. We had a $10 million partnership, but we only drew down $6 million of it. We ultimately distributed around $40 million, and that was through some very lean years. So it worked out well. I had decided when I came to California that I really wanted to make this a career because I just loved the economic activity and the entrepreneurial spirit. So as we evolved through the early '70s, Arthur and I talked about starting a second partnership. I had actually invited Tom Perkins to join us as a general partner before he decided to leave Hewlett-Packard. Arthur said he didn't think that getting Tom to join us was a good idea. Later, in 1977, Tom returned the favor, but it was too late for me to alter my course. So I was really frustrated. I wanted to build on the cornerstone we'd started and turn it into a good firm, a firm with perpetuity to it. Arthur didn't want to do that at all. I had the choice of starting a second partnership with him or personally building something. Ask anybody who has a touch of the entrepreneur in them whether they really have a choice. It's clear that you're going to say, "I want to build something."

Launching NEA

I'd known Frank Bonsal before I came to the West Coast. He is a wonderfully energetic guy who knows everyone and has a great understanding of the entrepreneurial process. He had helped bring Alex. Brown into the underwriting of new technology companies. Chuck Newhall grew up in the business and is passionate about it. His father had worked with Laurance Rockefeller, and Chuck had focused on venture capital when he attended Harvard Business School. He is a mountain of integrity with a devious sense of humor.

Anyway, these were two really terrific guys. I was philosophically aligned with them and thought that there were enough differences in terms of our experience that we could really start something of interest.

Chuck was running the incubator fund at T. Rowe Price at the time this happened. He had systematically met everybody of prominence in the venture business, and he said he'd really like to partner with me. And I had known Frank, and he and Frank had decided to work together.

So the three of us started talking. I said there was no way I was going to move to the East Coast. Out of that discussion came the concept of starting on a national basis when we founded the partnership in 1978. So we really had the challenge from the very beginning of determining how to make decisions, and how to communicate. We were stretched from the start. And the good news is that stretching helps you accomplish things you never knew you could do. It is easy to take things for granted. With Arthur and me and Marie, you'd think there'd be 100 percent communication. The reality of the situation is that even with Chuck and Frank on the East Coast and me on the West Coast, we actually had better communication over the entire range of the country than Arthur and I did in that little office because of our methods of operations, our communications, and our simpatico personalities.

What we have done is build upon that. In fact, now, we make all our decisions when we have partners' meetings on Friday from 9 A.M. to 1 P.M., West Coast time. All spending decisions are made in full view of the partnership on Friday. We try to keep it very clear and straightforward. We have perhaps twenty people involved in this audio discussion. Companies come in and make video presentations from, say, 9:00 to 10:00. We then switch off the video and go to audio. I have learned that audio is a much purer way of communicating than video. It's not distracting at all. And the quality of the content and the explicitness of the decision-making process is far superior. So that's how we decided to do it, and we've continued ever since.

3Com

When we began in 1978, we invested in companies we knew something about. Between '78 and '81, we went into a half-dozen or more companies that we had known well, plus some new ones. All those we knew caught the early '80s wave, and we were able to return the capital to the partners very early.

I was the first investor in 3Com, one of the new NEA I companies. Bob Metcalf, its founder, had been at Xerox PARC and had been a co-inventor of Ethernet technology. Bob was making the rounds of the venture people, trying to start his company. 3Com stands for computer, communication, and compatibility. He was starting the company with a group of fraternity brothers from MIT, most of whom were on the West Coast, with a few on the East Coast. He came to the office and diagrammed what he was doing in the ether. I was trying to understand how ether related to what he was doing. I knew it was communications, obviously. But he drew this schematic of all these clouds in the ether and how he was intending to take this concept and turn it into a company.

I had been fortunate enough to have been an investor in Apple in 1977. Apple was booming from the beginning, actually, and really couldn't supply the demand. It was just an amazing phenomenon. I had gone around and seen every one of the PC companies, by the way. None of them are around today. But Apple was the one that clearly had the graphics and the pizzazz to make a difference.

So, having been invested in Apple and the personal computer, the idea of using multiple resources around a work group made a lot of sense to me. And as he was describing this cloud formation that represented ether, I felt pushed into the technology. I made an offer to Bob. Bob went around the country and he was gone for about 60 days. One night I got a telephone call at home at 10 o'clock. It was Bob Metcalf. "Dick," he said, "you told me when we got together that your word is good. . . . I've been around seeing a lot of other people." I asked, "How many firms have you seen?" He said, "About thirty-five."

And then I said, "Well, what did you learn?" He said, "Well, without naming any names, what I learned is a deal is not a deal is not a deal. I actually had other offers which were numerically superior to yours, but when I got into it, I found there were all kinds of little gotchas and terms that I didn't really want to live with. You promised me a very straightforward deal." And I said, "You're right. That's the way we do business here." And he said, "Well, what do you advise me to do?" I said, "What I would advise you to do is to pick, out of those thirty-five firms that you have seen, one person, one firm that you really want to work with, go to see that person and tell him we'll split the deal with him." He said, "Great idea."

I got a call the next morning from Jack Melchor of Portola Ventures, who represented a group of HP executives. Jack was on the speakerphone. He said, "Hi, Dick. I'm here with Bob Metcalf, and he tells me we ought to do this deal together." And I said, "Right, Jack." And so we just split the deal fifty-fity. Paul Baron was the first person that Bob asked to join the board because he was one of the founders of Ethernet. Subsequently, we brought in Wally Davis from Mayfield. But that's how we got started. It was really just a classic situation where we had to help form the management and develop a business plan.

As 3Com took off, Jack advocated adding professional management, which resulted in bringing in Bill Krause from Hewlett-Packard to run operations. I had always backed Bob and wanted to keep his high-level involvement in the company. So we had a little tension going. Tension is not necessarily a bad thing—it can be a good thing. Bill was the president and chief operating officer and Bob was the chairman. Then Bob took on a number of different roles. The most brilliant of all these was when he was made head of sales. Bob had a wonderful reputation as the father of Ethernet technology. When he visited Bell Labs, for example, he'd have a room full of thirty-five or forty people, as opposed to a one-on-one sales call. It was a great missionary sales effort on Bob's part. He entered into an agreement with DEC and with Intel to make this a standard. Xerox had established license fees at $1,000. It was a Xerox, DEC, and Intel consortium that started the adoption and that's why Ethernet became a standard, a forerunner of the Internet. It was a phenomenal thing—our sales went from $1 million to $4 million to $16 million to $64 million over a four-year span, on time and within budget. It was the first company that went public with Morgan Stanley at under $10 a share. We didn't want to reverse split the stock. So it went public at $6 a share.

NEA Grows Up

After the first wave of successes at NEA, we had to enlarge the organization. We brought in several people with operating experience. Art Marks came in from General Electric. Woody Rea, who had been involved with Xynetics, which was acquired by General Signal, came in from General Signal on the West Coast. And Neil Bond joined. He had been on our investment committee, and he moved from the East Coast to the West Coast. So we were dealing with larger numbers of people and just more mass.

NEA-1 had been a $16 million partnership in 1978. NEA-2 was a $45 million partnership formed in '81. NEA-3, which was formed in '84, was a $125 million partnership. So we're now dealing with bigger numbers and more people. Then we had the idea of getting Vin Prothro, who I had known through my wife's family for a long time. He was at Mostek, the semiconductor company, and had been at Texas Instruments. He invited me down to see Mostek when I was with Arthur Rock, but as they were competitive with Intel they were out of bounds for us because Arthur was the chairman of Intel at the beginning. By the time we got to the early '80s, Mostek had been acquired by United Technologies and Vin had become president.

Vin was wondering what to do after Mostek. I thought if Vin organized a fund using his own network of people in the Southwest, supplemented by us, we would automatically create a much larger deal flow in that area from the ground up. So we formed Southwest Enterprise Associates, making NEA a fifty-fifty general partner with Vin. Out of that came Dallas Semiconductor; Convex; a company called NetSolve, which is going public this year; and about a dozen other companies. But Vin wanted to run Dallas Semiconductor rather than become a full-time venture capitalist. Leland Murphy ran day-to-day activities at SEA.

So the challenges were to try to bring these people up to date in experience. We had to train the operating people and attune them to the venture capital cycle. It was a problem. It takes about a half-dozen years to really learn this business. It doesn't seem like it's very complicated in certain ways, but there are a lot of subtleties involved. The onslaught of too much money and too little experience really created declining returns in a major way in the mid-'80s.

Industry Decline in the Mid-1980s

It was a classic situation where the prices went up and quality went down. The major problem at that time was lack of experience in the industry because there was a period of almost no activity until about '80 or '81, and there were no apprentices in our business. We'd gone through a decade of marginal activity, and then suddenly, there was an onslaught of capital, and a lot of people came into our business from the investment banking world and from operations. The industry had very little understanding of the subtleties involved in growing a new company that was incorporating new technologies.

You had all these characteristics: high prices, no experience, too much capital, and little liquidity at the end of the day because the stock market had declined in the face of rampant inflation and high interest rates during the Carter administration. We at NEA went

through an awful cycle, and venture returns went down to single dig-
its. We also started experimenting outside of our core competencies
in information technology and medical life sciences. We did some
retailing activities and financial services. Both were mistakes that we
cut off after we had enough experience to know that they weren't
what we wanted to do. By the time we got halfway through NEA-4,
which was a 1987 $150 million partnership, we said, "We're going to
get to core competencies, and we're not going to do anything that's
outside of our real sphere of experience." By that time we'd had
enough experience to know that we could scale this business and
have a consistent high level of return, as long as we didn't stray outside of our core competencies and dabble in other things. We had to
develop the experience level of our partners.

NEA Milestones

The West Coast people came up through technology, and had a lot of
operating experience. But on the East Coast, our people initially
came out of the financial world, so we hired Peter Barris who had
worked with Art at GE and had been president of Legent Software.
We actually started building generations of capability within the organization by adding Tom McConnell, for example, on the West Coast.
We trimmed our sails to focus on our areas of expertise, and we
brought in a balance of operating people with financial acumen.

We have kept on growing. The actual evolution was NEA-3, which
was $125 million. NEA-4 was $150. NEA-5, a 1990 partnership, was
$200 million. NEA-6, a 1993 partnership, was $230 million. NEA-7, a
1996 partnership, was $320 million. And NEA-8, a 1998 partnership,
was $560 million.

From 1978 to 1990 we had twenty-five IPOs. And from 1990 through
1996 we had seventy-four IPOs in seventy-two months. It was the most
by far in the history of our business—one a month for almost six years.
It was incredible. We also had a number of acquisitions along the way.
There were some fluctuations between 1990 and 1997, but for the most
part, it was a tremendous period for the venture business, and that has
continued through 1998 and 1999. We now are up to 115 IPOs with
twelve in the pipeline. We have had 130 companies acquired. We have
had $4.3 billion in distribution value, and our companies employ over
400,000 people. In my own case I have been fortunate to have been a

director of eight companies that have gone from start-up to well over $1 billion in value. These are 3Com, SGI, Dallas Semiconductor, Immunex Corporation, Macromedia, Ascend, Juniper, and Healtheon. My personal goal is ten, and I think I have a good shot at it.

So let's just take a few examples of things that have happened during recent times. One of the best examples was a company called UUNET Technologies. I'd gotten a call from Mitch Kapor in 1987. He was involved in a nonprofit organization called UUNET that was propagating the Internet. Ben Rosen had suggested he call me about this. I said, "Mitch, my view of this is, if you want to get capital, you have to convert it to a for-profit organization and really make a business out of it." Subsequently, in 1990, we were involved in Ascend (recently acquired by Lucent Technologies) and Telebit. Telebit eventually got acquired by Cisco. I began to see substantial demands for products from Ascend and Telebit by UUNET. And I said, "My god, that's the company that I talked to Mitch about a long time ago."

Totally independently UUNET had come to the attention of Peter Barris, an NEA partner based in Virginia. Peter put together a financing for UUNET with two other venture firms and recruited as president John Sidgemore with whom he had worked at GE. It was the most exciting damn thing because, as I said, we began to get tons of orders at both Telebit and Ascend for all these products out of UUNET. And they were growing incredibly fast. Their goal was to become a business-to-business provider, essentially an Integrated Service Provider (ISP). Microsoft agreed to build out the network and provide the capital—which was quite a bit of capital at the time—in return for a 15 percent interest in the company. They made a direct investment in UUNET. They would use the network at night; we would use the network during the day. So it got to be a fully utilized network from the get-go. And subsequently UUNET went public and got acquired by MFS Communications of Omaha. Ultimately UUNET has become a valuable part of MCI Worldcom. It was the first $400 to $500 million dollar hit for NEA.

Our Present Focus

This is our twenty-second year. In NEA-7, 42 percent of our investment is in communications data networking, the infrastructure for the Internet. That's clearly a major focus with us. Peter Morris has led this charge. Peter came to us from Telebit, where he'd worked as a product manager, and I worked with him very closely as he came into NEA. He learned the business over a four- to five-year period. He didn't start really doing any deals for three or four years. What he did, though, was get to know the infrastructure of the communications business extremely well. We diagrammed all the critical stress points in the communications infrastructure, and then tried to find the best-of-breed companies in each area or develop the area ourselves. We've done more than twenty companies all around the infrastructure. Examples include Juniper Networks, Gadzoox Networks, Packeteer, Fibex, and many others. At the same time, we didn't do that many biotechnology deals. What we did were more drug delivery deals, companies that didn't have to go through quite as much of the ten- or twelve-year FDA cycle. We did invest in a few biotech firms such as Immunex and Vertex. We went into several catheter companies with Dr. John Simpson, all of which have become the bedrock of Guidant Corporation today, including Advanced Cardiovascular Systems and Devices for Vascular Intervention. We did some medical devices. More recently Tom McConnell has led the charge at CardioThoracic Systems, as well as many medical device companies, ably assisted by Sigrid Van Bladel.

But where we are really focused, with Chuck Newhall, is in health care services. We felt there was a large rationalization that should take place there. And then that led into health care information services, where Ron Kase focuses his entire time. Health care information services would include companies like Health South Rehabilitation.

Now we're into a whole new level of rationalizing health care services using the Internet, hence our involvement in Healtheon, MedicaLogic, and a number of other companies. A huge inefficiency exists in the bureaucracy in health care services and we've got to cut through that, make it much more efficient.

The Challenge of Growth

As far as NEA is concerned, our challenge in the near term is how we turn a half-billion dollars of NEA-8 into $2 or $3 billion. We're still driven in part by achievement and numbers. Every deal that we're going into has to return at least $35 to $50 million. So that puts certain parameters on what you're going to do. We don't want to be locked into a minimum number of dollars per deal, be it $10 or $12 million. We believe you can still start small and grow organically.

Our challenge is to quickly ferret out those deals that we think have world-class opportunity and not get too distracted by deals that are not going to amount to anything. We have to be very skilled at process, which is what I think we've really gotten good at in the last ten years. Our process has gotten a lot sharper. We don't spend too much time on tertiary activities. We're really focused on the world-class opportunities around these tectonic paradigm shifts, if you will, things like e-commerce and the Internet.

Now, as far as the public markets are concerned, we've never felt any real competition from the captive venture organizations within the investment banking firms. This is what we do for a living, but for them it's a tertiary activity. As far as the acquisitions of the four horsemen by major firms, what's happened is that has raised the threshold for IPOs. And the consequence is a $50 million minimum IPO threshold for a major underwriter. The consequence of that in part is that there are a lot of orphans out there among companies that have gone public in the past that are still good companies with good people that are just further along. A lot of the biotechnology companies are actually at the point of delivery, ready to fulfill their promise: Venture returns can occur in the public marketplace.

Our challenge is to continue to realize liquidity events. We have to continue to deploy our capital very selectively, but we also have to keep our eye on distributions to our limited partners and liquidity events that allow us to do distributions. The term I like is quality velocity.

Narrowing the Playing Field

We need to continue to focus on individual issues within the context of the much larger environment in which we're playing. Each of our professionals will do one to three new deals a year. Not any more than that. And if you only do a few new deals a year, and keep your eye on liquidity events as the outbound side of the equation, you can continue to do an awful lot of quality work in a very traditional way. It's when you get swamped with four, five, or six deals a year that you begin to lose your head. You can't spend an adequate amount of time on each individual company to really add value.

So a challenge is to continue to refine, and continue to keep our eye on liquidity events. I don't consider the raising of the bar by the consolidation in the investment banking business to be a bad thing. What's going to happen as a result of that is a whole new level of distribution that's going to happen through the Internet. There's going to be an entirely new form of distribution and underwriting—for example, E*trade, e-Schwab and Wit Capital. It's going to take place where companies may do their own underwriting. It's going to be a Dutch auction system of the kind that Bill Hambrecht is espousing. It's going to be focused underwriting within specialties by boutiques. Maybe when Sandy Robertson[1] gets free and is able to do it, he'll do some of that. Tommy Weisel's[2] way ahead of his business plan already.

How much bigger can NEA get? Our goal is not size, but quality. From the beginning Frank, Chuck, and I wanted to create a partnership that would last 100 years. We are now organizing NEA-9 for late 1999. It will be slightly larger than NEA-8. This is getting very manageable, more manageable today than in the mid-'80s when we were really stressed. At that time we were dealing with a lot of new variables, a lot of moving parts, such as new and inexperienced partners, more dollars, and frenetic activity in the marketplace. Today we process in our core competencies. As Warren Buffett says, "This is not a three-strike game. We're going to wait till the ball is chest high. Swing at that one."

---

[1] Sandy Robertson is the founder of Robertson Stephens and featured in Done Deals.

[2] Tommy Weisel is the founder of Montgomery Securities, which now is owned by Nations-Banc. He now operates an investment banking boutique specializing in entrepreneurially driven, emerging-growth companies.

GRANT HEIDRICH AND KEVIN FONG
The Mayfield Fund

Among the venture funds in existence today, Mayfield is one of the more storied. Tommy Davis, one of its co-founders, was not only an astute and successful investor, but he also helped establish many of the conventions and practices of venture capital in Silicon Valley, especially strategies for technology transfer and commercialization. Mayfield's partners—from Davis and Glenn Mueller to Gib Myers, Grant Heidrich, Kevin Fong, and Yogen Dalal—have been some of the most successful practitioners of the venture capital business.

Like a lot of the more established funds—it was founded in 1969—Mayfield has always emphasized a generalist approach to technology investing,

focusing not only on technology but also on health care. Even though generalism has had its detractors at various times, Mayfield sticks by its philosophy, as evidenced by Kevin Fong, a computer technology specialist, and Grant Heidrich, a specialist in health care for much of his venture career. Heidrich and Fong together provide a view of how Mayfield Fund and the Valley developed an approach to venture capital that is both financially attractive and humane. They begin by discussing Tommy Davis and the role he played in getting the firm off the ground.

FONG: Tommy started off in the land development business working for Kern County Land Company out in the Central Valley in California. He was a blue-blood type, very properly educated in England and at Harvard Law School. He loved horses so this was a neat job for him because he got to go out riding the range. Kern County was doing oil development, cattle, horses, and land development. Then along came this little-known phenomenon of technology development in Silicon Valley. Tommy, who knew nothing about it, would sit around and scratch his head and say, "I don't know what traveling wave tubes are, but I think they are important."

So he started making personal investments. Then he would go back to his board of directors at Kern County Land Company and say, "We've got to get involved in this. This is the future. If you really want to make some money, we ought to do this." And the directors kept saying, "Tommy, go back out to the range. Go sell off some more land. Go punch another oil well. That's what we're here for." Finally Tommy got so frustrated he left Kern County Land Company and became one of the first angel investors.

In 1963, he hooked up with Arthur Rock and the two set up the Davis Rock partnership. They had one partnership cycle, and then they went their separate ways. In 1969, Tommy created Mayfield Fund with Wally Davis (who is no relation to Tommy). Even at the time, Tommy recognized the eventual institutionalization of the business, which is why he used the name Mayfield Fund rather than calling the firm Davis & Davis. He knew that it would be something that would continue in the Valley for a long time.

Mayfield got its name from a town near Palo Alto called Mayfield, which was the train stop to get to Leland Stanford's farm. As Leland Stanford started building Stanford University, he wanted to do certain things. Mayfield had its own city council and it didn't want to cooperate, so Stanford built a train station in Palo Alto. After that Mayfield started to wither away because Stanford did all his business in his own town and created the way he wanted things done. Finally Mayfield was annexed by Palo Alto. There's still a train stop today on California Avenue, which was once Mayfield's main street.

Working with Universities

HEIDRICH: The size of the first Mayfield fund was between $3 and $3.5 million dollars. That was typical at the time because there was almost no institutional venture capital around.

Tommy Davis was a visionary in many ways. He recognized the vital role that universities play in education. He formed a very close relationship with Stanford University in that first fund, and maintained close and collaborative dialogues with a number of the professors in the new technologies.

Stanford, I think, pioneered the whole model of universities having a close liaison with industry in its early mentoring of Hewlett-Packard. The university realized that it could play a vital role. Universities differ in how they think about working with industry. Some simply say that they are purely academic, that they publish papers and put them in the public domain. Others say, "We don't have anything to do with the technology transfer in that case." Still others, like Stanford University, will say, "We like to have this close liaison with industry."

By 1969, when Mayfield Fund was started, Hewlett-Packard had been around for twenty years. The Stanford Industrial Park had been around since 1960. Frederick Terman, then dean of the engineering school at Stanford, knew that collaboration between the university and business was very important.

That collaborative tradition has continued through all our funds. We have very close relationships with many leading institutions including Stanford, Yale, MIT, Harvard, Cal Tech, Carnegie Mellon, University of Rochester, Princeton, and Dartmouth. We really value these relationships for two reasons. First, they are smart people, they have a very long-term perspective, and most of their capital comes from their endowments. So that works well. Second, if you don't have your own relationships and you call and say, "Gee, I'd like to talk to somebody in the engineering department," they will make the introduction. That's been very helpful for us.

A good case study is MIPS Computer Systems, which was acquired by Silicon Graphics and recently spun out as a separate company again. John Hennessey, now the provost at Stanford, and two other Stanford Ph.D.'s had conceived the idea for MIPS and had developed it with funding from DARPA, the Department of Defense program that funds many high-tech projects. But when they went back for more funding, DARPA said, "John, we feel funny. We think this is an interesting project, but it's kind of a radical idea for the time." So we spent a lot of time talking back and forth. MIPS had no full-time employees. They had no capital. John Hennessey eventually ended up taking a leave of absence from Stanford—though he eventually went back. Jim Clark, who was an associate professor at the time, left permanently. Clark started Silicon Graphics. So there is a flexible model about how universities and entrepreneurship meld.

Another more recent example is Cytokinetics, a company Mayfield Fund incubated. An associate professor from UCSF, the chairman of the biochemistry department from Stanford, and a professor from UCSV were the founders. We brought them into Mayfield and incubated the company. We went to their open house recently and they've got this big, beautiful lab and well-defined projects. They've hired top scientists to work on these projects.

We had another guy here from Texas A&M who is a professor with joint appointments in computer science, electrical engineering, and math. He started off doing teleradiology with image compression and decompression. We knew something was there, but we didn't know what the right market was. We studied up, and he left the university and relocated here. We ended up realizing that the real play was over in the digital consumer world. Along came a group of guys from LSI Logic, a semiconductor company, who wanted to do digital TV. We said: "Wait a minute. Somehow, somewhere, this compression/decompression of images is important." The guys didn't even know each other, but we merged the two companies and then invested in the parent company.

FONG: It is important to remember that the things that we take for granted today were very unique and groundbreaking in the 1970s. How should a university think about a professor collaborating on a start-up? Today, at least at Stanford, we take it for granted that a professor might take a one- or two-year leave of absence. I think there are still a lot of universities that don't think of collaborating at all.

The other motivator is intellectual property and patents. The university has all these patents. It has to have an Office of Technology Licensing that knows how to deal with venture capitalists. What will you do with equity? The companies don't have a lot of cash to give the university. But universities understand that the companies give back to the university, and, in the long run, the university benefits from having these companies spin out. So we have Hewlett-Packard, Sun Microsystems, MIPS, and Silicon Graphics giving equipment or direct stock donations, or the founders themselves giving back. In a lot of cases, the professor-founders actually go back to the universities and, like John Hennessey of Stanford, they're much more productive.

Codes of Venture Conduct and Core Values

HEIDRICH: If you look at the Mayfield tradition, it goes back to one of the fundamental things Tommy Davis did. He set the highest possible ethical standards for how we deal with each other, such as respect for the individual, complete honesty, and complete integrity, as well as standards for how we treat people on the outside. This industry got started that way. These concepts have been an integral part of the Mayfield culture.

Mayfield is not a hierarchical organization. It is just the opposite of the way most East Coast venture firms are organized. That's because Tommy always believed that you establish leadership by what you do. While there is leadership at Mayfield, everyone is rewarded for his or her individuality.

FONG: In the mid- to late 1980s we at Mayfield recognized that there are core sets of values that we stand for, and that these values and philosophical approaches have worked for us in the past. We also recognized what segment of business we liked and were good at, which is early-stage investing.

What it means to be in this business focusing on the early stage of a company is that you can't get too large in terms of the capital under management because you don't want to drown a company in capitalization. It means that you have to be willing to stick with companies for a certain length of time. In order to do an incubation or a first-stage investment, you've got to be willing to work with that company for three to five years.

Today that time is greatly shortened with Internet companies. But in early-stage investing, you have to focus on the technology, whether it's health care or information technology, which has certain implications for our skill sets and our ability to understand and contribute in certain technical areas. It's the consolidation of these factors that makes our business interesting.

The next thing you have to do is to keep on top of the actual management of the firm. There are no templates for the venture capital industry. Venture firms are creations similar to law firms and other professional services firms. They are run as partnerships and are very non-hierarchical.

How do you manage a firm that is substantial in size and with a breadth of business? You need some kind of leadership. When you have four or five people sitting around the table, leadership involves getting everyone into the same room and deciding what do to. When you have ten, twelve, or fourteen people, you can't do that anymore. If you have billions of dollars under management, you certainly can't do that anymore.

One of the things we ask ourselves all the time is, "who is the customer?" Certainly our investors are our customers. But the other customer we could talk about is the entrepreneur. Clearly we have to serve the entrepreneur. We are absolutely part of the food chain and in some sense we are facilitators. But we are not necessarily the ones who get all the glory. In our business, there are sets of limited partners that at the end of the day are our customers. They measure us by financial returns. Their other need, by the way, is that they want to put a large amount of money to work, more than we can manage, actually. So we have to handle that tension, because every single one of our limited partners would like to be the largest investor in Mayfield. They would love to put more than $30 million to work. That's clearly one need that we cannot completely satisfy.

HEIDRICH: I think one of the things Mayfield has pioneered has been the different ways we work with people. We've brought in several people in the health care sector such as Mark Levin, who is now CEO of Millennium Pharmaceuticals, a large company based in Boston that we incubated here at Mayfield. We created a very unusual role for Mark—a role that is now being widely imitated throughout the whole venture capital industry. Mark principally invents businesses and then uses his unusual set of technical and entrepreneurial skills, along with the entire infrastructure and knowledge base of Mayfield Fund, to start companies. Today as CEO and founding investor in Millennium Pharmaceuticals, Mark is running a company that I think will prove to be a watershed company for this century.

FONG: We invest a lot of personal time in making sure we know how to work with each other. That personal time includes off-site meetings, workshops, and reviews in which every partner evaluates us. We spend a lot of time making sure we all understand how each of us works and what our motivations are. We talk about these things in a very open fashion. Issues about how succession or change should be dealt with are all discussed in an open environment. Simple as it sounds, proper compensation for work done and for success realized is something that is fundamental to the way we work.

Going Forward

FONG: When we talk about $1 billion of capital under management, that's the summation of all the funds since the beginning of Mayfield. The maximum per partner for each fund is about $25 million, and has been for a long time. One of the major issues will always be whether we can manage more money per partner, coupled with the concern that more money will change the way we've always done business.

We still believe in backing people who want to do things in partnership, not just with us, but also with their other founders, their employees, and their customers. Through rough times and different business cycles, people always come back to those values. There are certain groups of entrepreneurs who still want to do things that worked in the past.

Of course we would like to be in the top tier of companies when it comes to the number of deals we did this year and how much money we invested. But if achieving that causes us to fundamentally change our business, we'd rather not be the fund that does the most deals every year or invests the most money. If those numbers are going to be the measure of which is the best firm, we're not going to play that game.

When I first came to Mayfield, everybody was raising $150 million funds. Now funds are much larger—in the billion-dollar range. Back then, that was the number that you had to raise if you were a premier

fund. What is important to us is being recognized in terms of working with entrepreneurs and understanding their businesses on a per-
sonalized basis. That is what will carry our reputation forward with
entrepreneurs.

HEIDRICH: The best references we get are two-fold in my opinion.
When some group of entrepreneurs we've worked with, struggled
with, laughed with, and finally succeeded with comes back at the end
and says, "Grant, or Kevin, or any individual partner here, was terrific,
and give that reference to any other entrepreneur"—I don't care what
the press says. That reference is worth gold. The other reference we
value is when we see limited partners who have invested with us eight
or nine successive times turn around and say, "How much can I
invest?" If we get those two things right, we are doing the right thing.
You don't see these kinds of accolades in the press. But that is how
we know we're doing our jobs the right way.

LARRY SONSINI
Wilson Sonsini Goodrich & Rosati

 *Larry Sonsini, perhaps more than any other lawyer in the country, has shaped the venture capital process. As head of the law firm that represents some of the oldest and largest venture capital funds—predominantly ones in Silicon Valley—he has been involved with the formation of most of the major pools of capital. In addition, his firm has represented many entrepreneurial companies, helping to prepare them to go public.*

But Sonsini and his firm may be better appreciated for having helped establish many of the legal guidelines for the fledgling venture capital business, benchmarks that created a more uniform playing field for venture capitalists, their investors, and entrepreneurs. And although Larry Sonsini is not a venture capitalist, he clearly is one of venture capital's star performers.

Some observers believe that lawyers are too close to the venture capital business. Lawyers not only act as legal counsel to companies but often invest in those same companies; and hence, some argue that they lose their objectivity. In an industry that historically has operated through trust and handshakes but is now experiencing hypergrowth in terms of the size of funds, the number of investment opportunities, and the number of new entrants, the need for rules and standards has never been greater. Sonsini, whose own professional life mirrors the growth of venture capital in the Valley, is an expert commentator and observer.

I CAME TO Silicon Valley to practice law in 1966 when the technology industry was really starting. The industry may have started sooner, for example, in '47 or '57. But back then it didn't have an identity or a paradigm, and at that time there was no methodology to starting, funding, and building technology-based enterprises. The template that we used then is still used today. Any fundamental changes have been the result of growth in the industry as opposed to a change in methodology.

I came here in 1966 very much enticed by the idea of representing entrepreneurs and building companies. I guess I'm no different from any other entrepreneur, except my field was law, rather than technology. The thought of getting involved at a very early stage in the growth of a technology company *and* being able to practice the legal profession was very appealing. Back then this area was not well represented—there were very few law firms that had even heard of venture capital. There weren't many venture capitalists at all. My partner, John Wilson, was involved in the formation of Mayfield Fund and was once a partner there on a part-time basis. So, there was excitement in the idea of building an enterprise.

The West Coast model of venture capitalism has always been a very intense business partnership with the entrepreneurs. The providing of capital was one function of the venture capitalist. Being actively involved in developing the business model, managing the enterprise, and recruiting management was all part of what a Tommy Davis, an Art Rock, or a Tom Perkins did. They thought of more than investing money. They thought about mentoring, training, and providing business solutions. The goal was not only to make a successful investment but also to be a part of building a successful venture. That was similar to our practice of law. We started to represent entrepreneurs, and got caught up in the same thing. Instead of investing money, we invested a legal solution. But the legal solution wasn't the whole piece. The other piece was creating the business judgment, anticipating how to identify the land mines in developing an enterprise. I think that growing up with venture capitalists and being an entrepreneur shaped my model as a business lawyer. In the early days, we were described as venture capital lawyers. As the firm has matured our skill set has gotten better and bigger.

Viewing the East Coast from the West

What's happened on the East Coast is that the technology has expanded and the opportunity to build enterprises or to get financial returns is much greater. Now you can do leveraged buyouts of technology companies. You can do joint ventures of technology companies. You can do more pure financial plays, because you have large technology companies. You have billions of dollars that you didn't have before. So it's opened up the opportunity for the pure financial play to come into the venture industry. A lot of East Coast money, which is driven from a pure financial play perspective, is moving to venture capital, and I think a lot of venture capital is migrating to pure financial transactions. If you look at the kinds of transactions that many large venture firms do today, you'll see diversification. Now we have firms doing leveraged buyouts of technology companies. That was unheard of for a West Coast venture firm. But the idea is migrating, because that's where the opportunities are going.

We have done large start-ups that are venture-capital based. The structure of these large transactions often emphasizes financial returns—the securities may even have dividends.

Follow Technology

In the '70s we were doing primarily semiconductor start-ups—at least one a month. Everyone was doing a semiconductor deal. There was a certain way you did those deals. You knew how much money they needed. You knew the land mines that they would run into. In the '80s, the computer industry really kicked in with Apple Computer in 1980, and then you had the whole peripheral industry around it—disk drives, floppy disks, hard drives, printers, and modems. The '80s was just an explosion of the hardware industry built upon the microprocessor, the integrated circuit of the '70s, which kept going and got more complex, smaller in size, and so on. You saw the growth of the PC companies. That opened up more and more opportunities because those companies required a different kind of financing profile, with a large emphasis on distribution. The PC became a consumer product, so you had to know retailing. Then you saw the growth in the software industry. In the '90s, we see the result of software and now the Internet. These technology revolutions have each addressed a bigger market. These markets are getting bigger, more global, more competitive, and the cost to people is becoming higher, so the cost of investing is bigger. So it requires bigger dollars to play. That's caused many of the venture funds to have to consider how to do their models. If you're going to be a big player, you have to have a lot of money.

That has changed the environment a bit. But not because anything was broken, or needed to be fixed in the venture industry, but because the opportunity, the size of the issue, has expanded. It's made it a more sophisticated and more challenging industry.

Many venture funds have to put a lot of capital to work. To understand the issues this creates, you have to understand how a venture fund works. A venture fund has a very limited life—ten to twelve years for each partnership. A partnership has the very specific objective of getting its investments liquid and its portfolio securities distributed. It therefore only has a certain amount of time to put that money to work. If you're only going to live ten years, and it takes an enterprise maybe three to five years to get public, perhaps requiring several rounds of financing, you're going to get a lot of money invested in the early years and save some for second round financings. As the deal size has gotten bigger, and the amount of money has gotten bigger, it has forced a lot of these funds to put more money to work at a particular time. Rather than investing $1 or $2 million, they'll invest $5 or $10 million. That means that a lot of enterprises that only need seed capital struggle a little bit. The big deal mentality has resulted in the growth of a new kind of industry, a band of angels that is trying to address this perceived need.

As the opportunities have gotten bigger, and the technology play is bigger, many of these venture funds have started to either specialize or diversify. You go inside these venture funds, and you'll see that there will be partners who are dedicated to life sciences, to telecommunications, to microelectronics, to the Internet, and so forth.

The technology is changing so rapidly, the opportunities are so broad, and these entrepreneurs have so much venture capital to look at, that they want to pick partners who are going to add value. The decision of a venture capitalist, as I said before, is not just about the money.

Is There a Separate Venture Capital Law?

The kind of corporate law I practice is no different just because it happens to be related to venture capital. You still are dealing with tax laws, securities laws, contract laws, and state laws. You're dealing with corporate law.

What's different is the creation of this business enterprise, and helping mold its direction. How do you protect a trade secret? At what stage do you protect it? Should you patent the invention, or not patent the invention? That's not a pure legal question. It's a combination legal and business question.

First, is it patentable? A legal question. Second, does it enhance the business environment to have a patent? Should you license your technology, or sell your technology? There are legal consequences to both actions, but the decision is not solely a legal decision—it's driven by where you want to go.

Imagine, for instance that you are the founder of a business. You have $2 million of venture capital, you have a product in development, should you do direct sales? Or should you go through sales representatives or distributorships?

All of the problems involve legal issues, but they're the result of business problems. The legal problem just reflects the business on that day. And so all of a sudden we're having a conversation about really defining the business model in which the predicate is the law. It's not that the law is different, or that the lawyering is different, it's just that there's an opportunity to add value as a business partner.

Creating Incentives for Entrepreneurship

One of the most unique characteristics of this industry is the meritocracy system based upon great incentives. I was over in England last week talking to people there about how to replicate the technology industry in the States. One of the fundamental problems is the whole rewards system has to be turned upside down.

In the United States, the rewards system has many components. There's a lateral movement among employees that is unheard of in many nations. The idea of going to work for one enterprise while looking to leave to go to another enterprise is really contrary to many countries' work ethic. The idea that you would give up dollar compensation for future equity incentives is also unique.

Another unique characteristic of the U.S. technology industry is the emphasis upon equity incentive compensation. It works because there's a tax structure that allows it to work. The grant of a stock option is not a taxable event. There is a securities law system that allows it and there is a capital market that allows liquidity for these types of incentives.

We have entrepreneurial programs in universities. This law firm is involved with the Law and Technology Center at Berkeley, the Technology Enterprise Center at Stanford, and the Enterprise Center at MIT. My partners are lecturing in business schools, teaching venture capital courses, talking about how to develop a business plan, how to get financing, and how to structure financing.

Another unique thing about the industry is that there are a lot of founders who are re-treads. A lot of people come back. Another part of that, which makes us different from, say, Europe, is that failure is not a stigma. The fact that you started an enterprise and failed at it probably makes you more valuable as an entrepreneur. In Europe if you fail, you may have difficulty getting started again. So, there is a lot of experience, that's the second thing. Third, there's a lot of competition—venture capital competition and legal competition. So everybody is wanting to educate somebody quickly without the competitive edge.

Structuring Venture Partnerships

I think that you have to realize that the partnership structure has been around a long time, and it hasn't changed that much over time. The management fee component still runs about the same, from 2 to 2.5 percent. The carry still runs about the same, 20 percent on the low end, 30 percent on the high. The total flexibility of the general partner regarding distributions and liquidations hasn't changed. Funds have to be more accountable to their investors because the institutions have put more money at stake, but venture capital works best when the institution is truly a silent, limited partner.

The changes in the partnership structure to me are not material. Valuations are still done by the general partners. Very few investors are on the valuation team. The split of the general partner is dictated internally. The voting provisions, the indemnity provisions, the termination provisions, the distribution provisions—they're the same. The partnership structure as a legal structure has been evolutionary, not revolutionary.

The internal workings of the partnerships have changed some-what. The dynamics of the general partner have changed. You now have M.B.A.'s, associates, vesting, and side-by-side funds without carry. All of that has changed, because funds are managing more money and there is a need for more institutional accountability.

There's been a maturation of the role of a general partner. The size of their investment and their role has changed. Some of them incu-bate start-ups in their own offices. Some of them take management positions. So yes, the infrastructure of the general partner has changed, but the structure of the partnerships is pretty much the same.

There's a lot of pressure on liquidity. A great deal of emphasis on earlier IPOs. Reluctance to do later-round financing is causing a greater need for a mezzanine player to come in and help out. So, those fundamentals have caused change. It's created opportunities for financial players.

We have in the United States a capital market that will accept an early-stage enterprise without an earnings history that goes public. Now, that is unique. There isn't a capital market out there other than the United States that allows that. England has developed a market they call AIM for Alternative Investment Market. It's supposed to be the market for venture capital companies to go public with. You need a broad-based, efficient liquid capital market to make the venture capi-tal recipe work. The reason why venture capital works in this country is the U.S. capital market. Without the U.S. capital market, you wouldn't have venture capital. For the most part government has stayed away from intervening and this is paying off. People are doing well.

Capital Flood

How is all this capital going to be put to work? Clearly, you don't need $1.5 billion for a venture start-up. What's going to happen is that a lot of this capital is going to go into different kinds of investments. You'll see more leveraged buyouts. You'll see more investing in public enter-prises, as opposed to private enterprises. You'll see more later-stage investing. And you'll see less sharing of the risk with other venture firms, where one party solely finances a business.

Is it good for the industry? Yes. The more money we can put to work, the better for our enterprises. Is it a kind of a new model? Yes. The liquidity for these large investments is going to be different than it is for the ordinary $50 or $100 million IPO. Could it affect us? It could. One of the things that we have seen in this bull market is that sometimes it is easier to take a large cap company public—a company that had a $500 million or $1 billion dollar market—as opposed to a $250 million market cap.

Perils of the New Venture Capital

If we keep putting private money in, and we put it in at lower prices because we want the ROI, we are going to start to dilute management down to nothing. And if we dilute management down too much, we're going to upset the equation of the equity incentive to the entrepreneur. And, if you upset that, you're going to see fewer start-ups. That would be a problem in the industry. Another peril is that if you can't make an investment liquid through the IPO market, what are you going to do? You're going to start running companies to merge. Your business model is going to be sale. Your business model is going to be consolidation. It's going to drive a different business discipline, a different incentive, and a different management philosophy. It's one thing to build a company to be a worldwide, global, multibillion-dollar company, bringing in MIS systems, internal control systems, and so on—building a real enterprise. We might not do that. What we might do is build projects, rather than enterprises. Develop a particular market, a particular product, and then sell or merge it.

Sonsini on Sonsini

It's like building an enterprise. That's what we have done here. What I focus on are two things. One is the continuing maturation and evolution of my own legal skill. There is a continuing evolution of my expertise. The second piece is the continuing evolution of this law firm: driving the vision of this law firm, continuing to develop its brand. We are trying to be a law firm that leads the technology industry with a capability to service an enterprise from start-up to a multibillion-dollar global enterprise. I don't think you'll find a law firm that has that scalability in the technology industry. There are great law firms in this country that don't even get involved with venture capital transactions. There are wonderful venture capital law firms that don't service complex M&A transactions. But we do have that scale. That's unique in the industry. It's designed to mirror the growth of the industry. Because of the demands of these venture funds, as more money comes in and transactions become complex, we have to evolve the legal discipline that continues to service this emerging industry. So, that's what I'm about, both professionally and as a businessman helping to lead a large institution in this industry.

EAST
COAST

CHARLES WAITE
Greylock Management

Charles Waite got his venture capital education at Harvard Business School, at the feet of Georges Doriot, the master.

For Waite, the excitement of what Doriot taught was all-pervasive. But Waite simply didn't believe that others should make all the money while he did all the work, so when the opportunity to join a start-up fund came, he jumped at it. He co-founded Greylock in 1965 with $10 million from six wealthy families including the Watsons of IBM and Sherman Fairchild, the founder of Fairchild Semiconductor. Greylock has gone on to become one of the most venerated East Coast venture institutions, and Waite was involved in many of the fund's major successes.

Waite isn't active as an investor anymore, but he continues to be involved with some Greylock investments—both as an advisor and as a board member—as a Greylock limited partner. Here Waite recounts not only his days with Doriot, ARD, and later Greylock, but also the early days of venture investing on the East Coast and the early values and practices at one of the most storied firms on either coast. He talks about the venture capital industry that was and how it is changing as greater infusions of money, higher expectations, and greater successes leave the industry with an embarrassment of riches. His narrative is a candid description of how the venture business found an identity and how quickly it can lose it.

I WAS A STUDENT of Georges Doriot at Harvard Business School. He probably had more to do with the formation of this business than any other single person. Doriot had the practice of asking a high performer in his class to be his teaching assistant the following year. He only asked you to assist for one year, because he thought there was valuable exposure if you did it for one year, but he wasn't attempting to make you into a teacher. I took that post for the school year of '59 to '60. It was a grand year—the pay was low, but I had a lot of exposure to his students. It was a large class with 150 students, and there was a lot of activity. Doriot then asked me to join his venture firm, American Research and Development Corp. I liked him, and I had learned a lot about venture capital from him in his class. So after finishing at the Business School I went to work for him. I stayed there for nearly seven years. Then with Bill Elfers and Dan Gregory I founded Greylock in 1965.

Doriot took the first steps toward institutionalizing venture capital. As a young professor at Harvard, he knew a lot of powerful people including the president of MIT, the head of Mass Investors' Trust, and the head of John Hancock. They met in 1939 to define what was to become venture capital. In other words, they were asking if it wouldn't be useful if there were money and advice available to support the entrepreneurial effort. They actually held their meeting, as I recall, the night the Germans invaded Poland. With the war, they put the whole program aside for seven years. They met again after World War II and got the process started in 1946.

When I came to ARD in 1960, venture capital had been around for fourteen years or so. But it was still an academic experiment in some ways, because Doriot was head of it, and he was more than anything else a teacher. He was in the business to test a thesis. Making money wasn't really a very high objective. He wasn't opposed to it, but the salaries were modest. There was no ownership in the company for anybody. When others began to make serious money, ARD, unless it changed itself, would be unable to continue. At one time he tried to give options to ARD employees but the SEC wouldn't allow him to do that in the investment company format. He then tried to give options in the companies we invested in to ARD employees, and was able to do that in a start-up we did called Digital Equipment Corporation. But the SEC didn't like that either. There was really no way of having employees participate.

ARD started out being owned by John Hancock, Mass Investors' Trust, and a number of wealthy families, and then became one of the first publicly traded venture capital vehicles. It was founded under the 40 Act, and did a public offering in 1960. It raised $18 or $20 million, which was sizeable at the time, and was traded on the New York Stock Exchange. We invested our money as it is invested today, with a lot of legal hooks, a lot of careful analysis going into each investment, and a lot of time and effort put into the directoral, strategic, people-finding, and financial advice support areas. Doriot believed in working very hard at your investment portfolio.

Investing in Digital Equipment Corporation

Ken Olsen came to ARD two years before I got there. As I remember the story, he was working in the Computer Lab, or whatever it was called then, at MIT. Something was published about the work the lab was doing, and the youngest guy at ARD picked up the phone and called him. That fellow, very interestingly, never became a well-known venture capitalist or an industry legend. But he did find and help create one of the most successful companies ever. His name was Wayne Brobeck. He was a very studious person who didn't spend a lot of time at ARD. He found Ken Olsen and a couple of other ARD ventures, and then joined one of ARD's portfolio companies and moved out of the business. However, there were a number of people at ARD who were pleased to take credit for the Digital investment.

The investment made in Digital was $70,000. That bought 68 percent of the company. So in the early years, before subsequent financings, ARD owned 68 percent of DEC for $70,000. We subsequently lent $150,000 to DEC for no further equity position. But that was not risk capital. We did that because it was easier to lend the money to them than go to the bank, but it really wasn't capital at risk. So, it was a $70,000 equity investment. The end of that investment came many years later when ARD was sold to Textron and the DEC investment was distributed to the shareholders. It had a value at the time of between $400 and $500 million. Now, of course, there are many $400 or $500 million successes. But that was a time of different equity valuations, and a less inflated dollar. It was a huge win by any measure. Several of my then colleagues had a 1 percent interest in DEC that they'd received in options before the SEC closed that window to ARD and other investment companies. So those positions totaled $50 million to $60 million at the peak.

One other thing people have forgotten about DEC is that Ken Olsen had a partner who was every bit as important in the early days as Ken was. His name was Harlan (Andy) Anderson. Andy is still a private investor, living in Connecticut. He was a very, very valuable partner of Ken's. They had a falling out, a technology falling out some years later, and Andy left. But, of the founding equity, Ken had 60 percent and Andy had 40 percent. So, they were nearly equal partners.

Launching Greylock

Bill Elfers was the driving force behind the launch of Greylock. I think it was to prove himself, to see if he could do it on his own. He'd been in Doriot's shadow all these years. He was very important to ARD. He was the number two guy, and had been the number two guy for a long time. Doriot, being the professor, relied heavily on Bill for the everyday decisions. Are we going to make this investment or aren't we? Are we going to advocate the change in management in company X? Are we going to sell this investment? Are we going to put more money into this investment? Those were the kinds of things that Bill Elfers did on a day-to-day basis. I think Bill wanted to try his own game.

He left in 1965 and put together a group of investors—private families—and then asked me a few months later to come and join him. There was a third fellow who he had met along the way, Dan Gregory, that joined him. So there were three of us, essentially, from the beginning. Bill and I had already been working together for a number of years. So, we just did what we had learned how to do.

The first fund began at just under $5 million with five investors. Subsequently another family came in, and then several years later the same group put in some more money. That first partnership became a $10 million partnership that took us six years to invest. My colleagues now are putting money to work at a far more rapid pace. It's changed a little bit. We were investing $250,000 and $300,000 at a crack, and we looked at everything very, very carefully.

We did a wide range of deals at first. At ARD we often backed scientists that left MIT or elsewhere to make scientific instruments, often related to defense or to the space effort. There was pattern for many of these companies—there would be a professor who was working for the Air Force, or NASA, with an agreement that they would get a $50,000 or $75,000 research contract for some technology effort. After getting that contract, they would come to us for some operating money to get started. That would be the initial step of the company—funded with some research money from Washington and some venture capital. They would do the research and if it was successful, it would turn into some instrument they would sell to the Air Force. Then if the instrument had commercial application—as we always hoped it would—they would commercialize it. That sounds easy, but it was very difficult, because the markets were different, the configuration of the product had to be different, and it was often a very costly and time-consuming transition to make. But I'd say that was more of what we did than anything.

At Greylock, we said from the very beginning that we would do anything as long as it was legal and honorable. We obviously weren't going to back cocaine traffickers. And we wouldn't have backed a cigarette maker. But we were open to most anything else. Among the first investments we made at Greylock were a cable TV company, an insurance company, and a grocery retailer. Those weren't necessarily one, two, and three, but they were three of the first seven or eight investments. We were looking very opportunistically at a wide variety of things.

At Greylock in the early days, we weren't oriented to start-ups. That was basically because Bill Elfers felt much better, much more at ease, when there was more information to go on. And, of course, if a company had been around for a couple of years, there was more to analyze. One could be more confident. The risk was lower. That was one of the early tensions between Elfers and me, because I always believed that the odds of a great win were only there if you did start-ups. So I pushed very hard, and eventually the firm came around to doing start-ups, but it was not an easy transition.

The nation—particularly in Boston at that time—was beginning to develop an entrepreneurial culture. There was a company that ARD founded or supported called Tracer Labs. That's a name many people don't know. But, Tracer Labs was an early model for Fairchild in California. How many companies came out of Tracer Labs? You could make one of these branching maps today. It was a big number. Tracer Labs was never a great company. It was one of these companies that started making analytical instruments. But some scientist inside, some researcher, would come up with a new instrument. He couldn't sell it to his boss, so he'd leave and come to us, or others, and get funding to start his own company. That happened repeatedly.

High Voltage Engineering was another early success of ARD's after World War II. And by the late '50s, early '60s, those companies were producing an interest in high-technology capital gains, as well as an entrepreneurial interest. The companies were also the source of people who were leaving to start their own companies. It's nothing like the wave of today, but it was there. And, of course, the semi-conductor companies started. We had Transitron, which was the early one in Boston. The people poured out of Transitron by the '60s, and were starting little companies, either in California or Boston. And if they weren't coming out of these companies, there would be professors at MIT or Harvard, or elsewhere, that read the stock sheets and could see that there might be opportunities.

The Greylock Family

We started with around $10 million in '65 and '66, and the three of us went for about three years. We then added Henry McCance, who runs the firm today. This young person we hired—he's still a young guy to me—is in his mid-fifties now and has been with the firm about thirty years. We added Howard Cox a couple of years after that. They had both worked in an analysis group at the Pentagon. Henry was a civilian employee at the Pentagon. As a matter of fact, he worked there for a guy named Charlie Rosatti, who we later backed in a venture and who is today Commissioner of the IRS. The five of us went along for a while, and our next hire was David Strohm. One of the interesting things about Greylock is that no one on a partner track has ever left the firm. Not one person in thirty-three years.

Today there are ten partners. That doesn't include the three founders, who are all in one form of retirement or another. I still sit on boards of companies, but I'm not looking for deals on a day-to-day basis, or integrating with my partners on a day-to-day basis.

The size of the last partnership that we raised, which was done early in 1998, was about $250 million. We have a different philosophy than some about raising money. We've been one of the successful firms, so raising money has not been a problem for us. If we were to have a few bad years it would become a problem for us like anybody else. We're not alone, of course. A number of good firms have no problem raising money. We try to raise as little money as we can. I mean that sincerely. At the same time we want to be thought of as a player by other people in the industry, because the source of a lot of investments is other people in the industry. We don't want Sutter Hill or Kleiner Perkins to say, "We can't take this deal to Greylock, it's too big for them." So, we have to have enough money to qualify to be a member of the real club, but that's all the money we want.

Actually, we've disappointed some potential investors by saying, "we're sorry, we don't have any room." "Well, of course you have room," they say. We don't. We've turned down many families and university investors, because we want to keep a lid on capital so we have a higher confidence of our ability to create returns. Greylock was very successful with a $10 million fund, then with a $12 million fund, then with a $30 million fund, and so on, but there are some different things you must do when you start managing a $250 million fund, and still different things when you raise $1 billion. The people that are true venture capitalists, and are really working on these companies, aren't necessarily good at managing huge amounts of money.

Venture Capital, a Small '60s Community

When I started in the business, there were very few other players. If there were fifty people in the business in 1960, that was a lot. Today, I don't know how many professionals there are, but I think it's 7,000 or more. I used to know everybody in the business quite well. You didn't really compete with one another. I mean, if Venrock had a deal, it was Venrock's deal. If you really wanted in, you'd call Peter Crisp and ask him to let you in. But you wouldn't put another term sheet on the table. That was not very gentlemanly. If somebody was going to start a company, they wanted $250,000 or $300,000 and they gave up about 65 percent of the equity. The deals that we offered were all about the same. So unless you were some great man—unless you were Dwight Eisenhower wanting to start an infantry division—there wasn't much hurry to do the deal, which gave us plenty of time to research the market, the competition, and the quality of the people.

The president of a proposed company in these early days didn't have all the experience in high-tech firms that most entrepreneurs have today, but he had an education, and he had worked somewhere. So we looked at his performance, and talked to his boss. We didn't do that on the telephone. We would get on an airplane and go to Youngstown, Ohio. Which I've done. I've been most everywhere. And we would sit down across from the entrepreneur's boss and talk to him. It does make a difference. It is very hard to get a read on people today. People won't be honest with you. If there's anything negative to say, they won't say it, because they're afraid they'll be sued, and for good reason. And if you do it on the telephone, there's no way you're going to get any negatives. So if you are really interested in this entrepreneur, you better go and personally talk to the people who he's worked for. But people frequently don't do that. It's too time consuming, and it's too much work. The business has gotten too easy, even though it is very competitive.

There was time to do your due diligence, and we did our due diligence. We would make a lot of visits and calls, and really do our homework before we made an investment. And when you'd made that investment, there typically weren't five other companies created by your competitors to do the same thing.

We genuinely believed that companies benefited greatly by our serving diligently on their board. That diligence has been lost along the way by some firms to some degree. Our reason is that the numbers don't work anymore. You start out by raising a whole pot full of money, say $500 million, because it's available. How many boards can one person serve on effectively? Six, seven, eight, nine? That's about it. Beyond that it's a joke, because you don't know what's happening. You don't have time. You miss meetings. You try to do it by telephone, and it doesn't work, at least not the way that it's meant to work. So, what people can do to solve this problem is either raise less money—which they don't do—or make larger investments, which at some point in time aren't really efficient venture capital–type investments anymore. Or they kid themselves that they can handle a lot of boards by not really being on the board, just being available as an advisor, and so on. That's not what the classic entrepreneurial-venture relationship used to be, and I think still should be. So a lot of ventures don't work because they're not getting proper attention from somebody who has the relevant experience. Just because some young person has been to Harvard Business School and is now a fresh twenty-six years old, and smart as hell, really doesn't mean that he's much use to an entrepreneur. He probably needs four or five years of experience to be helpful. A lot of these entrepreneurs get young guys foisted off on them because there isn't anybody else in the firm to do it. In our early days at Greylock, and at the other good firms at that time, we wouldn't put a new hire on a board without his having first served with one of the partners. That substantially reduces the amount of money you can manage, as well as the rapidity with which you make investments. That's all been speeded up—not necessarily for the better—in recent years.

People today are placing high values and betting that these companies are going to achieve great success, and then the market value will be there, the performance will catch up to the market value, and it will be okay. But, in most cases, they probably won't be great successes, and those numbers will get punched back substantially.

Early Venture Capital: A Mission to Create

There was a kind of a missionary quality in venture capital years ago—or at least a feeling of doing something that was different and good—that remains to a lesser degree now. One reason for that was Doriot's philosophy. Many of the people in venture capital have some connection to him. For example, Tom Perkins and Peter Crisp were his students, and I'm sure there are many others. And he stayed in touch with these people. Not only were they students of his, but he had substantial influence on them.

Doriot's thesis was that if you took a team of people with business experience and a willingness to expend time and effort as well as money, and mixed them with an entrepreneur they could invest in, it would be greater than just the entrepreneur raising money from his uncle Fred. This pool of knowledge, money, and time would add materially to the mix. Back in the '50s and '60s, this was a new idea. Entrepreneurial efforts in the past had been done by wealthy individuals who would invest in a start-up now and then. Doriot would pick the entrepreneur he wanted to back, invest the money, and go away. A year or two later, he'd hear whether it worked or not. So this was a new idea. And, yes, there was a missionary zeal about it—that's how Doriot got away with underpaying us all, because we believed were doing something for the greater good, making America a better place. And it was true—we were doing something. I had a lot of good times, and felt like I was making the contribution that the great man wanted me to make.

Optical Scanning Corp.: A Turning Point

There was one company that changed my mind about this, or made me at least change the way I did it for a living. We had at ARD a company called Optical Scanning Corporation, which was a '60s company that was involved in optical scanning technology. It was a troubled investment for ARD, and some of my colleagues had lost confidence in it. Doriot kept trying to force them to put more money into it. He didn't want to be responsible for writing the check—he wanted them to want him to write it. The way he responded was to get me involved with it. I was still pretty green. I went on the board of this company, and I was the one that he used to get the checks written over the next few years—I was responsible for putting a lot more money in this company and working very hard with it. Optical Scanning eventually went public and was a large success. ARD went from an exposed capital position of about $3 million to having a gain of over $20 million, which was a lot of money at that time. It went from being a burden to a big win in about three years. I had made a very substantial contribution to that company. The way I had done it was by getting along with the entrepreneur. The other guys didn't do that. He and I had a lot in common, and he had confidence in me, and I in him. We made it work together. The CEO's net worth went from zero to $10 million, and I got a $2,000 raise. I agonized a lot over that. I loved what I was doing, but I thought I should be somewhere where I was compensated adequately. And, so that was what eventually led to my leaving the firm and moving to Greylock.

From ARD to Greylock

My partner Bill Elfers had been in the business by that time for nineteen years, and I had been in it seven. I had a good reputation. I was thirty-five at the time, Elfers was in his middle to late forties, and we knew everybody that was in the business. We knew Peter Crisp's Rockefellers and we knew Bessemer and Peter Brooke, and the people out here on the West Coast. So although Greylock was a new name, we had a continuing flow of opportunities.

We've had a very good record over the years, but in the early years we weren't doing start-ups, so we didn't have the huge wins. We were investing a little further along the spectrum, and were seeking to make four or five times our money. One of our investor founders was the Watson family. They asked us not to invest in the computer industry. If somebody said that to you today, you'd laugh about it. But we were willing to accept it in 1965 and 1966.

The Watsons were IBM. They viewed it as a conflict for Greylock to invest in the computer industry and it may even have been a written IBM policy. They didn't make us sign anything, but they didn't want us to invest in the business. Thus, we weren't looking at deals in the computer industry in the late '60s. Many thought at the time that the computer industry was over—it had been done, and IBM controlled it. And there were a bunch of other little companies like SDS that became XDS, and DEC.

Prime Computer really changed us. Prime came to us through one of the investor directors, who was also the father of my son's girlfriend. I was invited to his home one night. I thought it was a social function, but they were actually raising money for Prime. I ended the night with no dinner but a favorable introduction to Prime and its chief technology officer Bill Poduska. In order to invest in that company, we had to form a special partnership that excluded the Watsons. We thought enough of the opportunity to do that.

We've since followed Poduska through his entrepreneurial career. We did Apollo Computer, and, unfortunately, Stardent. He's still a great friend, having made a lot of money for us with Prime and Apollo. We gave some of it back in Stardent, but we're still way ahead with J. William Poduska.

Growing Big

How has Greylock evolved? We've gone from a $5 million partnership that became $10 million, to what is most recently a $250 million partnership.

We've tried to maintain the culture of the firm as much as possible. We expect people to stay. When we bring an investor on board we expect them to stay. In bringing people into the firm we've been careful. We don't want a bright person whose culture is all wrong for us— someone who wants the toughest, harshest, sharpest deal he can pos-

sibly make, who's going to be a little too sharp. Even though in the short
term we might make a lot of money, we just don't hire those kinds of
people. We try to hire mannerly, personable people with a good education who honestly want to make a contribution to the companies
they're involved in and are not focused only on making money. Most
firms say they do the same but my experience is that many don't.
They'll hire the smartest people they can get, people who have a reputation for making money but are often devoid of people skills and the
ability to help entrepreneurs. I'd say this is a principal element of our
culture. And that leads you to a number of other places. For example,
we've never lost an investor. We've now raised nine partnerships, and
not one of the original investors or of the other investors we've added
along the way has ever dropped out. Where people have died, their
sons or daughters or trusts are writing the checks today. That's part of
the same culture and we're very proud of it. The last time we made a
major change in our investor format was in 1978, when Harvard University, in the person of Walter Cabot, came to us and asked to invest
in Greylock. Walter was a classmate of mine, and a close friend of Gregory's. He told us he had just taken over Harvard's money management
and wanted to try to get some push in it, and had decided that venture
capital might be a place to put some capital. At that time, universities,
with a few small exceptions, really weren't investing in venture capital.

Once Harvard expressed a serious interest in Greylock, MIT, which
had been exploring an interest in us for years, wanted to invest—as did
Duke and Dartmouth. From this time in the late 1970s on, 50 percent
of our new capital in each partnership has come from these universities, along with Stanford and Yale, who joined us later.

We have subsequently had to limit participation in new partnerships because the appetite of our present investors exceeds our need
for new capital.

Our Grand Slams

We've had one of those recently. A company called Ascend Communications, here in San Francisco. The Ascend investment was made
for Greylock by Roger Evans. Some years before, Evans was COO
and CEO of a very successful Greylock investment, Micom Systems.
I worked on that company for Greylock with Roger. We sold the com-

pany after much success and some trials for about $400 million. Roger, a Brit with a liberal arts degree from Cambridge, was rich, forty-two years old, and trying to figure out what to do next. We persuaded him to join Greylock. He sponsored Ascend and contributed enormously to its success in terms of getting the right people in the right slots and defining strategy. The company was recently sold to Lucent for about $23 billion. Greylock's share of that counts on our records at about $800 million because of time of distribution. At any rate, Ascend proved to be Greylock's largest win ever.

Carried Interest

Firms in our business have carried interests of 20 percent or 25 percent—some even have 30 percent. And there are all kinds of different formulas. Alternatively, I can write a check for as much money as I want to give to Ned Johnson at Fidelity Investments and he'll manage all the money that I give him for somewhere between 0.5 percent and 1.2 percent. Think about that. Why should an investor give Greylock, or Kleiner Perkins, or anybody else money and pay them 25 percent if I can get Ned to do the same thing for 1 percent?

The only reason for investors to tolerate high carried interests is to receive superior returns. In the past, venture capital operators providing value-added services have shown, on average, higher returns than mutual funds or other investment vehicles. Recently, however, S&P average returns have been very high, placing pressure on venture firms to provide still higher returns. One of my concerns for the venture industry is that as capital pools get larger there is some tendency to provide less value added and over time I believe this will reduce returns. Not many people believe S&P or other similar yardsticks will continue to show such high returns. Nonetheless, the venture industry needs to remember that its investors are there for the returns. They also need to recognize that my friend Ned Johnson is always there to manage money for 1 percent.

Reprise

Would I personally do a venture capital partnership again at this time? If I were twenty years younger, I would. I wouldn't do it at my age largely because it is a young person's business. I would get together two or three other people, and I would raise about $100 million. I wouldn't want more, because I think $100 million is about the right size today to create the best returns. It is easiest to work with three or four guys. Working with eight or ten is more of a management burden. For example, my partner Henry McCance has to be a manager now. Henry loves deals. He loves to be on boards. And he hasn't stopped doing that. But he principally has to manage the firm. Everybody has an opinion. Someone must decide what we need to do now. Otherwise you have eight or ten guys running around doing deals on their own, with little coordination and no benefit to being together and having a culture and a management structure.

I think the venture business is still a good business. There is still an opportunity for experienced, motivated people to help entrepreneurs create wealth. There are probably, at this point in time, too many people in the business and there's too much money available to allow ideal venture returns, but adequate returns are still available. Young people are paid too much at the front end. They don't have the incentive to work hard enough to create the successes that will make them money when they become partners. Additionally, firms are pressured to make associates partners sooner than is ideal. There's also the problem that the business is much more competitive. That's good overall, but less attractive for each individual firm.

There's another factor. There are other classes of competitors—the Ciscos and the Intels—which are motivated somewhat differently than the Greylocks and the Sutter Hills. They are able to put $50 million into a company at extraordinary valuations if it has potential importance to their mainline business. That's very tough for us to compete with. You find that the prices make no sense. We lose often to this class of competition.

Today there is a significant advantage to having specialist experience in one or more of the areas in which venture capitalists concentrate. In the past, the investment spectrum was much broader and we generalists perhaps had an advantage. But today, if your firm doesn't possess software experience and talent, you should probably stay away from this lucrative area because the best and the brightest are already there.

RICHARD M. BURNES, JR.

Charles River Ventures

The history of venture capital on the East Coast is indelibly tied to the history of Small Business Investment Companies (SBICs), which were created by law in 1958 as part of an effort by the government to promote financing for small businesses. But in practice, SBICs turned out to be private investment companies that received leveraged capital from the Small Business Administration.

Many of the early venture capital firms started out as SBICs and developed their own identity, independent of the early, restrictive SBIC guidelines. Unfortunately, many East Coast venture capital firms that began as SBICs failed to make the transition to full-fledged independent venture capital activity. One investor who began within an SBIC but was able to make the leap into mainstream venture capital is Richard Burnes. Burnes began Charles River Ventures as an East Coast venture capital firm that would work closely with the Massachusetts Institute of Technology to commercialize new technology and new research. His success is as much a tribute to his ability to be a patient investor as it is to his ability to apply rigorous investment standards to early-stage technology companies.

Burnes has been at the center of Charles River's evolution from simply running with the pack to becoming a leader, and has played a large part in the firm's transition from a diversified capital provider to one that is focused on communications and information technology. His account mirrors those of other East Coast firms that struggled to find an identity after the first wave of venture capital had passed.

I N 1965, two years out of Harvard with a degree in history, I was assigned to Federal Street Capital Corp, a federally licensed SBIC, as part of Shawmut Bank's credit training program. Many banks set up or invested in SBICs at the time because it was the only legal way banks could make equity investments. During the 1960s, SBICs were actively making venture investments, and many of the early venture firms, such as Golder Thoma and Welsh, Carson, Anderson & Stowe, had their roots in the SBIC program. I joined Federal Street as its third employee, and we made $50,000 to $250,000 investments in a variety of businesses, ranging from a guard service to an electronics components manufacturer.

It quickly became apparent that investing in small companies was more interesting than working up the ladder at Shawmut Bank, and I convinced the chairman of Federal Street to hire me full time. I also realized that the emerging technical companies were the most profitable and interesting to work with. The financial orientation of Federal Street made it difficult to convince the directors to back new concepts or outstanding people with weak financial statements. We did, however, make an investment in Computervision and the board approved an investment in MCI New England. Bill McGowen had convinced Fidelity's venture arm to back the local MCI subsidiary and they were looking for investors to join them. McGowen was a terrific start-up CEO. I also recommended an investment in an early round of Jesse Aweida's Storage Technology, but the directors said it was too far away. I spent nearly five years at Federal Street, during which time I earned an M.B.A. at night from Boston University.

Launching Charles River

Jack Carter developed the concept for Charles River in 1969 while working as a special assistant to James Killian, the president of MIT. Jack was an aerospace engineer, a founder of Itek, and was interested in emerging technical companies. Peter Brooke, of TA Associates and Advent International, suggested to Jack that he contact me. Jack's original idea was to start a VC firm inside MIT utilizing the institute's resources, but the lawyers vetoed it. Instead we set up Charles River Ventures independently, with five MIT professors as limited partners and advisors. I felt that we needed marketing skills to be successful and found Jack Neises, the third founding partner, who had a wealth of sales and marketing experience at Xerox.

Jack Carter was a Stanford graduate, and while he was setting up Charles River, he was also working with Tommy Davis and Wally Davis, a friend from college, to set up a similar fund at Stanford, which became the Mayfield Fund. In the first Charles River and Mayfield partnerships all the partners—limited, general, and advisory—signed a pledge to return 15 percent of the capital gains to the respective universities. Also, the two venture funds each had an equity interest in the other to encourage working together. The advisors turned out to be very nice people who were useful in raising capital, but as with many professors their knowledge was deep but not very broad. If you happened to ask them about something they knew they were extremely helpful, but we seldom called on them and the concept was dropped in our second partnership.

We started Charles River to do something different. Financial people coming from SBICs, banks, family offices, or Wall Street dominated most of the venture capital activity in the '60s. Most of them did not have any operating experience with a business or with the emerging markets. The two major firms in Boston, American Research and Development and Boston Capital, were typical in that they had capable people, but no background in industry. We felt that people with operating experience would be better able to understand the issues facing entrepreneurs in growing companies and we used that concept to raise our fund. We had to sell the idea of venture capital, which most financial decision makers did not understand. In the '70s, as firms such as Kleiner Perkins were formed, the concept of operational expertise became well accepted.

The Start-Up Portfolio

Our first fund of $4.5 million was invested in a curious variety of what we thought were technical growth companies. At first, we were dilettantes grazing through the field of opportunity, picking the morsels we wanted. Investments ranged from a company producing components for the auto industry to two investments in innovative methods of pig farming. We ran into early losses from dumb investments, and overall, Charles River Partnership I was only a modest success. Fortunately, we made several investments in the emerging electronics industry which bailed out the fund. A later-round investment in Storage Technology and a Mayfield Fund–originated microwave communications company by the name of Avantek were our best investments.

CRP I showed enough promise to allow us to raise our second fund of $7.5 million in 1977. At the same time we convinced Pat Lyles, a Harvard Business School assistant professor and a friend of mine, to join us. He made a terrific difference in the rigor of the firm and really helped to launch us into the growth company world. He established many of the thought patterns that drive the firm today. Unfortunately, he died in 1983 at age forty-four, leaving a major hole in the firm.

Venture Capital—An Exclusive Club

In the '70s, there were only thirty to forty serious venture capital firms in the country. We all knew what the other firms were doing and it was not difficult to get into investments. We were all afraid of running out of our precious capital and relied on each other for support. It was even possible to get into successful companies like Apple Computer on the last private round. We declined to invest in Apple because we thought the microcomputer business was going to be dominated by big existing companies like Texas Instruments. We made a number of successful investments in the late '70s such as Applicon, and when the IPO market cycled back up in the early '80s we did very well, returning over six times the capital in CRP II.

The concept of developing a coherent investment strategy for the firm started to evolve in the late '70s. There was a debate as to whether we should focus on specific industries and market segments, developing real expertise, or remain opportunistic. The debate went on through the '80s and was really a battle for the soul of the firm. The diversity of the portfolio at that time reflected our indecision. The debate was not finally resolved in favor of specialization until 1989, when we raised CRP VI. We looked carefully at where we had made our money, and realized we should focus on early-stage information processing and communications companies.

Another shift in our strategy was taking leadership positions rather than joining syndicates put together by other venture capital firms. Large syndicates are hard to manage, give conflicting advice to management, and frequently lack adequate leadership. It was not until CRP V and CRP VI that we took lead positions seriously. When venture capital was a gentleman's club, it was easy to throw another $250,000 into a new round and expect your co-investors to do the work. One of my partners was excellent at finding his way into projects, but that mode of operation is not possible today.

Diversifying the Portfolio

An early CRP III investment was in the first round of Amgen. We were trying to figure out if the biotech industry was worthy of focus and we went to an investor presentation George Rathman made in Boston. He was most impressive, with excellent credentials and contacts, and we invested $300,000 without really understanding what it was all about. The company went public a year later, giving us more than double our money, and we decided to sell our stake—a terrible mistake in hindsight, given the performance of Amgen as a public stock. Later in the 1980s, we decided not to continue investing in biotech companies, recognizing our lack of expertise.

In the early '80s, I began to specialize in telecommunications. The first investment was Summa Four, a New Hampshire company working on microprocessor-controlled telephone switches. We had four different presidents and every problem imaginable—from drugs to deregulation—but Summa was ultimately successful, had an IPO, and recently was sold to Cisco. Summa holds the record in our portfolio—we were in it for thirteen years—but it produced an annual ROI of over 21 percent for the firm. Summa had excellent technology, but never could get their marketing function working properly.

Four other successful communications investments followed: Bytex, Xyplex, Chipcom, and Cascade, all of which had IPOs. We originally bought 75 percent of Chipcom for $250,000 and the business plan actually evolved in our offices. Right after we made the investment, our partner Pat Lyles died, and to reduce the workload several of my partners tried to back out of our commitment to Chip-com. I argued that it was not fair to the people who had left their jobs to join the company. Ultimately, the company was sold to 3Com for nearly $1 billion.

Cascade was the first investment that returned over $100 million to the firm. Several members of the founding team at Cascade had been at Bytex and thoroughly understood the emerging carrier-switch market. The carriers were beginning to rebuild their networks to handle data, creating a large market that Cascade came to dominate. It was one of the few companies where nearly everything unfolded as planned.

Milestones

One of the companies that helped establish the firm as an early-stage tech investor was Parametric Technology. Our general partner, Don Feddersen, had previously been CEO of Applicon, a successful CAD/CAM system vendor. Parametric came along with a revolutionary CAD/CAM package, and Don had the knowledge to back it. Parametric grew to dominate their market and at one point was worth over $10 billion.

In the early '90s, it became apparent that we needed more strength in the telecommunications area. We were successful in hiring Mike Zak, who has a deep background in the markets, technology, and people of the telecommunications industry. With his help, the communications area drove the firm's results in the '90s. Cascade was first, and then we had a major gain from CIENA, the leading optical transmission company.

The strength we had in telecommunications was not matched in software, and in 1996 we brought in Ted Dintersmith to remedy the imbalance. He has done a terrific job leading us into the Internet services and e-commerce fields, where we have been active and successful investors.

Changing Times

In the early years of the firm, capital was the scarce resource, but as capital has become readily available we've realized that our main resource we are allocating is time. Unfortunately, time is hard to leverage. We have done it by substantially increasing the size of each investment. We have been careful to continue to serve the same market segment: start-up, technically oriented growth companies. We are able to put more money into each company by limiting the number of co-investors and investing at each stage of a company's growth— from start-up to the pre-public round. Using this strategy, we have cut down the number of portfolio companies while increasing the size of each partnership.

As the '90s end, our firm has seven professionals, six of whom are engineers and have held significant operating positions. In late 1999, we closed CRP X, raising $500 million. We could have raised more, but we are cautious as to how firms like ours scale. We are growing, but slowly—we still have only one office. In recent years, we have focused primarily on start-up companies, taking lead positions. The operating orientation of the firm is a key component of our culture. We are a firm that supports entrepreneurs. We devote considerable time to working closely with our portfolio companies. The depth of knowledge our investment staff possesses—particularly concerning the nature of the emerging markets and the capable executives in them—has been a key to our success. This strategy has led several of our recent partnerships to be among the top-performing funds in the country.

PETER BROOKE
Advent International

The maturity of the venture capital industry is illustrated by the manner in which generational change has taken place and the way the industry has broadened its scope geographically. Peter Brooke exemplifies both the generational change and the geographical expansion.

Brooke was the founder of TA Associates and responsible for making it one of the preeminent venture funds on the East Coast. He also was one of the first American venture capitalists to attempt to export venture capital en masse. But what Brooke considered to be pioneering and entrepreneurially groundbreaking, many at TA considered a diversion of hard-earned institutional capital. In 1985 Brooke broke off from TA to start Advent, exclusively for investing in global venture capital.

The "experiment" has more than proved its validity. Advent today manages more than $4 billion in total assets in twenty-four countries, and the Advent model has been widely imitated by a large number of U.S. funds that now recognize the value of being an "international" venture capital fund.

Brooke may be one of the few venture capitalists to have studied venture capital as a global entity and to have understood its strengths and limitations. His prescription for Asia, where U.S. investment banks and investors have been both the catalysts to change and a cause of the trouble, is a remarkable insight into Asian business and U.S. aspirations in the region.

WHEN I GOT out of the Army in 1956, I joined the First National Bank of Boston as a trainee, and gradually worked into a position in the credit department where I was doing two things: making very advanced loans for a very famous dealmaker by the name of Serge Semenenko, a household name in financial circles at that time, and making loans to technology businesses that were bursting out of MIT and Harvard as a response to the the Sputnik challenge.

It seemed obvious to me that the business of the bank should be to finance the only valuable raw material we had in the region—namely brains. I felt that the bank shouldn't go around the country syndicating credits for General Motors and other national companies—it should concentrate on the core strength of the region in which it operated. The way to develop that business was to organize a lending program that would make small amounts of loan capital available to MIT and Harvard spin-offs and help build their businesses.

So very early on, I was lending small amounts of money to small companies, helping them attract equity capital, and helping them make management decisions. I was very much involved with some of these small start-ups—not simply as a lender, but also as an advisor. This was in 1958, 1959, and 1960. In effect, I was a venture capitalist using the bank's capital, and that was how I got my start. All of these companies were technology-based, and were responding to the technical challenges of their day.

At that time the federal government was contracting with small undercapitalized companies. They were front-end loading the contracts, providing the progress payments. For instance, a professor could leave with his prized doctoral student and begin an instrumentation company with a modest amount of his own capital—say $10,000—and manage a $250,000 contract for the federal government because the government would virtually prepay that contract. The first installment came before the work was even started. With very little capital, these companies were able to get into business. And there was essentially no risk because the contracting officer would accept almost any proposal as long as it pushed the science forward. So even though the lending appeared very risky, in effect it wasn't risky at all.

In working with these companies, I got very close to those who were providing equity capital at that time: American Research and Development and the wealthy families in New York such as the Rockefellers, the Phippses, and the Whitneys. I would lend money to a company, and if I thought it was particularly attractive and making good progress, and the loans were exceeding reasonable limits, I would take those companies to one of the family venture capital providers in New York see if they'd like to invest. That's how I came in contact with Bessemer Securities, the holding company of the Phipps family, in 1961. During that same year I went down to reorganize and run their venture capital operation in New York. I continued to do the same type of investing as in Boston, but with equity capital, not loan capital.

There was a good deal of altruism in what the Phippses, the Rockefellers, and the Whitneys did initially. They wanted to prove that advancing technology and making money were not mutually exclusive. So they started to make investments in the '50s, without knowing whether they would work or not, or what the exit would be. It wasn't until the over-the-counter market became somewhat more active in the late '50s and the early '60s that the investments were able to be taken public. There wasn't an expectation that they would make a lot of money in this field. Their first stabs proved successful, so they simply put one foot after another and did more of that kind of investing. Only in the early '60s, when Digital Equipment went public,[1] did the venture capital industry really take off. At that time, the New York families dominated the business—there was no real West Coast presence. Draper, Gaither & Anderson (a partnership formed on the West Coast around 1960), ARD, and the families—that was the ball game. The first real venture capital partnership in the current model wasn't formed until 1965, and that was Greylock here in Boston. That was followed rapidly by others on the West Coast, and TA Associates, which was formed in 1967.

I never moved from Boston to New York. I commuted on a weekly basis between August of '61 and January of '63. I was always about to move my family but I never could bring myself to do it. I was too confirmed a New Englander. So I quit Bessemer in January of '63. It was sad in a way because I had reorganized the firm—made it a much more hard-hitting effort—and the successes were beginning to show. The companies that I had invested in were going public and things were on the upswing. It was a job that I really knew how to do. So when I gave the job up, it was for lifestyle and family reasons rather than for professional ones. Back in Boston, Ogden Phipps, the chairman of Bessemer, and Jack Kingsley, Bessemer's president, gave me a contract to follow investments in the Northeast, which was a wonderful calling card for me.

---

[1] *DEC was a big winner for ARD and one of the most successful venture investments of its time.*

Beginning TA

I took that contract and approached three investment banking firms in Boston—Paine Webber, Hayden Stone, and Tucker Anthony and RL Day—asking if they would have an interest in starting a venture capital management company, a company that would first start putting together venture capital deals to sell to their clients, and then eventually raise capital for a venture capital fund. They all were interested. I selected Tucker Anthony and RL Day because they wanted to do it but didn't know who to do it with, and wouldn't interfere with the way I wanted to do it. The other two firms had an idea of how it should be done, but they didn't know anything about the business. We formed a company called Tucker Anthony & Co., Inc., that was jointly owned by the partners of Tucker Anthony and RL Day and myself.

We started that firm and put together deals that were quite successful. I began with a modest amount of capital, and at the end of a couple of years, the Internal Revenue Service came to me and said, you know, you're accumulating too much capital in this corporation and you have to pass it out as a dividend. That would have been prohibitive.[2] So we liquidated the company, took the residue after the partners paid their taxes, and then invested the remainder in Advent I, the first partnership managed by TA Associates. In 1967, Advent I was formed with capital from the partners of Tucker Anthony and RL Day and some of their wealthier clients. We organized a very small partnership, only $6 million. We made small investments, $50,000, $100,000, and $150,000 in size. And that was the beginning of TA Associates.

In 1972 we followed with Advent II, a $10 million partnership. Advent III began in 1978 with $15 million in capital. Advent IV followed in 1980 with $65 million in capital. And Advent V was formed in 1982, I believe, with $165 million. At that time it was one of the biggest funds. When we completed Advent IV, with $65 million in capital, we became self-supporting. You see, in the period from 1967 until 1980, when Advent IV began, I hardly had enough revenue to keep the team together. There was hardly enough revenue from a $6 million fund, a $10 million fund, and a $15 million fund to pay the six

---

[2] Because the firm was reinvesting its profits, passing the profits out as dividends would have cut off its source of capital.

young partners we had. In terms of people, it was a large partnership; in terms of revenue, it was a small one. So I had to do all sorts of consulting to keep the team together. And I was the only one who could do that since I was the only one with the name and the experience. The others were fifteen years younger than I. At that time Kevin Landry was a twenty-eight-year-old kid.

Not only did I consult for firms like DuPont (which had an interest in venture capital), Xerox, and International Nickel Company, but at the same time I started to investigate whether I could replicate our model in Europe. This was in 1972, and it pushed the envelope pretty early in the game. But I was fascinated with economic development. I had always thought of venture capital as the ultimate economic development tool, both for this country and for other countries that were underserved with capital. I felt that special programs could be designed to help these countries capitalize on what their people did best. I thought this could be done on a regional basis within the United States as well as on an international basis.

In 1972, when the Ministry of Industry in France wanted to investigate the forces that created venture capital around Route 128, they hired Arthur D. Little Inc. to do a study of what made these burgeoning technology-based companies successful. Part of the study was to look at the role venture capital played. They asked if I would write an appendix to that report describing the venture capital experience and the role that it had played in capitalizing these new ventures. In the course of writing the report I met the Deputy Minister of the Ministry of Industry, Christian Marbach. I convinced him that venture capital had been vital to the success of these companies and it could do the same in France. Marbach was a very innovative person. He returned to Paris and with the backing of Credit Nationale, the long-term lending institution in France, convinced the government to give tax incentives to individuals and institutions that invested capital in a new venture capital fund.

Taking Venture Capital to Europe

The venture capital fund Sofinnova was successfully launched in 1973. I became a founding director of Sofinnova. TA Associates became an investor and we put a young man in Paris to be the advisor to the company. I traveled to Paris five times a year, and spent a week of each visit with the companies Sofinnova had invested in, helping them to develop their business. Sofinnova, along with a few corporate clients, gave me the opportunity to travel throughout Europe to see if people would be interested in venture capital. I must say it was tough sledding because of the socialist environment. Economic growth was stagnant. There was no initiative. However, I developed some very good contacts, and when the Thatcher revolution occurred, we were in position to move rapidly to replicate the TA Associates model in various places in Europe, starting in the United Kingdom in 1981. That was our first foreign affiliate. Sofinnova was not an affiliate. We had an interest in Sofinnova by virtue of our investment. And I of course was an advisor and a director. But the first affiliate, Advent Ltd., was formed in Great Britain in 1981.

The affiliate was a management company owned one-third by TA Associates, one-third by David Cooksey, who was one of my partners, and one-third by another individual, Mike Moran, who was a partner of David's. We decreased our ownership position over time to encourage other people to join the management team. From England, we moved rapidly to Belgium in 1982, to Germany in 1984, to France in 1985, to Scandinavia (Sweden and Norway) in 1985, to Austria in 1986 and 1987, and to Italy and Spain in 1988. This was a very ambitious schedule. At that time that I was working on developing Europe and also expanding to Asia. We formed our first and only fund in Japan in 1982, and one in Southeast Asia in 1983. Until 1985, all these affiliates were owned in part by TA Associates.

Domestic versus International

I found myself in the 1980s trying to manage TA Associates, a domestic venture capital company, and trying to organize an international venture capital network at the same time. I determined in 1981 that I really wanted to concentrate on the international aspect and made two of my partners senior partners.

It became obvious in '83 and '84 that I had more of an interest in globalizing TA Associates than did my partners. I remember at the end of one year after we had raised a lot of money and the income was high that my partners said, "Well, how much money are you going to take out of our pockets and spend on advancing the company in Europe and Asia?" And I said, "Well, probably $1 million." There was a deathly silence. I knew then and there that if I was going to build a global company, I had to do it outside the profit-and-loss statement of the partnership; it had to be done in a separate company that was self-financing. That's when I arranged for the capitalization of Advent International and negotiated with my partners the transferal of the international program from TA Associates into Advent International.

When Advent International started in 1985, it inherited all of the affiliated programs that had been the property of TA Associates. With these programs and capital raised from European clients, Advent International was in a position to keep pushing forward.

The investors in Advent were families in Europe for whom I had made a lot of money. One was a very wealthy French family by the name of Bemberg that would have provided all the money we needed because of our successful investment performances in the past. There were two other investors—Sofina in Belgium, and Orange Nassau in The Netherlands. They put up the capital to allow me to follow my dream of making a global company.

Breaking off from TA

To this day, I'm very sad that we couldn't have kept the whole thing together as TA Associates. We had a powerful organization, not just in venture capital, but also in investing in the media and real estate sectors and in the international side. The year that we all went our separate ways, the real estate team, the media team, the venture capital team, and the international team raised $1 billion in total us for our various enterprises. So even way back in 1985, we were a very powerful company. And if it could have stayed together, it would have been the most powerful company in the world. Not that Advent International hasn't risen to a high level, but it would have just gotten there faster.

I wanted to build an institution, and frankly, the money was irrelevant. I wanted to build an institution that used venture capital as a national and international development tool, working with different cultures and different people to improve the way they managed their affairs. That was the underlying thesis: to have people in various parts of the world manage their human and raw material assets more effectively with the provision of capital and management assistance. If a company's competitive advantage was in raw material, we could help them manage their resources more effectively by capitalizing their companies more adequately, by working with them to develop export activities, and by managing their affairs better. That was my desire. I wanted to see if it could be done abroad the way it was in the United States. I thought it would be useful from both a financial and a societal standpoint.

A Formal Global Fund

What I set out to do was not to start an investment organization all over again, but to be an advisor to our affiliates abroad in running their investment programs, and to help them and their portfolio companies in technology transfer between Europe and the United States and between the United States and Asia. It wasn't until 1987, that some of my old investors came to me and said, "You know, you've got this fantastic network of people around the world who are making private equity investments, venture capital investments. Why don't we set up a fund that will co-invest with them? One that will capture those deals that your affiliates are syndicating to others." So in 1987 we started the first fund managed by Advent International, the International Network Fund (INF). The INF downloaded one third of its capital to its affiliates and network members, and co-invested the remaining two thirds with them in situations where Advent could add value.

Advent was represented on each investment committee of each affiliate and had the right of veto on any deal that was put forward. But that did not give us the quality control that we needed. What we really needed was U.S.-style due diligence. We were not getting the return on the International Network Fund that I wanted. So in 1990, we established our first office in London to coordinate our affiliates and to build a direct investment organization. I sent Doug Brown over to run that office. He established and executed a strategy for us, opening offices in Milan and Frankfurt, and then in Paris this past year. Now we are a direct investment organization only. When we do a deal, we work on the analysis with our affiliate right from the beginning and we sign off with our own people. We don't depend on our affiliates for due diligence. Every deal we do we will show to an affiliate, and if it wants to join that deal, it is free to do so. Our affiliates are the recipients of deals from us rather than us being the recipient of deals from them. We concentrate on different types of investments—recapitalizations and acquisition financings. We do not make early-stage investments as do our affiliates. We are into both financial and managerial restructuring.

Investing in Europe

Our affiliates in Europe were inclined to do business the way merchant banks still do business in that part of the world. When they get a deal, they subcontract out the accounting work and the management and marketing studies to outside vendors, gather the data, do some analysis, and then decide whether they're going to do the deal. That's not the way we do our business. Our people dig into all of the data on their own. We spend a tremendous amount of time training our people how to do in-depth due diligence, how to do the appropriate kind of checks with suppliers and customers. We use outside sources but we conduct a lot of market surveys ourselves. We do a tremendous amount of background checking on the management team. This is a method that was not known in Europe when we opened our first office. It's getting to be better known now. But still, on occasion the analysis of an affiliate is quite casual. I found myself, while on their investment committees, saying at the eleventh hour that I didn't want to do a deal. It created a lot of angst between myself and the affiliate analysts. So to get around that problem, if a deal comes through an affiliate, we now go to work on that deal together with our affiliate right from the beginning. We use a team approach. What has come out of this approach is much better analysis and much better performance.

Europe versus the United States?

Some venture capitalists in this country take pride in the belief that ours is the only culture in which venture capital can succeed. This is inaccurate. The institutional structures in Europe have impeded the development of entrepreneurship. But if those structures are changed in a way that will allow people to express themselves, they will. We don't have the corner on entrepreneurial drive or desire. I think that Europeans have suffered from a socialist culture over a period of time, but entrepreneurs have surfaced in virtually every country that we've operated in. Given enough encouragement, capital, and freedom, they will prosper.

Doing business across Europe is still difficult. Although you do have a common market, a prospective common currency, and common standards, you still do not have the type of homogeneous market we have in the United States. European consumers are still biased against products from other European countries in their home market. And there will always be some degree of protection for locally produced products. It is going to take a long time for Europe to be a common market the way we think of the United States as a common market. And so we still have to think of Europe as a series of smaller markets. The United States is the largest homogeneous market, the one that everyone always wants to invade if they have a particular piece of technology or product that they think they can sell. But getting goods from there to here is a challenge for any rapidly growing small company. It's always going to be a challenge.

Another challenge is an active market for the common stocks of emerging companies. There is a lot of talk about the new markets in Europe. There is movement in that direction but they have a long way to go. When we have exited an European company through an IPO it has usually been through a listing on the Nasdaq. The first company that we made a lot of money on in Europe was Scandinavian Broadcasting System, a group of television stations in Denmark, Sweden, and Norway. Our exit was through Nasdaq. We've exited a Polish cable company through Nasdaq. Nasdaq is still the route to liquidity for a lot of our European holdings. We recently had a successful offering on the Milan exchange, but that was an exception to the rule. If we have a company with all the attributes that would be attractive to U.S. securities buyers, Nasdaq is the place we'll go. It will take a long time for the European market to catch up.

Mergers and Buyouts as Exits

Two-thirds of our exits have been to trade buyers, and I don't think that will change. We've always made strategic investments in areas that have been attractive to others, whether they be a buyer of a public security or an acquiring company. But buyouts have always been a staple exit for our companies. The largest investment we've made was in the privatization of an East German company that manufactured railway cars. We sold that out to Bombardier for fifteen times cost, for cash, earlier this year. And that's the way historically we've exited our investments.

We will gradually move toward the globalization of the public equity markets. You will find that individual and institutional buyers in the United States are interested in buying securities of foreign countries that are in new and exciting areas. However, there is a hiatus in that interest now as investors recover from the recent turbulence in emerging markets. A lot of people have been hurt by recent sell-offs and by their exposure to emerging markets. When people are hurt, they don't make the distinction between international emerging markets and international established markets, or between developed and developing markets. They cast them all in the same mold. They're all hit with the same criticism.

Repairing Emerging Markets

Emerging market stock funds have done more to hurt emerging countries, and more to hurt investors, than any other asset class I can think of. I preach this constantly. Emerging market managers at Morgan Stanley or Goldman Sachs don't understand the depths of the management problems in Malaysia, Thailand, or wherever they invest. We do because we deal with them on a daily basis. We sit on the boards of these companies. We know about the lack of talent when we invest. We know what we have to add in terms of managerial support to make these companies successful. An emerging market manager has no concept of the challenges. The people who have been attracted to those markets, I think, have been ill-served.

The Morgan Stanleys and the Goldman Sachses have devastated some of these countries. They gave them the wrong idea about what was real. They were told, "Mr. Tiger from Thailand, you are something special, something that defies the law of gravity. So here's all this money." And the Thais said, "Okay, we'll go ahead and build plants, hotels, and so on." Then all of a sudden, it's not such a good story anymore. The money leaves and the Thais are left with an underutilized capacity that will take them years to work off.

The future of Asia will remain uncertain until the Japanese riddle is solved because Japan has historically been the economic engine and the supplier of capital to Southeast Asia. The Japanese will eventually be back to simply protect what they have already built. So eventually, when they complete the restructuring of their financial institutions, they will be back as a major supplier of capital to the region. Until that happens, I can't see that there's going to be any major recovery. Certainly U.S. institutions are not going to move in until they see some evidence of recovery. The only U.S. capital we can count on is from strategic investors, corporate investors, and multinationals that are looking to buy assets at a depressed price. Their investment will occur over a period of time. So eventually there will be a recovery, but it will be a long, long workout.

Up until now, the capital provided has been expansion capital. The capital we are employing or will employ now will be reorganization capital. It has to be, since there is contraction, not expansion. We will be investing capital to reorganize companies that have a good future but are hopelessly overleveraged or overcommitted.

Take the example of a feed mill company in Thailand, a fully integrated agri-industry and agriculture business. The group's core activities play a key role in every stage of production from seed supply to feed production to processing. More recently, the group diversified into international trade, the automotive industry, retailing, pharmaceuticals, real estate, and telecommunications. Now these peripheral activities have to be chopped off and sold. We're not going to invest in those activities. We're going to invest in the core business. And the price of investing in the core business is getting rid of anything that is non-core and focusing on what has been the company's strength over the years. Virtually every group was inundated with capital and said, "Well, gee. Why don't we try this? Why don't we try that?" And they expanded into areas where they had no knowledge. So the entrepreneur, if he accepts our capital, has to agree to de-leverage by selling non-core assets. We tell the owner that he's got to sell the stuff that's not relevant and concentrate on what is relevant.

In another case, we're putting up a fair amount of capital to enable a well-managed Hong Kong trading company to buy a very good distribution company in Southeast Asia. And the job there is to once again get rid of the stuff that doesn't make sense, cut out the related layers of overhead, and concentrate on introducing a different distribution structure.

A very formidable management team thoroughly trained in Western management techniques is executing this strategy. Without a strong management team I would not invest in any company in Asia. Complicating the situation in Asia is the fact that most companies are family owned. Many times the Chinese family is unwilling to give management control to professionals, relying on family members to run businesses that are becoming increasingly complex. In many instances the family members are not equipped to handle such a job.

The family unit can be seen as a limiting factor in the growth of a Chinese business. And not just Chinese businesses in Asia. There are examples here in the United States. My favorite example is Wang Laboratories. I was a director of Wang from the beginning and participated in its growth and its demise—a demise caused by the fact that the founding father wanted the business managed by his family. He did not attract or give authority to those who were more competent. That underlying risk exists in every company in which you invest in Asia. You have to be very careful. Getting back to the Hong Kong trading company, we are pleased with the investment because the company is professionally run and because we have structured the investment intelligently. We have crafted our investment vehicle such that it gives us a threshold return plus an upside potential that's significant—not unlimited, but significant. And we have assets to back up our position. In playing that game in Asia, we can't just put the money in the way we would in the United States. We have to invest it in a way that will give us protection and ensure our exit at a price that gives us the return our investors deserve. We are in a position to do that effectively now. This is why it's a great time for us, because there is no other capital available. The banks are out of the business. They have fired all of their people in the region, and won't be around for awhile. They're licking their wounds. And so if someone has equity money they can fill the gap—and if they're smart enough, they can start getting the terms they need to offset the risk they're running.

So I look at Asia—and I'm including Japan here—as one massive workout over a two- to four-year period. What we see as recovery is illusory. The underlying institutional problems have not been addressed. The necessary restructuring has not occurred.

KEVIN LANDRY
TA Associates

Peter Brooke founded TA Associates, but it was Kevin Landry, joining as a junior partner in 1967, who molded the venture capital firm into its present shape—a giant fund that specializes in providing late-stage financing to both technology and non-technology companies. The question for TA Associates, and other firms that thrive on big pools of capital, isn't simply whether they can continue to invest large sums of money in entrepreneurial projects, but how long they can continue to call themselves venture capitalists as opposed to a specialized mutual fund that invests in private and publicly owned companies. Some skeptics question whether such firms are capable of producing venture capital returns with LBO-style investing; still others consider TA more of a hybrid investment bank that provides private equity financing rather than a venture capital firm involved in financing entrepreneurially run companies.

Today TA Associates is one of the biggest of many such venture capital/private equity funds. TA, like most others, started investing in early-stage businesses, but as the money came in and the venture capital business became more established, it gravitated toward late-stage investments in companies that already had products and revenues. Some, such as BMC Software, have proven to be highly successful. Others, including Copley Pharmaceutical, a Massachusetts generic drugmaker, proved financially successful but developed giant business problems. TA even became active in buyouts of companies such as the mutual fund manager Keystone Group.

Landry explains why venture capital funds such as TA have migrated away from early-stage investments, and addresses what the future holds for such endeavors and whether they can compete with the large leveraged buyout funds such as those managed by Thomas H. Lee Company and

Kohlberg Kravis Roberts & Co. Landry maintains that there is a niche market for providing large sums of capital to a broad range of mature privately owned companies.

I INTERVIEWED WITH Peter Brooke in the spring of '67 for a summer job, and I can remember he said he was in the venture capital business. I said, "Oh, that's a great business," because I knew that was the right response, but I didn't have a clue what it was. Later that day I was interviewing with a large corporation. I really wanted to work for the large corporation, but when Peter offered me a job, I said to myself, "I've got this job, I don't have the other one. I'd better take it. I need a job." That's how I got started in the summer of '67. I was still in business school at Wharton. Peter asked me to stay, because that was when he was first putting together a fund. I declined and told him I would come back after I finished graduate school. I felt I needed to finish, because a job is something you do for three years, and then you change and do something else. That's what I thought. And, of course I came back and I've been here ever since.

I was making $10,500, plus a $500 bonus, in 1967. Most deals were from $300,000 to $500,000. We would put in $100,000 out of our fund and raise the rest of the money. When you have to raise money and charge another firm a fee, it brings a certain discipline to the process. You can't do something only because you've got a hunch it might work. You have to document it, which means you do probably a little more due diligence, and you are a little more thorough. That's how we operated throughout the '70s.

In the beginning we were a balanced fund. We were doing some start-ups, some intermediate-stage companies, and a lot of late-stage, profitable companies. That mix later shifted in the '80s to investing 60 percent of our funds in profitable companies. Around 1989, we looked at our data and realized we had always made more money investing in profitable companies than in early-stage companies. In any three-year period, profitable-stage investments always outperformed start-ups by a wide margin. So we decided to do only profitable-stage investments.

That strength may have developed because we were good at finding our own investments, so we could find good profitable companies we could invest in at attractive prices. You can always get profitable companies. Our companies were less dependent upon the capital markets, which ran in cycles through the '60s, '70s, and '80s, where sometimes you couldn't raise money for your companies. They were always ready to go public when the proverbial window opened. Well, it's been open since '78. It was a good strategy up until then, with less risk. The value added was in picking a good industry, finding a great management team, and getting into those companies at attractive prices. If you could do that part, the rest was fairly easy.

Chasing Deals

Since the beginning we've always been chasing management teams and entrepreneurs. I think the venture and private equity community only looked that way in the mid-'90s, when things got competitive. We have always chased them. But then when you think about what we're doing, we're investing in profitable companies.

Our target companies don't need capital. If you want to invest in the best companies in the country, by definition they don't need capital. We sell money to people who don't need it. That's a much tougher job than what a venture capitalist does. He sells money to people who do need it. We've always been more focused on selling ourselves, and on being proactive in finding our own investments.

Maybe we didn't do a good job in start-ups. Maybe we didn't have the right vision—the ability and the patience to distinguish between those we should stick with and those we should shut down. We just shut them all down. But we were doing something very right at the other end of the spectrum with profitable companies. We were finding them—not only Silicon Valley, but in all parts of the country—and we were specializing in industries and convincing entrepreneurs to bring us in as a desirable partner and at an attractive price.

Investing in Mature Technology Companies

Technology companies all want to go public. That's what they all associate success with. Usually they are broad-based ownerships and not family businesses. Everyone wants to get liquidity. The entrepreneur and management team may know a lot about their technology and a lot about their marketplace, but they don't know anything about the public markets. They want someone on their team who's going to help them go public—someone who's motivated by one thing, getting that stock price up. We try to explain to them that getting the stock price up is just one of the things we'll help them do. We'll help them go public. We'll help them get to the next level. And in the meantime, we'll give them some cash. Another thing that we were doing in the '70s and '80s that no one else was doing was putting money into entrepreneurs' pockets. We were buying stock from selling share-holders and, more often than not, from the CEO. No one else was doing that then. They all do it now. Curiously again, when you look at our data, you'll find that we had a much higher rate of return on investments where there was a secondary aspect to it—where we were buying out selling shareholders—than on investments where we were putting money into companies. Counterintuitive, but true. So, we invested in profitable companies. The less risk we took, the greater the rate of return. When we bought out selling shareholders our returns were better than when we weren't buying.

Our typical entrepreneur never had any money so didn't really take any risk. If you didn't start with any capital, you didn't have any to lose. You started with your wits. If you're in the software business, you probably got a couple of contracts. You had to make money from month one, because you had no capital. Suddenly, you have a valu-able business. Now you are taking a risk.

People want to take some of that risk off the table, and we let them do just that. When you first talk to people, they never admit they want to take it off the table. I think they're afraid they'll spook you if they say they're interested in selling. You just tell them, "We'll put $5 mil-lion, $10 million, or $20 million into the company. And if you want to sell some, we'll buy another $5 or $10 million." Sort of sheepishly they say, "Maybe we will." The closer you get to the closing, the more they start to come out of the woodwork.

Evolution

TA got bigger in '72. It started with $6 million, and then went to $10 million. Then in '75 $50 million was raised in the whole industry. It wasn't even clear at that point that we had an industry. No one believed in us in terms of giving us capital. At that point, Peter took the initiative and started going to Europe and developing European sources of capital. It was a big effort, but we developed some European sources of capital.

We raised another fund in '78, just before ERISA changed. By that point, we were moving from raising money from individual investors to institutional investors. Between the '78 fund and the '80 fund, we completed the transition. We didn't lose all the individuals, but their dollars didn't matter. Our '78 fund was $15 million, and then we had done some other $15 million funds offshore. By 1980, our fund was $60 million.

In 1983 we raised a $160 million fund, and then some more offshore. We grew tremendously from '78 to '83, certainly more than others in the industry.

We also began to diversify into a couple of different areas. Along with our investments in technology and traditional venture capital, we started an SBIC in '75 that expanded our investments in the media communications area, including cable, radio, and television. In the early '80s, Peter started to focus more on the international side of things, affiliating with groups internationally. At that point, we started an internal real estate group called TA Realty. All of these things were sort of bubbling along in the early '80s within TA, along with our rapid growth as a venture group.

Breaking Up

Eventually all those pieces went off in their own directions. Advent International went its separate way in the mid-'80s. Why did it do that? Peter had a vision, and it was a long-term vision. It was just something he wanted to do. Peter was less interested in making money than I am. I've always been amazed that people would give me capital to manage. I came from a family that didn't have capital. For someone to trust their capital to me is an incredible compliment and an incredible responsibility, which I've accepted. I just love making people money. I get a kick out of succeeding that way. Peter marched to a different drummer—he had a vision, and he wanted to see it succeed.

My team looked at that in the mid-'80s and said, "We've got a lot of money to manage here. We've got our hands full with lots of

responsibilities and opportunities. We don't believe in that dream."
We were correct for the next five to ten years. We were correct in the
short term. Peter was correct in the long term. So, Peter couldn't get
us to work on it. He had to develop his own team of people that was
dedicated to the international effort, and have his own organization.
Meanwhile, we had the venture group and the media group, with different personalities. We tried to motivate people by giving them more
ownership. If you're in the venture group, you're going to own more
of the venture fund. If you're in the media group, you're going to own
more of the media fund. It seemed to be a good way, but it was also
a divisive way, and people started forming their own groups.

The media group broke off in '86. They formed Media Communication Partners. We got a little piece of it, and then we went our separate ways. Advent International and the real estate group also went
their separate ways. We kept some ownership temporarily in the over-
rides, but basically they were on their own. At that point—in 1986—
TA was a "venture" fund, although we were predominantly investing
in profitable companies and in larger companies. We were only doing
a few start-ups through Bob Daley and Steve Gall. The rest of us were
moving on to larger deals. If you look back at our brochures, you'll see
that sometime in the mid-'80s we changed our description to private
equity capital. I don't think anyone else had used that designation,
but we wanted to design our material to appeal to those companies
that were profitable and didn't need money. We figured it was much
easier to sell down market—if we wanted to be a venture capital firm,
all we had to do was say we were one. We were always moving up, trying to work on larger companies and larger investments.

In the late '80s, we looked at all our data and said, start-ups don't
pay off for us. We make more money investing in profitable companies. And, we asked ourselves, Where are we spending our time? We
are in the free consulting business, that's the business we're in. We're
in the business of helping the weak and the lame survive. At that
point we had ninety companies in our portfolio. We did thirty-three
private financings that year. Raising capital privately for thirty-three
companies takes an enormous amount of time. With profitable companies, you don't have to do that. You go to quarterly board meetings.
I don't mean to say it's all easy, but in general there are fewer crises,
you have more time to invest, and the results are better. And we were

better at it. We then shifted entirely to investing in profitable-stage companies, shrinking our portfolio from ninety to sixty. In the last few years, we have raised money privately for only two or three of our companies—not thirty-three.

Focusing on Financial Services

Our most successful deal ever was Invescap. It was a leveraged recapitalization done by Andy McLane in 1993, in the financial services business. We already were a major player in the financial services industry. I started that move with Keith Stone.

Why did we like the financial services industry? Well, it was obvious. We were in the financial services business ourselves. During the recession, you saw every other business worrying about how to make payroll. We didn't have that worry. We asked ourselves, What businesses do we like? We didn't like manufacturing companies. This was when every manufacturer was moving to Asia. We didn't want to compete there. We liked brain businesses, and in that respect, software and financial services are the same. They're both dependent upon a few highly skilled people. That's what we had been doing in the software business—investing in businesses where the assets drive home every night, and if you treat them right they come back the next day. We wanted brain-power businesses. We wanted renewable revenue businesses, where you have a customer who stays with you day after day, year after year. We wanted businesses that had high profit margins. In the money management business, if you get an incremental dollar of revenue, it's probably ninety cents of profit. That's 20 to 50 percent pretax anyway. And we wanted businesses that had good underlying growth. In the money management business, business grows from having your assets grow with performance, and having your assets grow from gathering more assets.

In 1989, all the banks and insurance companies going out of business had to sell their nonstrategic assets at very attractive prices. You could grow them over a five-year period. By then, the banks and insurance companies would be healthy again and would want to buy them back at a higher multiple. It was pretty simple. That's how we started. We began with Keystone, and then moved on from there. Andy took over that effort, and in '93 he did AIM, which was our largest investment at the time. We put in $33 million. It was a great thing, because it happened as one set of funds was winding down and the other was starting up, so we could put it in two generations of domestic and international funds. It was a recapitalization where we bought out the stake of the selling institution, and bought some stock from management, shrinking the capitalization. So management took money out. They actually owned a higher percent of the equity after we came in. We put in a total of $35 million of equity, and then borrowed $120 million. The business grew, and we got a multiple play. All those wonderful things that are supposed to happen, happened. Sixteen months ago it merged with Invesco of Great Britain, formerly called Invescap. We started getting free of our stock in May of 1998. We got cash in part when we sold it. It was 26 percent cash, 74 percent stock. It will be twenty-five times the money. So, we used the B-word—Billion—for the first time on that one. That was certainly the biggest and best winner.

We've had other winners: Tandem, the disk drive company was 77 times the money. Emulex in the late '70s and early '80s, was 60 times, Biogen was 65 times, and we've had some other bigger multiples, but the combination of big dollars and a big multiples—that's Invesco.

TA Today

Today we are a private equity firm competing in profitable-stage technology venture deals from $10 million on up. We are not doing anything in the early stage. We're doing recapitalizations. Recap means we end up with a minority position, using some modest leverage.

We work with certain senior lenders in the high-yield market and with other firms, because it's a competitive environment and you end up splitting a lot of deals. We're also doing modest-size LBOs. We would like to become known as a specialist in technology LBOs. We've done a few of those, and they've been quite successful.

We did Diamond Networks in 1997, Fargo in 1998, and Trident in 1995. These were all profitable technology companies that we bought, and leveraged up modestly. The venture guys know the technology, but they don't know the debt market. The LBO guys know the debt market probably better than we do, but they don't understand technology. They don't want to combine financial risk with technological risk. It is dangerous, and you have to do it in moderate doses. Some of the deals we've done have been relatively short product life-cycle companies. So you have to make sure that you have a very strong current product, and you can see the next product cycle coming along. Then you hopefully take them public early, so that you can get the leverage reduced, and at least get the leverage risk out of it early in the game.

Ultratech Stepper was a buyout from General Signal of a piece of semiconducting capital equipment. It had turned the corner and made a little money the year before. You could see they were at the right place in the semiconductor capital equipment cycle. We invested—I don't remember how much. I think the Bank of Boston was the senior lender. Took it public a year later, and it just continued to grow. I think we made twelve to one on that. We bought at the right point in the cycle, at an attractive price. The company itself had turned around and was profitable. We could see it had a nice backlog. And then, as it ramped up, we could get it public a year later. We could get the back debt paid off and then get our capital return. From then on we're working in profits. The deal ended up having more upside than we thought.

Our Competitive Advantage

I think I probably came at venture capital with a bit more ambition than normal, and all my partners are pretty competitive. So we wanted to grow more than other people. We have the skill set—the judgment that you need in our business—combined with a lot of ambition and a vision of where we wanted to go. We wanted to be larger. We wanted to manage more money. You can't do that holding the hands of the start-up guys. So we moved into the profitable-stage area. Once you're there, it's a logical step to move into the leveraged area. We've continued our migration. In some sense you need it just to stay fresh, and to stay interested.

I stopped going on boards in the mid-'80s. At the same time I stopped spending the majority of my time doing deals and started spending more time helping other people here at the firm with their deals. In the '80s and early '90s, some of that was troubleshooting—trying to work our way out of bad deals, and trying to figure out if we should finance them, sell them, or just shut them down. In the '90s, we just haven't had many problems, so I haven't had to do that as much. We've expanded the firm, and so I help to raise the money. I work on virtually every deal we do, but in a small way. As you get into leveraged buyouts, the deals become more complex. You have to work with banks, and it takes a huge effort to get them closed. So I'm involved in a couple of meetings at the front end, when we're trying to decide if we should do it, and when we're trying to sell ourselves to the management team. And I drop out of the picture after that.

WILLIAM EGAN
Burr Egan Deleage

 *Like many of the venture capitalists on the East Coast, Bill Egan began at TA Associates and then eventually set off on his own. In 1979, together with Craig Burr and Jean Deleage on the West Coast, he set up one of the first bi-coastal venture capital operations, Burr Egan Deleage. Today, the firm manages over $700 million in assets, focusing on a few selected business areas such as computer technology and the life sciences. Still a firm of generalists, it copes with specialization by building rela-*
tionships with smaller, more focused venture capital firms.

Egan is part of the old guard, which recognized the need for two things: independence and specialization. A generalist himself, Egan nevertheless realized that the industry had become too sophisticated and complex to keep investing on the basis of contacts and networks. Without the ability to understand technology and provide some level of technological assistance to entrepreneurs, the value of the firm would erode. To answer this need, he set about hiring new associates and creating relationships that would position the firm for the new era.

In this interview, Egan describes the evolution of venture capital on the East Coast—from SBIC roots to generalized venture capital to specialization—and offers a lesson that firms have had to learn in order to maintain their position in a highly competitive market.

I CAN REMEMBER going to one of my kids' school events in 1970 and being asked, "What do you do?" I said, "I am with a venture capital group." And someone said, "Well, what's that?" I tried to explain to them that we invested in companies, and the woman looked at me and said, "Oh, you're a stockbroker."

I said, "No." But I couldn't explain it. I got so tired of trying to explain what venture capital was—this was the early '70s—that I would just say I was in the investment business. My wife used to say it sounded like I was a Mafia guy or something, because the term was so amorphous.

I knew the venture business had absolutely come to a whole new level when I went to one of my kids' college events. Someone asked, "What do you do?" I said, "I'm in the venture capital business." And the woman just nodded and said, "Oh, my cousin does that." It was like being a consultant. Everybody was in the business. Even if they weren't in the venture capital business before, they were now. The whole business has changed.

Starting at a Small Business Investment Company

I started as the gofer for Arthur F. F. Snyder, the executive vice president of the New England Merchant's Bank. He was the guy who made all the loans in the late '60s and early '70s. He had the responsibility for technology loans on Boston's Route 128, which then was America's technology highway. Arthur Snyder was a great guy. He was an engaging guy, but as I have told many people, being his gofer was like being an ashtray in a no-smoking restaurant. You were present but useless. After about three or four months, he let me go into the workout loan department of the bank. And I did workout loans. I actually restructured a couple of companies for stock—I guess this was 1970—and ended up going to run the bank's Small Business Investment Company.

The Small Business Investment Company was a great investment vehicle at the time, because there wasn't a lot of capital around. It was basically a way to leverage capital with the help of the government, and in a format that makes sense to me, where private capital was being risked to get some government capital. Almost by definition, when you had an SBIC, you had to have a more broad-based approach. You couldn't just make early-stage investments because you had to pay the interest on your debt. So, we'd invest in some later-stage, more developed companies that could pay a coupon, and then we'd make some early-stage investments. Then I went to TA Associates after I had actually brought them a couple of early-stage deals and they had invested in them. Peter Brooke asked me to come over.

In the early '70s, I would say venture capital was an opportunistic business. We did everything from early-stage to very late-stage investing across a range of sectors. Under the roof of TA Associates, we did everything from disk drives to Federal Express and Levi's jeans stores, because there was a small universe of money and not many players.

Our approach to the business wasn't a grand strategy. It was to see interesting companies. Interesting being defined as, Are there some decent managers with relevant experience that you can back? Are they in a market that's growing like hell? Because high-growth markets will cover up all sorts of sins. I mean, never confuse a great market with a good manager. And, then, can we find either a product or service that has either a technological unfair advantage or a license for some sort of legal unfair advantage? This is why I always loved the media business—radio, TV, and all that stuff—because you have an unfair advantage. If you're there at the right time, then the rest of it's money.

I've seen more companies fail because we were too early than because we were too late. We invested the money before the world really needed the product. So to me, the wonderful part of the venture business is that, as we've evolved, we now have huge amounts of capital, and a lot more people talent in the firms than before. We've absolutely evolved from a time when we were clearly not money managers to where many of the firms are money managers. But the base activity hasn't changed all that much. You follow four steps: You get a good management team, in a high-growth market, with a product with good gross margins, and if the time is right, you'll make money. It's not that complicated.

Breaking Away

At TA I was a user of capital. I had nothing to do with raising it. In 1979, a guy who I had done some work for, David Hile, said to me and Craig Burr, "You guys ought to go out and raise your own fund. I'll tell you what, we'll put up some money to let you do it, so at least when you come in town, you won't think you're out of work. You'll have a paycheck."

Maybe I'm an entrepreneur in that sense. To me, I wanted to bake the whole cake—to get the experience of raising the capital and of investing it. This is a business that lends itself to trying to put your own imprint on what you've done.

I often tell people, if your goal is just to make money, be an entrepreneur. If your goal is to meet a hugely diverse group of interesting people *and* make plenty of money, become a venture capitalist. This is the best business in the world. It's like owning a sports team. I meet hundreds of entrepreneurs annually, most of whom we don't end up financing. Yet, most of them are far more interesting than the heads of major companies I've met. That's why young people want to be in the business. It's a no-brainer. I don't care how successful you are at investment banking, you're still in a service business. When the client calls, you jump. How high depends on how big the client is. The reason I love this business is that I actually like to see my kids play sports. When you write the check, you get to set the time of the meeting. It's a lifestyle thing. You get to be able to say, I'd just as soon meet with you Thursday afternoon at two. Now, when we go out to raise a fund, I'm in reverse mode. If the guy at CalPERS[1] says he can see me Tuesday at three, that's when I see him. But, it's a wonderful sort of business, because you meet incredibly bright people who clearly believe they've got the answers that will change the world in their sector. They're probably wrong 98 percent of the time.

One of my early deals at Burr Egan Deleage was a company called National Demographics, which was then called The Lifestyle Selector. It was a very interesting little company that had developed a database, or was developing a database, for list rental that was psychographically driven, not demographically driven. It was an interesting company, because when you talked to their potential customers, you'd realize that the customers needed them but didn't realize it. In other words, you would talk to someone who was going to create a new sports magazine, a tennis magazine, and they would want a list of people they should mail this offer to. They would normally create the list using demographics such as age and income. What National Demographics did was provide a list of people who were interested in tennis. The information was developed from warranty card data given when a consumer bought some hard goods. National Demographics would give the hard goods manufacturer (G.E. Appliance Division,

---

[1] *The California Public Employees Retirement System.*

for example) a profile of their customers' interests. But, for doing that, National Demographics would get to keep the data as part of a larger database for their own use. Today, they're owned by R. L. Polk.

That's the kind of stuff I get a kick out of, because it was a little tiny company that started out with five people. I don't know how many employees they have now, certainly hundreds. Same thing with Tandon.[2] When Jugi started Tandon, there were four people—Jugi, Jerry Lembus, and two others—in about 6,000 square feet at Chatsworth. Seven years later, he had literally thousands of employees in the United States and Singapore.

Early Venture Capital

In the beginning venture capital was definitely a collegial business. It was what I would call a sound business in the early days from the standpoint that there was collusion, in the best sense. If there was a little deal that took $2 or $3 million, we might put a half a million up and Mort Collins's group might put a half a million. The entrepreneur would say, "Gee, for $3 million dollars we want to give away 20 percent of the company." But, I'd call Mort or someone else, and we'd say, "Gee, $2 million for 20 percent, that's a little high. We were thinking more like $2 million to buy 35 percent of the company." So clearly, collusion went on. But it was constructive because we financed companies on the basis of leaving slack in the rope before the entrepreneur hung himself. Because you didn't really believe the projections. You knew they weren't going to work. We got into a period in the '80s where you competed for deals so much that you were almost forced to buy into deals at prices you knew were only good if the entrepreneurs made their forecast, which you knew they couldn't make. So, you were almost setting up the entrepreneurs to get their heads cut off. It's actually interesting. In telcom today—because it requires so much capital—we've moved to some degree a little more back to this collegial, or collusive, style.

We have a rule here that we don't do second rounds unless we can get a co-investor with us. Because we're not the only people in the

---

[2] Tandon is a peripherals company of the early 1980s.

world who know everything. I think the West Coast is insanely competitive. We've picked a sector where, frankly, there just aren't as many players, so we don't face that kind of competition. Years ago you would see three of four venture firms working together. What you tend to see now is a venture firm with maybe one or two limited partners who have a venture activity investing with them. But that venture firm, or buyout firm, is really making the calls. They're not necessarily getting as many of the other guys to come in.

Venture Capital's Competitive Advantage

In the '70s, deals came from the local banks or the attorneys and the accounting firms. You didn't see well-prepared or slick business plans. One of the major changes you see now is that we do very few deals that come from some kind of private placement. There's a lot of that business out there. Our theory, and I think it's right, is that if you've got an investment banker working on a private placement, you've probably taken much of the market imperfection out of the pricing. The reason I've always contended the venture business is a great business to make money in, versus the public market, is that it's an imperfect market. In some degree, we as venture capitalists are in the enviable position of being both the buyer of a security and the market maker of that security.

I told someone jokingly one day, "Listen, if the venture business ends up over the Internet, getting a bid-and-ask auction going for financing new companies, you will have ended the venture capital business as we know it."

That's why lots of firms are becoming more and more specialized. By specializing, they understand a sector far, far better, and what that allows them to do is to react more quickly. So, the time value. We get radio, TV, or cable deals where they could send it to six different venture firms. But we can give them a legitimate answer in a week. I'm not saying we can do all our homework, but we can tell them if we're interested or not. Now, we may want sixty days to do due diligence, but we can say, "That's a deal we want to do. We'll sign a letter with you, subject to due diligence. If this checks out, if everything you're telling us is right, we'll do it." Well, if you've never seen a radio station before, it will take you a while to understand it. When I first got into the business, we'd spend a month to six weeks just learning about a sector when a deal came in—learning the terminology and so on. Well, you can't do that today. One of the advantages of specialization is that people are committing more quickly to deals. If they know the sector, they ought to be able to commit more quickly. Right?

Continental Cablevision: Our Best Deal

My biggest success has been Continental Cablevision. One of the two guys who started Continental, Irv Grossbeck, now teaches at Stanford Business School. He's been voted by the students as one of the best teachers there. He didn't start off as a great teacher—he taught himself how to be better. Amos Hostetter, who was with the company through the end, and Irv, who left earlier, were just extraordinarily capable people, and hired extraordinarily capable people.

Hostetter worked for an SBIC in Cambridge. One of the first deals he looked at—he may have still been attending Harvard Business School—was a little cable deal in New Hampshire. "This is an unbelievable business," he said. So, he said to Irv, who was a teaching assistant at the time, "We should get into this business." They went off to Tiffin and Fostoria, Ohio, two little towns, bought their cable franchises, and built them. The interesting thing is they were classic entrepreneurs. They did the early-stage stuff on their own, and they just kept growing the business. When I made an investment they already had around 25,000 customers.

The fundamentals of the business were so good. It's a business where you have good people. You have an unfair advantage. You have the license for the community. And you're sitting in Ohio where you can get maybe two conventional TV channels without this cable system. Give them cable at that time, and you might be able to give them twelve channels, because there's no satellite or anything. But, most importantly, one of those channels might give you the Ohio State football games on Saturday, which I'm told is the closest thing to sex you can have in Ohio. As a financial person you could understand the opportunity very easily. You build the system, and you hook the homes up. It was almost that easy.

A Love Affair with Venture Capital

I love this business. I'll make investments until I die. I love making investments. My father actually ran a laundry business. The thing I love about the venture business is that I've never had any desire to run a business. Some people in this business view going in and taking over troubled companies as a badge of courage of some kind. I want to back the best people I can back, and put the best people on the floor. If I never have to play a minute in a game, that'll be the greatest. Because I love trying to help people build their business.

There are lots of people who were great players, and they could never coach. There are some people who were pretty good players, and they can really coach. I think there are lots of entrepreneurs who, once they were successful, said they were going to be venture capitalists. Many of them don't do very well at it, because it's a very different skill set. To be in the venture business, you have to be able to compartmentalize. You have to be able to go from a meeting where you've got a fabulously successful company—things are going great and you're trying to figure out how to take them to the next level, which usually involves a tweak of a better person here or there—to the next meeting, where you've got some disaster, and you've got to figure out, Am I going to let it go? Am I going to stay with it? And then on to the next meeting, which is a new deal you're looking at, which is clearly better than the disaster and may even be the best deal that you've ever done.

New Deals

We have a company down in Atlanta, a shared tenant services company called Cypress. It's run by a couple of young guys. We put the seed money up to get it started, did a first round, and we're just now closing a new round. We put up, with Centennial, three quarters of a million dollars. Then together we put up about $7 million. And now we're closing on $15 million.

The shared tenant services sector is very interesting. You go into a building, and then you offer a range of aggregated services—local, long-distance, cable, and Internet—to smaller tenants who wouldn't have information services or an information technology officer who would do these kinds of things. The former vice chairman of Continental, Tim Neher, met one of the founders in Atlanta who told him what he was going to do. Neher said, "You ought to call this guy Bill Egan in Boston. This could be an interesting business to him." When the guy called me and told me what was going on, I said, "I don't think so." Twelve years ago I looked at the shared tenant services business, and it wasn't interesting at all. The reason it wasn't interesting was that you needed to put a million-dollar switch into the building. And at that time, for all the happy horseshit, the only thing you had to sell was long-distance. You couldn't give them a local-access alternative. You couldn't give them Internet access—we didn't even know the Internet existed. You basically had a very expensive piece of equipment that at the end of the day you couldn't provide much with.

These guys came up to see me. They sat down, and we went through their proposal. And, all of a sudden we realize that in these buildings you can have the capability to provide PBX, local access, long-distance, voice mail, and Internet and cable television access for maybe a $50,000 investment. And all of a sudden you say, wait a second. I'm certainly not a technologist, but from a revenue-per-unit basis, you might be able to get $125 to $130 a seat. We have buildings now around the country where we have maybe 12 to 14 percent penetration of a building and we have an operating, positive cash flow on the building. That's an enormously attractive business.

There's a real opportunity, if you can get in that position, where you're the interface with that customer, and you become the person who's helping to solve problems for them, and you're going to help them make decisions. For example, if six months from now the long-distance deal they have with, say, AT&T, can be done a lot better with MCI WorldCom, we'll make sure they get that.

Diversity

Jon Flint and I have been trying to figure out how to organize this business going forward. I always loved the original model we had at Burr Egan, in which we concentrated on three areas: medical, namely, biomedical and device technology; IT, which is information technology software; and media communications. In any given fund, one of these sectors was a laggard, one of them was very good, and the other was pretty good. In fact, in our third fund IT was so bad that a number of our limited partners said, "You shouldn't be in that business anymore. You guys do so well in media and medical, just give up on IT. Just don't do it. It's too competitive. There's too much going on." Well, of course we listened to our own thoughts instead of theirs. And, in our fourth fund, IT was the blockbuster. We had Premisys and Powersoft in there—two companies into which we put $2 to $4 million investments, and on each of which we made close to a $100 million. That's a sector we could have been out of. But I loved the model. And, interestingly, when we split into three entities, I personally put money in all three entities. I wanted a presence in all of those areas.

A sector fund, in a good market, will absolutely outperform a balanced fund. But it will also underperform a balanced fund in the wrong period of time. I think we've got enough people in the venture industry, providers of capital, who have figured out how to allocate. For instance, when I say to our limited partners, "I don't think this area will be as good as it has been the last five years," they know I'm really saying, "Our sector may not be as good, but I think we will do better than average in our sector."

It's hard for me to believe that this is going to continue to be as good a business as it has been. When I tell my limited partners, I don't think we'll do as well in the next five years, they think that's a very strange sales pitch. But I'm not making a sales pitch. I'm simply responding to the question of how we'll do. I'm giving an honest answer, which I hope is wrong. We'll work as hard as possible to prove it wrong. But, with all the capital, with all the resources, we are moving back closer to a commodity. Money is fungible. If you ask me, in today's environment, I'd rather be an entrepreneur than a venture capitalist.

STEVE ARNOLD, JONATHAN FLINT, AND TERRANCE McGUIRE
Polaris Venture Partners

Expect venture capital to look a lot different in the years ahead. To be sure, there'll be more venture capitalists, more competition, and more scrutiny; the need for differentiation will never be greater. Venture funds, especially those that are newly formed, will have to establish an identity for themselves that goes beyond that of other capital providers.

Newly formed funds such as Benchmark and Polaris have been among the first to quickly articulate a position for themselves and set about establishing it. Polaris, with partners based on the East and the West Coasts, and with a wealth of experienced investors and entrepreneurs, has positioned itself as a fund with a nationwide reach and a philosophy that brings together the best of the two coasts—the financial discipline of the East with the technological adventurousness of the West. And like Accel, another small fund that now is acclaimed as one of the "hot funds," Polaris has created a network of successful entrepreneurs and industry experts who can provide a quick read on changing technology and business strategies.

Since its founding in 1996, Polaris has shown that small funds can also deliver significant financial returns, especially if they are willing to be creative in their investment style. Polaris's early successes—Classifieds2000, Allaire, Exchange.com—have come from investments in ventures and entrepre-

neurs that others had neglected or ignored. But perhaps its—and the industry's—most remarkable success came at the end of 1999, when Akamai Technologies, an Internet technology firm that allows for rapid transmission of Web data, went public. The $8 million investment Polaris made in April was worth over $2 billion by the end of the year.

Polaris partners Arnold, Flint, and McGuire aren't newcomers to venture capital or to entrepreneurship. They've all served apprenticeships at other funds and in other contexts. But their backgrounds and their reasons for starting their own fund serve as clear reminders that venture capital is just as exciting today as it has been in the past, and that the industry continues to attract a remarkable mix of backgrounds and practitioners.

McGUIRE: I got the bug to be a venture capitalist in a very unique way. When I left college in 1978, I was fortunate enough to win a Thomas Watson Fellowship, which gave me the chance to live in a different culture before pursuing a career. The fellowship provided year-long support to live on the west coast of County Donegal, Ireland, an area where Irish Gaelic was—and still is—the first language.

Donegal's remoteness and relative poverty is both a curse and a blessing. The Irish language still lives because the English and the Anglo-Irish never made a serious attempt to colonize Donegal's beautiful, yet infertile land. To illustrate how removed it is, back in 1969 many of the locals doubted that men had actually landed on the moon because the lunar terrain they saw on TV so closely resembled the landscape where they lived.

I found myself in a place known as the Donegal Gaeltacht—so designated by the Irish government because it is one of the few areas where the indigenous language survives. My project was to learn to speak Gaelic and study the one or two remaining Seanachie, or elderly storytellers, who were the last surviving link to Ireland's great oral tradition.

Donegal's remoteness preserved the native tongue, but also compelled its young people to leave in search of employment. For more than 100 years, many of the young men and women left to find work in Dublin, Glasgow, or New York. When they left, they carried with them the energy and sense of purpose every community needs to remain vibrant. When Donegalmen returned to the Gaeltacht, they often had every intention of raising their children to speak Gaelic in order to help preserve native traditions. But their children often preferred to speak the English they learned in Great Britain or the United States. Their need to find work had the unintended effect of eroding their cultural traditions. Obviously, jobs were needed to keep people in the Gaeltacht in the first place.

But not just any kind of jobs—the best opportunities would be those that could harness Donegal's unique culture and history. I left the Gaeltacht convinced that the way to save this island of Irish tradition was to work in the area of new ventures, that I might one day return to help put in place the very infrastructure needed to create a sustainable and thriving economy. I returned to the United States and to Dartmouth College and pursued a degree in engineering. Following Dartmouth, I became the first employee of a start-up software company. My academic and experiential journey led me to the Harvard Business School, where I discovered this great field known as venture capital—and, I thought, Donegal's solution.

My smattering of Gaelic didn't fail me when the time came to find my first job in venture capital. At that time, entry-level positions in venture capital were just as scarce as they are today. Fortunately, I had been elected president of the HBS Venture Capital Club, which opened a few doors. However, even my combined engineering and M.B.A. degrees didn't guarantee a slot. My lucky break came during an interview with Golder Thoma & Cressey, a Chicago venture capital partnership and one of the few venture firms recruiting on campus.

My initial interview was conducted by Jon von Schlegell, an associate with the firm who would soon become a partner. The interview was going well, if not spectacularly, when Jon blurted out, "An bfhuil se fluic, amach?" This is Gaelic for "Is it very wet outside?" I responded, "Ta, ta se fluic angus fuar amach—it is wet and cold outside." Jon, too, had studied Irish one summer in Dublin. We hit it off. He went on to champion my candidacy and subsequent job offer from GTC. So off to Chicago I went.

Eventually, I returned to Boston and for seven years worked with Burr Egan Deleage. During my last year with the firm, several partners left to found venture capital funds of their own. We, too, decided to take the entrepreneurial plunge.

Launching our own venture firm gave us an opportunity to use the advice we had given to many of our clients. We had to convince investors to share our vision of what Polaris Venture Partners could become. We've taken substantial risks to ensure the success of our company. If I didn't have compassion for entrepreneurs before starting on this adventure, I certainly have it now.

I'm fortunate—I work with great partners and we share a common vision of our firm's mission and purpose. An essential component of that mission—the belief that supporting the entrepreneur is one of the keys to a successful venture—was vital to our founding in 1996, and has proved to be esssential to the great success and sense of achievement we are experiencing now.

FLINT: I was a litigator with Testa Hurwitz & Thibeault, the major venture capital law firm on the East Coast. It was there that I came to know about the venture business, which seemed much more interesting and attractive to me than being a lawyer!

My background is pretty eclectic. I worked in the film industry briefly, and was involved with several well-known projects. I was also an investigator and researcher for the Watergate Special Prosecution Force's impeachment inquiry staff, which was an arm of the House Judiciary Committee.

Watergate was the best and worst thing ever to happen to me. On the positive side, I had a tremendously educational experience working with some truly exceptional people on the impeachment inquiry staff. Bill Weld, who later became governor of Massachusetts, was a staff member, as was Hillary Rodham Clinton. I learned a lot about the need for intellectual rigor, how to investigate and evaluate, and how to make appropriate judgments about people. At the same time, my time on the Watergate staff was also detrimental because it was difficult to discover anything else in my career that could replicate that level of excitement and interest.

After my time with the Watergate Committee, I went to work for a Wall Street law firm, where I became involved with the IBM antitrust litigation. This was my first exposure to computers, software, and the related technology issues.

I was one of the many young lawyers working on the IBM case. My first assignment was to prepare the direct examination of Digital Equipment Corporation as a witness for IBM. IBM sent us to

Armonk, New York, for a month, where we were taught the basics of technology and capital markets. Ironically, the preparation for this case led me to my present career, because DEC was backed by General Doriot, founder of the legendary venture firm American Research and Development. I fell in love with the idea of creating and championing new companies.

While at Testa Hurwitz, I had discovered that I liked creating business solutions, instead of litigating business problems. For two years, I continued to practice law as I attempted to enter the venture business. Bill Egan and I had worked together on one deal. Finally, I went to him and said: "Look, I can do this. I'm willing to take a huge risk and I'll work for nothing." Here was an offer he could not refuse. For three or four months I worked for Bill, free of charge.

Honestly, I would be very skeptical about hiring a lawyer for the venture business. However, I wasn't a typical lawyer. Really, I wasn't! I view myself as eclectic and entrepreneurial. I wanted to use the experience investigating people, products, and markets that I had gained from my work as an attorney and as a member of the House Judiciary staff. Part of my strength has been my good fortune to work with people of great ability and achievement. In addition to working with Bill Weld and Hillary Clinton, I also had the opportunity to work with John Landis, the well-known director, on his first feature film. Through these experiences I became convinced that venture capital was about identifying great people with exceptional talent and putting good teams together. In our industry the most important capital is human capital. This philosophy certainly propels us at Polaris.

ARNOLD: I've been involved in the technology industry since 1982. My first job was at Atari during the period when it was the fastest-growing company in the world. Atari was moving so fast that I had a new job and a new boss every three months. I left Atari in the fall of 1983, after the company had crashed and was attempting to recover.

When I left Atari, I didn't expect to remain in the technology arena, but I was recruited by Lucasfilm Ltd. to run their games and entertainment group. The group began as a research and development project that collaborated with Atari to build games based on the kinds of creative impulses that George Lucas had in his movies and that Industrial Light and Magic demonstrated in their special effects. I ran Lucasfilm's games and entertainment group from 1984 to 1991.

We evolved into LucasArts Entertainment Company, which became one of the top three privately held software companies in this emerging industry.

In those days, we were developing software for PCs rather than the video game platform. We developed a number of very innovative products, including "Lucasfilm's Habitat," the first multi-player graphically animated online adventure game. The game was a joint venture between LucasArts Entertainment and Quantum Computer Services, the forerunner to AOL.

I left Lucasfilm in 1991, when Bill Gates recruited me to run his private company, Continuum Productions, now known as Corbis. Continuum's mission was to figure out how to build what we called at the time "navigable information systems." The goal was to make a broad array of images and information—and eventually sound—available to users as an integrated and easy-to-use database. My first focused encounter with the venture industry came during this time, when Jon Flint, then at Burr Egan Deleage, asked me to consider becoming CEO of one of his portfolio companies.

My conversations with Jon gave me an understanding of vision and the goals of his company. Even though I didn't take the position with Jon's portfolio company, I became intrigued by the workings of the venture capital industry, and the opportunity to help create the future—something we were doing at Continuum.

There were many similarities between venture capital and my work at Lucasfilm and Continuum. At each company we looked forward into new and emerging markets, trying to figure out where the interesting business opportunities would be. Then we worked to build a team of talented people, and then with that team we worked to build a business that addressed those markets. In conversation with Jon and his partners at Burr Egan Deleage, I could see how they were doing similar things with a range of companies, and I found that I really liked the notion of "inventing the future" across a portfolio of early-stage, leading-edge companies.

Around this time I went to work at Microsoft as vice president of broadband applications. While my work with Microsoft was very rewarding, I found myself still drawn to this idea of creating new ventures. I had enjoyed a number of opportunities to be a pioneer in new technologies and new markets; yet, I still wanted to build something of my own. To me, that was a greater challenge than improving the performance of an already successful company. So, I left Microsoft and joined Jon at Burr Egan Deleage as a special advisor. When we formed Polaris, I finally completed the transition from running emerging software companies to venture capital.

The Genesis of Polaris

ARNOLD: My friendship with Jon and Terry grew during my time with Burr Egan Deleage. We talked about the flood of opportunities in the information technology and medical sectors, and how great it would be if we could create a small team of entrepreneurs that could harness these opportunities. We all realized that it would be extraordinarily satisfying to build and champion companies, work with creative, passionate people, and invent devices and processes that change the way people live. Each of us had experienced this somewhat through our work. But the thought of uniting all of these goals under a new company was inspiring to all three of us.

FLINT: We started Polaris because the venture capital business is a great business. We had a lot of fun and success at Burr Egan Deleage. Terry, Steve, and I thought we could create even more opportunity and satisfaction by doing the same thing ourselves.

We wanted to do what Bill Egan, Craig Burr, and Jean Deleage accomplished when they spun Burr Egan Deleage out from TA Associates in the 1970s. Like most entrepreneurs, we wanted our own sandbox. We wanted to have the fun of creating our own brand, finding our own office space, and growing our own organization.

We believed that our approach to the business was unique. We observed that medical technology and information technology were converging. We predicted that platform shifts with the Internet would create a bonanza of opportunities for entrepreneurs who had innovative ideas—and who would need capital to make their ideas a reality. We thought our backgrounds would be highly beneficial in this environment.

Each of us was a generalist, without deep technological knowledge. Terry and I had been investors for more than twelve years. We had invested in medical, service, and pharmaceutical companies. We had invested on the IT side, in media, and in broadcasting. We felt our breadth of understanding and diversity of experi-

ence in these markets would prove helpful when investing in portfolio companies.

McGuire: As a venture capitalist, you live in an entrepreneurial
environment. We, too, became infected with the need to create.
Founding Polaris empowered each of us to build a firm that embodies our philosophy, goals, and passion.

I took great comfort in the fact that we had a core partnership. Jon
and I had worked together for many years, and together we had had
the chance to work with Steve for three years. When I helped create
Polaris I wasn't simply an individual walking out to start a new and
untested fund. I was part of a group that had been successful and
would continue to be successful.

Arnold: We never questioned whether Polaris was the right thing
to do or whether or not we would be successful. Our question
was: What level of success would Polaris achieve? Market conditions
would greatly influence the level of success we would enjoy. But
we all agreed that the momentum to establish a partnership was
there.

Strategy

Flint: At the core of Polaris's strategy is the requirement that we be
great partners to entrepreneurs. When you back and support great
people, wonderful things often result. This approach to partnership
was in direct contrast to the prevailing view of venture capital. The
venture industry had developed a bad reputation. On the West Coast,
the tendency was to micromanage companies. People complained
that venture capitalists did not stick with things for the long term,
and that they did not build company cultures. On the East Coast,
venture capital had the reputation of being too financially oriented.

We wanted to unite the best attributes of the East and West
Coasts. Of course, we also wanted to provide outstanding returns on
investment. And we could do this by creating long, loyal relationships
with the entrepreneurs who created and ran the companies within
our portfolio.

Steve was our West Coast guy, located in Seattle. Having run LucasArts with George Lucas and then Bill Gates's private company, he was experienced in the more creative way of business typical on the West Coast. As we established our other founding office in Boston, our goal was to unite the traditional financial and corporate discipline of the East Coast with the entrepreneurial, innovative traditions of West Coast firms. We felt that it would be fun to create Polaris and bring in talented young people and mentor them, just as we had been mentored. Polaris would also be a home to experienced entrepreneurs and venture capitalists.

Our strategy is also based on seeking diversity within the portfolio. At a time when most of the other players were leaving the practice of investing in medical technologies, we felt that the new paradigms that were occurring in the information technology domain were also occurring in the medical arena. Perhaps the public markets were not captivated by the medical business, but these things run in cycles. In 1990, for example, Burr Egan Deleage was told to get out of the IT business for its fifth-generation fund. Of course it did not take that advice, and the returns for that fund from its IT investments just blew the roof off. Those IT investments in highly successful companies such as Powersoft and Premisys returned five times their original cost, because the investments were made at a time when prices were very discounted.

ARNOLD: We believe that supporting entrepreneurs and their ideas is the best model for creating value. In a nutshell, that's how Polaris works. Today, there is a real edge to the competitive aspect of the venture business. There's a lot of money around and events move very quickly. Syndications and teamwork among VCs are occurring less frequently. Yet, everyone is still looking to establish a relationship with *the* great entrepreneur.

An Investment Blueprint

FLINT: When we went out to raise our first fund as Polaris, we told our investors we'd do what we had been doing for fifteen years—get into our companies early, complete an array of seed deals, and support a lot of entrepreneurs who were working out of their garages. And we're doing just that. For example, in Polaris II, we are either the lead or co-investor in every deal. Often we are the sole institutional investor, and Polaris is usually the first venture capital firm. We are extremely active investors. We want to build companies. Allaire is a good example of our philosophy in action. When we first met with Allaire's staff, we found a group of fourteen twenty-five- and twenty-six-year-olds with a great idea. We gave then the choice of moving to Boston or the Silicon Valley. Thirteen of them chose Boston—which was the right decision, because the talent pool there was right for what they wanted to do.

We found their office space, accountants, and lawyers. We recruited their CFO and their vice presidents of development, marketing, and professional services. We created a board of directors. We used a recruiter to retain Allaire's CEO. Four months into our work with Allaire, we helped them raise $10 million—at four times the value we originally paid. Together with Allaire, we created a company with a $2 billion dollar valuation in less than two years time.

ARNOLD: Sometimes venture capitalists push their portfolio companies to go for the gold, when maybe the silver is a great outcome. A good venture partner establishes a realistic picture of the marketplace for their entrepreneur.

Classifieds2000 is a good example of establishing a realistic model of success for the VC and the entrepreneur. Classifieds2000 is a provider of classified advertising on the Internet. They grew very quickly and had a very important strategic place in the market. But it was evident to the entrepreneur and to us that there were a lot of giants who were coming into that part of the marketplace.

As other major players in the Internet industry awoke to the opportunity, it became clear that a small, independent company might have a hard time growing in the years ahead without the right partner. So we talked to a number of possible partners, and a found one where there was a great fit and the opportunity to accelerate Classifieds2000 to the next level of its development. We sold the company to Excite. We were in that investment for less than a year, and it was a success for everybody.

McGUIRE: Working with Advanced Inhalation Research (AIR), we re-invented the model for investing in medical companies. AIR developed a proprietary system for delivering drugs by breathing dry powder into the lungs. We co-founded the company and invested at every stage of development. Although we are a large fund now, we still make strategic early-stage investments in increments of $250,000. We call this cradle-to-altar support life-cycle investing.

The biggest challenge in the medical arena, however, is to find a product that can generate commercial sales sooner rather than later. The market isn't patient with interesting biology that needs a decade to develop into a commercial product. Companies like AIR with more immediate technology are able to generate commercial sales quickly. AIR wasn't going to require $20, $30, or $40 million in equity to move the company forward. What it needed was a good partner to help with the heavy lifting. I worked very actively with the two founders of the company in the areas of business development and in the process of negotiating the deals. I had the capability to talk with our corporate partners and tell them that I was not prepared to accept their offer. We would accept the right deal, or no deal at all. We didn't need their money at any cost. Having the necessary capital allowed us to be selective. We had created a company without a huge burn rate that possessed great science and attracted corporate interest. Being a strong partner was what made the difference.

Partnerships

McGUIRE: This idea of being successful by growing great companies is the fundamental idea we communicate to our entrepreneurs and investors. We begin a relationship by inviting entrepreneurs to perform as much due diligence on our firm as we would on theirs. They understand our idea of partnership and how a strong relationship between the VC and the entrepreneur adds value. In fact, this kind of understanding between Polaris and entrepreneurs is at the foundation of a good working relationship. Their confidence in our commitment to their enterprise helps build the value of the company.

Our philosophy is that we want to create companies that will change the world. This is one of our core values and is evident with every company in our portfolio.

FLINT: We have probably thought more about how to build an enduring organization than anyone in this industry should have. We strive to surround ourselves with people more accomplished than ourselves. Because we have been able to recruit some great talent into Polaris, Terry, Steve, and I joke that we aren't sure if we could land a job with Polaris anymore!

ARNOLD: Are there limits to our investment strategy? I believe that we have to be careful not to overcommit to too many companies. We aren't limited simply by money, but by the number of deals we as a group or as individuals can accommodate wisely. Different companies need different kinds of resources, depending where they are within their life cycle. Companies undergoing their initial stages of development often need significant time and attention, while other companies later in their life cycle may need much less. Some companies may be developing information or medical technology. They may need to pass a certain threshold before they are deemed credible enterprises. We observe and see which companies require our expertise and at what level of their development our involvement is useful. Ideally, when a company matures, it should possess an experienced management team. As a company achieves this stage of development, our involvement often becomes more episodic.

We scan the horizon for challenges and opportunities. We then offer our entrepreneurs our perspective on the challenges or opportunities that may impact their company and try to advise and coach them on ways to marshal their resources, so each situation is resolved in the most advantageous manner.

We have always told our limited partners that we will substantially outperform the market. Each of us has lived through market cycles, and we realize that if you build great companies, your efforts will be rewarded. We believe that if we work with the entrepreneur and build a great company, excellent returns will follow. AIR is a great example. We didn't expect to sell the company. But the technology was right, the environment was right, and we found a strong partner and buyer in Alkermes.

Billion-Dollar Deals

McGuire: There is a fear in the entrepreneurial community that every venture capital deal must possess a billion-dollar valuation. We have built billion-dollar companies and we are delighted with them. However, we've also been invested in opportunities where we've approached an entrepreneur and said: "This is the time to sell. You won't have a billion-dollar company, but you will have a company valued in the hundreds of millions."

We have entrepreneurs who ask us: "Does this have to be a billion-dollar company?" Their fear is that venture capital firms have become so obsessed with the idea of a billion-dollar company that they don't know when it is prudent and advisable to sell the company for something less. One entrepreneur we met with was particularly concerned that we would just drive for the billion-dollar mark, with nothing in between being an acceptable valuation.

Our philosophy is simple: If you build good companies, guided by the vision and goals of the entrepreneur, you will be paid for your hard work.

MORTON COLLINS
DSV Partners

Until recently, few East Coast venture capitalists had technology backgrounds; most came from the world of finance. Some had worked for banks and converted bank SBICs into venture capital partnerships such as Charles River Partners. Still others, backed by family wealth, took on the role of venture capitalist.

Morton Collins of DSV was one of the few East Coast venture capitalists with a degree in engineering. Indeed, when he founded DSV in 1968, in Princeton, New Jersey, Collins was among the first of the old guard to attempt to set up a venture capital organization outside of Silicon Valley and Massachusetts. His attempt to create a venture fund specializing in electronic data processing ventures was one of the first specialized venture funds in the business—on either coast.

In his unusual location, Collins had the advantage of access to Princeton University's vast technological resources, but he also found himself out of the deal stream that ran between Route 128 in Boston and Wall Street. Yet, a large number of early technology deals on the East Coast depended on Collins's due diligence to make them happen. He was one of a handful of the early East Coast investors who really understood technology.

In introducing DSV's third venture capital fund in 1981, Collins said he would concentrate on embryonic technologies embodied in digital electronics, molecular biology, and renewable energy. Very few early East Coast venture capitalists were as adventurous.

I GREW UP in New Jersey. I was the only child of immigrant parents who died when I was very young. My mother died when I was two, my father when I was eleven. I became a ward of the State of New Jersey. I've been on my own since age eleven. Since my parents came here from different countries, there weren't other relatives around to look after me.

My father was from Konigsberg, East Prussia, and my mother from Baden Wurttemberg, near Stuttgart, Germany. They emigrated separately, and met and married in the United States. I ended up, by good luck, and with the help of a very dedicated grammar school principal, going to the University of Delaware and getting a bachelor's degree in chemical engineering. Everything that matters from the standpoint of all things cultural and material I learned there.

I came to graduate school at Princeton University, having already decided that I wanted a career as an academic. I got a master's degree and a Ph.D. here at Princeton in chemical engineering, and I was on the faculty for some years. But something happened very soon after I came here. I was working on my Ph.D. research and I derived a very difficult differential equation that I needed to solve, but I couldn't figure out how to do it—and I was pretty good at those things. So I went to my advisor, Bill Schowalter, and he said, "Well, it's non-linear. That is why you can't solve it. But there's a new computer that just arrived two weeks ago that is getting set up—you ought to go meet and talk to those people. This problem will have to be solved numerically; you can't solve it by hand." I followed his advice. The computer came in to be used on a general basis, but nobody wanted to claim it. So, they set up something called the Statistical Techniques Research Group, with representatives from various departments, and I became the representative from the Chemical Engineering department to teach the rest of the university what it was and how to use it. I got hooked very quickly. Not only was I much more interested in the computer than I was in chemical engineering, but it was like differential or integral calculus. Suddenly you look out the window and see what it is—its potential power. The same with computing. I immediately thought computing was going to have a dramatic impact on our society.

I was becoming very frustrated as a faculty member by the fact that I couldn't change things. I couldn't get the department to accept industrial sponsorship much in the way that MIT does. We were sitting around all the time worrying about what our graduate students were going to be doing and how we were going to pay for it. I knew exactly how, because I was a consultant to Exxon, then called Esso Research and Engineering Company and American Cyanamid Company. They would have been happy to pay the university large amounts of money to work on some of the real problems they had, as opposed to the straw-man problems that we used to invent. So I got very frustrated with that, and I left academia to work for Esso.

As a result of my work at Esso on high-energy rocket fuels, the government came along and asked me to manage a special project. For two years, I managed the project, which was basically a re-design of certain weapon systems based on the new computer techniques that I had been a part of developing at Princeton.

Entrepreneurship 101

At Esso, I had also been working on overlaying economics on engineering calculations of plant designs to optimize profit. I decided to start a company that did that, and it grew quite quickly. But after two years, I discovered I was spending 80 percent of my time dealing with cash flow and personnel problems. I sold the company to a West Coast software company, and it was moved from Princeton up to River Edge, New Jersey.

My intention was to start another company, because, after all, I knew how to do that now. But I thought about it for a minute, and realized I had made enough money through the sale of my company that I didn't have to start earning a salary right away. I could wait a year or more before I really had to go back to work. So, I thought about it for a little bit and decided not to go down the same path I had been on three years earlier. Since I knew about computers and data processing, people I had met here in Princeton who worked on Wall Street in various firms had asked me if I would do some work for them to answer certain technical questions. For example, a new company named Memorex had been founded to manufacture disk drives. Did I think those drives were going to come along and put a dent in the tape drive business? Or, would I go look at a technology company and tell them what I thought about it, and so forth.

I began to do that on a consulting basis, and I was seeing a number of small companies along the way, in various EDP-related businesses that couldn't get financed. There wasn't any venture capital of the sort that there is now, or of the sort that I think I played a role in creating.

Learning from American Research and Development

I learned about American Research and Development quite by accident. Sam Bodman, who's now the CEO of Cabot Corporation, was on the Chemical Engineering faculty at MIT at the same time that I was on the Chemical Engineering faculty at Princeton. We met and became very good friends. He worked part-time for American Research and Development while he was on the faculty at MIT. He would evaluate deals, go out and look at companies, and so forth. We were looking at the same company—I was looking for some Wall Street group, and he was looking for American Research and Development. So he took me up to Boston, had me meet General Doriot and Bill Congleton, and showed me how they did business. I was really fascinated by it. I thought it was really a nice way to do things and the way that technology should progress.

There were a few people around the financial community and some partnerships that would invest in some of these small companies. Mostly they put money into companies that had been operating for some time. They invested in early-stage companies from time to time, but not really start-ups, whereas the people at American Research and Development would really get involved in start-ups. I was fascinated. So I started thinking about the fact that electronic data processing was going to one day be the biggest business in the world, a big subset of the total economy, which would lead to specialization in investment. At this time—pre-1968—there was some specialization in investment, but not much. There was oil and gas, real estate, and everything else. That was about it, I think. So I said to myself, We have this business that I know a lot about. I know most of the players. I'm interested in start-ups, in early-stage investments. I'd like to do the things American Research and Development does. What I would really like to do is become a venture capitalist.

But I had certain caveats that were critically important. I wanted control. And in order to have control, I needed my own capital, which

I didn't have. On the other hand, I had made a few investments in some of the small EDP companies that were doing very well, and the public market was also doing very well at that time. I figured five years was my time horizon. In five years I would have enough capital to start my own venture fund. I figured that I needed around $2 million dollars. I'd put $100,000 or $200,000 in a given deal, and do about ten or more deals in my fund.

How did these ideas become real, and how did it all come about for me? Well, continuing forward, I thought, What an ideal situation. I'm being paid very handsomely to do this consulting work. I'm travelling all over the country. I'm meeting everybody involved in the businesses that I want to be in. I'm getting to understand more and more about the business, other than the parts of it that I know about from my previous experience, and I'm making enough money that I'll have the capital that I need in five years—what a wonderful world.

Starting Data Science Ventures with Eli Jacobs

Well, one thing came along to change the picture. I did a study for White Weld and Company. They then had their offices down at 20 Broad Street, where the New York Stock Exchange is located. I went to a partners' lunch to give a report. There were perhaps twenty people in the room. When the questions and answers were over, one fellow said, "I'm going up to the midtown offices, does anybody want to share a cab?" I said, "I will, I'm going to midtown." So, the two of us—who had never met before that moment—got in a cab together. His name was Eli Jacobs. The last thing he is known for, that I am aware of, is owning the Baltimore Orioles. He was a young partner of White Weld at the time. So, we got in the cab, and we started uptown, and he said to me, "Gee, that was really an interesting presentation that you gave today. Do you do this often?" We had some rambling conversation, and then he asked, "What do you plan to be doing in five years?"

Fateful question. I replied, "I know exactly what I want to be doing in five years." I described my idea of a start-up venture capital company specializing in EDP technology. He asked, "Why do you want to wait five years? The world needs that now." I said, "I want to wait five years because I want to control it, and I won't have the capital that it takes for five years. Besides, I'm learning more and more about what

I want to do as I go along." He responded, "If you write a business plan, White Weld will help you raise the money, and I think we can overcome all of the problems you mentioned."

I did write a business plan, and they decided to help me raise the money for what became DSV—Data Science Ventures. We set out to raise $2 million, but we were oversubscribed almost immediately, and in a brilliant piece of investment-banking decision making, White Weld raised the size of the offering to $6 million. I wasn't necessarily thrilled by the idea. Now, hindsight tells me that it was good, but at the time, I wasn't sure it was. However, they did two or three things that were very important.

First, and most important, they made up a list of investors for me to go and make presentations to. I had mostly never heard of these investors—Rockefeller Family and Associates and E. M. Warburg being typical ones. The very first meeting was with Rockefeller Family and Associates. I called up a friend of mine in the economics department at Princeton, and asked, "What do investment bankers do?" He said, "Investment bankers have capital clients, and what they do is find things for the capital clients to make investments in, charging them a commission along the way, which is how they get paid."

So, Eli Jacobs takes me to Rockefeller Family and Associates, and we go up to the fifty-sixth floor, to the big conference room on the left side of the office complex. I was seated at the end of the conference table. There were probably fourteen people in the room. Eli was seated directly on my right. What I had in my head was that Eli would make this presentation, and then I would answer questions. But suddenly everyone was looking at me, so, I stammered out a disjointed idea of my plan, not being prepared to make a presentation and not having any slides to show or papers to pass out. Rockefeller Family and Associates (this was pre-Venrock) committed almost immediately.

Eli then marched me around, and within a couple of weeks, we had $6 million dollars raised. I controlled the company, which was a corporation. They put up all the money on day one, and I took it to the bank.

There was no management fee structure. Whatever the costs were, they were. I owned a third of the stock, but I had control of all of it, so the investors couldn't liquidate it or anything. As crazy as it may sound, not a single one of them, including the Warburg folks,

ever asked why it was a corporation. I didn't know enough about partnerships to realize that a partnership would have been a much better
structure, in that day and age, given the body of securities law and tax
law. But I did know something about corporations, so I made it a corporation. Nobody asked me why. ARD was a corporation, after all,
and I was emulating ARD in large part.

Looking back on that time, I had ten monolithic groups that had
never really worked together before—E. M. Warburg, Newcourt
Securities (the Rothschilds), and Rockefeller Family and Associates,
to name a few. They had never worked together on anything. It was
an interesting amalgam. DSV was, if not the first, then one of the first
venture groups that brought together capital from other investors to
be managed by an independent manager in a venture capital early-
stage start-up way. Through DSV those groups got to know one
another and ended up working together on other projects.

The Arithmetic of Dealmaking

DSV planned to operate in the world of electronic data processing.
For us that meant that all of the CEOs or would-be CEOs of these
companies would be engineers by training. I was an engineer and the
people I hired were usually engineers with M.B.A.s, or had degrees
in the pure sciences with an M.B.A.; one was a math major with an
M.B.A. The people I brought on all had business school training,
which I think is invaluable for some of this activity.

I approached each deal logically and fairly. I would say, "Here is
what my investors expect to earn as a return on this investment. I'm
probably going to have to earn twice that return on paper to actually
earn that return, because some of the companies are not going to
work out, and so forth. So, if I just pick numbers out of the air, if my
investors expect a 25 percent compound return—not a bad number—
I have to earn a 50 percent compound return at the DSV level in order
to produce a 25 percent compound return for my investors. Now, let's
go through the business plan. How much capital do they require? On
what schedule do they need it? How is this business going to grow?
Let's project this business out. Let's see in five years what its revenue
and earnings are going to be. Let's also apply some rules of thumb to
the revenues and earnings, to get an estimate of what the company is

going to be worth." So we did it strictly like engineering, by the numbers.

We looked upon working with entrepreneurs as a partnership. I never raided other firms for people. I always grew them myself. I said, "I want you to learn it our way. We're going to be partners with these entrepreneurs and we're going to negotiate with them, hopefully, only once." Unfortunately, we had to negotiate three or four times, but the idea was to only negotiate once.

We had some of our own little rules. You couldn't be on more than six boards of directors, for instance. We would go through the numbers of how many hours you should be spending as a director of a company. When we got to six companies, there weren't any hours left. So, we were always very involved. I felt that on the board of a young company, you had to spend at least one day a month at the company. Additionally, you had to spend at least one day a month, or the equivalent of one day a month, on the company's business. So, that's two days a month per company. With some companies it was more than full-time, and with others it was hardly any time, depending on the size of the companies and their problems as they grew up.

The First Successful Deal

In the first fund, the most successful deal was Tempo Computers, a minicomputer company, like DEC, that got acquired. The company was a West Coast company located in Fullerton, California. It was a start-up that was doing very nicely. Along came GTE, which was just starting their Information Services Division in Connecticut. They came in and made us an offer that we couldn't refuse. It was way more than we would have thought the company was worth. That was probably the most successful company in DSV I. We made ten times our money in about two years, which was unusual. It wasn't unusual to make ten times your money, but it was to do it in two years.

The success with DSV I helped us get DSV II financed in 1974, faster than many others doing their second fund. But DSV II was only $4.25 million. We also changed to a partnership structure. The $4.25 million was not new money. We rolled the old corporation into the new partnership, and anybody who wanted out could get out. But most of our investors didn't want out. The only ones that did were some tail ends from the original deal, because White Weld took a piece of it themselves and hacked it up among their various partners. Those people were just making an investment and were very happy with the result and the liquidity.

With DSV II, we had a partnership structure and a 4 percent fee. There was also an increment based on asset appreciation. So, it was 4 percent of the original capital, plus this increment for asset appreciation, and the assets appreciated very quickly. Then we cut the 4 percent down because of the rapid appreciation. We ended up with a rational fee, but it was always high by any current standard.

Building Companies First

A lot of venture capitalists aim their companies at IPOs. We didn't. We had a rule, or an idea, that we tried to foment in our companies, which was that you don't even think about going public until you have $500,000 in net after-tax earnings. Later we upped it to $1 million. The reason was that we had seen, in the experiences we had with companies that did IPOs early on, that the marketplace had an expectation of sustained quarterly earnings growth. If you didn't produce that, you were going to be punished severely. If you were public and had a low-priced stock that nobody wanted, you had a real hard time raising money any other way as a young company. Being public also had other costs—both real and opportunity costs. Being public took management time and so forth, and produced all these costs over which you had no control. Legal costs, accounting costs, printing costs, certificates, and so on, all of which hurt your business until you really could assimilate those kinds of costs. It was only after the companies became very successful that we thought it was appropriate to go public. But, remember, back in those days you didn't get a real big bite at the apple. If you went public, you raised $4 million dollars, not $40 million, which is on the small side these days.

Exploring Fiber Optics

I became very enamored of fiber optics as a solution to the coming need for bandwidth. There didn't seem to be any way to get bandwidth with copper, and sure, you can go to coaxial cables but you really needed to do something different. So I got very excited about fiber optics as a big thing of the future, and looked hard for an entry. But there were no deals around.

We spent a lot of time circling around Bell Laboratories, and we could neither get in nor get anybody out. Bell Laboratories was a national treasure and a prime place to be employed—the best of the best. Finally, we talked two guys into leaving Bell. One was an expert on how to make fiber itself, how you actually pull fiber from a boule. The other was an expert on making the electronic devices that operated on the ends of the fiber. We decided to put this company together and called it Fiber Communications, Inc. We located the company in a loft up in East Orange, New Jersey. My partner Jim Bergman was the chief financial officer of the company. We had a total staff of three—the two Ph.D. scientists and Jim Bergman. He wrote the checks, and took care of everything. We knew that the fiber business was going to be a long time coming, and we didn't know exactly when it was going to come. All these futurists told us that it was going to take off, but nobody knew where it would start or where the knee of the demand curve would be.

We decided to start making a superior fiber because it was cheap to make. There are not a lot of economies of scale in the fiber optics business. You can make a hundred miles of fiber, or a billion miles of fiber; it costs almost the same amount per mile. The idea was that we would keep the cash outflow of the company as small as possible. We would sell market development samples for pretty high prices, and we wouldn't have any expenses. DSV's money was there to pay the difference in cash flow. We structured a deal with the two Bell Labs guys that really had to do with the growth of the company. It was what we called in those days a formula deal. We started out with most of the stock, and then we would give it back to them as certain milestones were achieved.

At the time the CATV industry was looking for an alternative to coaxial cable. The ducts in New York were all filled with it, and they couldn't get any more in the street. Here, we thought, was one possible application for fiber. We made up five miles of fiber and sent it out to Belden Company in Illinois to get it made into a cable. They took a standard cable that had nine conductors in it and replaced one of the nine copper conductors with glass, and Teleprompter put it in the street in New York City. We modulated thirteen broadcast TV channels—analog, not digital, which was very wasteful of bandwidth—and Ron, one of our guys, built the devices on both ends. It worked like a charm. They were thrilled, and we were thrilled.

The first thing we did was ask Belden Company if we could enter into a contract, to get them to make up hundreds of miles of cable. They said no; they weren't in that business. So we tried to do that ourselves. We bought a cabling machine, and made some other equipment investments. But we just couldn't do it. In the midst of trying to make the cable, we found out that Times Wire and Cable, a division of Insilco, made the cable for Teleprompter. So, we went up to Meriden, Connecticut, met the people, and showed them what we were doing. About a week later, the chairman of Insilco called me up and he said he would like to have lunch with me in New York. I went to New York to have lunch with him, and he said, "We'd like to buy your company." I asked, "What do you mean? This isn't a company; this is two guys in a loft in East Orange. We're in the venture capital business; we're not in the business of selling companies at this stage of development." He said, "Well, I'll make you a deal. You put in Fiber Communications Inc. and I'll put in Times Wire and Cable, and we'll form a new company. We'll own it fifty-fifty." Times Wire and Cable had about a $100 million worth of assets on the balance sheet, and a lot of machinery that was written off, that was worth a huge amount of money. The deal was just too good to be true and I didn't believe it. I said, "I won't do a deal I don't understand. It doesn't make any sense." He responded, "I'll tell you why I'm willing to do this deal. The reason is that we, Times Wire and Cable, are perceived as a boutique. We make all these cables for the CIA, for NSA, for all these people. We were perceived by the CATV industry as being on the front edge of the technology. We sold more coaxial cable than anybody else did, even though our coaxial cable was no better than theirs, because people believed that we were on the front edge of the technology. We're no longer perceived that way. Buying this company will put us back there." He was absolutely right. Times Wire and Cable sold untold quantities of copper coaxial cable before the first fiber was even pulled.

We did the deal. The company is called Times Fiber Communications and is still located right on I-95 in Meriden. That was probably our most successful company of all of the investments, as far as multiples. I think we made at least 100 times our money.

Pioneering in Biotechnology

In 1981 we made our first investment in biotechnology in the Liposome Co. There were two things I liked about the company. Its potential to develop animal products as well as human products was one. The idea was that you could sell things into the animal products world and use that cash flow to develop human products. Second, the application of the Liposome technology was not limited in the way that most biotech ideas were. There were a million ways to win. God knows, there were all kinds of things that liposomes might work for. I liked that this was a multiple-product idea. I came back here and told my partners I really liked what I had seen and was really interested in pursuing it. I wanted them to visit the company and hear the same presentation I had heard. If they came back and said forget it, I would forget it. If they said go for it, I'd go for it. And I did. We put together a standard venture financing with DSV as the lead along with Kleiner Perkins, Venrock, Adler, and Inco. I'm still on the board after all these years. I was the CEO for a year, after a huge battle with Ed Mertz, its chief executive.

Before coming to Liposome, Mertz ran Dairylea Enterprises, a big dairy cooperative. He had beaucoup management experience, which we badly needed. Marc Ostro, the CEO and chief scientific officer, never pretended to be a manager. He was what he was, and he was terrific. We needed a manager. Ed Mertz's résumé came across my desk. Guys like us get hundreds of résumés. Mertz's résumé came across my desk and across Tony Evnin's desk at Venrock at the same time. Tony Evnin and I were working on hiring a manager. I said to Tony, "I got this résumé from a guy named Ed Mertz." Tony said "Yeah, he looks pretty good, let's interview him." So, he interviewed him, and I interviewed him, and we hired him. Then we proceeded to further finance the company, take it public, and do all the usual things. Ed Mertz was a good manager and hired a lot of good people, building the company substantially.

The problem with Ed Mertz was that he couldn't make a deal. Every time he got into the final negotiation of a big pharmaceutical deal, the deal somehow died. He didn't have a realistic idea of what a company such as Squibb would be willing to do. So, in the final phases of the negotiation, he would end up wanting too much or trying to get too much and lose the deal. We just lost one deal after another. I ultimately concluded the reason was that he wasn't one of the good old boys. He didn't know the pharmaceutical business and they didn't know him.

Mertz began heading for the cliff at about 1,000 miles an hour. Here we are, approaching Mach 1, and we're approaching the precipice at the same time, and I'm saying, "Jesus Christ, Ed, what are we going to do here? We've got to cut back some of this research." We had thirty-six research projects. He would finally decide he wasn't going to do anything. We were always going to make this big deal the week after next, with some company. The big deal never came, but the truth was coming. So, finally we fired him. He decided he wanted to have a proxy fight. I said, "I have the votes, Ed. We don't have to go to the public. Let's just add up the votes right here in the room." He added them up and decided he was going to lose, so he left relatively quietly. I became the CEO and worked very hard to cut the flow of blood and focus the company. It didn't help that my wife of more than twenty years, Eva, was diagnosed with leukemia and died within five months.

If it weren't for venture capital, the Liposome Company would not exist today. Not because of the money; they might have gotten the money somewhere else. But somebody had to get hold of that company, put it in a rational format, and put the right people in charge. It was venture capitalists who did that. I was one of them. The products of the Liposome Company are now saving lives every single day all over the world and the company is worth $1 billion in the marketplace. We've done that time after time in companies—that's the value we add. It certainly has made a difference in many, many young companies as far as I'm concerned. I worry that this kind of added value isn't there in the venture capital community anymore.

Shaping DSV

Let me go back to the early DSV days. We were the only East Coast firm that said we specialized in something, namely computers and computer-related technology. We integrated backwards over time. We went from computers to semiconductors, because semiconductors became computers. We went from semiconductors to semiconductor capital equipment, and then to semiconductor materials.

Biotech was a leap, but not such a great leap at the time we did it, because somebody else had shown us the way, and I was emulating him. I was calling Tom Perkins and regularly asking him for advice during this time. Tom and his partner, Brook Byers, were the pioneers in biotech.

We sat in this very spot, and almost every deal in the country that said technology on it—especially computer technology—came here. We didn't have to ask; they came here. Yes, I went around and I got to know all the guys on the West Coast, the few guys who were in the venture business in San Francisco, and so forth. There wasn't any Silicon Valley yet; it was mostly a prune orchard. I was calling investors in Los Angeles with Westland Capital's help, because Jim Bergman and Kip Hagopian had been fraternity brothers at UCLA. That's how all those contacts happened.

I don't know exactly when, but the day came when that stopped happening. What began happening was that we would spend two months with an entrepreneur working on the technology and all the stuff in the deal, and then we'd do a term sheet, and three days later, the entrepreneur would come back to me and say, "Well, everything's fine except the equity split is off by a factor of two." I'd say, "Wait a minute, we went through all that. I showed you the arithmetic of why it has to be that way." They would say, "Oh well, XYZ group, some new venture group, is willing to give us the money on that basis." So, we got to the point where we were doing all this work, and as soon as we made a positive decision and created a term sheet, somebody else would improve on our term sheet without even having investigated the deal.

So, we asked ourselves how we were going to deal with this. Then, of course, it came to the point that everybody had so much money to invest, including us, that we didn't want or need any partners. In our first decade, before 1978 or 1979, there was a shortage of capital. Then suddenly, in 1979 or thereabouts, there was much more capital than the system required.

I was one of the people who worked on capital availability. In other words, I was one of a committee of five from NVCA who worked with the Labor Department to restructure the ERISA (Employee Retirement Income Security Act) rules. We called ERISA Everything Rotten Invented Since Adam. It used to be so crazy at the Labor Department that I would say that the best part of that building is that you can escape fast using that tunnel underneath, because the people in here are all nuts. You know what we never did in all of that? We never calculated out what would happen if we were successful. If we had, we might not have done it. It never dawned on me that if there were ten times as much capital available, it might not be a good thing. But, anyhow, all this capital became available because of our success. I happened to go to the National Venture Capital Association meeting in Washington in the spring of 1980. I bumped into Stan Pratt when I was going to get a cup of coffee. I asked Stan, "How's the fund-raising going this year?" "Well," he said, "I think maybe $5 billion will get raised this year." I said, "Wow, $5 billion—that's enormous." It went right over my head. I got up really early the next morning and was sitting there doing some calculations. Five billion dollars? Let's see, nobody's putting up that money if they don't think they're going to get at least a 25 percent return on it. I did some back-of-the-envelope calculations, although I didn't know what to relate the values to. I was then on the board of Tandem Computers, which had just become a Fortune 500 company, so I tried that out. My calculations showed that you had to have roughly 1,000 new Fortune 500 companies ten years hence to achieve the return. They also showed that if you went back twenty years, ten had been created. Ten new Fortune 500 companies had come about in the preceding twenty years from venture capital investment. I had them all named. The next day, NVCA had something called The Three Wise Men, where they take three old timers from the venture business and put them on the stage to talk about the present situation in venture capital, where it is headed, and all that. So, the three wise men spoke and then it was time for the audience. I raised my hand and said, "Trust me on the arithmetic, you know I'm good at that." And, I went through my calculations: "I'll tell you what this means, it means returns are going to go down, it can't mean anything else. Because there's not going to be 1,000 new Fortune 500 companies, that's all there is to it. It's not credible." The audience of venture capitalists booed me out of the room. Before long, the blood was flowing in a serious way and, in many cases, the returns became negative!

Venturing in a Changed Environment

How did we at DSV cope with the day when the deals stopped coming in? We decided that we would create deals. We knew how to do
that. We would create deals, and we would invite our friends that we
had invested with over the years to join us in those deals. Then they
would do likewise with us. That was the idea. So, we created the first
deal. We got what we call a world-class idea. It didn't come from here.
It usually came from Arnie Levine over in Molecular Biology, or the
Mafia that we know very well at Harvard and MIT. Arnie is now president of Rockefeller University, but he was formerly the chairman of
Princeton's Molecular Biology department. It's always been in
biotech. So, first we get a world-class idea. We then develop it, create a company, get some scientists, and then we get a little working
space. We put up a few dollars. We get a little space up in Cambridge,
or someplace, put together a nice board, and start discussions with a
major pharmaceutical company while beginning the search for a
CEO. Next, we and a few of our venture friends put up $2 million
each and the company is created.

Alkermes, now public, was done exactly that way. Alkermes was
invented by Michael Wall and flowed from the fact that Michael
became very interested in brain chemistry while taking a course at
Scripps. Only Michael, the arch-entrepreneur, would take a course in
brain chemistry as a vacation. We shook hands on the deal in the
Brooklyn Battery Tunnel, a curious anomaly, but true. In fact, my
requirement that biotech CEOs be "good old boys" from the pharmaceutical industry nearly kept us from hiring the very able CEO of
Alkermes, Richard Pops. He had been interviewed by everybody else,
but I refused to even meet him because he was not from the industry. Finally, in desperation, Michael Wall got Hubert Schoemaker,
then CEO of Centocor, to call me and try to soften me up. I said,
"Hubert, just name one successful biotechnology CEO who isn't
from the industry." He responded, "Well, there's me, there's Bob
Swanson," and he went on to name six others. So, I quickly cried
uncle and interviewed Richard. We hired him quickly and in hindsight I can tell you that it was a good move.

We then waited for the phone to ring with deals put together by
others. Well, needless to say, it didn't ring. I got pretty angry because

we had put a lot of energy into a couple of these deals. So I called Venrock, Warburg, and others, and asked, "Why isn't my phone ringing?" The basic answer was that others were not originating deals in this manner. They were still reacting to the deals brought to them.

So we changed our plan. The way we did our deals after that was to do exactly the same thing, except now we would put significant money—half a million—up front. Half a million would typically get us six to twelve months into the project. One of us would be the CEO. We would do everything. We would hire scientists. We would talk to pharmaceutical companies, based on the technology. We'd have Alex Rich, Paul Schimmel, or somebody equivalent as directors, fronting for us. Then we would go out and search for a CEO. Just about the time we were hiring a CEO, the big pharmaceutical deal was coming to roost. When all of that was done, we would do a standard venture financing with the same group of friends, each putting up $2 million, except that we had a lot of equity in that first $500,000. That's how we got paid back for doing all the work, by taking it out of the first piece.

Where Are We Now?

The venture capital business has undergone a dramatic change in the thirty-plus years since DSV had its first closing on October 1, 1968. Then, venture capital meant high-risk, high-reward, early-stage, long-term, high-technology investing. Now the words seem to cover almost any form of investing. The change has two major origins—the huge influx of capital from the pension funds, and a wildly exuberant stock market. As a consequence of the new source of funds, venture capitalists have been transformed into mouse hunters. They formerly were elephant hunters. The pension funds have a target IRR that they are trying to achieve, say 16 percent per year. They drive for liquidity and they are anxious to receive distributions of cash and securities, which they usually sell immediately. The exuberant stock market has provided returns without the creation of underlying intrinsic values such as revenues, earnings, and cash flow. Each of these things is a force acting against long-term commitment and long-term investment. The net is that the pension funds have investment goals that are incompatible with those of what was formerly called venture capital. The other major new source of capital for venture firms is the university endowment funds. They are not looking for cash, and if they have an investment in their portfolio that is earning an appropriate return, they are happy to stay with it as long as that remains true. They are truly long-term investors and their goals are completely aligned with the old-style or "value" form of venture capital investing.

The great majority of venture capitalists in the '90s are making investments with a lower risk-and-reward profile than those made in the '70s, satisfying the needs and desires of their major source of capital, the pension funds. Fortuitously, the highly valued stock market has enabled them to earn attractive returns. This will not last. A similar phenomenon occurred in the '70s with computer-related stocks, and in the '80s with the biotech stocks, although neither of these periods became as excessive with respect to valuation as today. Can Internet stocks be different? Can Amazon.com, with a history of huge losses and no profits ever, really be as valuable as Anheuser-Busch with net after-tax earnings in excess of $1 billion per year? I don't think so, unless the market capitalizations are telling us that the public is going to give up beer drinking to take up book reading. Take a look at the present values in computers and biotech—they have shrunken considerably. In many cases now, venture capitalists serve on twelve boards; in still other cases, they don't serve on any boards because there just is not enough time. Additionally, the so-called "gatekeepers" advising the pension funds have successfully reduced management fees for venture firms to the point where the fees for most venture funds are lower than the fees for most mutual funds. Is that crazy? No wonder venture capitalists are behaving like managers of securities rather than like managers of companies! The Catch-22 is that a venture firm has to manage a very large asset pool to earn sufficient fee income to pay the bills; therefore, it must make many investments per professional—and the larger the investment, the better. Naturally, the heavy involvement and partnership with entrepreneurs that was in style in the '70s, along with its value added, cannot occur in most cases. Elephant hunters are still out there—take a look at Venrock on the East Coast or Asset Management in Silicon Valley. But their numbers have been substantially reduced.

DSV celebrated its thirtieth anniversary on October 1, 1998, and is now in its final year of liquidation. A successor firm, Cardinal Venture

Partners, has been formed and financed. John Clarke, a DSV partner for seventeen years, is Cardinal's managing partner. Jim Bergman and myself are special limited partners. I have made a number of personal investments in electro-optics and wireless communications and am spending the bulk of my time working with these companies in the old-fashioned, value-added venture capital way. I believe that this approach still adds value. We shall see. Having been a pilot for most of my life, I have also taken up modest aerobatics in which I am using an open-cockpit WACO biplane. I am also building a very high-performance experimental airplane.

The future, as always, is unpredictable. It will be very interesting to see the impact of all the technology that has been developed with funding provided by the venture capital industry. Things are changing very fast, and my guess is that the rate of change will continue to accelerate.

EDWARD MATHIAS
The Carlyle Group

Ed Mathias has been a player at almost all points of the venture cycle. At T. Rowe Price, the Baltimore-based financial services organization, he was responsible for buying IPOs and stocks of emerging-growth companies during the '70s and '80s. He was also involved in helping T. Rowe Price seed the formation of New Enterprise Associates. After leaving T. Rowe Price in 1993, Mathias began investing in entrepreneurial businesses himself and finally ended up overseeing the venture capital operation of The Carlyle Group, a Washington, D.C., investment bank.

Mathias, like Mitch Kapor, has seen many sides of the venture capital business. His vantage point as an investor in other venture funds provides invaluable insights into institutional investing, and his proximity to the entrepreneurial process allows him to compare the role of both the angel and the institutional venture capitalist. Most important, Mathias has lived through both downcycles and the buoyant years of the 1980s and the late 1990s.

I HAVE BEEN around venture capital, in one way or another, for almost thirty years. This has included being a buyer of the venture capital product while an investment manager, forming and managing venture funds, and being active as a private investor in numerous start-ups and early-stage situations. The latter has required hands-on involvement, which broadly translated in my case has meant helping raise money or dealing with personnel or strategic problems. My background differs significantly from most other practitioners in that I come to this arena with much more of a macro view and public market orientation.

It's been fascinating to experience the industry's growth and its cycles, all of which have occurred in a relatively short period.

Remarkably, a large number of the participants who created the industry and sustained its growth are still alive and active.

A Cottage Industry

Early on, venture capital was a cottage industry and certainly not a glamour business. Looking back to the late '60s and early '70s, wealthy individuals, SBICs, banks, and insurance companies were the major participants. There was a lot of money raised coincident with the technology craze and speculative markets of the late '60s, but it was nothing like the industry we know today. There were relatively few participants, the pools of capital were small, and everyone seemed to know each other and work together. In those days, the industry totaled perhaps $1 billion in aggregate. Venture activity peaked in 1969 as the market reached a major top and the capital gains tax was increased, I believe, to 49 percent. A five-year bear market and the destruction of small company valuations followed.

My own indoctrination to entrepreneurship started with my father, who was an active small businessman and investor. In the Navy, I was a Supply Corps officer, in effect running a small business onboard a destroyer. I was formally introduced to venture capital at Harvard Business School in 1970. A number of my classmates were interested in small business opportunities, and the course Starting New Ventures with Pat Lyles, who later went on to be an active partner at Charles River Ventures, was exceedingly popular.

The companies we studied seem mundane by today's standards. People typically started on a shoestring and usually financed growth with positive cash flow over a long period. The most distinctive memory I have is of families coming to class with the husband—since mostly men started companies in those days—saying how great it was, and the wife saying what a disaster it had been to live through.

At the same time, we were confronted with stories of General Doriot. His legacy played a major role at Harvard Business School, although he had retired by the time I got there. Everybody talked about Digital Equipment Corporation (DEC) and the fact that American Research and Development (ARD) had turned something like $70,000 into $400 million by the time DEC was sold to Textron.

Between my business school years, I worked with a classmate on two mundane ventures that gave me additional insights. One idea was to consolidate beauty shops. The other involved providing leased equipment to Blue Cross Blue Shield. Neither of these went anywhere, but the experience proved highly worthwhile and, importantly to me, the individual for whom we worked happened to be a senior person at T. Rowe Price Associates. This relationship indirectly led to my choice of a career and my first job.

T. Rowe Price and NEA

I joined T. Rowe Price Associates in 1971, as did Chuck Newhall, who later went on to establish New Enterprise Associates (NEA). At the time, T. Rowe Price was a small firm but an established leader in small public company investing. The New Horizons Mutual Fund, managed by Cub Harvey, was one of the only public vehicles focused on emerging-growth stocks. Chuck Newhall was charged with preparing T. Rowe Price to enter the venture business, and I joined as an investment counselor, or portfolio manager. Through a total fluke, as seems to characterize most careers, I ended up house-sitting with Cub Harvey during my first summer. He subsequently asked me to work on the New Horizons Fund, which turned out to be an extraordinary opportunity and one that greatly influenced my future. Chuck also worked on the fund, establishing what we termed as an incubator portfolio, which was devoted to very small public companies. His efforts were to be a prelude to T. Rowe Price Associates launching its own venture capital product.

About this time, having an entrepreneurial itch, a friend and I established a chain of ice cream stores. As a result of the riots following Martin Luther King's death, none of the established firms would go near the inner city. We tried to take advantage of this, and let's say, charitably, that we lost a small amount of money and a lot of time. Our failure resulted primarily from not selecting and being willing to pay for premier real estate locations.

At the time, although it wasn't readily apparent, there were significant structural changes occurring that would lay the groundwork for venture capital's growth. The Nasdaq was created, and this eventually provided a robust public marketplace for small companies. ERISA was passed in the mid-'70s, which over time enabled fiduciaries to diversify into assets other than bonds and large blue-chip equities. ERISA didn't have much of an initial impact, but down the road it proved to be extraordinarily important.

As institutions became more aggressive and adventurous, a number of regional brokerage firms emerged which were very much oriented to technology and venture capital. Firms such as Hambrecht & Quist, Robertson Stephens, and Montgomery Securities come immediately to mind. Alex. Brown, with its long history, sensed the opportunity and positioned itself to participate. The firms were primarily in California, and came to play a powerful role. Initially, a lot of them had extremely close, sometimes incestuous, relationships with the venture community.

T. Rowe Price Takes a Stab at Venture Capital

From the depths of the bear market in 1974, the investment environment began to improve. In 1977, T. Rowe Price tried to establish a venture capital arm. At the time, though, there were some real problems with the Securities and Exchange Commission in terms of whether a registered investment advisor could have a profit participation or a carried interest. Also, the idea that one element within a large firm oriented to public securities could invest in venture capital with the principals having a direct profit participation raised significant internal issues. Finally, given the problems trying to do this internally, we worked with the potential partners and created New Enterprise Associates (NEA). The initial partners were Chuck Newhall from T. Rowe Price and Frank Bonsal, a legendary deal finder or "bird dog" at Alex. Brown. Finally, NEA attracted Dick Kramlich, who had been Arthur Rock's partner and was a friend of Cub Harvey's. Dick wanted to stay in San Francisco and thus NEA became bi-coastal. T. Rowe Price became a special limited partner, and forged a long-term relationship that proved to be mutually beneficial. It seems hard to comprehend in light of today's conditions, but NEA struggled mightily to raise $15.6 million. I recollect that there were only two other funds raised that year. Had it not been for a fortuitous event in which a Midwestern family put up close to $5 million, I question whether NEA would have gotten off the ground.

In any case, that was the start of New Enterprise Associates and my direct involvement with traditional venture capital. As it turned out, it proved to be an extraordinarily opportune time to start a venture capital fund. New technologies were coming rapidly to the forefront and this—coupled with a shortage of capital, experienced investors at the ready, low public valuations, and time in which to build companies—created a great investment opportunity. Together with the clarification of ERISA, the growth of Nasdaq, and an advancing market, this set the stage for the ensuing boom years.

Coincidentally, the capital gains rate was reduced, thus providing a further impetus for investment. Venture capitalists have always considered the capital gains rate extraordinarily important, not just for the investors but as related to their ability to attract and motivate workers. As we've come to see, the incentive compensation system with a heavy emphasis on options that venture capital spawned now permeates the U.S. economy.

We began to see a number of leaders emerge in the venture community. Some of the early venture capitalists who come to mind include Peter Brooke, Arthur Rock, Tommy Davis, and the principals at Kleiner Perkins, Sutter Hill, and Mayfield. Interestingly, a number of the early firms have grown and maintained their preeminent positions. On the institutional side, GTE, IBM, General Electric, Harvard Management, AT&T, and the Hillman Family, among others, were early to the game and laid the path for others to follow.

T. Rowe Price was fortunate in attracting Paul Wythes, an extraordinarily successful venture capitalist at Sutter Hill, to join the board of the New Horizons Fund. We felt that Paul would be useful in helping us understand the industry and in providing a perspective that differed from our public market vantage point. This certainly proved to be the case, as his inputs and contacts proved invaluable.

The late '70s and early '80s were still a period in which not a lot of money was being raised by today's standards. There were something like seven new partnerships in '79 and perhaps ten in 1980. But as the market started to advance, people started to see the spectacular returns being achieved by the venture capital partnerships. This stimulated interest, with the result that around 100 venture funds were raised over the next three years. Much of this was institutional money, primarily from private pension funds, which had begun to grow enormously.

By the early 1980s, venture capital had become significant—not within the context of the overall financial markets, but in terms of its impact. The industry then had almost $7 billion under management. Venture capitalists raised almost $900 million in 1981 alone. The stock market rebounded strongly starting in the summer of 1982, and from 1983 to 1985 we had an IPO boom of then-unprecedented strength. This enabled venture realizations, created an outstanding performance record for venture capitalists, and permitted them to raise more money. Almost $4 billion was raised in 1983. Throughout this period, the pension market came to see venture capital as an increasingly attractive asset class and as the mutual fund industry grew, there was tremendous interest in owning shares of venture companies that became public.

High-Tech Investment Bankers: The Four Horsemen

One cannot consider this period without mentioning what came to be known as the "Four Horsemen." This group, which issued a majority of the hot technology deals, included Robertson Stephens, Alex. Brown, Hambrecht & Quist, and Rothschild, Unterberg & Towbin. Bill Hambrecht was something of a cult hero at the time—not only did he run one of the most powerful firms, but he was also one of the most visible venture capitalists. His name alone would generate a lot of interest. The Hambrecht & Quist conference, dating back to the early '70s, became extremely popular as a gathering place for public and private investors.

At T. Rowe Price we watched what was going on and decided that it would be an opportune time to launch what was then called a mezzanine fund, which would invest in companies just prior to their public offering. Previously, brokers had often given these deals to favored clients, or had formed what then were called bridge funds to participate. Now, big institutional clients that generated large brokerage commissions wanted a seat at the table. We raised approximately $80 million for the T. Rowe Price Threshold Fund. At the same time, Hal Bigler,[1] working with Rogers Casey,[2] a then-prominent pension consulting company, launched a similar fund called Crossroads. Today, this is a well-defined segment and numerous such later-stage funds exist.

---

[1] Hal Bigler was one of the first gatekeepers of venture capital—a financial consultant responsible for investing institutional money in venture capital funds and in monitoring their performance.

[2] Rogers Casey was also a gatekeeper of venture capital.

We soon learned that you could not invest in deals by simply piggy-backing on top of brokerage or venture capital relationships. Doing your own work was critical. Most of all, this brought home the real differences between the public and private markets. There are basically no regulations in the private market—it's caveat emptor. Also, terms have to be negotiated, as opposed to being pre-established. Unlike a public company, there is much less credible and analyzable data. Finally, there is virtually no liquidity in problem situations. As a portfolio manager, I could always get some bid on a public company. For private companies, if there were a major problem, it often would require a great deal of work, additional funding, or simply pulling the plug. None of this is particularly fun, and the time drain can be substantial.

It turned out that what was happening during this period, as is often the case, was that many were putting money in at a peak. Too much money had come into the market and venture prices had increased greatly based on public valuations. If you look back, it's interesting to see that the funds formed in the '83 to '87 period, with few exceptions, provided returns that were significantly below historic norms. In general, the venture capital returns from this period proved to be considerably less than 10 percent annualized. This highlights the cyclical aspects of the industry, something that today seems to have been forgotten.

During this time, as the funds experienced growth and became institutionalized, a myriad of unanticipated issues began coming to the fore. Were venture capitalists holding public stocks and getting paid venture fees? Were they distributing at the top with the stocks immediately going down after distribution? Did the brokers know about the distributions and were they somehow taking advantage of this to front-run clients?[3] What were the internal conflicts and those between different funds within the same organization? Internal issues pertaining to the general partner's operation also came under scrutiny. There were no easy answers and a number of the issues remain relevant today, although the industry has developed many standard guidelines and accepted practices to deal with them.

---

[3] *Front-running is when a broker provides key financial information to a company's shareholders in advance of the general market.*

Venture capital again peaked in terms of fund-raising in 1987 following the bull market and ensuing IPO boom. Performance is historically followed, with a delay, by money into venture capital. Coincident with the '87 market peak, the venture industry raised $4 billion. For perspective, and as further testimony to the historic cyclicality, fund-raising declined to $1 billion in 1991 as performance of the mid-'80s funds lagged. There was virtually no IPO market, with the cumulative amount of IPOs from 1988 to 1990 being less than was done in 1986 alone. I believe after the crash in 1987, there was only one deal done for the balance of the year.

I remained at T. Rowe Price, but as the '80s progressed, I became increasingly interested in private equity. As competition increased, I could see it was becoming increasingly difficult for individuals to distinguish themselves in the public market. As a frame of reference, when the New Horizons Fund started in the late '60s, we were one of two or three small-company institutional investors. In the mid-'90s there were almost 500 emerging-growth mutual funds, not to mention other pools of capital available for this purpose. Despite what people say about venture capital and competition, it's still a business characterized by huge inefficiencies where the practitioners continue to live by their wits and relationships. Also, the opportunity to distinguish yourself is just enormous if you can build companies that grow into substantial enterprises. It really struck me that the differences between the creation of wealth and simply money management, along with the fee structure and the appeal of a profit participation, would lead talent toward venture capital and other forms of private equity.

The '90s: Venture Capital's Golden Age

As the '90s dawned, venture capital was poised for a major resurgence. This was to mark the beginning of what became the golden age of venture capital—a period unlike any we have ever seen in terms of the build-up of assets, wealth, and enterprise value. We had a great backdrop: a rising stock market, low inflation, falling interest rates, good economic growth, and lots of liquidity. Add to that yet another change to the capital gains tax, which had risen in '87 to equal the tax on ordinary income and was now reduced to a much lower level.

Venture capital by now had become an accepted institutional asset class. There were large amounts of new money seeking superior performance and diversification. It was also an exciting place to invest. The institutions also liked the way the accounting was done, eliminating volatility by holding values relatively constant. This was a time when tax-free investors began to truly dominate the market. In addition, the baton was passing slowly from the traditional defined-benefit plans of major corporations to state and local governments, which were funneling enormous sums of money into this arena. As an example, the State of California allocated billions of dollars to alternative assets and became a significant force in the marketplace.

All in all, it was a very hospitable environment. We again started to see new, exciting industries emerge—networking, wireless communications, the Internet, and others. What we have seen—and continue to see—is that the venture community is a very good allocator of investment capital. When the need was for hardware, that's where the money was going. When networking and the Internet took off, venture capital was there. It's interesting that if you track venture capital flows, you track the growth areas in the U.S. economy.

Expanded Venture Capital: A New Structure

Once again, the industry started to take on a new structure. As institutions played a much more prominent role, gatekeepers, fund-of-funds, secondary markets for partnership interests, and so on, came into being. The infrastructure developed as venture firms grew larger and the bigger investment banks began to show more interest in their output. Venture capital began to get much more recognition as the business press focused on it and high-tech millionaires were highly publicized. Venture capitalists even began taking on a political role concerning issues that were important to them. However, I think it is important to note that in the overall context of the financial markets or alternative assets the amount of venture capital is not all that significant. Leveraged buyout and real estate funds are much, much larger, and their impact even greater if you consider the use of financial leverage. However, it can be argued that venture capital has far more impact in terms of job creation and economic growth.

I decided to leave T. Rowe Price in 1993. I liked the idea of becoming more focused on private equity, working with smaller companies without having to worry as much about potential conflicts of interest, and being involved with young entrepreneurs. In doing so, I wanted to remain active, be taken seriously, have a credible platform, and work in smaller situations where it would be possible to make a difference. I was fortunate to have a number of opportunities that enabled me to move in this direction. I had been instrumental in founding The Carlyle Group, a Washington, D.C.–based merchant bank, and this provided me an outstanding platform from which to operate. At the outset, I helped to establish and become a special limited partner at Trident Capital, a venture pool focused on information systems, and assisted in the founding of several other funds. I also invested directly in a number of individual deals—some in conjunction with venture firms, others not. My whole idea was to spread out, get into the traffic, and establish a lot of interlocking relationships. I saw myself as something of a server, in computer parlance, where a lot of things would come my way, and I would distribute them to others and then figure out how to participate in one way or another. As an interesting sidelight, Jim Clark gave me one of the first looks at Mosaic—which subsequently became Netscape and is now part of AOL. I missed participating for a variety of reasons, but this opened my eyes early on to the Internet's potential and led me to a number of related investments, including iVillage and Wit Capital.

An Angel in the Beltway

As contrasted to most venture capitalists, I have had to repackage myself at a relatively late stage in my career and shift focus from a primarily public market orientation. What has evolved is an extraordinarily exciting and challenging multifaceted role. As time went on, I helped establish and now oversee The Carlyle Group's venture capital pool, with assets now totaling well above $500 million. I am also a special limited partner in a number of other firms and serve on other advisory committees. This outreach program gives me a window on industry conditions, provides deal flow, and generates a wide range of personal contacts.

Probably the most interesting—and challenging—thing has been private investing in individual companies. I don't like to use the word *angel*—it seems almost too benign. I was fortunate early on in tapping in with a few young entrepreneurs outside the traditional venture capital world. Through a series of circumstances, I had become acquainted with Jon Ledecky, who early on promoted the concept of consolidating or rolling up industries. I became the first investor in U.S. Office Products, which soon went public and eventually reached over $4 billion in revenues. I also became involved in several other companies—USA Floral and Sirrom Capital—that quickly went public.

As a private investor, I see a number of relatively small situations with people who do not want, for a variety of reasons, to go the traditional venture route. A lot of those deals are too small for the large funds, creating opportunities below the so-called radar screen. This, together with the wealth creation of the '90s, has led to the development of the angel networks. You cannot fail to be impressed with the amount of activity that's taking place at this level. In some ways, these bands of angels are disintermediating, or at least competing with, traditional venture capitalists.

This occurs in a period during which we are starting to see an evolution in the world of venture capital. We have gone through a tremendous boom—an unprecedented creation of wealth. This has been accompanied by an explosion in the aggregate amount of venture capital raised. New Enterprise's first fund was $16 million in 1977. Their most recent fund, NEA-9, is over $800 million and the next fund is expected to far exceed $1 billion. Billion-dollar venture pools, unthinkable just a few years ago, are becoming almost commonplace. Large institutional investors continue to allocate small percentages, which amount to extremely large dollar amounts, to the area. The preference for well-established firms or brand names that can effectively manage large money is quite remarkable. The large firms have more than maintained their market share.

There exists a tremendous aversion to first-time funds. To me, this represents an inefficiency in the market. I have personally tried to get involved with them and found this to be financially and professionally rewarding. Typically, those with a first fund are experienced, motivated people that either have a new idea or a proven expertise. The amounts of money are small, which tends to better equate with high rates of return. There's no doubt that such funds are highly focused and dependent upon establishing an outstanding record to ensure the viability of their firm.

We are also seeing something of a redefinition of the traditional venture capital system. There's less camaraderie, less syndication, less sharing of information, and more geographic dispersion. The large firms have a much harder time funding and working with very early-stage companies. With size comes an inviolate trade-off: more deals or bigger deals. It's now not just competition between firms, but also competition from small investors who are no longer really that small. That's particularly true in technology, where tremendous amounts of wealth have been created. This, together with high prices in the public market and the funds available to traditional venture firms, is driving up valuations. Today, entrepreneurs are much more knowledgeable and sophisticated in terms of selecting partners and setting the financial terms for their deal. The ample availability of funding, together with intense competition for deals, fosters this kind of environment.

Marketing Venture Capital: Gaining a Competitive Edge

Venture firms are now confronted increasingly with the issue of how to establish competitive advantage. We are seeing various responses to that as the industry matures and segments. Many firms now have more of an industry focus. There have been numerous other responses, including a regional focus, the incubation of start-ups where venture capitalists originate and nurture an idea, the use of platform companies as a basis for consolidation, housing entrepreneurs in residence, the allocation of small amounts for overseas investment, and so on. Also, we see numerous major corporations spraying large sums around. Both Microsoft and Intel have put significant amounts of money into individual companies, not so much to earn a financial return but for strategic purposes. Other technological companies such as Oracle and MCI WorldCom have recently announced moves in this direction. There's no reason to think such activity will diminish.

New hybrid models have also emerged. One that immediately comes to mind is Roger McNamee's Integral Partners, which has used his knowledge of the public market and a relationship with Kleiner Perkins to forge a new type of firm that invests in both public and private companies. Roger worked with me at T. Rowe Price and has been very innovative in identifying market opportunity. Recently he established Silver Lake Partners, the first firm to focus on technology buyouts.

We have been in an environment where an amazing number of big companies—most of which came out of the venture capital community—have been created. Cisco, Yahoo!, Amazon, CIENA, eBay, and innumerable others have come out of nowhere and emerged as leaders in rapidly growing—and often new—markets. The speed at which this has been occurring has not been lost on venture capitalists, and it has had a dramatic impact on the industry. Today's venture funds have become much larger and the rapidity of investment has increased exponentially. There is almost an inexhaustible appetite for capital, as many deals—particularly in telecommunications—require substantial funding. The potential for wealth creation within the venture community has become enormous. With over $120 billion of allocated capital in the venture business today, the derivative incentive compensation (based on a 20 percent-plus profit participation) is almost mind-boggling. It is also important to note that, when you look at the number of highly successful companies and initial public offerings, the preponderance of such companies that have been venture-backed is quite remarkable. While venture money may be the tip of the iceberg within the financial markets, it really has driven the IPO market and been a significant force propelling the U.S. economy.

Paying for Venture Capital

Some things, however, have not changed. Perhaps most significant is the venture capital fee structure. This was put in place to solve very specific problems and has endured. In many ways it is no longer as relevant to today's business with many organizations layering funds and managing huge amounts of money. Nonetheless, it's been impervious to very strong pressures from the institutional community and today we even see the best funds increasing to either a 25 or 30 percent carried interest. Perhaps the reason for this is a perceived shortage of top-flight venture capitalists that can effectively manage large sums of money. Such firms have not had to bow to the fee pressures that have hit other parts of the investment management industry. Also, Silicon Valley continues to be dominant. The region has the capital, the technology, the role models, the major universities, and the infrastructure. We've recently seen pockets of venture capital emerge in other areas such as the northwest, Texas, and the mid-Atlantic region. But while vibrant, they pale in comparison to Silicon Valley. Overseas there have been fledgling efforts to establish venture capital centers, but this remains primarily a U.S. phenomenon.

Today the industry has become institutionalized in a way that none of us could have imagined thirty years ago. However, it has not become larger in the context of the financial markets of the U.S. economy, where $40 billion of annual funding and total assets exceeding $100 billion are relatively small sums. That would suggest that this is an industry that still has room to grow and attract more capital.

Initial Public Offerings: Venture Capital's Crunch Factor

As I look back over history, the IPO cycle remains a point of particular fascination and importance. There is overwhelming evidence that most people don't make money in new issues. But the infatuation comes and goes, and periodically provides the window that allows the realization of huge value for venture capital. As I look back on my career, one of the most interesting things is how investors react to hot new issues. A love affair with the new, and the idea of getting in on something exciting with huge potential and some scarcity value,[4] seems to be eternal. The underwriters and the companies are very good at whipping up enthusiasm for new issues. This can be an extraordinarily important component of venture capital returns, although over longer periods perhaps two-thirds of venture companies are sold or merged rather than taken public.

The new issue market is not just a factor in realized returns. It provides a very inexpensive form of capital for companies, which in turn

---

[4] *Underwriters have historically boosted value of IPOs by selling only a limited number of shares at the offering. Thus, price often becomes a function of demand rather than inherent value.*

provides a huge competitive advantage for the new companies that can obtain it. I've always looked at the financing cycle of venture capital companies as being something like an accordion. It expands and compresses based on the availability of public capital. If the public markets close, you have various rounds of financing at fairly expensive prices. When there's a very robust new-issue market, capital can be extraordinarily inexpensive. Thus, we see opportunities come and go in various stages of the financial cycle as a result of stock market conditions and the outlook for new issues.

Despite its success and widespread appeal, the industry is not without challenges and issues, both for investors and practitioners. Performance, truly spectacular in recent years, is always a question mark and a challenge. It goes without saying that expectations today are extremely—perhaps unrealistically—high. Venture firms are dealing with increasingly large sums of money, and current public and private valuations have risen dramatically. Historically, such conditions have augured a period of lower returns, although this is counterbalanced today by an abundance of opportunity in the U.S. economy. There are also generational issues facing the industry, as the people who built the firms are migrating to other areas, or taking on more limited roles. Another important question is: Will institutionalization lead to sterility? The successful venture investors in the past were really people who had ideas, made a leap of faith—not an intuitive judgment, but an instinctive reaction to people and ideas—and then worked to build companies. Process was not that important. More and more, it seems that venture capitalists are acting like traditional money managers rather than investors. This is something that I saw happen as the money management business grew and became institutionalized. It poses a true danger to the larger firms and could provide an opportunity for smaller, aggressive new entrants.

Looking ahead, it seems that the risks in venture have gone up as a result of high valuations, an abundance of capital, and increased competition. This should eventually result in lower returns than those experienced in the late '90s. However, there is no reason to think that venture capital will not continue to provide superior rates of return over longer periods. There seems no shortage of new ideas nor of those willing to take an entrepreneurial risk. When you look at the number of companies that have been formed over the last four or five years, a tremendous pipeline of opportunities exists. There is a huge need for venture capital to sustain and grow these companies. Interest is growing on the part of individuals and institutions, and this should provide adequate funding for the foreseeable future.

As in the past, some cyclicality in returns and funding levels seems inevitable, but the industry looks to be on very solid ground. Clearly, there's no reason to be discouraged about the long-term outlook for venture capital. It remains a great business, and I can't imagine a better career venue.

VISIONS

JAMES BREYER
Accel Partners

Succession will always be a major issue for venture capitalists. Making the transition from one generation of investors to another has not been easy. Many funds such as Merrill Pickard, Anderson & Eyre, and TVI couldn't make the changeover and faded away. One fund that has made the transition from one group of successful venture capitalists to another is Accel Partners.

Accel Partners was launched in 1984 by Jim Swartz and Art Patterson, two venture capitalists who began their careers in venture capital with New York's Adler & Co. Swartz and Patterson built Accel into a respected technology and telecommunications fund.

Jim Breyer, who joined as an associate in 1987 and now is the managing partner, has successfully continued the tradition. More important, with a network of entrepreneurs, technology professionals, and corporate investors such as Microsoft, Dell, Compaq Computer Corp., Lucent, and Northern Telecom Ltd. in its most recent venture fund, along with a style that has made Accel one of the most successful funds—and most accessible—Breyer has given the venture fund a new image and identity.

Accel always has focused on software and communications, and its focus hasn't shifted in recent years. But like most others, its biggest hits in the recent past have come from Internet companies such as Redback Networks, Foundry Networks, Portal Software, RealNetworks, and UUNET (acquired by MCI WorldCom). Still, Breyer believes in a diversified strategy that encompasses a wide range of businesses involved with the Internet and its infrastructure, along with the "bricks and clicks" initiatives of new investments such as Walmart.com and Accel-KKR Internet Company.

I 'LL START from the very beginning, or perhaps, before the beginning. The personal history starts with my parents. My parents are Hungarian immigrants; they left Budapest in 1956 during the revolution, settled in Vienna for one year, and attended University of Vienna. My mother had been a very successful mathematics student in Hungary, and had attended the same college as Andy Grove. My father was an engineer, and he received a scholarship to Yale. They came to the United States in '57, and I was born in New Haven in '61. My parents spent all of their working careers in the high-tech industry in the Boston area. I grew up in Natick and Weston, a couple of towns outside of Boston.

My mother worked for Honeywell for twenty years, and eventually ran their design automation group. My father was at Honeywell as well, but eventually left to join Pat McGovern at International Data Group. Both my parents were very much a part of the Route 128 technology world of the mid- to late '70s and early '80s. I grew up with a cultural emphasis on technology, with a focus on Intel because of the Hungarian background of Andy Grove, Les Vadesz, and a number of the people leading Intel.

Going West

When it came time to go to college, I was accepted by both Yale and Stanford. My family very much wanted me to stay close by, but I became completely enamored with Stanford for a couple of reasons—its California and Silicon Valley location, and the opportunity to study both computer science and liberal arts. I journeyed 3,000 miles to Stanford in 1979.

Very early on, I became very intrigued with computer science and computers. During my sophomore year, I sent out 50 résumés and received one job offer. Fortunately, it was from Hewlett-Packard. During the summer and fall of 1981, I worked in HP's data systems division in Cupertino, doing product management work and technical work. I came away from the experience with enormous respect for HP. One event stands out: the time I had the audacity to schedule a lunch with John Young, HP's CEO. To his credit, he met with me, and I offered him my opinions on what HP should be doing differently in the computer business. I smile when I look back on what he must have been thinking during that lunch.

In 1981, Steve Jobs was on the cover of *Time* magazine. Figuring I had nothing to lose, I sent a letter and résumé to Steve. I had already gone out and purchased an Apple II, and was deeply passionate about the Apple II experience. Steve, fortunately—as I've said to him several times since—did take a look at the résumé and forwarded it to his director of marketing, Alan Oppenheimer. Alan called, brought me in for an interview, and offered me a job. I started working part-time, and then for a summer, at Apple Computer in 1982, one of the defining years in the computing business.

Rookie Years at Apple

It was the summer when IBM entered the business—the same summer that Apple ran their famous *Wall Street Journal* ad welcoming IBM to the business. Apple's stock, at the beginning of the summer, was trading at $11, and by the end of the summer the stock price was north of $60. It was truly an amazing time at Apple and in Silicon Valley—in many ways a frenzy that we did not see again until the Internet era of the late 1990s.

Apple was attracting the most unique, innovative people in the business—it was an extraordinarily young organization. I was twenty-one at the time, and fit right in. My peers were in their mid-twenties, and of course, Steve Jobs was the spiritual and de facto leader of the company. In many ways, it was similar to what many premier Internet companies feel like today.

After the Apple Computer experience, I had a strong visceral feeling that I wanted to spend my time in the technology business, but decided to apply to business school. I was accepted at Harvard Business School, and chose to go to work for McKinsey & Company in New York for two years prior to Harvard. I consulted to very large, bureaucratic Fortune 50 computer and communications companies. Although I had a wonderful experience, and developed enormous admiration for McKinsey, after two years I was absolutely convinced I didn't want to be a management consultant. One day stands out. At 9:00 P.M., we had just finished some presentations, and the director of the project thought it would be a good idea for me to hand-deliver the presentations to the homes of the ten executives who would be attending the meeting the next day. For the next three hours, I went to each of the executives' homes in N.Y.C., Connecticut, and New Jersey, and dropped off the packages. A true learning experience! The next day, as I pulled into the conference center, I saw ten limos waiting outside the building—a sight that never would have occurred at Apple or HP.

Prior to attending Harvard Business School, I went to Europe with my girlfriend—now my wife. I spent several weeks at Cambridge University writing short stories, and although I'm not particularly talented as a writer, it remains a personal passion.

I was at Harvard Business School from 1985 to 1987, a period when Wall Street mania was ubiquitous. There was very little interest in technology. I went through business school with a very strong focus on getting involved deeply in the technology business. I had a limited idea of what venture capital was all about. Professor Bill Sahlman was instrumental in providing that introduction. Mitch Kapor came to speak to our entrepreneurial finance class at Harvard. Not surprisingly, everyone gave me similar advice—spend five to ten years in a technology company, and then enter the venture capital business.

Choosing Venture Capital Over a Start-Up

As I graduated, I had a decision to make—join Oracle as a director of product management or enter the venture capital business. Tom Siebel, who founded and has built Siebel Systems into one of the premier software companies in the world, would have been my boss. As he was recruiting me, he emphasized that it would be foolish to go directly into venture capital. His words still resonate: "Jim, you can come work for me for ten years, and you'll be investing your own money—not someone else's." In retrospect, he would have been right. Tom is an exceptional individual, and it would have been a great experience. However, I decided that I wanted to pursue venture capital, knowing that it might be for only a year or two, and that afterwards, I could join an entrepreneurial venture. I received several offers, and decided to accept a position with Accel Partners in San Francisco, working very closely with Arthur Patterson and Jim Swartz.

Arthur and Jim started Accel in 1984, and had built a very unique and successful emphasis on software and communications investing.

I had a passion for the software business and communications-oriented technologies. Therefore, it was a tremendous fit. In addition, I viewed them as very strong mentors, and indeed, they have been terrific. Venture capital is still an apprenticeship business, and mentorship is at the heart of learning the venture capital business. My compensation level was anywhere from a half to a quarter of what my other job offers were coming out of business school. Yet, I felt that there are certain fundamental businesses that one joins thinking about the long-term potential—both financial and personal. Venture capital and real estate are two businesses where fundamental value is being created, and over time, if fundamental value is created, positive things happen.

I went in with low expectations. In my heart I felt that I would spend two or three years in the venture capital business, and then join a Tom Siebel, or some start-up, and pursue that path. Eleven years later, I'm finding venture capital to be a great ride. I have not been bored at any time. I never thought I'd be doing it for eleven years, but it's been a terrific experience. I left Harvard Business School in 1987, a very important time. It was the year of the crash. Investment banking hired the highest percentage of Harvard Business School graduates in the history of the school—33 percent of my class. In terms of the technology business, 1987 was rather slow relative to today, to put it mildly! There were few fundamental breakthrough technologies, and there was considerable doom and gloom about the venture capital business as well.

In 1987, when I joined the business, there were a number of articles suggesting that the venture capital bubble had burst. For me, this simply indicated that this was an excellent time to get into the venture capital business. I am a contrarian by nature, and all of the negative articles, combined with all of the people advising me that it was a terrible time to join, strongly fueled my interest and desire. From afar, it looked like an extraordinarily compelling business, and the contrarian characteristics suggested to me the timing was right.

Venture Capital in the '80s

What was unique about the venture capital business in the late 1980s was the declining base of venture capitalists. Every year in the late '80s there was a 20 percent drop in terms of the number of venture capitalists and venture firms in the business. There was limited competition for deals, although the competition to back the best entrepreneurs is always fierce. If we made three times our investment on an acquisition, it was viewed as heroic. Obviously, we were in a completely different cycle from 1999, where we're at the other extreme. Today there is euphoria—in many cases a mania—that will inevitably come to an end. In today's environment, it is easy to confuse brains with a bull market.

The rapidity with which some of these returns have been generated is unlike anything we've ever seen. In May 1999, we had four companies go public, creating over $10 billion in market capitalization. The Internet has dramatically impacted all parts of our professional lives, and has fundamentally altered Silicon Valley and the venture capital business forever.

Hitting Cyberspace through UUNET

Fortunately, I became very interested in the Internet in 1992, largely through Mitch Kapor. Mitch deserves an enormous amount of credit for being one of the first individuals in the world to recognize the commercial importance of the Internet. He'd been a personal investor in a small Internet service provider in Virginia called UUNET. I met Mitch at an industry conference in 1992. We stayed in touch, and in 1993 Mitch introduced UUNET to us, and emphasized that it was an explosive opportunity. We had also looked at PSINet, a competitor of UUNET, as a potential investment. In early 1993, we came to the conclusion that there was a fundamental investment opportunity in the Internet. We also felt going in that UUNET's Internet service provider (ISP) business wouldn't be the only upside. We believed that the ISP business would commoditize over time, and that the real upside was in the value-added services that UUNET would provide. We were wrong about the ISP business commoditizing quickly, but fortunately we made the investment. That's true of many of the deals that one does. The initial thesis is often a little bit off.

UUNET not only made money, it was one of the first and best venture capital investments in the Internet. In our case, we invested $4 million in UUNET in 1993, and after the mergers with MFS and later

WorldCom, the as-carried value was well over $1 billion (at the time of the WorldCom merger, the value was $500 million). It also was a terrific team effort where several of the partners played a significant role in the spring, summer, and fall of 1993 in finalizing the investment.

As I said, we felt that there would be a fundamental business for UUNET around value-added services, and this will turn out to be the case in the longer run. However, for the first five years, there was an enormously valuable business in providing high-speed Internet service capability to businesses, and UUNET established category leadership. UUNET also gave us unique insight into other investments. In 1994, I was the only venture capitalist at Internet World. I walked the tradeshow floor with Mike Odell, the VP of technology, and we talked through every one of the interesting deals. This strategy is a clear example of how an early franchise deal can lead to "prepared mind" thinking around many other related investment opportunities. In addition, it is vitally important to remember that in nine cases out of ten, the first business plan is not the business plan that ends up being pursued by the company. Therefore, the intangibles around the team, market, and position within a turbulent wave are so critical. In almost all cases that I can think of, Internet businesses have created enormous value in a very different way from what was proposed in the original investment thesis that was circulated within the partnership.

Investing in Confusion

Perhaps the defining characteristic of what we look for, taking all this into account, is confusion. Confusion is an enormous positive for the businesses that we participate and invest in. Massive confusion indicates to us that established leaders such as Microsoft, Cisco, and Intel are unlikely to put together a detailed, implementable plan on their own. They can buy into the market, but they won't innovate and lead the market when there's a very high degree of confusion. Therefore, we look for dramatically growing markets where confusion is a defining characteristic. This increases the odds substantially for the start-up venture. Venture firms approach this confusion from the standpoint of risk reduction combined with opportunity maximization. The operating assumption is that opportunities can be realized by eliminating the risks to their achievement. Obviously, risk can never be fully eliminated; however, there are definite benchmarks in technical and marketing accomplishments that represent the lowering of risk.

It's very clear to me that the only way to generate home runs is by building franchise businesses. Occasionally, we get a unique IPO environment where it's possible to generate a significant return without building the business. But these are abnormalities. There's simply no doubt that it is all about building businesses with strong underlying fundamentals that achieve market share dominance. Our returns are generated through the big hits, and the big hits almost always come from building great businesses. As I said, we may get lucky in times like today where extreme sales and earnings multiples are applied to our companies, but we cannot generate high rates of return over a long period of time without building fundamental new businesses. We have been in a fortunate time: Our 1993 fund has generated an internal rate of return after fees and expenses of 90 percent per year, and our 1996 fund's IRR is well over 100 percent per year.

Any entrepreneur or venture capitalist who as part of the investment thesis says this company is being created to be sold to Microsoft or to Cisco will inevitably fail in my view. We simply won't back entrepreneurs who view it in this manner. Now, clearly a merger will be one of the outcomes in a lot of cases. However, it is important to fundamentally attempt to build an underlying business that will stand the test of time. They don't all become franchise companies, but the ones that do are the investments that generate the disproportionate share of returns for our investors.

The Importance of Corporate Partners

One area of the venture business that has fundamentally changed is the view of corporate partners. It will be interesting to see how it turns out. We've taken a very proactive stance around corporate partnering. In our latest fund, which we closed in April 1998, we brought in Microsoft, Lucent, Nortel, and Compaq as direct investors—all major corporations, but Microsoft in particular has received the most attention. Our view is that because of the Internet, a young start-up has minimal time to establish escape velocity. It used to be that a company could spend a year developing product, and another year putting together a sales and marketing plan. If there was a mistake made it was possible to recover. Two or three years into a company's life, that company might think about a strategic corporate partner. Today, on day one we're asking ourselves, Who is the appropriate corporate partner? What is the right distribution, OEM, or technology deal that needs to be put together? How do we as venture capitalists ensure that we are putting together an optimal deal for the portfolio company? This does not mean our exits will change over time. The goal is still to build an independent entity, but Microsoft, Cisco, Intel, and others have changed the rules of the game. They are the leading companies of the '90s. They are also the leading minority equity investors in Silicon Valley. Contrast that with the '80s when IBM and AT&T were the dominant companies in their spaces. They were truly horrible at business development. They simply did not understand start-up entrepreneurial cultures, or how to co-opt some of the innovation that occurred in young companies.

The fundamental difference today is that the technology leaders are venture-backed companies, and in some cases the founders are still leading the firms. These leaders completely understand the importance of partnering effectively with start-ups. Therefore, our role as venture capitalists has changed. There's controversy today in Silicon Valley around the importance of strategic partnering. One camp believes that strategic partnering is not fundamentally important, that independent companies will grow without strategic partners, and it's business as usual. Another camp—which we are firmly a part of—that believes that entrepreneurial company building has fundamentally changed from five or ten years ago. The right deal, on the right basis, with the right corporate partner, and at the right time is often the difference between home-run success and failure. UUNET is a perfect example. The Microsoft deal in 1994 was fundamental in UUNET's history, and in its ability to distance itself from its competitors. Without the Microsoft deal, you could question whether UUNET would have been the ISP that garnered 60 to 70 percent of the market capitalization of that space. We see that again and again in the market spaces that we're investing in.

The increase in strategic partnering does present certain dilemmas. People always want to buy the exceptional companies. The most difficult decision we have to make, in most cases, is a Las Vegas–type bet: do we let it ride or not? We may be receiving an enormous valuation offer from a major company for a certain portfolio company, and yet for the very best companies we need to let the bet ride. We need to pursue the independent home-run opportunity, because that's the business we're in. We're not in the business of hitting singles and doubles. We're in the business of hitting home runs and grand slams.

Quintessentially Internet

One deal worth talking about, because it illustrates a number of defining characteristics of the Internet, is RealNetworks. In some sense, Rob Glaser, the founder and CEO, is the perfect entrepreneur. Rob graduated from Yale in 1983—the same year I graduated from Stanford. He was also a computer science and economics major. Rob decided to go directly to Microsoft as his first job out of school, and stayed ten years at Microsoft, eventually becoming the vice president of multimedia. He left in 1994, and started a company called Progressive Networks.

I have always been passionate about rich media and multimedia. I learned about what Rob Glaser was doing at an Esther Dyson Conference in Phoenix in 1995, and from the beginning I pursued the investment aggressively. It took six months to eventually arrive at an investment agreement, and we made a $5 million investment in Real-Networks in the fall of 1995. The final negotiation was memorable: Rob was at a Yankees–Mariners playoff game in New York. I was at home in California watching the game on television. Between innings, Rob would call me from his cell phone—with wild cheering in the background—and we'd negotiate pricing and other terms. After six or seven calls, we agreed on the deal. I cannot remember who won the game, but I hope it was the Seattle Mariners since I'm a die-hard Red Sox fan.

Rob's personal characteristics in many ways define exactly what an Internet entrepreneur needs to be. In real estate, it's all about location, location, location. In venture capital, the axiom is people, people, people. The major characteristics we look for are leadership, integrity, vision, and dedication. Rob is brilliant from a strategic standpoint. He is off scale in terms of IQ, deeply technical, and passionate about the business he's pursuing. He immerses himself completely in the business. He is able to completely internalize that an Internet business is not about one specific discipline, but about a multidisciplinary approach. That is the fundamental shift in the Internet. In every successful Internet business today, there is a strong core technology component, an e-commerce sensibility, and a broadcasting/media strategy. The franchise businesses sit at the intersection of these different markets.

This is fundamentally different from five or ten years ago, when the entrepreneur would often have a very deep, specific skill. Businesses rarely sat at the intersection of colliding worlds. The enterprise or client server software business was defined as a business where the individuals came from an Oracle or an IBM and the strategy was often a continuation of that set of experiences. What is dramatic, exciting, and challenging about Internet investing is that the home runs are all about interdisciplinary interaction.

Rob combines a set of sensibilities in a way that is extremely rare. Today's entrepreneurs are defined by deep strategic capability, IQ, and personal characteristics—not their résumés. Five years ago we spent considerable time with résumés. We simply don't place emphasis on them today. We care about personal characteristics. I'm much more interested today in getting to know how the entrepreneur personally views the opportunity and what their level of passion is. It wasn't Rob's experience that led me to pursue the investment so aggressively—he possessed the set of personal characteristics that I believe define outstanding entrepreneurs today. Today, RealNetworks has a market capitalization of over $12 billion. It's been an enormously successful investment for us, but more importantly, we also feel that we've started to build a business that matters.

What's very interesting to me as a venture capitalist is how RealNetworks has developed a defining set of relationships. Microsoft is an investor in Accel Partners. Greg Maffei, the CFO, is the point person. I spend a very significant amount of time in Redmond with various Microsoft senior and product executives. The relationship with RealNetworks is one that I helped define. It was Father's Day, 1997. We had heard that Microsoft was pursuing an acquisition strategy in the streaming media space. I flew up to Seattle on a Friday. Rob Glaser, Bruce Jacobson, and I brainstormed about what an appropriate deal might be with Microsoft. That evening, Rob, Bruce, and I met with Greg Maffei and Paul Moritz. Over that Father's Day weekend, we put together an equity and business deal with Microsoft that helped fuel RealNetworks' rise to prominence. At the same time it became a cause célèbre; by 1998, it had clearly evolved into an untenable business relationship. Microsoft and RealNetworks today have become direct competitors in the rich media space.

Strategic Partnering Ambiguities

Strategic partnering is a clear example how our business has fundamentally changed. Strategic partners can be highly valuable. At the same time, the wrong deal can destroy value. If we don't have a built-in, graceful way out for both sides in a deal from the beginning, it's potentially a disastrous scenario. Mistake number one that venture capitalists and entrepreneurs make when building strategic partner deals is that the deals are too often based on a successful outcome. What has to be built into these deals is how to manage the relationship when unpredictable things happen. RealNetworks and UUNET are two wonderful examples of different outcomes. Microsoft was the strategic investment partner in both cases. In the case of UUNET, it turned out to be a deal from heaven. Microsoft contributed enormous amounts of capital and value and helped UUNET achieve a multibillion-dollar value in the space of three years. In the case of RealNetworks, Microsoft and RealNetworks embarked on a journey where everyone knew going in that there was a significant likelihood of collision. Both sides knew that going in, but still went ahead with the deal. The rapidity with which the worlds collided was a surprise to both. However, the fact that the two companies became competitive over time was not a surprise. Microsoft provided enormous distribution leverage through Windows early on in the deal's history. RealNetworks provided to Microsoft a very important part of the overall rich media experience. Today, however, Microsoft believes that streaming media is a very large future opportunity. In the venture business, we like to say that, as the grass grows taller and passes a certain height, the strategic partner often takes a look at the market and decides that it needs to be in the business. It's no longer a niche market. When the lawnmower comes directly at us—whether it's Cisco, Microsoft, or Intel—we need to understand that the relationship is unstable, and that it's time to quickly move in separate directions.

As the Microsoft relationship publicly fell out of bed during the summer of 1998, it was up to us on the RealNetworks side to go out and form fundamental business deals with America Online, Netscape, Intel, and IBM Lotus, which we successfully did that autumn. The nature of the Internet investing business is that today's strategic partner is tomorrow's competitor.

Partnering with and Competing with Microsoft

Surprisingly, during this period of time, we became the first venture capital firm to receive a direct investment from Microsoft. Microsoft specifically approached me in November of 1997. Greg Maffei knew we were potentially going to raise a fund, and he proactively suggested that Microsoft would like to be a direct investor in Accel. We thought long and hard about it. Microsoft brings some tremendous value and strengths, but at the same time if there are any strings attached to a corporate relationship with an investor, it becomes a non-starter. There were no strings attached to the Microsoft investment. Like our other strategic partners and financial partners, they received no confidential information regarding technology, business plans, and so on. Our conclusion was that Microsoft is a factor in every business we invest in. In some portfolio company cases we will compete vigorously and directly with Microsoft. In other cases Microsoft is an exceptional strategic partner.

While they have been an investor, we have worked together on a number of new deals as well as on existing deals. Greg Maffei was the point person on the investment in both Accel Partners and RealNetworks. This leads to obvious complexity. At RealNetworks, my role is one of board member and significant shareholder. I do everything that I possibly can to help RealNetworks beat Microsoft in the rich media space. However, at the same time in other segments, I have to ensure that there are positive relationships that come out of the overall relationship with Microsoft. This is typical of the venture business. One day I will be in competition with venture capitalists on a particular deal. The next day, we're working together as board members on another deal. This continuously shifting role between competition and cooperation is part of the nature of venture capital, and is becoming more pronounced. I find myself constantly competing with, as well as working with, a handful of exceptional venture capitalists including John Doerr, Bob Kagle, Vinod Khosla, Doug Leone, Mike Moritz, John Walecka, and Geoff Yang. I'm juggling more potentially conflicting relationships than ever before. And I have access to more confidential information than ever before. We as venture capitalists are part psychologist, part investor, part agent, and part entrepreneur.

The New and Future Venture Capitalist

In a venture capitalist, there are nine or ten different elements of personality that need to be pulled together in a coherent way. Everything is happening an order of magnitude more quickly. Therefore, the venture capitalist needs to be able to juggle these different challenges and decide, with management, what the critical path is. We used to talk about two or three balls in the air. Today, there are nine or ten balls in the air. It's our job as venture capitalists to help prioritize the balls, and make sure that we're catching the really important ones. This is very different from five or ten years ago, where the challenges and the execution were far more defined. This balance between strategic partners, entrepreneurs, and venture capitalists has fundamentally altered our ecosystem.

We are also much more hands-on, but not necessarily in day-to-day management. We are far more hands-on when it comes to recruiting, strategy, and defining business relationships. I'm on two boards with John Doerr. As busy as John is, he is absolutely remarkable at being able to cut right to the critical-path issues for a company, and devoting his enormous energy and talent to helping a company achieve its critical-path milestones. That is the business we're in today. There are a lot of ways to waste time. Being able to determine what is critical path is a matter of survival. One month it may be recruiting a key individual; the next month it is cementing a corporate partnership. Our job is to be insanely rigorous about what that critical path is. So, if there is a defining characteristic of the venture capitalist today, versus five years ago, it's analytical—being able to help management form conclusions around critical-path items, and helping management achieve the core milestones. This is where the hands-on element exists today, and why you're seeing even greater concentration in the venture capital business today than ever before. I think of the venture capital business as a series of individual personalities, as opposed to a series of firms.

Defining Jim Breyer

I would certainly prefer that the entrepreneurs, rather than I, talk about what my strengths and weaknesses are—and my weaknesses are substantial! Here's how I think one needs to think about the venture capital business, and how I think about myself in the business.

Venture capital is a team-oriented business. I grew up playing soccer, hockey, and basketball. I received as much satisfaction from assists as I did from scoring the goal or basket. At Accel, we strongly believe in working on deals as a team. Redback Networks is a perfect example. Sequoia Capital introduced the deal to me. I led the due diligence process, negotiated the deal, and championed the investment. The company needed significant operational help so my partner, Jim Flach, became the board member and interim CEO. Without Jim's efforts, the company would not have completed its successful IPO in May 1999—the deal was priced at $23 a share and finished its first day of trading at $84 a share.

Venture capital is a humbling business. For all the successes, there are humbling events that occur on a daily basis. When we're looking to hire people at Accel, one of their defining characteristics needs to be an ability to laugh at themselves and not take themselves too seriously. We're in a highly competitive, highly intense business. There are always failures along the way. They might not be investment failures, but failures in terms of the people we hire and our business relationships. So, there has to be an ability to look at each event, learn from it, and rebound from it. First and foremost we have to laugh at ourselves, have a sense of humor about the day-to-day lives that we lead. Second, there's an enormous amount of luck in this business. Anyone who says otherwise is delusional. The fact is that we can do everything right as venture capitalists—in terms of identifying an investment, building a management team, and defining a market strategy—but external variables beyond our control still help define whether we've hit a home run, a single, or a double. I view my greatest strength as being passionate about building businesses, and passionate about building something that we can all be proud of. If we take the Real-Networks example, we're on a journey where the outcome is unclear. There's an enormous market capitalization. More importantly, we have an 85 percent market share of a business that I think is going to be enormous over the next five years, and we are innovating in areas such as digital music and media delivery.

Nonetheless, Real's outcome as a major defining entity is still in question. I'm very bullish, but fundamental challenges lie ahead. How does RealNetworks play in the broadband world? Will the Internet truly turn into a mass medium? How do we take RealNetworks from a leader in a small, defined business today on the Internet—streaming media—to a true leader and enduring franchise? It's not just the outcome that I enjoy. I love the process of getting from point A to point B. I get bored extremely easily. Like many in the business I suffer from Attention Deficit Disorder. I need to be challenged constantly on an intellectual basis. For my type of personality there is no other career that would be as fulfilling. The entrepreneurs quickly figure out who are the venture capitalists who are passionate about what they do, who can make a real strategic contribution, and, most important, who can bring the right set of values over a period of time. This isn't about creating a company to sell to Microsoft or Cisco. It's not about generating enormous returns. It's not about trying to take a company public. It's about creating businesses and cultures that we can feel proud of. They don't all get there, but what's so compelling about the venture capital business is that there's the opportunity to make a huge difference. Not as a CEO, but as a CEO's business development partner. This is what I try to excel at. I'm constantly asking, How do I as Jim Breyer, or we as Accel, help the entrepreneur build a truly world-class company? We must have personal passion around human resources as a strategic advantage to a company. There are numerous CEOs who view human resources management as follows: If the stock price is going up, I have a good culture, and I don't have to worry about anything. That's not what it's all about, obviously. I'm trying to help put together an innovative program where we help entrepreneurs view HR strategically from day one. I want the entrepreneurs to be thinking from the beginning about how to build a culture that's enduring, that scales, and that is one to be proud of. Mitch Kapor and Bud Colligan have been personal mentors in this area. This has not been a historical focus of venture capitalists or entrepreneurs, but going forward, as the public markets inevitably pull back, recruiting and retaining great personnel will become the single most important factor in the success of a company. Helping entrepreneurs build a culture that allows employees to achieve dramatic personal growth and that encourages employees to stay when the stock price is clipped in half is a personal passion. It is where we as Accel can help innovate.

At the end of the day, I define my success or failure by the answer to the question: Are we the first phone call that an entrepreneur makes when he or she goes off and starts a new company? If we're not that first phone call, we have not done our job. If the entrepreneur does not believe that we genuinely assisted in building a franchise company that stands for integrity as well as financial success, we have failed in our mission.

JON CALLAGHAN
@Ventures

The success of Internet companies such as Netscape, Amazon, Geocities, and Lycos have become the talk of investors everywhere. In the process, Wall Street and many investors have gotten excited about CMGI, a publicly traded database marketing company, that early on chose to make investments in Internet companies through a company-funded Internet-only venture capital pool, and chose to sell shares in that pool in the public market.

Venture capital funds historically have been pools of capital whose value cannot be accurately pinpointed. That is because they mostly own shares in privately owned companies whose price has not been determined in the manner that shares of publicly owned companies are. Indeed, the combination of CMGI and @Ventures, the venture capital arm of CMGI, is a fascinating experiment in how to publicly value a portfolio of public and privately owned entrepreneurial companies. CMGI, which is publicly traded, had a market valuation as high as $16 billion in 1999. CMGI owes much of its success to its investment in Lycos, the search engine company, but it also has been an active investor in Internet start-ups such as Chemdex and Critical Path, and more established companies such as Alta Vista.

At a time when many venture capitalists—both experienced and inexperienced—have chosen to jump on the Internet bandwagon by creating Internet-only funds, @Ventures stands as the granddaddy of them all—in cyber-time, of course. Jon Callaghan, a managing partner of @Ventures, talks about the industry's first Internet-only venture fund and the benefits of such a focused strategy.

I GOT INTO venture capital in a unique way. I joined Summit Partners straight out of college. Prior to that I started a small business and ran it for about eight years. It was a chain of retail sporting goods stores in Jackson, Wyoming, called Mountain Bike Outfitters. I ran that during college and after, even while I was at Summit. I got into the venture business from the entrepreneurial side, although I joined pretty young in my career.

When I joined Summit it was about a $400 million fund. When I left, it was probably triple that. Early on, we were doing what for Summit were early-stage deals—$2 to $5 million investments. For Summit today, an early-stage deal is a revenue growth company with profits. It's definitely later stage by the industry's definition. I spent four years there, and then went to business school at Harvard Business School. While I was at HBS, I worked for America Online's Greenhouse, which is now AOL Studios. At the time, the Greenhouse was a $10 million pool of capital that was put aside to find and seed content opportunities for the online service. With my bike shop background, I was much more interested in working with young companies.

I did a lot of other work in the Internet at business school, including a field study called Chemdex in which we wrote the business plan for an online market for specialty chemicals. I got exposed to the Internet, and actually hooked up with the guys at CMG way back when CMG was a Summit investment. I knew David Wetherell, and knew what he was doing in the Internet, and joined the company to do early-stage Internet venture capital.

CMGI

Structurally, we're not CMGI but its venture arm. CMGI was the sole limited partner in our first two venture funds, @Ventures One and @Ventures Two. We're structurally like any other fund, in that we take and carry from our limited partner on the gains that we create. So, I joined as a general partner in @Ventures One and @Ventures Two. At the time there were me and four others in @Ventures—Peter Mills and I on the West Coast, and David Wetherell, Guy Bradley, and Andy Hajducky on the East Coast.

CMGI initially was in the database marketing business. Then in 1994, Dave Wetherell put a small development effort together under a division he called Booklink Technologies, which had developed a browser designed to let people read books remotely over a network. It used HTML and HTTP. Booklink was sold to America Online for about $30 million in AOL stock, which traded up to $70 million very quickly. We took $50 million of that and put it into @Ventures One, which became the first Internet-only venture fund.

The Early Bets

The thinking for us has always been that the Internet was going to be big. We didn't profess to know where it was going, nor did we profess to be experts on the Internet. It's far too big and it is going in too many different directions. From the very beginning, however, all of us knew that the Internet was going to revolutionize the way that people communicated, accessed data, and stayed in contact. So, a lot of our early bets were on three areas: content and community, electronic commerce, and enabling tools. That's been our mantra since day one.

We chose those three areas because we thought there was a need for content in communication, which is part of creating a community. We also thought that there needed to be people building the structure of the Internet, so enabling tools and technology were very important to us. Lastly, we had the vision early on that people would conduct business on the Internet, either business to business, or business to consumer.

Lycos fit everything. It's an enabling tool and a component of the Web infrastructure. We saw very early on that there was this tremendous growth occurring with Web sites and we figured there was a need to index all of them. We knew that the directory/search engine space was going to be a place where most people started their experience on the Web—whether they needed to find something or do something.

Lycos

We invested very early in a technology that we licensed out of Carnegie Mellon University. I think we put in $4.5 million. We brought in a CEO by the name of Bob Davis, and basically built Lycos. We still own 18 percent of Lycos, and at one point owned somewhere in the high 50 to 60 percent range. It was a very successful investment for us. The investment was obviously as early as it gets: we literally licensed code out of a university, negotiated that license, and built a company around it.

Did it take a lot of thinking to put $4.5 million—10 percent of our total fund—into one deal? This gets back to your risk tolerance. We have an exceptionally high tolerance for risk. We acted very quickly to get the competitive advantage in this space. We saw Lycos as being fundamental to the building block of the Internet. It was a very complicated deal to do—and it was super risky—because we were negotiating with a university to pull a piece of technology out, relying on researchers who had never been in the private sector before for the code. It was a very risky venture deal.

Lycos was an East Coast deal. We are split geographically, because our mode is to be very operationally oriented, very hands-on. When we work with companies, we work with them day to day. We always give exposure to companies like Lycos on the West Coast, and others, but they need lots and lots of handholding, which we provide.

We also were the first professional investor in Geocities. David Bonet had approached twenty other venture capitalists, and got turned down by all of them before he met us. We invested something like $5 million in Geocities. At its acquisition by Yahoo!, our investment in Geocities was valued at somewhere between $1 billion and $1.5 billion in Yahoo! stock.

Geocities was something really fascinating. We fundamentally believed that the Web was a great place for people with common interests. Birds of a feather flocking together. We thought that David Bonet had something major in his paradigm of allowing people to build Web pages.

The Rookie Syndrome

How can a new fund break into this ultra-competitive world? Every single venture fund is doing Internet investments, including Kleiner Perkins and Sequoia. All the big and very successful names in the business are in Internet investing. So how do we compete in such a market?

We compete by virtue of our focus. Our value is that we do only Internet investing. A few things result from that focus that are more valuable than capital in the competitive Internet markets—not in the market for Internet deals, but in the competitive market that is the Web. One is familiarity with the problems of rapidly scaling Web companies. We've not only seen Lycos and Geocities, but we're also investors in Iconic, which was sold to US Web; Netcarta, which was sold to Microsoft; Planetall, which was sold to Amazon; Real.com, which was sold to Hollywood Video; Chemdex, which exploded growthwise and is doing great, but is still private; and Critical Path, which went public in February 1999. We've got forty investments that we've worked with from early-seed stage to maturity. We have experience with a lot of the specific challenges and pitfalls that these companies are facing for the first time.

A lot of the challenges and pitfalls are uniquely related to the Internet. They can be as simple as deciding whether to do a big portal deal with Yahoo! for $2 million—or with AOL for $5 million—or putting that money somewhere else. Or it can be as complicated as determining how we should think about customer acquisition costs or an OEM strategy. We've lived through all these things, specifically on the Web. That's one result of our focus.

Another is business development opportunity. We invested in Planetall early in its development, then helped forge strategic alliances between Lycos and Planetall, and between Geocities and Planetall. Both alliances drove their membership growth overnight and dramatically contributed to the success of the company. The same can be said for Critical Path. We have Planet Direct, Nabasite, Raging Bull, Ancestry.com, and a couple of others, all of which are customers of Critical Path. In a way we're the keiretsu of the Internet.

Our Own Keiretsu

We've done probably five to ten strategic deals with Yahoo! on behalf of our companies. We've done that many with AOL. We've done that many with Inktomi and Excite. Across the portfolio, all of us partners have had direct interface with many different companies, so it's very easy to figure out who to talk to at Yahoo! for a deal with a new portfolio company. It's easy for us to pick up the phone and make that introduction. Externally we work very hard to provide strategic resources to our entire portfolio. For example, we work tightly with Compaq to make sure that every company in the portfolio gets close to cost pricing and rapid deployment of hardware. They did that with us because they see forty companies growing rapidly and think it is a great way for them to get an inside track. I don't want a CEO of a start-up wasting his or her time on these types of administrative issues. I can pick up the phone, get a team of Compaq or Inktomi people there, and basically allow the company to focus on the important stuff.

We're getting into a third area we call building-block technologies. Within the portfolio, CMGI owns a company called Nabasite, which provides hosting co-location and bandwidth. Raging Bull is a great example. By hooking them up with Nabasite, we took Raging Bull from one server in a dorm room to a fully redundant and scalable architecture within a hosting facility within a month. Ancestry.com is an even more dramatic example. We installed and went live with fifty servers redundant for the Web site within about four to six weeks. So, we can deploy building-block technology.

Another example is our advertising suite of companies, owned by CMGI—Interpreter, Engage, Adsmart, Youcan, and Eyepro. If there is anything to do with advertising at any one of these start-ups, we can deploy a technology, whether its an ad network, a serving solution, or a traffic profiling engine. Again, it's a very easy way for a company to get up, out, and on its way to being a real business without spending a lot of time on some of the lower value-added decisions.

@Ventures Two, which we closed in 1996, had roughly $50 million. It was very successful. We had investments like Planetall and Real.com. We still have 70 percent of Critical Path, and are in several others that are still live and active. We invested that very successfully, and then in December 1998 we closed @Ventures Three, which has $280 million in capital.

In @Ventures Three, CMGI is one of many investors. We also have investments from Microsoft and from LVMH, a European company. We also have Bank of Boston Capital and other financial investors. We want a deeper access to capital, because we think the market is accelerating and we want to do more large investments. More than that, CMGI has been a great keiretsu partner. Within their stable they have companies like Nabasite, which we've mentioned; Planet Direct, which is great for distribution; Engage, which is great for tracking; and Activerse, which is great for the chat-type thing. We thought by getting companies such as Microsoft, Sumitomo, and several large media companies to invest, we could have access into their networks.

It is part of the whole theme of providing more than just capital. If capital is a commodity in a competitive market, and we don't have the name and longstanding record of success that a Kleiner Perkins or a Sequoia has, we need to work harder and more strategically for our portfolio companies. So, we saw fund-raising as a way not only to bring in more capital for these companies, but also as a way to add additional strategic resources and contacts. It has worked quite well.

Do we worry that more money will change the way we invest? We had always thought, even in the early days, that we would trend up with the industry's growth. Initially, we were doing early-stage investments, and we still do a majority of those. But as more companies mature, there are opportunities for some larger investments, or perhaps some investments in companies that already have a Web site. We've been very active in doing those types of investments, and with good success.

There is a lot of competition and a lot of money. But for venture capital funds that are not focused on the Internet—just like for companies that are not in the Internet—it becomes harder and harder to catch up. Our keiretsu is number two in total live hits all time, number two in total reach. When we go to any company that's interested in reach and distribution that's a meaningful statistic, especially if the entrepreneur's making the decision based on how to add the most resources to his company, and how to ensure success in the Internet world. Funds might be able to do one or two successful companies, but it's pretty hard even today to create a successful keiretsu on the order of forty companies. That's not to suggest that there isn't time and room for other venture capitalists to come into this space. We think there is. We have a tremendous amount of respect for some of the more traditional venture firms that have shifted their resources to the Web.

Internet Only

Our intent is to focus entirely on the Internet industry. We don't have the distraction of also having to monitor a health care portfolio, or a hardware portfolio. We're fully dedicated. I think that enables us to be much more nimble as a partnership.

I've talked to a lot of folks on Sand Hill Road, and they tell us that when they're having a problem with Internet investments, their health care partners just don't get it. Or some of the more traditional partners just don't get it. So, as a partnership they have trouble reaching a decision.

The nine of us at @Ventures get it—at least the big picture. We all believe in this opportunity. It's not a question of figuring out whether this whole Internet thing is going to be real, but of evaluating the vision of the investment opportunity. It means we can act very quickly and decisively. We can bring in resources that others can't, and we can add value that others can't, because we've lived through several companies in the industry—both successes and disappointments.

The Internet is too powerful for businesses to ignore. It's too powerful for it not to proliferate into every single aspect of most companies. We have evidence that it costs certain companies upwards of $100 per purchase order. It costs us around $3. We're doing an investment in the health care side—an e-commerce company that sells specialty medical devices to hospitals. The cost in the industry per purchase is in the range of $300. We're doing it for dollars or pennies. The Internet is absolutely too powerful for any profit- or growth-motivated business to ignore. For that reason, and because the pace of business is accelerating and there's no faster way to communicate, I'm quite confident that the technology will expand into pretty much all aspects of business and our economy, which is what's so exciting about it from our perspective. We believe that in 1999, we're in the first inning of a long game.

Building an Internet company is also going to get more expensive. It costs somewhere between $25 and $50 million of private capital to get a standard e-commerce company up either to an IPO or to a larger strategic round. Our philosophy is that when we're behind a company, we like to not only protect but enhance our position. Clearly, we need financial resources to do that. We think we can very successfully and rapidly deploy this capital into good deals, since the opportunities are just tremendous. Again, that points to the opportunity being here now if we raise a larger fund, because there are good and prudent places for us as investors to put it.

Do I think the Internet will last forever? I think the Web will proliferate. I think it will become more of a mature business, and you'll see probably fewer of the home runs. By the same token, you're going to see much more consistent business models, much more consistent revenue models, and much more consistent profit models.

I don't think this type of explosive growth will last forever for investors or for the industry, because it will mature. The Internet is not just an industry, it's a layer on top of our economy and society. It's bigger than just one segment. So I don't think it will end or slow down soon—or mature soon. But over time it will follow the path of other nascent industries, and grow up.

STEVE LAZARUS
ARCH Venture Partners

Technology has always been the cornerstone of venture capital investing, and university research and national laboratories such as Argonne, Ames, and Los Alamos have long been the source of those technological innovations. Indeed, for universities such as Harvard, MIT, Stanford, and the University of California, licensing technology has been a very lucrative source of revenue. Still, for all the value resident in these institutions, few venture funds have been formed to specifically mine and commercialize their technology.

Steve Lazarus founded ARCH Venture Partners in 1986 to transfer technology from the University of Chicago and Argonne National Laboratories, one of the nation's twelve national energy laboratories. Since that first $9 million fund, ARCH has expanded—both in terms of managed capital and in terms of its geographical reach.

As a fund that started in Chicago and now has partners in Seattle, New York, Austin, and Albuquerque, ARCH is attempting to institutionalize the process of technology transfer. With successes such as NEON, a developer and marketer of software for business enterprise applications, and Everyday Learning Corporation, a provider of educational material for mathematics classrooms, it has proven that seed investing, especially in the area of untested and unproven research technology, can succeed. But ARCH also has shown that such investing requires building bridges with other venture capitalists and research organizations, as well as a commitment and a passion that sometimes go beyond traditional venture capital practice.

S O MUCH OF venture capital begins from a university perspective. Prior to World War II there was no substantial level of organized university-based research, not in the physical sciences nor in the life sciences. In the life sciences, you only had the advent of the sulfa drugs in the '30s. World War II was a watershed of enormous proportion. After World War II came the founding of American Research and Development (ARD) headed by General Georges Doriot, based at Harvard. While Professor Fred Terman had been at Stanford for some time before that, venture investing began broadly only after World War II. When William Shockley, co-inventor of the transistor, moved from the east to Palo Alto to start Shockley Electronics, the foundation was laid for a transistor-based electronics industry in northern California.

The University of Chicago evolved during the '50s and '60s as a research university doing work in both the physical and life sciences—probably at about the twentieth research dollar position in the United States. It didn't have an engineering school, so what actually occurred there over the years were a number of covert or hidden engineering organizations.

Chicago was not a Hopkins, a Columbia, a Harvard, or an MIT, but it was respectable. However, there was no organized technology transfer. The first reason for this was that there was the usual ambivalence within the faculty about doing anything that diverted from pure research or that had the flavor of a profit motive. There were arguments about this in the senate of the faculty. But one extremely important decision had been made—that the university and the faculty took ownership of all discoveries that were made by individual faculty members. Even today in 2000 that concept is still in dispute on many campuses. But it was clearly settled at the University of Chicago. The second thing that was going on in the late '70s and early '80s was a growing concern in Congress that the nation was not getting a payoff for all the investment that went into national laboratories and research universities. There are about 700 national laboratories, with the largest concentration in defense and energy. Many of the energy laboratories for decades had been operated by management designates such as the University of Chicago. The University of Chicago managed the Argonne National Laboratory on behalf of the Department of Energy, with a $500 million annual budget in basic research. A lot of ideas were sitting in that laboratory, and nobody was looking at them for commercial purposes. In the early '80s, Congress passed the Stevenson Wydler Act and the amendments to the Bayh Dole Patent Act and essentially the two pieces of legislation together gave the University of Chicago the opportunity to take title at no cost to discoveries at Argonne. So, you had a faculty that was doing productive research, and a potential at the Argonne Laboratory for a lot of valuable intellectual property.

The catalyst for all this, I believe, was the fact that the drug Erythropoietin, the red blood cell stimulating factor, was synthesized by Gene Goldwasser at the University of Chicago. Nobody protected it. It went into the public domain, and ultimately Amgen cloned it and it became a billion-dollar drug. Many people at the University of Chicago wondered why Stanford and UC San Francisco could participate in the revenue stream of the Cohn Boyer recombinant DNA inventions but Chicago got nothing as a consequence of Erythropoietin. All of these things came together in the mid-'80s, under the aegis of Walter Massey.

Walter was a high-energy particle physicist. He had been director of Argonne and was the VP of research at the University of Chicago. Later he went on to be head of the National Science Foundation and provost of the UC California system, and today is the president of Morehouse College. Walter was not only an excellent scientist, but he also had exquisite political skills. He pulled the basis for ARCH together, getting buy-in from some very powerful trustees, some important and influential people in the faculty, and some local businesspeople. He also designed ARCH as a not-for-profit corporation, wholly owned by the University of Chicago. Its main interest would not be in licensing technology, which was the conventional way of doing technology transfer at the time, but rather in starting new companies. At that time, I was retiring from a Chicago-based company called Baxter Laboratories, and I was thinking about teaching. Walter and the fellow architects of ARCH designed a job that was simultaneously a president of a corporation, albeit a small one, and associate dean of the Business School at the University of Chicago. So I came down to Hyde Park from Deerfield, and found myself the first employee of ARCH. I had a very small budget. We had the responsibility to do all patenting for both the university and the laboratory from that budget, which was enough to sustain me and a secretary, but not much else. We had a substantial amount of technology to examine.

The 57th Street Irregulars

The placement in the Business School turned out to be extremely fortunate. The student body was made up of a large number of young people who had been out in the workforce and who decided that they did not want to continue as salary men—in the Japanese sense of the phrase—but wanted to become owners. They wanted to build net worth; they wanted to control their destiny. Therefore, they wanted to go into small new enterprise, and build up from there. Several of them found me, and asked, "Is there any way we can work with you?" I said, "I can't pay you." They said, "That's okay, we'll do it voluntarily." Thus began what we first called the 57th Street Irregulars, and later—when we decided people needed to take us more seriously—the Group of ARCH Associates. I think it's coincidental, but very fortunate for me, that the two earliest members of that group, Bob Nelsen and Keith Crandell, are today my partners in ARCH Venture Partners. Clint Bybee, who came a year or two later, is the fourth general partner of ARCH Venture Partners.

What the young people started to do was go into the halls of the institution and locate the stars. I realize that's an elitist comment, but it's just like salespeople qualifying sales. Who is most likely to buy? Who is most likely to be productive? There are a lot of fairly mundane ways of finding out. Who has the most grant money? Who has the most publications? Who has the most citations? Who are members of the national institutions, the scientific elite structures who elect people? And finally, who did other scientists admire? Out of that, one could narrow it down to the 10 percent of the research faculty who were likely to yield inventions that would have intrinsic, and ultimately extrinsic, economic worth. Over time we have continued with that technique and refined it. This form of triangulation truly works.

I think the second technique we evolved was learning how to first identify the unique invention that was not going to have much follow-on, and that was best licensed to a third party. After syndicating out the licensing candidates, we concentrated on the technologies and inventions that could be platforms for new companies. When we licensed an invention there was no certainty that a revenue stream would result. For example, all too often a molecule licensed to a Bristol Myers, or a Lilly, might engender initial interest, but over time would be displaced by interest in other targets. It would then stay on the shelf. Which was another reason to start creating companies over which you have a greater degree of control. There was, however, very little venture capital in the Chicago area. I'm talking specifically of seed and early-stage high-risk capital with which to start new companies.

We made several trips to both coasts, carrying our portfolio of technology. Everyone was interested in a number of the specific deals but nobody had any enthusiasm about getting on an airplane and flying to the middle of the continent to shepherd, nurture, and incubate an early-stage deal. This is one of the demanding characteristics of seed and early-stage investing.

So, quixotically, we set out to raise our first venture fund. That was in '87 and '88. I made something in excess of 100 visits to foundations, other venture funds, and university endowment people. Everybody thought that the idea had merit. Nobody was interested in investing. I was told over and over again that my track record was all ahead of me. There was no denying that—it was the absolute truth. There's a Catch-22 to getting started in venture capital. If you don't have experience it's hard to get started, and if you haven't gotten started, you don't have any experience. Fortunately, a friend suggested that I call on Jim Bates, then the vice chairman and chief investment officer of State Farm. So, on a Saturday I drove out to meet Jim, who had been playing tennis, at the International House of Pancakes for lunch. I talked without interruption for about an hour, at the end of which he said, "That sounds like an interesting idea, we'll put $4 million into it." Suddenly I had my first investor.

The university endowment matched that, and soon we had a $9 million fund. We invested that fund in twelve companies. We made horrendous mistakes in some of those investments. Five of them failed. But seven of them were successful, and a couple of them were quite successful. We had a first fund that was returning a respectable return to its investors, and we were now considered legitimate venture capitalists. Not experienced, but legitimate. The university examined that set of occurrences and said, "This is no longer an experiment. We as a university are not at all comfortable with continuing as a general partner of a venture fund, so why don't we divide the entity we have created? The technology transfer and commercialization organization will remain inside the university, with the venture capital partnership going outside." At that point, in 1992, Keith Crandell, Bob Nelsen, Clint Bybee, and I stepped outside the university, created ARCH Venture Partners, and started to raise ARCH Venture Fund Two. We still had friendly relations with the university, and an opportunity to have early examination at both the University of Chicago and the Argonne National Labs. About that same time, we were invited by Columbia University in New York to take our model and open an office at the University in New York City. Some commercial interests in Albuquerque, New Mexico, helped us take the model and open an office in Albuquerque that was focused on the two huge national laboratories there, Sandia and Los Alamos. Those two labs represented $2 billion worth of basic research every year and had never seen a venture capitalist. Clint Bybee went to Albuquerque. We hired a young M.B.A. to operate in New York with Keith Crandell frequently coming into New York to supervise the operation. Bob Nelsen, who was born and raised in the Washington area, relocated to Seattle to open an office, on the assumption that the latent technology in Seattle—physical sciences, information sciences, and life sciences—was largely unexplored. There were very few venture funds in Seattle, and therefore we had an opportunity at the University of Washington to apply our same set of techniques.

ARCH Venture Fund Two proved to be an extremely successful fund. We created twenty-two companies. Six of them were follow-on investments in Fund One companies. We realized that what we were becoming was a seed and early-stage venture fund that also did later-stage investing in companies of its own origin. This had two consequences. One, it reduced the overall level of risk in the portfolio. Two, it started to shorten the time to recovery of the investment.

We started to be written about. Other universities heard that we were active, realized we knew how to interact with universities, and invited us to come out and look at their technology. We started to do a lot of flying. We violated our early rule that you had to drive to the deal. What we found we could achieve was an operating relationship either with the technology transfer function in a university or with a local, small venture capital fund. For example, at the University of Michigan, we worked with the Enterprise Development Fund, which is located in Ann Arbor. In Boulder, Colorado, we worked with Boulder Ventures. We do that today in more and more locations around the country. We found there were certain other funds who had similar characteristics to ARCH—some of whom had been around longer than we had.

Mining the Corporation

After focusing on university and laboratory technology primarily, we started to see opportunities in technologies that had been developed by corporations but were not being pursued by those corporations. In Fund Three, which is a $107 million fund, we dealt with several companies that are spin-offs of technology from company research and development locations. The techniques are quite similar to doing university research. We still take pure technology, act as entrepreneur or general manager—until one can be recruited in—and then nurture and support that concentration of technology. That appears to be a portfolio-expanding idea, getting away from just purely doing universities and laboratories, and having a different set of opportunities that balance the deal flow.

We tried to come to grips with the question of specialization versus generalization. It was being argued in venture capital circles that technology was becoming so sophisticated and so granular that you had to restrict yourself to life science or information technology, for example, or sometimes a subset of information technology. Because we were casting our net so broadly at a university, or in an industry, we felt that that specialization would be a mistake for us. What we decided was that the general partners should become reasonably knowledgeable in one or more technological areas. Then we would hire a group of very, very sharp consultants—Ph.D.-level academics or practitioners who understood the subsets of technology very, very well—and then pair the consultants and the partners together while working the deals. We felt that this was a successful approach to the generalization versus specialization problem.

In Fund Two, a $31 million fund, we recognized that we were sub-optimizing our capability for return by only raising the fund levels that were traditionally associated with seed and early-stage investing. We would do the start-up investment in the fund, the seed investment. We would invest substantially in the first round, but when the second, third, and fourth rounds were required, we would take an increasingly smaller position, and turn the control investment position over to a larger fund like Venrock. Essentially, that meant that we were doing the heavy lifting, and then inviting the larger fund in after a great deal of the risk had been washed out of the project. Although the price was somewhat higher, it wasn't all that much higher. So giving Venrock—who were great investing partners—that kind of a position was ceding to them much of the value of the deal. We determined when raising our third and subsequent funds that we would raise enough money to allow us to invest proportionately through all rounds to liquidity. We have 25 investments in both Fund Three and Fund Four, and these larger funds have enabled us not only to remain true to our seed and early-stage investment approach, but also to maintain a position that allows us to have somewhere in the vicinity of a 20 percent ownership by the time a deal goes to liquidity, either through an IPO or through a sale to a larger entity.

A Success out of Left Field

There was, in the mid-'80s, a project going on at the University of Chicago managed by a combination of the Department of Education and the Department of Mathematics. When you set yourself up as technology investors, you don't normally think in terms of going to the mathematics and education departments looking for a core, or a seed of a new corporation. But within this project, which was aimed at reforming the mathematics curriculum in the United States for grades kindergarten through six, there were materials being crudely published. These materials were being made available through what they called summer boot camps to mathematics coordinators all over the country. There could be twenty large urban centers represented on the campus of the University of Chicago for three or four weeks every summer, and they would want these materials. The project people were trying to operate out of the basement of the Department of Education, copying these materials and sending them out for cost. Finally, one of the professors in this project asked Bob Nelsen, then one of the 57th Street Irregulars, if there was any way the business school could help bring order to the chaos.

A couple of our young people went over and examined what was going on, and came back and told us there was money to be made. These people received royalties of $40,000 operating out of a closet last year. Furthermore, the product was getting publishing industry kinds of margins, it was a disposable product, and the essentials were there for a business. So, we organized a business, first staffed with four students, and started to recruit for a CEO. I should point out that this was before we had raised the venture fund. We were recruiting for a CEO without the venture money in hand. We were also extraordinarily lucky in our hire, because Joanne Schiller, the CEO of that company, proved to be a superb manager. We put in a little more than $250,000, and the company never needed another venture dollar. It broke even early in its second year of operation. The product was renewed each year. It actually violated all tenets of academic publication. It only produced a grade at a time, rather than spending $20 million and developing an entire curriculum and publishing it at one time as Simon & Schuster might do. But there was a great niche—the reform-minded market in the education community—that loved the product.

At the end of about five and a half years, that company was sold to the Chicago Tribune for $26 million. Joanne Schiller is today a group executive at the Tribune. ARCH's return on its $250,000 investment was something like a twenty-two multiple. The university, which had substantial ownership for having licensed that product to the company, got a return in excess of $10 million. It was an enormous success. We had started from a situation where the university had realized perhaps $200,000 each year for commercialization of products. Now they were seeing seven-figure numbers.

The Biggest Success to Date

Our biggest success to date has been New Era of Networks Inc. (NEON), a company for which we help to bring the technology and the entrepreneurs together.

Rick Adam founded NEON, an Internet infrastructure company. Even though he had come out of the financial services industry, he thought the great need was in health care. That turned out to be a mistake. Health care was not mature enough or ready to buy. But because Rick knew the financial services marketplace, he found very quickly that there was a demand for the product, shifted resources almost on a dime, and started to penetrate the financial services market. That propelled NEON's great success. It's either knowing where your market demand driver will be when you go in with your product, or having the background and the knowledge to sense where it's going to come from. If you don't go there first, you go there second. So Rick had a track record, deep market experience, and experience in having supervised some people before, having done a lot of hiring and some firing. That's helpful, because you're going to have to fire some people in these small companies. You can't afford to hesitate and wait until they really do damage. If you've got a vice president of marketing or sales who is not penetrating with your product, you cannot afford to stay with that person very long. The general manager has to be able to make that change. We've learned some other lessons. We're going more toward formal executive searches, where the executive search companies have exhaustive records on people. Modern techniques of interviewing, a lot of reference checking, and exhaustive due diligence can go a long way toward making ideas bear fruit.

Still Collegial

We're a highly collaborative organization. We see that as an element of great strength. We are a group of people who have now worked together intensely for 14 years, and while we don't think homogeneously, we have great respect for each other's judgment, and so are very supportive of each other. I think a 14-year partnership is becoming increasingly rare in this day and age, as people spin out from venture partnerships to form new partnerships. We're still pretty comfortable with each other, and that seems to be an important factor in our fund-raising efforts. Another part of our methodology is that although seed investing is conventionally considered enormously high-risk investing, we invest at the beginning with a teaspoon or an eyedropper. We are adherents of Tom Perkins's creed of investing early to wash a particular kind of risk out of an opportunity. I was very influenced by his story of how he invested in Genentech at the beginning. He put small packages of money in scientific institutions to replicate the Cohn Boyer science, and when he saw it was replicable—when he felt that the major risk had been put aside—he could confidently invest larger amounts. We try to do that all the time. We invest small amounts to achieve specific milestones. We cooperate in helping those milestones to be achieved, but we do not invest $5 or $10 million at the outset. Our level of investment in our companies, in the aggregate, is going to be somewhere between $7 and $15 million in each company. But we do that over several rounds. That's another part of our style.

Spreading Out

We've found, particularly in Seattle—which has proven to be a very productive location for us—that there are underserved locations that have companies emerging in a number of disciplines, including information sciences, as you might imagine, the life sciences, and the Internet in particular. We have taken advantage of that position. Now we are working out of Albuquerque. We're journeying not too far to Texas. We've done three investments in Austin, one together with the local reigning Austin venture partnership, Austin Ventures. We mentioned Ann Arbor and Boulder before. Denver is a third. We have done a company in Ames, Iowa, where I think we are one of maybe two venture funds that have invested in that area over the last thirty years.

We also have refined a technique that we call the technology roll-up. One of the reasons that biotech investing is so difficult is that early in the game one tended to make a bet on a single molecule. In order to develop a single molecule to a product, one goes through not only the FDA gauntlet, but the general research gauntlet, which could fail at any stage. A lot of money has been lost, and one of the reasons that biotech has been slow to return its investment is because of that early style of biotech investing. What we learned to do, once we saw an interesting molecule, was range around the country to find corresponding, associative, or complementary molecules that we could bring into the same company. So, it was a roll-up in the sense of not only beginning with science at the University of Chicago, but pulling in complementary science from the University of Indiana or the University of Pennsylvania or one of the national labs. One of our companies, a microfluidics company called Caliper, has technology from nine different institutions in it. (Caliper had a very successful IPO in December 1999.) The roll-up also preempts a competitive response to your idea if you have all the relevant technology in your company. The other strategy in doing this is if you have early-stage inventions—or in the case of biotech, molecules—that are probably looking at six, seven, or eight years to move through the laboratory and testing, you want to match that with later-stage molecules in the same general discipline that are in the clinic, or at least close to the clinic. That's part of the roll-up strategy as well. All our biotech investments have this characteristic.

Breaking from the Past

In the early days, we did the jobs ourselves. That proved to be too onerous a demand. You could not be acting CEO of even two companies at the same time. It was more than a seven-day, twenty-four-hours-a-day job. So we learned to recruit earlier and earlier. Our recruiting has had the same characteristic over the fourteen years we've been doing this. That is, we've been right more often than we've been wrong, but not by much. The old cliché truly pertains— the best predictor of success is track record. If you recruit a CEO or acting entrepreneur who has no relevant experience, you are taking a very long chance. I don't think that has changed very much in the fourteen years I've seen this, though I think we have become a lot better at finding people.

The first trick is to find a natural affinity, as illustrated by Joanne Schiller and Everyday Learning. Thinking back to our early interviews with Joanne Schiller, nothing in those interviews would have predicted the rich level of success that she ultimately had. She had not done it before, but she had experience in the industry. She knew the marketplace. Her personality and her stamina just fit what had to be done in that company. I hesitate to call it luck, but there was certainly a lucky aspect to the marriage of Joanne and

that company. Apart from a track record, probably the most important factor is really knowing the marketplace. Not just having
the Rolodex of names of the people who are in the marketplace,
but really understanding what aspect of the marketplace would
become a driver for your product. This is critical to long-range
planning and positioning of a company.

Does a Seed Fund Mean Staying Embryonic?

I think the classic venture investing pool of capital is a hybrid. You
start a company and you stay with that company to the point of
liquidity. You do not hand off the entire destiny of your investment
to a IVP or a Chase. Rather, you remain in position, not only to
realize the level of return that allows you to go back and raise the
next fund, but because you want to stay in control of the deal.
Everything you've learned about that business at the beginning
becomes more and more valid and valuable as the company
matures. You don't want to put its destiny in the hands of someone whose background may be in an investment bank, because it's
a different style of thought than the development of enterprise. I
think that eventually bankers are useful, but not in driving the
project. So I believe that the best model for people with personalities like ours is a fund of a size that allows you to do a certain
number of investments and stay in those investments to liquidity,
sale, or disposition of some sort.

Now, what's the right number when you're starting companies all
the time? When I was going around the circuit and trying to learn
what the masters knew about this business, Tom Perkins said that he
felt that the start-up bandwidth was one, maybe one and a half companies at a time, and probably that meant one to one and a half a year.
You could probably have ideas simmering on the back burner. Think
in terms of a guild: If you have some really good journeymen, and
some clever apprentices, the master can leverage himself or herself
beyond the one and a half to some degree. But I think it's still a number that has merit, in order to calculate how many early-stage deals
can you really start in a given time period.

Ultimately, we have an exploration mentality. We think the land is
out there, the way is uncharted, but the reason we leave the port and

sail uncharted waters is because of the belief that there is an undis-covered continent or a route to the Indies. There used to be very few real seed and very early-stage investment funds, but now the enor-mous and unique phenomenon of the Internet space has midwifed a gold rush generation of seed investors into existence. We're glad to have the company.

JOHN DOERR
Kleiner Perkins Caufield & Byers

John Doerr began at Intel in 1975 as an engineer and for the next five years became versed in everything technological—from engineering to the marketing of technology. He couldn't have had a better company or a better mentor: Andrew Grove. When he left Intel to join Kleiner Perkins in 1980, he started at the beginning of a decade in which "we witnessed (and benefited from) the largest, legal creation of wealth on the planet," he says.

The value was in new ventures based on the microchip and personal computer. The then-new PC companies (the Compaqs, Suns, Microsofts, and Dells) grew from $0 to $100 billion in revenues and market capitalization.

As the 1980s ended, Doerr was looking at a new world of opportunities, a world that he has greatly helped shape. With investments in Netscape and Amazon.com, and the launching of the Java Fund, an Internet-only fund fully financed by Kleiner Perkins, he was helping create companies in what clearly has been the biggest industrial boom in modern history.

Doerr, the young venture capitalist, became one of the first flag bearers for the Internet generation, where most entrepreneurs were in their teens and twenties—younger than Doerr himself. He adopted a new mantra, declaring the Internet had been underhyped, that everywhere we turned, the Web was changing everything, and that the benefits, contributions, and value of the new Net companies would dwarf the $100 billion created in the first decade of new microchip and PC ventures. And do so faster!

Here Doerr talks about his path to venture capital and ten important ventures that Kleiner Perkins Caufield & Byers has backed. He looks forward to venture capital in the twenty-first century and in the new economy and shares his personal passion for education reform and the New Schools Venture Fund for education entrepreneurs.

WHAT LED me into venture capital? Luck, a fascination with innovation and entrepreneurs, plus the ambition—inspired by Lou Doerr, my dad and hero—to one day start a venture with friends.

In 1974 I moved to Silicon Valley after finishing my first year of business school. Venture capital, I'd heard, had something to do with building new companies. So I cold-called Silicon Valley's venture groups, hoping to apprentice myself to one. But the timing was terrible. In 1974 there were only two new ventures funded with more than $1 million—Playboy Enterprises and KP's Tandem Computers. Venture groups were not making new investments; instead, they were struggling to keep existing ventures funded and afloat.

Somehow, several venture capitalists found time to offer advice, including Brook Byers,[1] who was then working with Pitch Johnson,[2] Bill Draper,[3] Burt McMurtry,[4] and Dick Kramlich,[5] then working with Arthur Rock.[6] Their advice was to forget about venture capital and to go out and get a real job working with a good company. A few suggested a small new chipmaker called Intel.

Luckily, Bill Davidow,[7] then VP/General Manager of Intel's microcomputer division, agreed to meet me. I interviewed and landed a summer job.

Intel: 1974

The summer of 1974 was pivotal in my career. Intel was a promising, well-managed, $130 million revenue company with 3,000 employees. They had just introduced the 8080 chip, the first 8-bit microprocessor.

That summer Andy Grove taught new employees the first course on "Intel's Organization Philosophy and Economics" (iOPEC). Andy's management genius and personal commitment to education were evident even then. By summer's end Andy and I had trained Intel's sales

---

[1] *A partner at Kleiner Perkins, best known for his investments in biotechnology.*
[2] *One of the early venture capitalists, a partner at Asset Management.*
[3] *Another early Valley venture capitalist, a partner at Draper, Gaither & Anderson.*
[4] *Venture capitalist at Technology Venture Investors.*
[5] *A founding partner of New Enterprise Associates.*
[6] *The lead investor in Intel and Apple.*
[7] *Engineer at Intel, and later venture capitalist at Mohr, Davidow Ventures.*

force in the U.S. and Europe. Our benchmarks showed the superiority of Intel's 8080 processor versus Motorola's 6800. And even more fun, we won major design contracts selling major customers like Siemens and ICL. I promptly forgot about venture capital and decided to build a career at Intel.

I returned to grad school to finish a degree in business and continued working twenty hours a week for Intel as the field engineer assigned to DEC. We dragged DEC kicking and screaming into the brave new world of microprocessors. DEC's engineers were skeptical of computers on a chip, but that's another story.

After business school my next job was at Intel's factory "headquarters," working first with engineering and then product marketing. However, my friend and marketing manager, Jim Lally, advised me that if I someday wanted to be a successful marketing or general manager, I'd better learn how to sell and how to motivate a field sales force. He told me to "get out into the field, and carry a bag!"

So I transferred to Intel's Chicago sales office and had a blast, calling on small accounts in farming and industrial communities. It was the one of the best and most educational of jobs: solve a problem, get an order. Then I was called back to Intel's factory to be a marketing manager, still working with microprocessors, software, and people.

Kleiner Perkins Caufield & Byers: 1980

In 1980 a friend introduced me to Kleiner Perkins. They wanted a gofer to help check out new business plans. I was still interested in someday starting a venture, but I wasn't so sure about venture capital. During my interview, the KP partners—Eugene, Tom, Frank, and Brook—promised that if I worked for them, they would someday back me in starting a new venture. They pointed to their success backing Bob Swanson, an associate who incubated Genentech, and Jim Treybig, who incubated Tandem Computers.

Kleiner Perkins offered me a job and within the first year I was fortunate to meet two professors at the 1981 Cal Tech VLSI Conference: Carver Mead from Cal Tech, and Jim Clark from Stanford. Carver and Jim would later play key roles in ventures that KP backed.

Carver Mead told us about his research into new tools for chip design. He called it "silicon compilation." True to their word, the KP partners backed Carver and me in co-founding a new venture, Silicon Compilers. After eighteen months we recruited a more qualified CEO from Intel, Phil Kaufman. Later, Silicon Compilers merged with Silicon Design Labs, and in 1991 Mentor Graphics acquired Silicon Compilers for $142 million.

Meanwhile, Jim Clark was developing his geometry engine, which led to Silicon Graphics. Jim later worked with KP in building great companies like Netscape, Healtheon, and currently myCFO.

Throughout the 1980s, the microprocessor was the common denominator—the base technology—for successful KP ventures, from Compaq to Lotus, and from Sun Microsystems to AOL. None of these new digital, personal computing, information, or network products would have been possible without the microchip.

Compaq: 1982

The first business plan from Compaq founders Rod Canion, Jim Harris, and Bill Murto outlined their intention to market hard disk drives for the original IBM desktop PC, which desperately needed more storage. Ben Rosen and L. J. Sevin (the lead investors) and the KP partners didn't think that was a durable business, so we passed on the hard disk idea. But the founders had already resigned from Texas Instruments; so although they were devastated, they didn't give up. Instead they "worked the problem"—which is a Compaq attitude and slogan. They sketched out a new plan at a fabled meeting at the House of Pies in Houston.

Their new vision was to build the first *transportable* PC—similar to a computer that Regis McKenna and I had advocated unsuccessfully at Intel a few years earlier. The first Compaq was sewing-machine sized, with a nine-inch diagonal green screen, two floppy disk drives, and a handle. It was 100 percent IBM compatible. Thirty-five pounds. Portable—or at least luggable. I fell in love with their idea and advocated we invest and help build the team.

Their timing was terrific. IBM was unable to supply all the demand for PCs, and the Compaq was in many ways better. Further, the genius of Compaq's marketing was positioning Compaq as complementary to IBM, not competitive. Compaq did neither intellectual, emotional, nor economic violence to the commitments and success of the IBM dealer chain.

To sign up and serve the dealers, we recruited Sparky Sparks, one of the original "Dirty Dozen" founders on IBM's Boca Raton PC team. Sparky had set up the IBM dealer network, making numerous dealers millionaires by awarding them the IBM franchise. So when Sparky phoned to sell Compaq's high-quality, IBM-compatible product, the dealers took his word. They signed on and promoted the Compaq, and delighted their customers. Compaq's dealer network, including Sears, Computerland, and Businessland, remained one of its strengths for many years.

Revenues skyrocketed. Compaq sold $110 million of portable PCs its first year. Over the years it became the fastest new venture ever to achieve $1 billion in revenue and the fastest to enter the Fortune 500.

Sun, the Stanford University Network: 1982

While I was at Intel in 1980, Stanford professor Forrest Baskett visited and described the "Sun: Stanford University Network" research project led by Andy Bechtolsheim. They were building an affordable version of the much-admired and envied Xerox "Alto" workstation. After I moved to KP, I followed Sun's progress by hanging around the second floor of Margaret Jacks Hall, the mother lode for computer science innovation at Stanford.

The four co-founders of Sun were twenty-seven-year-old entrepreneurs—backed by a couple of thirty-year-old venture capitalists. Fortunately, none of us really knew what we were doing, or what we were up against. If we had, we might not have violated the then-conventional wisdom about computing.

Sun adopted and promoted "open systems": standard networking, commodity microprocessors, and Berkeley's UNIX operating system. In comparison, rival Apollo Computer in Boston had far more experienced, respected management and proprietary systems. Although starting later, Sun's founders—Vinod Khosla, Scott McNealy, Andy Bechtolsheim, and Bill Joy—and their team decisively beat Apollo. Vinod, Scott, Andy, and Bill remain lifelong friends, and Vinod is one of my most talented partners.

Sun's original business plan, written by Vinod, was a model: just seven pages covering the mission, four months' objectives, a tentative two-year plan, the product, the market, their competitors, and their people. Brief business plans are best.

GO, a Fiasco in Pen Computing: 1987

GO's failure in pen computing is well-chronicled in Jerry Kaplan's *Startup*. It could have been titled *Screwup*. GO failed—but not for lack of vision or good corporate partners. IBM, AT&T, and KP backed some of America's smartest, most passionate entrepreneurs who were convinced that pen computers were the next big thing. But our implementation was just wrong. We misread the market and picked the wrong price point, and the handwriting recognition was too ambitious.

A few years later, Jeff Hawkins and Donna Dubinsky introduced the Palm Pilot hand-held computer. Jeff and Donna sold four million units in 1998 before leaving 3COM/Palm to start Handspring with KP backing.

Three important lessons stand out despite GO's failure. First, the importance of leadership and teams: Bill Campbell and GO's people were extraordinary. We've subsequently backed dozens of them in building other successful, important companies. GO alumni are now CEOs, founders, or VPs of ventures such as Netscape, Intuit, Sun, Verisign, Amazon.com, Handspring, OnSale, and others. Second, a terrific team is necessary but not enough. Don't confuse a great team with a great business. And third, the ethos of Silicon Valley: It's okay to try and fail, and try again—just don't make the same mistakes twice. We want to encourage risk taking. When important risks are removed, there can be great rewards.

Intuit, a "Speedup": 1990

Intuit was founded in 1983 when Signe Ostby, VP of Marketing for a large software company, complained to her spouse, Scott Cook, about the time and hassle required to balance a checkbook. Scott sought funding from over twenty-five Silicon Valley venture firms, all of whom passed on the investment. So Scott's savings account, his father, and his friends were Intuit's first-round investors. They struggled, missed payroll for four months, but by 1988 Intuit's Quicken was the leading personal finance software on DOS.

By 1990 Intuit had one million happy customers and revenues of $33 million. Then Scott decided it was time to take Intuit to the next level. The company had only inside members on its board of directors. Scott wanted the strongest possible outside board—one that would pay a lot of attention to Intuit, challenge it, and help grow it to $1 billion in revenue. He viewed Quicken's number-one personal finance software as just one leg of a stool. Scott wanted to add small business finance, and possibly taxes. He wanted to strengthen his team for impending competition with Microsoft Money for Windows.

KP invested $4.7 million for 12 percent of Intuit, promising to speed up—instead of start up—the business. We helped recruit management, get Quicken for Windows to market, launch the important Quickbooks business application, complete a public offering, merge with the leading tax provider (Chipsoft's TurboTax), recruit Bill Campbell as CEO, and attempt a merger with Microsoft. Intuit didn't need KP's money; in fact, our $4.7 million never went to the company's bank account, but purchased shares directly from founders.

After Microsoft withdrew its acquisition offer, Intuit rushed its products to the Web, forged alliances with Excite and AOL, and developed leading online sites for personal finance, tax, and small businesses. Under Bill Campbell's watch, Intuit grew from four million customers and $120 million revenue in 1994 to eighteen million customers and $1 billion in revenue in 1999. A whole book should be written on the leadership, integrity, character, and legacy of "Coach" Bill Campbell. The teams Bill assembled and coached at Apple, Claris, GO, and Intuit today lead many of Silicon Valley's best businesses.

Netscape: 1994

Alan Kay, a Xerox Palo Alto Research Center scientist, said, "The best way to predict the future is to invent it." Well, if you can't invent it, you can finance it. Or help piece it together.

Every year, usually in December, Bill Joy and I think ahead five to ten years and discuss the largest, most important new opportunities in science, communications, society, computing, and commerce. In 1991, Bill predicted that one day KP would back a nineteen-year-old kid who wrote software that would change the world.

On a Sunday afternoon in January 1994, at the MacWorld Expo, Bill Joy and I met with Will Hearst, Scott Cook, John Gage, and Chris Gulker in the San Francisco Examiner boardroom. John Gage demonstrated Mosaic, the first Web browser, and Bill Joy admonished us all to dive in. He declared that this was moving so fast, if we didn't get going, we'd be behind forever. Sure enough, Netscape redefined time. It created Web time, characterized by rapid change, growth, time compression, and shifting strategies.

In early 1994, Jim Clark was thinking of leaving Silicon Graphics. Jim was being "classic Jim": frustrated, restless, imagining the huge potential for multimedia over networks, possibly the Nintendo 64 game platform. Jim has always had an incredible sense of taste for technology, teams, and market opportunity. Bill Foss suggested Jim meet Marc Andreessen. Shortly after their meeting, Jim offered to fund the start of Mosaic Communications if Marc and he could hire the University of Illinois team that developed the prototype Mosaic browser. They flew to Champaign-Urbana, interviewed the programmers at the University Inn, faxed offer letters to the front desk, and signed all five engineers. Mosaic Communications was born.

A few weeks later Jim Clark called and asked me to meet with Marc, who was then twenty-two—the almost nineteen-year-old genius prophesied by Bill Joy.

Netscape's team was nimble, bold, and frame-breaking. KP partners, particularly Kevin Compton and Doug Mackenzie, helped rapidly recruit world-class senior executives including four VPs (Jim Shaw, Mike Homer, Todd Rulon-Miller, and Rick Schell), numerous directors, and an awesome CEO, Jim Barksdale, in less than twelve weeks. I can't overstate the impact of Jim Barksdale on Netscape. He was tough, but revered. He's ruthlessly honest, selfless, and a tireless leader and team builder. He has extraordinary integrity and courage, a sense of humor and the power to bring out the best in others.

It's astounding to stop and realize that just a few hundred weeks ago there was no Web. The introduction of Netscape's Navigator created unprecedented and unanticipated opportunities. Navigator simplified the Web, making technology previously the domain of academics accessible and ubiquitous. Remember the contributions of Navigator 1.0? It supported forms and encryption, enabling e-commerce. All you had to do was point and click.

On August 9, 1995, Netscape went public. Their IPO raised $140 million, with their price per share zooming from $28 to $74.75, valuing Netscape at $2.2 billion. It was the first Internet IPO—the shot heard round the world. The IPO was the starting gun in the race to develop technology, attract talent, build brands, and offer all kinds of new Internet services.

On December 7, 1995, Microsoft gathered financial analysts and declared they were going after Netscape. Microsoft would offer browsers, which were $150 million of Netscape's revenue, for free (more or less). Analysts wrote Netscape's obituaries. But Netscape morphed from a browser company to a browser plus server company, then from a browser plus server company to a collaboration and open standards mail company, then to an e-commerce software company, and then to Netcenter, a growing portal with nine million members. If America Online was the "nighttime online channel" for consumers, then Netscape's Netcenter became the leading daytime channel for business and professional users.

In mid-November 1998, Netscape and America Online, with Sun Microsystems, announced that Netscape would be acquired by AOL. Over the next six months AOL's market value increased $120 billion. Sun's market cap increased $25 billion. Netscape's market cap leapt from $4 billion to over $17 billion.

@Home: August 1995

@Home was incubated in Kleiner's offices with KP partner Will Hearst as founding CEO. We dreamed up the idea, the co-branding, and even the name, thinking it would be really cool to have an e-mail address that reads janedoe@home.net.

Will says that at the heart of every great venture is a technical genius. @Home needed a networking genius. So we asked our friends, "Who is the very best Internet guru?" All of them pointed to the infamous and elusive Milo Medin, who at the time was running Mae West and the government's Internet at NASA Ames. We called Milo several times a day and sent him mail messages for over a month. He didn't respond. One day, by chance, Milo answered his phone. While we couldn't disclose that the cable companies were our partners, we got his attention with the prospect that he could deliver the Internet into millions of homes thousands of times faster than ever before.

Two days later, Milo met with Will Hearst and me at the Good Earth restaurant in Palo Alto. We sketched our idea, Compaq-style, on the back of a napkin. We explained to Milo that we would recruit a world-class Silicon Valley technology team that would build the biggest, fastest network ever. But the idea was more than a fat, dumb pipe. The vision for @Home was an extremely popular, co-branded, always on, high-speed Internet service. All the high-speed Internet you could eat—for $20 to $40 per month. Milo laughed and said, "Nice try, but it won't work."

We had hoped to simply put cable modems in homes and then stitch them through cable head ends directly to the Internet. Our fatal flaw was that the fastest Internet backbone at the time was only forty-five megabytes per second. To deliver a full-screen video clip, for example, could consume a megabyte and a half of bandwidth. In other words, if just thirty people hit the carriage return on a video clip of a shuttle launch, they could bring the Internet to its knees.

Milo insisted we couldn't just connect with the Internet. Instead he proposed a parallel managed Internet exploiting an important idea in computer science: caching. Milo put proxy servers to keep copies of the most popular pages in every cable system head end. Also, Milo didn't believe the first cable modems were manageable, or would scale. He helped redesign them with industry architects at Cable Lab. The second-generation modems offered security, encryption, and manageability. Milo insisted the cable modem networks be very high performance and reliable, up 99.99 percent of the time.

In 1999 Excite and @Home became Excite@Home, a merger valued at $7.2 billion. Excite@Home would have failed merely as the idea of venture capitalists. It needed the genius of Milo Medin and the leadership of Will Hearst, Tom Jermoluk, and George Bell, who Will hired to run the company. Ideas are easy, but execution is everything, and teams win.

Amazon.com: 1996

The best ventures are big and simple. They serve large markets with strategic focus and a simple, powerful value proposition. When Amazon.com opened its bookstore in July 1995, there were many other stores on the Web. But none had so thoughtfully and rigorously obsessed about creating a compelling customer experience. Amazon.com offered huge advantages. They weren't merely putting a catalog online. Nowhere else could you find two million books, books in print, books out of print, with low prices and next-day delivery from an authoritative, trusted source. Amazon.com built its brand with a voice—with a light, playful, but respectful attitude.

The company fanatically focused on scale, on having happy customers, and on building a community of book lovers. Every ninety days was a Web year. But for the first twenty-four months—think of it as eight Web years!—the look of Amazon.com's Web site barely changed. All its effort went to recruiting the team, building the brand, and making sure the site would scale. Business was growing at 6 percent a week, faster than anything we'd witnessed.

Jeff Bezos and our partners immediately had a mind meld. The number one goal was GBF—get big fast. Inspired by Microsoft, we hired only incredibly smart people to lead this brave new world of e-commerce. We didn't hire senior management from the book industry. KP's Doug Mackenzie helped recruit a world-class CFO, Joy Covey, who is an incredible athlete and a great leader and competitor. She became not only CFO, but also one of Amazon.com's chief hiring officers. We hired not one, but two VPs of development: Dave Risher to run the front end of the store, and Rick Dalzell to run the back-end IT and logistics.

Under the covers, Amazon.com is a software company. Today, over 600 out of 3,000 people work on software. Jeff deserves enormous credit for insisting that Amazon.com execs hire better people at every level. That way, the quality of the organization is raised with each person hired.

How do you sustain an ultra-high growth user web? You keep hiring great people. Jeff Bezos says that KP's important contribution to Amazon.com wasn't the biggest check we'd ever written—$8 million for 15 percent. Instead, we helped hire more great people faster.[8]

So value-added venture capital is *not* about the money. Because of Amazon.com's positive cash cycle (customer pays in two days, vendors are paid in fifty days) the company barely used the $8 million we invested.

Less than a year ago, Amazon.com was only a bookstore. Today it is the leading book, music, and video store. In 1999, it launched stores for toys, consumer electronics, auctions, electronic greetings, games,

---

[8] *In just the last 120 days we helped Jeff recruit Joe Galli, a new president; Warren Jensen, a new CFO; Jeff Wilke, VP of Operations; Bill Price, VP of Customer Service; Daryl David, VP of HR; Mark Britto, VP of Development; and Jaheh Bisharat, VP of Marketing.*

software, Z-stores, home improvement, wish lists, and a Sony store-within-a-store. Further, Amazon.com has been savvy and aggressive by investing in strategic affiliates. Amazon.com's mission is to be the best place to find, discover, and buy anything online.

Amazon.com does regular, ruthless triage on a list of insurmountable opportunities. These are projects that ought to be pursued, projects that compete every day for finite resources. Jeff is an extraordinary founder and entrepreneur. And together, Jeff Bezos and Joe Galli are exceptional leaders and executives. They communicate clearly and effectively throughout the organization, by word of mouth, and through the press about the Amazon.com's mission.

We're witnessing at Amazon.com the creation of a gigantic, extraordinary service for discovery and commerce. In less than a decade, Amazon.com should be recognized like Wal-Mart, GE, or Microsoft for its contributions: pioneering e-commerce, lowering prices, building communities of happy customers, and delivering products and services that are really wanted. Amazon.com is shifting power back to the consumer.

Healtheon/WebMD: 1996

Just as Amazon.com puts the consumer in charge of their purchases, Healtheon puts the patient and doctor in charge of the health care system. Healtheon's premise is that the Internet will be the standard communications platform for health care. In my opinion our health care system is the second most screwed-up segment of the American economy. Americans simply want the best health care that other people's money will buy.

Until Healtheon, health care information systems were incompatible islands of minicomputer automation. These legacy systems mostly manage claims and adjustments ricocheting back and forth between payors and providers. The health care industry has historically invested a miserably low percentage of revenues on information technology. Medical records are not online, and they are incomplete or lost; lab data results are unavailable or delayed; and specialists incorrectly diagnose the needs of patients. Health care is more than the second largest segment of the economy; it is also a matter of life and death.

Jim Clark, Pavan Nigam, and KP's associate partner, David Schnell, founded Healtheon in January 1996. The first business plan was to use the Web for medical plan eligibility and enrollment. As with Netscape, we immediately began a search for a world-class CEO. And like Netscape, the business changed many times, responding to and ultimately transforming the market.

After many many months of recruiting, Mike Long, a world-class executive from Austin, Texas, agreed to become Healtheon's CEO. At the first board meeting Mike declared, "John, I'm in a hurry." Mike swiftly redefined the business to serve the information needs of a dozen large market segments, from diagnostic test results to doctors and providers. He scaled the business and team, completed an IPO in 1999, and closed dozens of joint ventures. In May 1999, Healtheon rocked the health care community by announcing a fifty-fifty merger with Jeff Arnold's WebMD, valued at $9.8 billion.

Healtheon/WebMD helps health care providers create their own portals for consumers. It helps consumers (patients) assess their health risks and take charge of their own medical care. Health care is, in the end, an information business. With data, you make better-informed decisions for yourself and your family.

So, Healtheon/WebMD meets KP's prescription for a great venture. It uses new technology to serve an important market with large, unmet needs. Although health care institutions are slow to change, the Web lowers costs, can profoundly improve outcomes, and most of all, puts power in the hands of users. That's the dynamic of the Internet.

The Java Fund: 1996

There have been just a few big ideas in computer science—one is the idea of caching, which was a pillar concept of @Home. A second important idea is Java. Java lets you write a safe, secure program, based on objects, that is small and can run anywhere. That the program is safe and secure and, in fact, provably correct, is incredibly powerful. It is as important an idea for software as the integrated circuit was for designers of electronic systems.

Bill Joy, James Gosling, Arthur van Hoff, Jonathan Payne, and Patrick Naughton created Java, building on decades of first-rate research in computer science. They said it was too hard to make computer systems work reliably—especially distributed systems, which are most of the really interesting systems. So they invented a new, needed language. Kim Polese[9] brought marketing savvy to the team. And Eric Schmidt, Bill Joy, and Mike Clary broadly licensed Java technology to gain worldwide adoption. They got Netscape to include it in Navigator 2.0. That was the slingshot that spread Java to millions around the world and motivated Microsoft to license it.

KP formed a Java Fund, inviting its partners to invest. The fund, led by partner Ted Schlein, focused on ventures creating new distributed applications. It looked very, very risky at the time. However, the fund returns have been spectacular. And Java has been broadly accepted as a key technology. KP has pioneered whole new industries before, succeeding with Genentech—recombinant DNA—and failing with GO—pen computing. With the Java Fund, we again tried to help create a new industry. This time it worked.

Drugstore.com: June 1998

Four years after the founding of Netscape, and three years after Amazon.com, drugstore.com illustrates well the new high standards for second generation Internet start-ups.

Peter Neupert signed on in July 1998 as CEO of a three-month-old organization with one employee. Drugstore.com made its debut on February 24, 1999.

In just thirty-two weeks, Peter accomplished the following: He concluded a strategic alliance with Amazon.com. He assembled a team of 250 exceptionally smart, aggressive people. They created from scratch an authoritative, scalable e-commerce service. They photographed and entered the instructions and warnings for 15,000 pharmaceutical, health, beauty, and personal care products—twice! They created order-processing, merchandising, inventory, purchasing, vendor integration, credit card, and fulfillment systems. They established certified pharmacies able to ship to customers in all fifty states. They staffed and offered 24/7 advice so you can "ask your pharmacist" online, anytime. They focused, correctly, on commerce

---

[9] *Kim Polese is a marketing executive at Sun.*

instead of content. And they raised $121 million in four private venture rounds.

In July 1999, just fifty weeks after Peter joined, drugstore.com filed for its IPO. After the filing, they forged a strategic relationship with Rite-Aid/PCS/GNC which ensured that all pharmaceutical purchases at drugstore.com could be reimbursed by health plans. They revised the prospectus to disclose the Rite-Aid alliance, and raised another $90 million in the IPO.

At year-end 1999, drugstore.com was clearly the leading online drugstore, with over 700,000 customers and four times the revenue of its nearest competitor. It is setting the pace in a $71 billion industry, with analyst forecasts for revenues of $1.1 billion in 2003.

The drugstore.com story shows the whole KP team serving great entrepreneurs. Associate partner Dave Whorton incubated the idea. Russ Siegelman suggested and helped recruit Peter Neupert as CEO. Brook Byers brought key insights into the pharmaceutical industry. He and I helped work out the Amazon.com relationship. None of this would have been possible without the team led by Peter Neupert, Kal Ramon, Susan Delbene, and partners at Amazon.com and Rite-Aid.

Kleiner Perkins Caufield & Byers: 2000

What's the outlook for venture capital and KP in the twenty-first century? How will venture capital change in the next two decades? Those are great questions that challenge us at our off-site strategy sessions. Venture capital, like every industry, is changing rapidly. And the change is accelerating because of the Internet and globalization. Venture capital remains first and foremost a service business. Advice, help, judgment, recruiting, and networking matter more than money.

Over $11 billion of venture capital was invested in Silicon Valley in 1999, up from $3.5 billion in 1997. An estimated 300 ventures in Silicon Valley are currently recruiting CEOs. Entrepreneurs, technology, market opportunity, and venture capital are in abundance. What's in short supply, what's dear, are great teams. Again, it's teams that win, because it takes teams to build a great business.

Great entrepreneurs and great CEOs are team builders. And good venture capitalists must help build and grow teams. We believe venture capitalists should have significant venture operating experience. The right to advise great entrepreneurs and to serve on their boards is earned, not purchased. And each partner and associate at KP is better because we're part of the KP team and network.

There's no reason a venture group need be more than an episodic collection of talented individuals. But since its founding in 1972 by Eugene Kleiner and Tom Perkins, KP has been committed to the training, development, and transition of generations of partners. We want to build and honor a long-lasting network of relationships with the best entrepreneurs and executives. And develop our own strong team with several generations of venture capitalists.

KP's venture keiretsu has been widely misunderstood by the media. Unlike a leveraged buyout firm, or a true Japanese keiretsu, KP doesn't control *any* of the ventures we back. So the KP keiretsu is a particularly American, Western, and entrepreneurial version of the Japanese keiretsu. The difference is that there's no central controlling bank, no interlocking boards of directors. Instead, there are strong, independent ventures led by smart, aggressive entrepreneurs who are tops in their field. They know they can't do it all on their own. They seek alliances with other ventures. They see the advantage of accelerating growth and success by partnering with others. The keiretsu is a network and entrepreneurs want to be part of the network.

There are too many alliances, investments, and outright mergers between KP ventures to list completely. But there's no denying their impact on technology and the new economy. Consider:

- Compaq and Microsoft's making the first 386 PC a year before IBM.

- Netscape's decision to include Sun's Java in Navigator 2.0, and the AOL-Netscape-Sun alliance.

- AOL's investments in Excite, Preview Travel, and HomeStore.com, and its acquisition of Netscape.

- @Home's merger with Excite to accelerate broadband Internet.

- Amazon.com's strategic investments in della.com, drugstore.com, homegrocer.com, and wineshopper.com, and its acquisition of accept.com.

- Cisco's $7 billion acquisition of Cerent, their largest acquisition to date.

- Broadband collaboration by Corvus, ONI, Juniper, Cerent, Siara, New Access, Qwest, and Rhythms to enable application service providers such as Asera, Broadband Office, Corio, and others.

- Microsoft's catalytic role in Healtheon's $9.8 billion merger with WebMD.

K-12 Public Education

Question: If health care is the second most troubled sector of the American economy, what is the worst? Answer: K-12 public education.

Crisis *is* the right word to use in discussing the state of education. Among America's eight-year-olds, fully 40 percent are reading below grade level. When kids aren't getting it—when they're not learning or making progress—they turn off to education. They fall further and further behind. And then, all too often, we lose them forever.

Our K-12 public education system is, in the strictest sense, a state-run monopoly rife with social promotion. As long as you don't make too much trouble, you ride the conveyor belt from grade to grade regardless of how much you learn or whether you learn at all.

Outcomes don't matter until you get to college. Then, suddenly, outcomes matter—a lot. In California, for example, an astonishing 50 percent of incoming college freshmen are forced to take remedial English or algebra classes just to stay afloat.

Why does this matter? Because in the new knowledge-based economy, even the jobs on the factory floor require fairly sophisticated symbolic reasoning. You can't run a wafer stepper at Intel without being able to do statistical process control. And you can't do statistical process control without the ability to do algebra. You can't work for a dot-com Internet company without being able to read, write, and think critically.

By failing to teach more than half our kids the most elementary of skills, America's K-12 system leaves them ill-equipped to survive in this new economy. We're wasting whole generations of kids, especially in poor, urban school systems. The kids know when they're not getting it. They end up on the streets, in gangs, and then in prisons because they think they don't have options or opportunities. It's hard to imagine a more searing indictment—or one with more dangerous consequences for the new economy and for all of us.

The New Economy

Let's be clear. Americans will not achieve their dreams through welfare or by redistributing wealth. Instead, we must ensure that opportunity is fairly distributed and available to all. Education is the key. Every kid in this country ought to have a shot at a great education.

Education reform is deeply in our self-interest. Left alone, technology will widen the digital divide, the gap between the haves and the have-nots, the knows and the know-nots. Without education reform, the new economy will face huge obstacles.

By now, everybody has heard about the new economy. Its pillars are the microchip, the PC, the Internet, and genomics. Between 1980 and 1990, the new PC companies grew from $0 to $100 billion in revenues and market value. The industries emerging around the Net are expanding at least three times as fast. For Internet entrepreneurs, normal growth is 6 percent a month.

Such growth is unprecedented, and so are the broad economic benefits. In Silicon Valley unemployment is at 3 percent. Wages are at an all-time high. Upward mobility is not just for those on the upper rungs of the ladder. Almost everyone seems to be moving up. This isn't happening only in Santa Clara, California. It's also happening in Austin, Denver, Seattle, Boston, Raleigh-Durham, Pittsburgh, and South Dakota.

The new economy, we're discovering, isn't a strange phenomenon that flourishes exclusively in Silicon Valley. But if the benefits of the new economy are going to be felt everywhere, big changes in education are necessary. In the new economy, the scarcest and most precious commodities are intelligence, resourcefulness, and innovation. The new economy's ability to achieve its full potential will be retarded if it doesn't have a continuous and voluminous supply of strong minds.

The System Is the Problem

I can already hear the cynics sneering, "Yes, yes, okay, John. Everyone agrees that improving education would be a Good Thing. That's apple pie. But what do you 'techies' know about getting there? You haven't the foggiest clue about school boards and teacher's unions and education policy. Consider all this talk about wiring the classrooms. We don't need Cat 5 wiring. We need the roofs repaired. We need more money. And we need shorter school days for overworked teachers. Go back to your garage start-ups. Leave public education alone. You guys just don't get it."

To which I reply, "With all due respect, *yeah right*." For decades, public education has been the sole province of powerful, entrenched bureaucracies of self-styled experts who supposedly do "get it." Look at where they've gotten us. The problem isn't with teachers, many of whom are dedicated, caring, and energetic. The problem isn't with parents, who want nothing more than for their children to succeed and are willing to work to see that happen. And the problem certainly isn't with our kids, who desperately want to learn.

The problem is the system.

What are the solutions to reforming the system? The first thing to realize is that there is no silver bullet. There never is. Education is complicated, subtle, and demanding. But this isn't rocket science. All over the country, experiments have produced affordable, scalable programs with tangible results. We don't know everything, but we do know some things that get kids reading, writing, and learning math:

- smaller classes and smaller schools

- teachers who have the time and the incentives to be better prepared

- intense parental involvement

- excellence and equity

- charter schools

- accountability—it's crucial to hold schools and teachers responsible for their students' performance and testing

- choice and competition

- leadership

Ultimately, the quest for education reform will fail if it's left to the politicians. They're necessary but not sufficient. This is a movement that needs to be driven from the outside by those who have the best understanding of the new economy and the greatest stake in it. It means encouraging and supporting a new breed of entrepreneur—education entrepreneurs.

The New Schools Venture Fund: 1998

The New Schools Venture Fund (NSVF) was founded to support education entrepreneurs.[10] It helps with funding, recruiting, advising, and expertise. It helps scale really big ideas to improve public schools, whether for-profit or nonprofit, tackling system problems both inside and outside the public school system.

Charter public schools—Advantage Schools, Learn Now, and University Public Schools—are one such idea. Success for All, another powerful idea, is a research-based, structured program for whole school reform that gets *all* kids to read. Greatschools.net, an online *Zagat's Guide* to the actual performance and needs of schools, is a third big idea. Volunteer programs like NetDay are a fourth big idea. They have wired tens of thousands of schools, and are now designing new "NextDays" to wire classrooms, train teachers, and connect parents in impoverished communities.

Reed Hastings is both an education entrepreneur and NSVF investor. After selling Pure Software for $750 million in 1997, he began a new career in education reform. He went back to school at Stanford's School of Education. Reed embraced the idea of charter public schools. He is leading the charge on California's Proposition 26 to allow a simple majority to approve school construction bonds. Reed is a co-founder of nonprofit University Public Schools. He led a $4 million campaign to take the caps off charter schools in California, resulting in

---

[10] *Says Doerr: "Leading each of these great ventures are passionate, committed, even angry entrepreneurs: Don Shalvey, Bill Jackson, Julie Evans, John Gage, Michael Kaufman, Gene Wade, Jim Shelton, Nancy Madden, and Bob Slavin. The New Schools Venture Fund is a network of America's education entrepreneurs. Its president, Kim Smith, is herself an eduction entrepreneur and a co-founder of Teach for America.*

"New Schools investors include Jim and Sally Barksdale, Ann Bowers, Brook and Shawn Byers, Scott Cook and Signe Ostby, John and Elaine Chambers, Steve Merrill, Halsey and Deb Minor, Ted Mitchell, and numerous others. NSVF is building the first network and community of education entrepreneurs."

AB 544, which will fund 100 new charter schools every year for the next decade. The result of his efforts could be 1,000 new competitive public schools in California, changing the lives of perhaps 500,000 kids a year—public schools that can be innovative, and that are accountable for high performance, with as much as $4 billion in funding. That's a more valuable return than the venture investment in Amazon.com!

The Net of It All

We're still very early in the development of this new networked economy—just a few milliseconds after the Big Bang. This new world is expanding rapidly. Only a few laws and forces are clear. But this is a long boom. And faster than industry leaders can consolidate, new ventures are emerging—technology is creating more opportunity. The markets are larger, but less forgiving. The universe of possibilities is expanding. Competition is intense—for talent, for ideas, for customers, and for alliances. There's never been a better time than now to start a new venture, to get great venture capital assistance, or to better educate American children.

INDEX

About the Editor

Udayan Gupta is the founder and CEO of Biztrail.com, a Web-based provider of news and information for entrepreneurial and growth companies. Gupta began writing about venture capital for *Venture* magazine in the late 1970s, when the industry was still in its infancy, and he subsequently covered the topic for a number of national publications. He was one of the few national correspondents to write about entrepreneurship within the minority community and was a contributing editor to *Black Enterprise* and *Hispanic Business*. After completing a Walter F. Bagehot Fellow in Economics and Business Journalism at Columbia University, Gupta joined the *Wall Street Journal* as a senior special writer focusing on venture capital and entrepreneurial issues. At the *Journal*, Gupta was the first to provide wide-ranging as well as specific coverage of venture capital, profiling venture capitalists and breaking news of key industry events.

In 1996, Gupta left the *Journal* to write independently and to work with some venture capital funds and entrepreneurial companies on communications strategies. Biztrail.com was launched in 1999 to provide more news and information about venture capital and entrepreneurship.

In addition to managing a small film production company in India and writing about film for a number of publications, Gupta has served on the board of Asian Cinevision, a national organization designed to promote Asian film and video. He also has been on the board of advisers of UCLA's Center for Entrepreneurship Leadership Clearinghouse on Entrepreneurship Education, an organization that promotes entrepreneurial education.